S0-ATP-671

Bessie

Bessie

Chris Albertson

REVISED AND EXPANDED EDITION

Yale University Press New Haven & London

Original edition published in 1972 by Stein and Day.

Printed in the United States of America.

Library of Congress Cataloging-in-Publication Data
Albertson, Chris.
Bessie / Chris Albertson.— Rev. and exp. ed.
p. cm.
"Original edition published in 1972 by Stein and Day"—T.p. verso.
Includes bibliographical references (p.) and index.
Discography: p.
ISBN 0-300-09902-9 (clothbound : alk. paper)
1. Smith, Bessie, 1898?–1937. 2. Singers—United States—Biography.
I. Title.
ML420.S667 A7 2003
782.421643′092—dc21

2002155414

A catalogue record for this book is available from the British Library.

The paper in this book meets the guidelines for permanence and durability of the Committee on Production Guidelines for Book Longevity of the Council on Library Resources.

10 9 8 7 6 5 4 3 2 1

Contents

Author's Note

The original edition of this biography saw light in 1972, at a time when published information on Bessie Smith was so scant that if one eliminated duplicated information and myth from existing books and articles, there would remain no more than ten to fifteen pages. Volume clearly exceeded substantive information in what then amounted to two biographical books, numerous chapters, and hundreds of magazine and newspaper articles. Most writings about Bessie Smith were based on her discography and recorded performances, leaving the reader with little knowledge of the person behind the voice. One's image of Bessie, the woman, was easily reduced to a stereotypical blues-singing fat mama who drank herself out of a career and seemed not to have had much of an offstage life. The truth, as those who experienced her in person were quick to tell me, was that Bessie Smith's persona commanded as much attention as her music did and that what we hear on her recordings is but one aspect of her talent, albeit the most striking.

My own interest in Bessie Smith dates back to the late 1940s, when I was a teenager living in Copenhagen. One night, as I surfed the ether on my radio dial, Bessie's big voice popped in and tested my tiny speaker. Although I spoke English, having spent most of three years in New York as a child, I did not understand the words as Bessie sang them, nor did I have a clue as to what kind of music I was listening to. But there was a compelling sincerity in Bessie's voice, an indefinable quality that drew me in and made me want to hear more.

When I learned that her name was Bessie Smith and her music was the blues, I began a search that soon led me to the United States Information Service library, where I borrowed books on blues and Afro-American music in general. The USIS also boasted a sizable record department, devoted to "American" music, but neither jazz nor blues seemed to qualify as such. All I found was two Lennie Tristano 78-rpm discs and, tucked away in a dark corner, three or four Library of Congress discs containing field hollers and chain gang songs — it was like reading the introduction and final chapter of a book. Not much, but it heightened my curiosity and opened the door to an eclectic love for jazz that over half a century of listening and exploring has not diminished.

By January 1970, my interest in African-American music had brought me back to the United States as a permanent resident. I thought I knew a lot about the music at this point, having spent more than twenty years listening and reading with no genre bias, and Bessie was one of the artists I had studied with particular interest. I had listened several times to every recording she made, read all the published stories, and seen the usual photographs. I had also spent more than two years trying to persuade Columbia Records that it was time to reissue Bessie Smith's entire recorded output, which they owned. My persistence paid off, but when the nod finally came, and Larry Hiller, my assigned Columbia engineer, and I began our restoration work, I began to realize how little I actually knew about Bessie. For nearly two years, Larry and I spent thirty-five hours a week listening intently to Bessie's legacy of 159 sides, a remarkable experience that only the raw power and emotion of an artist like Bessie Smith could keep from becoming mind-numbing. When I began preparing the liner notes, my research hinted at a life that was as nuanced as her singing, but I'm afraid that my album notes cast only a glimmer of new light on Bessie. Still, they brought me a decidedly undeserved Grammy award, which I can only attribute to show-biz politics.

The Grammys, the publicity generated by Columbia, and the temper of the times combined to spark a book publisher's interest in Bessie, which led to the original edition of this biography. It gave me an opportunity to fill in some of the many blanks left us by previous chroniclers. One reason why the lives of many jazz performers had been treated so superficially is that there was so much ground to cover and writers had a natural tendency to concentrate on contemporary artists. Another reason is that neither early writers nor those whom they interviewed felt sufficiently liberated to be forthright. Bessie, in its first incarnation, could not have been published in the 1940s, and probably not in the 1950s, at least not without stirring up controversy. In 1972, we were urged to "tell it like it is," but few jazz writers did, so I decided to throw political correctness to the wind and concluded — by way of convenient rationalization, perhaps—that the Empress of the Blues probably would have been no less candid had she lived to write the book herself. Expecting some flak from the prudish jazz press, I was pleasantly surprised when only one reviewer took offense.

In the 1930s and 1940s, when jazz literature was limited to the occasional book, one would not have had difficulty finding people with personal recollections of Bessie, but that may also be why writers dealt with her so superficially—there was no sense of urgency. Consequently, much information vanished as people passed away and memories dimmed. Still, a remarkable number of recollections were preserved, mainly because the folk and blues revival of the late 1950s and early 1960s sparked renewed interest in the origins of all African-American music and those who had helped shape it.

Were it not for a chance meeting with Ruby Walker a few months earlier, I might not have accepted the offer to write a Bessie Smith biography. Ruby and I had become friends, and our many conversations about Bessie, with whom she toured for fifteen years, had made it clear to me that a book needed to be written. At that point in time, I don't think a meaningful biography of Bessie could have been written without tapping Ruby's extraordinary memory—it would certainly have been seriously undernourished without her input.

Black performers—especially older ones—exercise understandable discretion when speaking to white writers; there are aspects of black life that many feel are best unshared. It's not that they have any sordid secrets to hide, but being black can be very much an "in" thing, and it behooves many African Americans to preserve at least part of the mystique that years of racial division has formed. As I began work on the biography and faced Ruby Walker over a microphone, she surprised me with her candor. It helped that we had already established a solid personal friendship and that the times were indeed a-changing in 1971. The Flower Generation loosened us all up and Ruby knew that it was now possible—and, indeed, trendy—to let it all hang out, as the saying went.

There are incidents in this book that show Bessie Smith in a decidedly unfavorable light; others are either favorable or unfavorable, depending on the reader's mind-set. I included them because they reveal aspects of her personality that are essential to an understanding of her. Other incidents, some far more sensational, were left out because they seemed irrelevant. One television interviewer asked me why there was so much sexual content in the book. I replied that I had probably dealt conservatively with that subject, that I had included only a few of incidents of backstage promiscuity, and that I had—for example—left out any mention of the German shepherd. The interviewer decided that it was time for a commercial break.

Bessie Smith cared remarkably little for the good opinion of others; she sought acceptance as a human being, but she would not alter her ways in order to gain it. As I have indicated, I like to think that a Bessie Smith autobiography would have held very little back.

In 1971, writers were beginning to face the reality of drugs on the jazz scene, but jazz artists were generally portrayed with Hollywood-like detachment; they were there, they played, they recorded, and one presumed that they had a life beyond music, but no details were offered. I knew, therefore, that the candor of this book might offend and that its dispelling of myths might disillusion. Having read a number of superficial biographies and heard performers laugh at their naïvété, I felt obliged to paint as accurate a portrait of Bessie Smith as could be produced at such a late date, and although the early 1970s was a confused period of ethnic polarization, I felt that the ethnic disparity between me and my subject should not be inhibiting. No writer, black or white, had undertaken a serious, researched biography of Bessie, and too much valuable time had already been wasted.

As Bessie's lifestyle unfolded before me, I reasoned that it would shock or offend only those whose precepts are based on outmoded, puritanical values. Of course time has since altered such values, and we entered a new century with eyes wide open. Yes, Virginia, Ella and Louis did make regular trips to the bathroom, and much of the jazz world's macho image is but a veneer. To gain as deep an understanding of Bessie as could be had at such a late date, I knew that I would have to portray her, warts and all. This would make it easier to understand why Bessie did some of the things she did. In one postpublication interview, I was asked why I thought it necessary to mention Bessie's bisexuality; I replied that it was more than a passing fancy, that it was rather common in Bessie's show-business milieu, and that it so went against Jack Gee's simple concept of life that it contributed to their marital problems. Would we not have gained a deeper understanding of Langston Hughes if his biographer had not tried to hide the fact that he was gay? Do we not know Billy Strayhorn better because of biographer David Hajdu's honest approach in *Lush Life?* We have seen several Miles Davis biographies, including one in which he collaborated, but none have been wholly truthful regarding his personal life, which leaves rumors to circulate and be embellished upon. Granted, much of Billie Holiday's *Lady Sings the Blues* was the work of collaborator William Dufty rather than Billie's own, but Doubleday's editors severely distorted her story by deleting segments that were deemed too controversial—they remain unpublished forty years later.

Today, tell-all books are common if not always acceptable, but shattering myths is not always easy, especially when they are as indelible as the alleged circumstances surrounding Bessie's death. That particular one took on a life of its own, often overshadowing all other aspects of Bessie's life. Shortly after the original edition of *Bessie* appeared, Florynce Kennedy—the feisty civil rights attorney, who was a friend of mine—seemed to have forgotten my phone number. When I finally caught up with her and asked why she had given me the cold shoulder for several years, Flo replied, "It wasn't necessary to change the story of Bessie's death—you shouldn't have done that." I told her that all I did was dig up the truth. "I know," she said, cracking a slight smile, "but you should have left it where it was."

Ruby's reminiscences and the natural way in which she related them removed my inhibitions and eased considerably the task of writing; as she, Maud Smith, and others relived good and bad times for me, I became so wrapped up in Bessie's story that I did not give prevailing jazz literature conventions another thought. I did not set out to break new ground, only to be honest in my reporting, and it was only when reviewers pointed it out that I realized how far beyond the conventional borders of jazz literature I had strayed.

But I hope this book also casts a new light on Bessie Smith as a performer. The very fact that it was possible to write a book about her in 1972 and include so much hitherto unpublished material regarding her character and career clearly illustrates that stones were left unturned. This is, not to say that everything contained in this book is gospel truth; it is quite possible—and, indeed, probable—that I have failed to detect an occasional embellishment, but I believe that I have captured at least the essence of this remarkable woman's life and that my margin of error is a thin one. Here I should point out that although attempts were made to discredit Ruby as a source, such accusations came from people who were discomforted by her frankness, and none offered proof to the contrary. Conversely, evidence supporting Ruby's recollections repeatedly surfaced in the years that followed the book's original publication.

Although a certain amount of repetition was unavoidable, I did not want this biography to be a mere rehash of previously published material; too many questions remained unanswered, gaps needed to be filled, and logic needed to be applied to deep-seated stories. I obtained some of the missing material from press clippings that seemed to have escaped the eyes of previous researchers and from the recollections of Bessie's few surviving associates. The clippings would of course always be there, but the memories would not; time depletes valuable recollections at an accelerated pace, and it was running out. Had my research started today, in the new millennium, I would have been hard put to find more than a handful of people with personal recollections.

Besides her vivid descriptions of events, Ruby Walker contributed immeasurably to this book by weaving into her reminiscences names and places that triggered new searches; often the casual mention of a person once associated with Bessie, but long since forgotten, led me to a valuable source of information. It all combined to bring a blurred portrait into focus.

Jack Gee, Jr., was one of several key persons whom Ruby casually mentioned in the course of our interviews. Bessie, who nicknamed him "Snooks," adopted this boy in 1926, when he was a small child. Since the original edition of this book was published, it has come to light that the adoption was unofficial, but that has not diminished Jack, Jr.'s importance to the story nor lessened the value of his recollections, which added a new dimension to Bessie's biography. It was Jack, Jr., who, in turn, led me to Lionel Hampton (who would have thought there would be a link between Hampton and Bessie!) and to Maud Smith, widow of Bessie's brother, Clarence. Maud Smith toured extensively with her sister-in-law and proved to be extremely helpful in substantiating information already learned from Ruby Walker. Maud also added details of Bessie's childhood and relationships to Jack Gee and Richard Morgan. On the rare occasions when Jack Gee, Sr., spoke to writers about Bessie, his agenda was clearly to trounce stories of a rocky marriage and to leave the impression that their union had never really ended. It is significant that he never mentioned Jack, Jr., Ruby, Maud, or Bessie's sisters, all of whom he maintained some sort of contact with. Consequently, historians never tapped these vital sources.

Newspaper and periodical accounts, mentions, and advertisements are a jazz biographer's guiding light; many microfilmed pages were carefully scrutinized in preparation for this book, with a concentration on African-American publications from 1915 to 1937. They yielded approximately three hundred relevant—if not always reliable—items, some of which substantiated information obtained through interviews. It should be noted that the black press of that period relied heavily on volunteer writers—often people who themselves were performers—and that these reporters and columnists sometimes received remuneration from the theater owners or the performers they reviewed. Thus a glowing write-up did not necessarily reflect its author's true opinion or a performance's true merit.

Unfortunately, not all the gaps could be filled. Although I was able to shed some new light on Bessie's activities in her formative years, information regarding that period of her life was, at best, spotty, and almost nonexistent when it came to her childhood. However, the publication of a biography has a way of generating more information, for it inspires people to come forward. That happened in 1972, when the Tennessee Arts Festival invited me, Snooks, and singer Pearl Murray, a dedicated Bessie fan, to come to Chattanooga for a long-overdue tribute. A local newspaper threw a cocktail party, extending an open invitation to anyone who had known Bessie during her childhood and early years in the city. Several people showed up; some had attended school with Bessie, others just remembered her from the neighborhood. Their recollections helped to fill in an important gap; we already knew much about Bessie's adult personality, and now we also had some idea of what had shaped it.

Jazz critic Rudi Blesh told me that he had come close to writing a Bessie Smith biography in the late 1940s; it all hinged on the cooperation of Bessie's family. For a price, Jack Gee and Bessie's sisters, Tinnie and Viola—then still living in Philadelphia—agreed to cooperate. As if to prove that their price was reasonable, Bessie's sisters showed Rudi a couple of her costumes and a trunk full of rare photographs, letters, sheet music, and other items. "It was a real treasure," said Blesh, "including some wonderful early pictures of Bessie." He eventually reached a financial agreement with the three relatives, and a major publisher drew up a contract, but just as he was about to sign it, Gee demanded more money. His unrealistic figure killed the project and reignited a long-running feud between him and the two sisters. "I was ready to go without Jack," Blesh recalled, "but he made the sisters so angry that they decided not to do anything that might in any way benefit him. Consequently, they destroyed the trunk and its contents—all that great memorabilia disappeared forever. It was heartbreaking."

A similar frustration befell me during the two years I spent on the original edition of this biography. One night, while working on the Bessie Smith LP reissue series, a Columbia Records technician named Doug Pomeroy handed me a time-worn ledger containing the company's log of artists' contracts and correspondence from the 1920s and 1930s. He had stumbled upon it in a pile of papers and hanging files that formed a trash heap gathering dust in a corner of an air-conditioning room at the Thirtieth Street studio. As it turned out, the ledger was just one item from a treasure trove of information that included interoffice memoranda and correspondence from Bessie's days with the label. This was an extraordinary and timely discovery of material that would surely have shed light on the relationship between Bessie and Frank Walker, who served as both her manager and Columbia's director of "race" records. It might also have given us a hint of the company's attitude toward its "race artists" at the time. The ledger contained valuable information: a session-by-session log of Bessie's recording activities, the terms of her contracts, payment details, and intriguing notes on advances paid, and other items. Unfortunately, it turned out to be the only document salvaged, for when I went to the Thirtieth Street studio on the following day, full of anticipation, there was not a sign of the remaining material. The maintenance crew informed me that the "old junk" had been thrown out and was beyond retrieval. Now I knew exactly how Rudi Blesh felt.

The line separating misinformation and conjecture is often a thin one, and it would be almost impossible to write this book without occasionally resorting to the latter. The reader will note that the text contains a good amount of dialogue that obviously did not take place in my presence, so some clarification of that is in order. The direct quotations and verbal exchanges are not of my own making but, rather, either taken directly from, or based upon, firsthand recollections; they may not give the actual words spoken, but I believe they capture the essence of what was said. In some cases, such as the Carl Van Vechten party incident, my description is a composite of several eyewitness accounts. (Ruby and veteran film actor Leigh Whipper gave almost identical accounts of Bessie's dramatic departure from the Van Vechtens' apartment; Ruby's and Maud's description of an incident involving Bessie and a gun was identical except for one detail: each claimed to be the one Bessie asked to go and fetch the gun.) Sometimes people, although interviewed separately, recalled an almost identical exchange of words.

Several no-holds-barred jazz biographies were published in the 1990s, but there are many important figures in black music's past whose true stories remain untold, and the job of correcting that becomes more difficult as sources of information fade with time. The understandable reluctance on the part of African Americans—especially older ones—to speak freely to a white interviewer is still in evidence, and although there is now a more reasonable racial balance, whites continue to dominate the field of jazz writing. Over the years, control over the commercial and, sometimes, creative aspects of black music has mostly rested in white hands, and it is still possible for an outspoken performer or determined writer to face closed doors.

The music industry is not all Grammy smiles and glitter; its closet is a veritable graveyard of skeletons, and when record companies point their collective finger at dot.coms like Napster and yell "Foul!" a hollow ring is heard by the thousands of artists who for decades have been unscrupulously shortchanged by some of these very same finger-pointers.

"If you dare to criticize him," trumpeter Rex Stewart once told me, "John Hammond will go out of his way to prevent you from working." I can attest to the veracity of that comment, as could Ruby Walker, whose career he once vowed to block.

In the early 1970s, as writer Linda Kuehl immersed herself in research for a Billie Holiday biography and delved into the singer's contracts and royalty statements, she began to receive anonymous threatening phone calls, suggesting—in strong terms—that she concentrate on the musical aspects of Billie's life and leave the business side out of it (she once played for me a tape recording containing such a threat).

In 1971, I optimistically pointed out that the old clique of writers, club owners, record company officials, and impresarios, who for decades literally ruled over the world of black music, was breaking up and that performers themselves were filling some of the vacated spots. My optimism was premature, for I failed to foresee mega-mergers that have since reduced the record industry to a handful of corporate giants, manned by number-crunchers and attorneys whose vision stretches only as far as the next favorable bottom line. An industry that once had at its helm caring, music-loving people was reduced to selling "product," forsaking artistic goals for material gain.

Although the recording industry's lack of ethics and creative pursuit has brought it to a low level, greed has also affected jazz journalism, spawning a rash of irresponsible, hastily assembled books that flirt with plagiarism and reflect a callous disregard for the truth. But jazz journalism has also changed for the better, for we have seen the emergence of a new, multiracial generation of writers who, in a climate of literary permissiveness, are slowly but surely bringing into proper focus their predecessors' blurry snapshots. This new generation of jazz chroniclers sees the importance of delving into concurrent events, attitudes, and social habits—important ingredients that their predecessors tended to ignore.

In writing this biography, I sought to do just that: capture the social and cultural climate of Bessie Smith's years as well as nonmusical aspects of her life. In 1971, as I caught myself getting carried away with historical and sociological asides, I became keenly aware the fact that an adequate social history of black Americans in the first four decades of this century had yet to be published. In his otherwise excellent books on America's twentieth-century growing pains, Frederick Lewis Allen all but left out African Americans, treating them rather naively when he recognized their existence at all; Gunnar Myrdal's *American Dilemma* reveals a far deeper understanding of the plight of Bessie Smith's generation in a racist society, but in such scholarly works the nitty-gritty of black life easily gets buried in exploration of a social phenomenon's broader consequence.

A case in point is the phenomenon of the "buffet flat," which the nature of this book allowed me to touch upon only briefly. Sociologists have dealt with numerous consequences of these establishments, but I have yet to come across a book that describes them or explains their significance to the black community. In Claude McKay's *Home to Harlem* and other works by African-American writers of the period, one finds numerous references to buffet flats, but in the atmosphere of 1920s and 1930s their salacious character was not something one wrote about, nor was there a need to explain what they were.

Buffet flats, speakeasies, white Hollywood goddesses, and a Florida real estate boom may seem like incidentals when speaking of Bessie Smith, but art is a reflection of the times and the milieu in which it is created. Imagine a biographer of a 1950s rock-and-roll star leaving out teenage gang wars, motel and drive-in romances, skinny-dippers, and panty raids, a 1960s or 1970s pop icon's story without Vietnam protests, racial riots, cross-dressing fans, and the disco drug scene. Similarly, a 1990s hip-hopper's tale would be incomplete if violent lyrics, drive-by and school shootings, and presidential indiscretions were omitted from the narrative.

Bessie Smith's story unfolds during a period when America was beginning to discover what the subculture she moved in already knew: the impact of African-American culture on the entertainment business. But no one could then have predicted how far reaching that influence would become. Bessie played a small but significant part in the history of American popular music. Her story is not complete as told here, but—thanks to the people named in the acknowledgments that follow—I believe this to be as close to a full account of Bessie Smith, the woman and the artist, as can be written at this late date.

Besides the aforementioned details regarding Bessie's childhood, I corrected a few discrepancies and went back to my interview tapes to find material that I—for reasons I now cannot fathom—omitted from the original edition. I also elicited further recollections from Ruby when the original publication gave her memory another jolt, and I have included material received from her in typewritten form after she relocated to California; some of it was intended for an autobiography, but she was unable to stir up publisher interest, and when she was diagnosed with a fatal disease, she asked me to "do something with it." Finally, I searched through other Bessie Smith material written by me in recent years, adding to this edition that which seemed to belong, including more about Bessie's recorded performances.

I am forever indebted to this extraordinary lady, who reached out to me with her artistry so long ago. Hers was the voice that opened the door, led me to the music of black Americans, filled my head with sounds that memory may dim but will never fade away completely, and ultimately led me to America. It is a debt that I can never repay, but I hope that I have done Bessie Smith justice and that my work here may inspire further efforts to enlighten us about major figures in African-American music, regardless of their ethnic heritage.

Acknowledgments

For giving their recollections and putting up with questions that sometimes were personal, and often naive; for contributing the dialogue this book contains, and for general encouragement, I remain indebted to Lil Hardin Armstrong, Lovie Austin, Eubie Blake, Lucy Brenner, Ida Cox, Demas Dean, Thomas A. Dorsey, Brick Fleagle, Juanita Green, John Hammond, Lionel Hampton, Katherine Handy, Alberta Hunter, Eddie Hunter, J. C. Johnson, Lonnie Johnson, Will Johnson, Jo Jones, Allan McMillan, Irvin C. Miller, Isabel Washington Powell, Gertrude Saunders, Frank Schiffman, Zutty Singleton, Elmer Snowden, Bucher Swan, Earle Sweeting, Leigh Whipper, and Sam Wooding.

For many hours spent scrutinizing the fine, faded print of hundreds of newspapers and periodicals, I thank Henri Berrings, Anthony Davis, Judge Mattocks, Lloyd Peerman, and Sheila Waters. For the tedious job of typing endless pages of manuscript for the original edition, I am indebted to Harold Hanson; for transcribing Ruby Walker's second round of recollections, I owe a debt of gratitude to Edward Hall; for detective work in Philadelphia, I thank my faithful friend of forty-three years, Bertha Stowall Waters; for clues and phone numbers, I owe much to the late Linda Kuehl—American music lost out when she was unable to finish her biography of Billie Holiday. For his extraordinary insight and social analysis—from which I confess to have borrowed freely—I am indebted to Billie Holiday biographer William Dufty; for enhancing my vision of black gospel music and introducing me to some of its most distinguished exponents, I shall always be grateful to Tony Heilbut and his authoritative book on the subject.

I also wish to acknowledge the help and cooperation I received from the late Walter C. Allen, whose exhaustive research into the life of Fletcher Henderson remains a definitive resource; Walter was with the Institute of Jazz Studies at Rutgers University when I began this project, and it, too, has earned my gratitude. Also most helpful were the staffs of the New York Public Library's Schomburg Collection and the Lincoln Center Research Library of Performing Arts; Valdo L. Freeman of the Negro Actor's Guild; the American Federation of Musicians, Local 802; Ernest F. Dyson of Federal City College, Washington, D.C.; Jerome A. Ford of Barber Scotia College, Concord, North Carolina; Willie Hamilton of the *New York Amsterdam News;* Rudi Blesh, whose book this should have been; Milton Kramer of Empress Music, Inc.; Mr. J. Seaman of the National Biscuit Company; and Doug Pomeroy, Pug Horton Wilber, and Ronald Francis.

A very special thanks is due to the late Jack Gee, Jr., whose reminiscences gave the original edition of Bessie an added dimension, and the late Maud Smith Faggins, who so fondly remembered her former sister-in-law and was able to fill in important gaps. Of all the myths that were generated around Bessie Smith over the years, none was more deeply ingrained than the alleged circumstances of her death; Dr. Hugh Smith brought that blurry picture into focus when he graciously shared with me his vivid memory of a fateful night in 1937. I also owe a debt of gratitude to the late Larry Hiller, a dedicated restorer of sound who burned the midnight oil at Columbia's studios, continuing our work on the Bessie Smith reissues when much of my time was absorbed by work on this book. I also wish to thank my editors for the original edition, Rennie Browne and Mary Solberg, who put up with missed deadlines and bad prose, some of which I think they pretended not to have read. For this new edition, I am grateful to Mary Frisque, my dear friend and hawk-eyed agent—who proofread my initial revisions and meticulously checked them against the original text—and to Laura Jones Dooley, who applied just the right finishing touches and became a Bessie Smith fan in the process; and let me not forget to express thanks to the late Henry Pleasants, who literally steered me right, making sure that the route of the funeral cortège this time did not lead into the Schuylkill River.

This note of thanks would be incomplete if I did not make special mention of the invaluable contribution from Ruby Walker. Without this remarkable woman's enthusiastic help, phenomenal memory, and gift for storytelling, I simply could not have written this book.

Finally, I note with great sadness that all but a few of the many wonderful people named above left us during the past thirty years. May they rest in peace and may their memory live on in these pages, as it does elsewhere.

1

No time to marry, no time to settle down;
I'm a young woman, and I ain't done runnin' aroun'.
"Young Woman's Blues"

On Monday, October 4, 1937, Philadelphia witnessed one of the most spectacular funerals in its history. Bessie Smith, a black superstar of the previous decade—a "has-been," fatally injured on a dark Mississippi road eight days earlier—was given a send-off befitting the star she had never really ceased to be.

Two days earlier, on a cold Saturday morning, Bessie's brother Clarence, his wife, Maud, and a prominent local funeral director, William Upshur, Jr., quietly awaited the arrival of Bessie's body at Philadelphia's Thirtieth Street station. They had waited there since early evening, reminiscing about Bessie while a succession of delay announcements rang from the loudspeakers. When the train still had not arrived at two thirty, Sunday morning, they decided to go home and return a few hours later. It was almost ten o'clock before the train finally pulled into the station, hugged the platform, and came to a steamy halt. "I'll never forget it," said Maud in a 1972 interview for this book, "as people got off the train, I kept expecting to see Bessie, but it was Richard [Morgan] who walked off that train, and I remember clearly the grief in his eyes."

Bessie and Richard had known each other for close to twenty years. They had been romantically involved for the past six, traveling thousands of miles together before making this last trip home from Clarksdale, Mississippi. Maud never got along with Bessie's husband, Jack Gee, but she liked Richard and now felt closer to him than ever before. As they embraced that morning, she noticed a small tear in the left shoulder of his dark suit, and it made her hug him just a little harder. "I still can't believe that Richard was in that car," she said, "he would have been killed, too, the way that car was smashed up."

Only Upshur seemed unmoved as they waited silently for the pine box of Bessie's remains to be lowered to the platform — to him, this was business with a nice promotional edge; to Richard, it marked the end of a short, sometimes bumpy trail; to Maud, the railroad station setting unleashed a floodgate of memories, good and bad; to Clarence, it was also a painful reminder of good times shared with Bessie on the road, but, above all, it brought home the fact that he had lost his favorite sister.

The Empress of the Blues lay in state at Upshur's funeral home on Twenty-first and Christian Streets. No one came to see her on the first day. But word of the funeral soon circulated, and when the black press published the details,[1] the body had to be moved to the O. V. Catto Elks Lodge, which more readily accommodated the estimated ten thousand mourners who filed past her bier on Sunday, October 3.

What they saw told them little about the remarkable woman whose last performance was being played out; Bessie's serene face gave no hint of the turbulence that had characterized her life. "They said she looked good and peaceful, poor Bessie," her niece, Ruby Walker, recalled. Her final costume was a long silk gown described by one newspaper as a farewell gift from Jack Gee, her estranged husband. She had recently admired this dress, the paper said, but not been able to afford it. "That should be turned around," suggested Maud thirty-five years later. "Maybe *he* was wearing a suit he never could afford, which Bessie bought for him." Actually, Bessie's life insurance paid for the gown.

Bessie's moments of artistic triumph and prosperity were eight years in the past, but the insurance policy helped bring back some of the glitter, affording her a grand exit in a five-hundred-dollar silvery metallic coffin, trimmed with gold and lined with pink two-tone velvet. The lining, suggested a reporter, matched Bessie's "flesh-colored" gown and slippers.

The auditorium of the O. V. Catto Elks Lodge at Sixteenth and Fitzwater Streets had on happier occasions resounded with Bessie's powerful voice and the cheers of those who came to hear it. Now some of the same people quietly filled the hall, testing its capacity long before the Reverend Andrew J. Sullivan mounted the pulpit and intoned the ceremony's opening words.

Sobs competed with Sullivan's ministerial voice, which rose solemnly from behind a pyramid of forty floral arrangements and bounced off the ceiling. When a Mrs. Emily Moten read a poem called "Oh, Life," a small commotion in the rear sent two registered nurses rushing to revive a swooned sobber. Three other mourners, including Bessie's oldest sister, Viola, passed out before dancer (and sometimes female impersonator) Rubberlegs Williams and a choir brought the service to a tearful conclusion with an emotional rendering of "My Buddy," a pop song that the day's gay subculture referred to as the lesbian national anthem. The song had been a hit in 1922, when Bessie, living in that same Philadelphia neighborhood, stood at the threshold of success.

Many people from Bessie's inner circle resented Jack's presence. They knew that his marriage to Bessie had been a continuous contest of physical and emotional strength, with only a sprinkling of blissful moments, and they saw his attendance as being hypocritical. Bessie and Jack had been separated for seven years, and each had established a new relationship during that time, but neither had seemed ready to put an official end to the marriage. Some friends optimistically took that as a sign of simmering love, but more levelheaded people labeled it a procrastination. Bessie and Richard Morgan enjoyed a more harmonious relationship. To be sure, there were bumps in their road, but arguments never turned physical, and it appears that each had remained faithful to the other. Of the two men, Maud decidedly preferred Richard and, in retrospect, felt that he should have been a greater presence at the funeral. This, however, was 1937 and society did not regard common-law husbands as members in good standing, so Richard stayed in the background during the funeral. Jack Gee took full advantage of the situation; as Richard's presence went unnoticed by the press, he unashamedly made himself the focus. Seeking out journalists from the black press, he put his own spin on the relationship, leaving the impression that he and Bessie had never lost touch and that she never ceased to regard him as her "man."

Leading a small group of close relatives[2] and friends—including Bessie's three sisters, her brother Clarence, his wife, Maud, and Thomas J. Hill, a nephew—Jack moved slowly toward the open casket for a final look at his wife. Some papers fancifully reported that he threw himself at Bessie's still form, that he wept, and that forty-five minutes passed before the six young pallbearers could lift the casket onto their shoulders and bear it out into the street. "Jack didn't throw himself over no casket," recalled Maud, "but he was good for putting up a cry, he'd cry in two minutes, and I'd have to say 'Stop those crocodile tears, Jack,' because he was just putting on a show."

The crowd outside was now seven thousand strong, and policemen were having a hard time holding it back. To those who had known Bessie in better

This Baltimore *Afro-American* photograph shows Bessie's casket being carried from the O. V. Catto Elks Home auditorium to the hearse on October 4, 1937. Photo by Edward Elcha, New York, from the author's collection.

days, the sight was a familiar one, but this was undoubtedly the largest crowd she had ever attracted.

As the front doors of the hall opened, mourners broke through police lines and pressed forward for a final glimpse. In the shoving match that followed, a woman and her child were knocked down and injured before calm could be restored and the ritual continued.

As the professional pallbearers,[3] who had never known Bessie, ceremoniously carried her casket a block down Sixteenth Street to the waiting hearse, the procession began to take shape; at its head, flanked by a tight-packed mob of mourners and onlookers, a choir softly intoned "Rest in Peace."

It was 4:20 P.M. before the cortege of thirty-nine cars began to move; another half hour before the last car passed in front of the Elks Lodge. The procession did not head straight for the cemetery but—as if to give South Philadelphia a last look at the Empress—crawled along Fitzwater Street, turning right at Eighteenth, and right again at Lombard. Making another right at Twelfth Street, it moved south into Bessie's neighborhood, past the Standard Theater at South Street, and across Kater, coming within a block of Bessie's house. Everyone seemed to know whose final journey this was, and all who stopped to view the procession seemed to be touched by it. A journalist reported seeing men dressed in rags bowing their heads and watching teary eyed as the procession disappear from their view.

Today, photo opportunity alone would guarantee the presence of celebrities at a star's funeral, but Bessie was laid to rest without the presence of major show business personalities.[4] Several celebrities, including Ethel Waters, had promised their presence, but no major star showed up. Performers, promoters, and others in the entertainment field who later claimed Bessie as friend, idol, or inspiration were conspicuously absent. Although Claude Hopkins, Duke Ellington, Noble Sissle, Buck and Bubbles, Bill "Bojangles" Robinson, Ethel Waters, and the cast of the Cotton Club Revue sent telegrams, only a handful of local show people and a few of her former chorines represented the industry of which Bessie had been such a big part.

At dusk Bessie's body was laid to rest in grave number 3, range 12, lot 20, section C, of Mount Lawn Cemetery in nearby Sharon Hill, Pennsylvania, where a hundred and fifty people watched a small group of mourners form a semicircle around a sunken, marble-finished burial vault.

A reporter dramatized the scene for *Philadelphia Tribune* readers:

> Two heavily veiled women wept steadily. In the strained silence, the breathing of the men was plainly audible. The clergyman cleared his throat softly, "I am the resurrection and the life . . ." The casket slid down into the grave. A woman screamed, and the broad shoulders of Jack Gee heaved and writhed as he buried his face in his hands. Hoarse sobs broke from his lips. "Bessie! Oh, Bessie . . ."
>
> "Earth to earth, ashes to ashes . . ." The minister closed his book. The mourners faltered forward to cast their flowers into the grave. Bessie Smith Gee, late "Queen of the Blues," was but a memory.

The airtight vault was guaranteed against corrosion or leakage for a hundred years. The funeral had cost approximately a thousand dollars, about half of what Bessie made in one of her better weeks. The grave remained unmarked for thirty-three years.

Jazz documentation was in its infancy at the time of Bessie's death. In Robert Goffin's *Aux Frontières du jazz,* published in 1932, and Hughes Panassie's *Le Jazz Hot,* published two years later, both writers plunged naively into their subject, led only by enthusiasm and curiosity. Lacking detailed information, their books offered an occasionally blurred view of jazz, but they inspired new writers who gradually pieced together the details of African-American music's development. By 1937, jazz had entered a new phase of development, and the hot, highly rhythmic sounds of swing groups and big bands was beginning to attract an impressive following that would eventually—for the first and only time—make jazz America's most popular music. Although a small cadre of dedicated writers sought to put it all into perspective, the main focus of the press soon shifted to the activities of the big swing bands and their star instrumentalists. In the process, historical data came to light by default; pioneers related amusing stories, but little effort was made to verify them, so myths were inadvertently planted. Some of these stories found a life of their own and have endured into the next millennium.

Bessie Smith was acknowledged as an important figure, but details of her life and career were overshadowed by the controversy surrounding her death—a controversy that, it turns out, had its genesis in sloppy reporting.

The pioneer jazz writers—all white and mostly European—embraced the music with tremendous enthusiasm, but showed little understanding of its social significance, and even less of the African-American culture that fostered it. They wrote of the music with awe and admiration, treated it with a reverence one might accord Bach or Beethoven, but all too frequently spoke of black artists in patronizing terms. By the late 1930s, the first American jazz critics had signed in, but extraordinary artists were still being portrayed with condescension and their personal lives trivialized—Bessie's death, the writers seemed to say, was tragic not so much because a human life had been lost as because it meant she wouldn't be making any more records for blues fans to collect.

It was not until the mid-1940s that writers began looking in earnest into the details of Bessie's life. Even then it was the blues singer and not the woman who interested them. The research was superficial and focused largely on her recording career, but some significant memories were recorded before it was too late. People remembered Bessie as crude, tough, or ill-mannered; irresponsible, passionate, kind, or generous. She was all these things, but the most vivid recollection was that of her extraordinary powers as a performer. Bessie's commanding singing voice, her superb timing, and her thoroughly musical approach to even the most banal material was something no one in her field could match. Her vocal material was often written by Tin Pan Alley[5] tunesmiths, but she reshaped their songs and charged them with joy and sorrow that appeared to be born of personal experience. She was also a natural entertainer who danced with flair if not grace, and she performed comedy routines with enviable skill.

Throughout her life, Bessie moved in a subculture that white America fostered but has only in recent years begun to understand. Her unique talent and unflagging quest for a good time took her into a third world of segregated black entertainment where, in an atmosphere of make-believe, she stubbornly remained herself.

If she had a goal, no one knew just what it was, but it was clear to those close to her that Bessie Smith yearned for acceptance rather than acclaim and that she did not see the two as being one and the same. Without playing the usual show business games and lacking the benefit of a modern-day promotional machine, she ascended to a level that no other African-American artist of her time and genre had reached. And when she tumbled from the pinnacle she landed without bitterness, gathered up the pieces, and began another climb.

Between the climb and the fall, Bessie Smith turned six glorious, eventful years into a love feast with millions of followers who clamored for her songs of romance, misery, and joy, and marveled at her ability to embrace fame with her feet firmly grounded.

Before 1972, when this biography appeared in its original version, those few years of costly glory had been the most frequently, if not accurately, chronicled. Less had been written about her last seven years, when she paid the price, and virtually nothing about her first twenty-five years, when she stood in the wings.

Bessie[6] Smith was born in Chattanooga, Tennessee, on a date that will probably never be verified. It was a time when Southern bureaucracy made little distinction between its black population and its dogs, so official records, such as a birth certificate, were not always deemed necessary. African-American people often recorded such events themselves, in the family Bible, but no such registry has turned up from the Smith household. Bessie was known to lower her age a bit in later years, but April 15, 1894—the date given on her 1923 application for a marriage license—is probably a correct birth date.

Located 138 miles southeast of Nashville, on the Tennessee River, Chattanooga was settled as a trading post in 1828. In the mid-nineteenth century, when railroads reached it, the small settlement grew in importance and population. By 1900, it had become an important trade center with a population of thirty thousand, almost 50 percent of which was black. In the 1890s, less than thirty years after the Thirteenth Amendment officially abolished slavery in the United States, most black Americans accepted poverty as a fact of life; in a very real sense, their enslavement continued, albeit in a veiled, more subtle form. By the turn of the century, a black middle class—mostly composed of teachers—was emerging in Chattanooga, but—in the minds of whites—education did not alter their status as second-class citizens. Most African Americans faced a bleak future of servitude with low-paying, demeaning jobs.

Abject poverty hardly describes the economic status of the family into which Bessie was born. William Smith and his wife, Laura, had met each other while both worked in Alabama, at the Owen plantation. When Bessie was born, they lived on Charles Street at the foot of Cameron Hill, in an area of Chattanooga known as Blue Goose Hollow. A laborer and part-time Baptist preacher, William Smith ran a small mission near the one-room wooden shack that was their home; Bessie remembered it as "a little ramshackle cabin" that would have been tight quarters for two adults, let alone a family of eight. Actually, the size of the Smith family fluctuated, for when there is little food and no medical attention, death becomes a frequent visitor: a seventh child, known only as Son, died before Bessie was born; she lost her father while still an infant, and by the time she was eight or nine, her mother had also passed. It was left to Viola, the oldest child, to raise her siblings: Bessie, Bud, Tinnie, Lulu, Andrew, Clarence. The last two soon became self-supporting, but now there were new responsibilities, for Viola and Tinnie became unwed mothers at an early age.

When an opportunity arose, Viola moved the family into a tenement apartment on West Thirteenth Street, in a rough, poverty-stricken neighborhood known as Tannery Flats. Taking in laundry, she generated a Spartan income to which everybody who was big enough to work contributed. "Viola was a hard-working woman," recalled Lucy Brenner, a neighbor. "She worked so hard taking care of them kids that she looked twenty years older than she was, and she never seemed to have any fun in her life. I don't think she knew what it was like to party—she didn't have time." Viola became an old maid prematurely when the burden of running the family was placed on her shoulders, and she never got over a brief romance that left her disillusioned and pregnant with her daughter, Laura. "Bessie said that guy ruined her sister's life, because she hated all men after that," Ruby remembered. "Sometimes I think she hated Laura, too, but—come to think of it—I don't remember Viola liking anybody. She was a nasty woman, and she even was nasty to Bessie, who did everything for her."

Clarence, the oldest male, worked odd jobs as a handyman but harbored loftier aspirations; Bessie and Andrew became street performers—she sang and did a few dance steps, he accompanied her on the guitar. Will Johnson, a friend of Andrew's who frequently saw them perform in front of the White Elephant Saloon on Thirteenth and Elm, remembered a feisty, uninhibited young girl: "She used to sing 'Bill Bailey, Won't You Please Come Home?' and whenever someone threw a fat coin her way, she'd say something like 'That's right, Charlie, *give* to the church.' I always thought she had more talent as a performer—you know, dancing and clowning—than as a singer, at least in those days I don't remember being particularly impressed with her voice. She sure knew how to shake money loose from a pocket, though."

Although she spent much of her time entertaining in the adult milieu of Chattanooga's seamiest streets, Bessie experienced at least the semblance of a normal childhood: she attended the West Main Street School, where she is believed to have gone as far as the eighth or ninth grade, and she found time to play with the neighborhood children, some of whom recalled her frequently being bullied by her playmates. This may account for the extraordinary pugnacity she exhibited as an adult.

While she accepted the money Bessie and Andrew brought home, Viola took a dim view of Bessie's street entertainment activities. Clarence had made his show business ambitions known, and Bessie seemed mesmerized by her older brother—it was clear that she, too, was priming herself for bigger things. While uneducated Southern blacks resigned themselves to a life of ill-paid labor, show business offered a tempting alternative to those who were so inclined.

Today, blacks dominate the American cultural scene to a higher degree than ever before, exerting a sometimes subtle influence on everything from music and dance to language and fashion. The story of black public entertainment in America begins in the early 1800s when—in a field at Orleans and Rampart Streets, in New Orleans—slaves were permitted to assemble on Saturday and Sunday nights for a tribal orgy of music and dance, a lively mix accented by religious chants and the mesmerizing rhythms of drums called bamboulas. These gatherings in what is now known as Congo Square, became a popular tourist attraction and, from contemporary descriptions, could well be considered precursors to the jam session.

"A dry goods box and an old pork barrel formed the orchestra," wrote a New York journalist. "These were beaten with sticks or bones, used like drumsticks so as to keep up a continuous rattle, while some old men and women chanted a song that appeared to me to be purely African in its many vowelled syllabification. . . . In the dance, the women did not move their feet from the ground. They only writhed their bodies and swayed in undulatory motions from ankles to waist. The men leaped and performed feats of gymnastic dancing. Small bells were attached to their ankles. Owing to the noise, I could not even attempt to catch the words of the song. I asked several old women to recite them to me, but they only laughed and shook their heads. In their patois they told me—'no use, you could never understand it. *C'est le Congo!*' "

Allowing slaves to express their spirituality at Congo Square may have seemed like an act of generosity on the part of their owners, but this gesture was, in fact, a preventive measure: whites, fearing a unified, voodoo-inspired uprising, thought it prudent to allow their slaves to vent.

By the early 1840s, an American phenomenon known as the minstrel show was also beginning to take place. Racist in nature, it was originally a form of intermission entertainment wherein white actors in blackface portrayed demeaning caricatures of African Americans. Minstrel shows eventually developed a distinct structure within which such characters as Mr. Bones, Mr. Tambo, and Mr. Interlocutor performed specific roles, a chorus harmonized songs by Stephen Foster and others, and so-called end men swapped comedic lines. Besides castanets and tambourines, these shows featured the banjo, an instrument of African origin that also formed a conspicuous part of the music heard in Congo Square and was commonly used by black street minstrels. As these shows toured the country, they firmly embedded in the minds of white America a racist stereotype of black people that Al Jolson and Eddie Cantor perpetuated in the following century and that still lingers as we enter a new millennium. By the mid-1800s, the original blackface routines had been relegated to the final act of shows that now featured a more varied program, including parodies of European opera—the foundation for extravagant variety shows had been laid.

So began a long tradition of looting black creativity. A quotation from an 1845 issue of *Knickerbocker* magazine offers early recognition of this problem: “Who are our true rulers? The Negro poets, to be sure. Do they not set the fashion, and give laws to the public taste? Let one of them, in the swamps of Carolina, compose a new song, and it no sooner reaches the ear of a white amateur, than it is written down, amended (that is, almost spoilt), printed, and then put upon a course of rapid dissemination, to cease only with the utmost bounds of Anglo-Saxondom, perhaps with the world. Meanwhile, the poor author digs away with his hoe, utterly ignorant of his greatness.”

In 1885, two white Boston businessmen, Benjamin Franklin Keith and Edward Franklin Albee, initiated the vaudeville era with a production that promised wholesome family fun from morning to night and allowed patrons to stay as long as they wished for a mere quarter. Nine years later, the Keith-Albee concept had evolved into a grand entertainment presented in lavishly appointed theaters designed to resemble the most opulent palaces of Europe. By 1900, vaudeville (a name Keith and Albee are said to have originated) had spread to other cities, spawned new theatrical alliances and theater circuits, and become the primary American entertainment. As vaudeville proliferated, it proved also to be an important springboard for black American entertainment, for it showed white impresarios that booking black talent could be lucrative. When that realization was put into practice, the doors of the rapidly growing entertainment industry opened wider to blacks, lines began to form, and the exploitation began in earnest.

Black touring companies—most of them rag-tag storefront affairs—hit every town and hamlet throughout the South with comedy patter, music, dance, and assorted hokum. When you are surrounded by poverty and hemmed in by hopelessness, even the tackiest little entertainment troupe can seem glamorous; it didn't matter if the costumes were raggedy hand-me-downs and the scenery a piece of cardboard—the keyword was freedom, a chance to escape to a more promising life. That gamble is what attracted Clarence Smith to every shoestring touring company that came to town—he was determined to some day leave Chattanooga with one of these shows.

The opportunity finally presented itself around 1910 or 1911, when the Moses Stokes company came to Chattanooga for a brief run in a storefront theater. Clarence auditioned and was hired as a comedian and master of ceremonies. Very much aware of the added burden his departure would put on Viola, he avoided the inevitable scene and quietly slipped out of town without notice. Although Bessie looked up to him, shared his dreams of escaping to better stages, and often fantasized that they made the great escape together, Clarence also kept his departure a secret from her. "If Bessie had been old enough, she would have gone with him," said his widow, Maud, in a 1972 interview, "that's why he left without telling her, but Clarence told me she was ready, even then. Of course she was only a child."

Clarence's sudden departure left everybody bereft: Bessie, having spent so much time daydreaming with her brother, felt a void. She was deeply disappointed, and if she felt betrayed, it was probably something Viola put into her head, for Viola saw Clarence's venture as a desertion and vented her anger and frustration on the rest of the family. Now more than ever, she came to rely on the money Bessie and Andrew generated on the city's sidewalks, yet she continued to resent their activity—for someone who had never known happiness, there was something sinful about earning money in an enjoyable way. Viola also knew that it was only a matter of time before Bessie and, possibly, Andrew followed in Clarence's footsteps. "Viola did some terrible things to Bessie," said Maud. "If she did something bad, she'd punish her by keeping her locked up in the outhouse all night." Ruby confirmed this, recalling that Bessie used tell people that she "was raised in a shit house."

Bessie's move to better houses, as it were, began with Clarence's return to Chattanooga in 1912. He was still with the Stokes company and he had told its managers, Lonnie and Cora Fisher, about his talented sister. They agreed to audition Bessie and, not surprisingly, hired her, but principally as a dancer. Viola had one less mouth to feed, but the loss of Bessie added to her hardship, and that was soon compounded by the violent death of their brother, Bud, allegedly in a street brawl.

The Stokes company's cast included Gertrude McDonald, Son Riggins,

Wiley Teasley, Len Collins, Isaac Bradford, Abner Davis, Will Rainey, and his wife of eight years, a singer named Gertrude. No one knows how long Bessie stayed with that show, but a few months later she was seen appearing twenty miles away, in Dalton, Georgia, with another troupe that also included the Raineys.

Bessie would undoubtedly have tasted success without Ma Rainey, but her direction might have been different if fate had not brought them together. Born in Columbus, Georgia, on April 26, 1886, Ma Rainey was Gertrude Pridgett when she made her stage debut at the Springer Opera House, in a local production called *Bunch of Blackberries*. In 1904, she married a dancer comedian, William "Pa" Rainey, who also became her on-stage partner. Together they toured the South and Midwest with a variety of companies, notably the Rabbit Foot Minstrels and Silas Green shows. She was soon being billed as Madame Gertrude Rainey, but she would forever be known as "Ma" Rainey, the Mother of the Blues, a pioneer of the genre whose place in jazz history was secured by nearly one hundred remarkable recordings. Since jazz and blues first became subjects of scholarly assessment, critics and collectors have regarded Ma Rainey as one of the greatest female blues singers, second only to Bessie. The tag Mother of the Blues was probably dreamed up by a record promoter, but it was appropriate, for although jazz boasts many legendary figures in its early, unrecorded history, the blues claim no predecessor to this extraordinary woman. She did not invent the idiom, but she appears to be the single or at least earliest link between the male country blues artists who roamed the streets and back roads of the South and their female counterparts, the so-called classic blues singers.[7]

In an interview conducted in Nashville by Professor John Wesley Work, Jr., of Fisk University,[8] Ma Rainey recalled first hearing blues in 1902 while appearing with a tent show in Missouri. "She tells of a girl from the town who came to the tent one morning and began to sing about the 'man' who had left her," wrote Work. "The song was so strange and poignant that it attracted much attention. 'Ma' Rainey became so interested that she learned the song from the visitor, and used it soon afterwards in her 'act' as an encore."

The song elicited such response from the audience that it won a special place in her act. Many times she was asked what kind of song it was, and one day she replied, in a moment of inspiration, 'It's the *Blues*.'

"She added, however," Work continues, "that after she began to sing blues, although they were not so named then, she frequently heard similar songs in the course of her travels."

In her well-researched book *Mother of the Blues: A Study of Ma Rainey*,[9] Sandra Lieb disputes the notion that Ma Rainey actually christened this musi-

Gertrude "Ma" Rainey was probably the first of the "classic" female blues singers. Bessie met her in 1912, when she joined the Moses Stokes company and launched her professional career. This 1923 photograph shows Ma Rainey with her Wildcats Jazz Band: David Nelson, cornet; Al Wynn, trombone; Eddie Pollack, alto saxophone; Thomas A. Dorsey, piano; Gabriel Washington, drums. From the Institute of Jazz Studies, Rutgers University.

cal form, pointing out that the term dates back to the late eighteenth century, when it was used to describe depression or despondency, and that—by all indications—the blues form was heard in various parts of the South around 1900. Given all the known facts, it is conceivable that Ma Rainey named the idiom, but she clearly did not invent it.

Among the many colorful myths that have clouded the facts of Bessie's life in the past is the story that she was literally kidnapped by the Raineys, made to tour with their show, and, in the process, taught the art of blues singing. One overly imaginative writer further embellished this story by describing a "cursing, outraged" eleven-year-old Bessie being dumped out of a burlap bag at Ma's feet!

Somehow, early research did not turn up the Moses Stokes company, nor the fact that the Raineys didn't have their own show until 1916, by which time Bessie had been on her own for several years. Early jazz writers made the apocryphal assumption that Ma Rainey taught Bessie to sing, a scenario that Hollywood screenwriters might embrace but flies in the face of fact. Ma Rainey may well have passed on to the younger singer a few show business tricks, and she probably taught her some songs, but Bessie was, by all accounts, a good singer before she left Chattanooga. "I remember one time when we were in Augusta, Georgia," Maud recalled. "Bessie and Ma Rainey sat down and had a good laugh about how people was making up stories of Ma taking Bessie from her home, and Ma's mother used to get the biggest laugh out of the kidnapping story whenever we visited her in Macon. Actually, Ma and Bessie got along fine, but Ma never taught Bessie how to sing. She was more like a mother to her. I have read so many things in these books, I don't know how people make up all those stories."

Irvin C. Miller, a theatrical producer who became a major force in black entertainment during the 1920s, had two shows touring the South around 1912. Bessie was in the chorus of one of them, but not for long. "She was a natural singer, even then," Miller recalled, "but we stressed beauty in the chorus line and Bessie did not meet my standards as far as looks were concerned. I told the manager to get rid of her, which he did." Miller's failure to see Bessie's physical beauty is explained by his well-known slogan, the theme of all his shows: "Glorifying the Brownskin Girl." To put it plainly, Bessie was too black.

Miller saw Bessie again in 1913 when she performed on the stage of the "81" Theater in Atlanta. So did veteran film actor Leigh Whipper, who—as manager of Newark's Orpheum Theater—hired her twelve years later. "It was in the early part of the year," said Whipper, recalling his 1913 encounter. "She was just a teenager, and she obviously didn't know she was the artist she was. She didn't know how to dress—she just sang in her street clothes—but she was such a natural that she could wreck anybody's show. She only made ten dollars a week, but people would throw money on the stage, and the stage hands would pick up about three or four dollars for her after every performance, especially when she sang the 'Weary Blues.' That was her big number."[10]

Bessie spent so much time at the "81" that its owner, Charles Bailey, told Jack Gee that she was "practically raised" in the theater's backyard, a small area that she used during the day to train girls for the chorus. Just how long she stayed with the "81" is not known, but this was one of the key venues in the Theater Owners' Booking Association (TOBA) chain, a major black vaudeville circuit whose star attraction Bessie would become. At this point, she was still relatively unknown, but she enjoyed considerable local popularity in the pre–World War I years when—with modest billing—she began making regu-

Clutching her pearls, young Bessie struck a sophisticated pose for this circa 1920 photo. Photo courtesy of the late Rudi Blesh.

lar TOBA tours using the "81" as her home base. Thomas A. Dorsey,[11] who sold soft drinks in the aisles of the "81" before becoming Ma Rainey's accompanist, witnessed Bessie's rise and shared some of his earliest recollections in a 1971 interview: "It was about 1913 or 1914 and Bessie was already a star in her own right, but she really got her start there at the '81'—I believe that's really where she made it—and I don't recall Ma Rainey ever having taken credit for helping her."

In a later interview for *Living Blues* magazine,[12] Dorsey was not specific when he credited Ma Rainey as a mentor: "When I worked at that theater in Atlanta, Ma taught Bessie Smith," he said, adding that numerous artists learned from Rainey, "the ma of all of 'em."

Bessie also toured with a popular troupe known as Pete Werley's Florida Blossoms and with the better known Silas Green show. An advertisement in

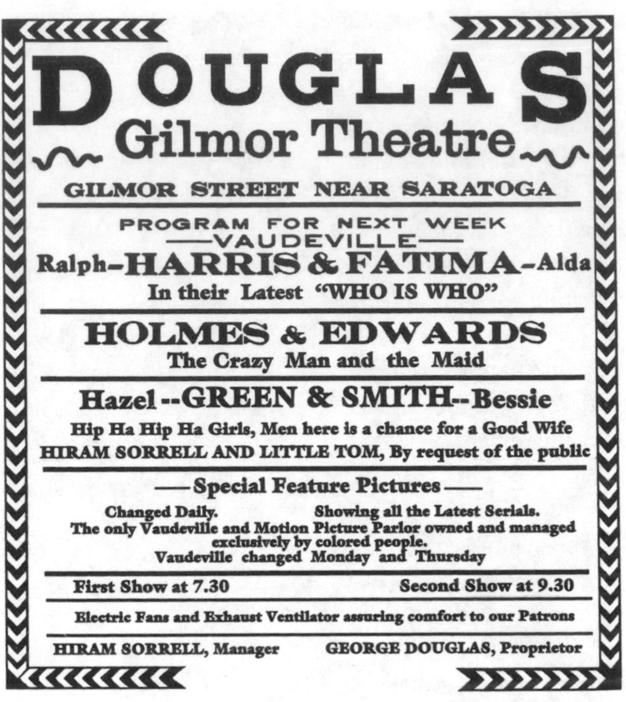

This print ad for an early Baltimore appearance appeared in the September 18, 1918, issue of the *Afro-American.* Bessie's partnership with Hazel Green appears to have been short-lived. From the author's collection.

the *Baltimore Afro-American* shows her scheduled to open at the city's Douglas Gilmor Theater on September 16, 1918, with a partner, Hazel Green. No other mention of this partnership has turned up, but Bessie is said to have performed with several female partners during this period. Perhaps more intriguing is the possibility that Bessie Smith was a wartime bride. There is no actual proof of this, but Bessie confided to friends that she had—in the early years of her career—married a man named Earl Love. Ruby remembered being told that he came from a prominent Mississippi family, that he was a soldier, and that he died young. Maud, who never met him, said that she could not be sure if Love had been in the military but added that, if that was so, Love was probably a World War I casualty. It has also been suggested that Love relocated to New Jersey from Meridian, Mississippi, met Bessie in Atlantic City, and died not long before she met Jack Gee.[13]

The World War was now in its final weeks. After America entered the fray, the year before, President Woodrow Wilson sent a segregated army—including the all-black "Harlem Hell-Fighters" (369th Infantry)—to Europe to "make the world safe for democracy." It sounded good, but those who survived found little evidence of democracy when they returned home. Blissfully ignorant of social injustices in their own backyard, most white Americans thought democracy had triumphed, but black Americans knew how meaningless Wilson's slogan was: they had been betrayed. America's "melting pot" continued to receive immigrants from the rest of the world, but there was not a lot of melting when it came to African Americans—they, it seemed, were in a separate pot, and it was beginning to boil over. Postwar race riots were more widespread than the press of the day indicated; thousands of blacks rallied in Harlem under the red, black, and green banner of Marcus Garvey's back-to-Africa movement, which white segregationists also supported, but the struggle for racial equality continued to leave most white Americans unconcerned. What interested them more was a new law, the Eighteenth Amendment, which went into effect January 17, 1920, and prohibited the manufacture, sale, and consumption of alcoholic beverages. It was prohibition with a capital "P," and it polarized the "drys" and the "wets" (or, as Florence Sabin[14] put it, "divided the nation, like Gaul, into three parts—wets, drys, and hypocrites"). The lifestyle it generated and the criminal activity it encouraged became the hottest issues of the decade.

Bessie had long exhibited an immoderate taste for alcohol, but its official banishment did not directly affect her, because—like many Southerners—she preferred homemade liquor ("white lightning"), maintaining that "anything sealed" made her sick. To most Americans, however, Prohibition offered a new challenge, and to the underworld, a major new source of revenue.

Ironically, Prohibition came just as a new generation of Americans unlocked the shackles of Victorian restraints and ideals. Given the mindset of the day, it was doomed to fail—as indeed it did, although alcohol consumption is said to have dropped some 60 percent. But how could anyone really know? Men and women on every social level broke the law routinely; speakeasies sprang up throughout the country, and well-established clubs—like Chicago's Dreamland—hiked the price on mixers and closed their eyes to bottle-toting patrons. Gangsters like Al Capone kept the "hootch" flowing by either smuggling it in across the border or distilling it covertly. "I wasn't drinking then," said pianist Lil Armstrong, who worked at the Dreamland, "but you could look around and never know that it was illegal to drink. One heard a lot about bad liquor being sold—some people got sick, or died—but they got to be pretty good at making it before it all became legal again." Americans were drinking as hard as ever, perhaps even harder than before; no self-respecting collegian would be found without a hip flask, and no member of law enforcement was so naive as to think that the cork could be kept in the bottle—government raids became little more than annoying pro forma events that today might qualify as photo-ops. It was a decade-long drama, a period piece with a leitmotif of machine-gun rattles and syncopated rhythms.

"The uncertainties of 1919 were over," F. Scott Fitzgerald observed. "America was going on the greatest, gaudiest spree in history." Part of that spree was a spending frenzy that had a well-to-do segment of white America luxuriating. For those who could afford it, there was more to buy than ever before: automobiles, refrigerators, Victrolas, brightly colored bathtubs, and, just around the corner, radios. If you didn't have it in the bank, there was something new called the installment plan. Although blacks experienced few changes for the better, the lifestyle of middle-class whites was improving conspicuously, and the contrast brought into even sharper focus the financial and social inequities that continued to feed the simmering racial divide. The entertainment industry also had its imbalance, but a smattering of inherent glamour made it less obvious; Bessie probably worked as hard as Viola, but she was having fun doing it, and there was a reward in every burst of audience applause, every gale of laughter.

Information regarding Bessie's activities during the postwar prelude to the flapper era is scant. She may have had less work during this period, because a deadly flu epidemic that killed thousands throughout the country forced the closing of many theaters and clubs, but it is clear that she was on the move (as far as Muskogee, Oklahoma, in May 1920, according to an item in the *Chicago Defender*) and that her career was heating up. The year also brought Bessie the sad news that her brother and erstwhile street corner partner Andrew was dead. Viola had been convinced that Andrew would eventually follow Bessie and Clarence out of town and join the entertainment world, but he opted to remain in Chattanooga, where—at the time of his death—he was comfortably situated with a family of his own and a good job as a prison turnkey.

Singer May Wright, the wife of pianist James P. Johnson, recalled seeing Bessie in Atlanta around 1920:

> I was playing at the "81" Theatre on Decatur Street in Atlanta, and Bessie Smith was at the "91" just down the street. The "91" was a smaller and rougher theatre, Bessie had her own show there, and I still fall out with laughter when I think about it, even today. You won't believe this, but Bessie was the smallest woman in that show. And you know how big she was. Well,

> that opening number was the funniest thing I ever saw. The curtain went up, and the floodlights came on, and there was the entire chorus dressed in close-fitting bloomers, bent over with their backs to the audience. The orchestra struck up "Liberty Belle," and there was that whole chorus shakin' every muscle in their bodies. I tell you I couldn't even keep a straight face when I was doing my own show after that.[15]

Bessie did not always have her own show during this period. In 1921 she appeared as a single with her band at the Standard Theater in Philadelphia, and in the summer of 1922 she worked in a production directed by pianist-bandleader Charlie Johnson at the Paradise Gardens in Atlantic City, New Jersey. Since the 1870s, Atlantic City had been a popular resort where the well-to-do promenaded on miles of boardwalk, amused themselves with coin-operated machines and mechanical rides, and cruised each other in the palm courts of its crystal palaces. When Bessie appeared there, the seaside town was under invasion by the period's leisured classes: liberated, flat-chested flappers and carousing collegians, strutting their stuff in the face of vanishing Victoriana. "Hot" music was all the craze, and there was plenty of it, for the popular resort had become a little Mecca for black musicians and entertainers.

One of the liveliest spots in town was the Paradise Gardens, where Bessie appears to have spent several seasons. Her presence in the club's 1922 lineup is verified by a photograph in which she is seated on the raised dance floor, surrounded by five young ladies, the Johnson orchestra, and comedian Frankie "Half Pint" Jaxon. A close friend and admirer of Bessie's, Jaxon began a nine-year summer residency as the Paradise Garden's entertainment director in 1918, and admittedly fading memories placed Bessie there around that time.

By 1922, Bessie had built up a loyal following throughout the South and along the Eastern seaboard. She was now living in Philadelphia, one of the cities that had been hardest hit by the 1918 flu epidemic, and she was ready for prime time. As America experienced a cultural revolution and countered the mindset that fostered World War I, times were changing in Bessie's favor. A societal transition was under way, the stiff-collared, pince-nez generation was being shown the door and the new generation that lined up had a very different look, for lurking in all of this was fodder for a feminist movement that would resurface in full force almost half a century later. After years of protest and demonstration by pioneering feminists, Congress finally passed the Suffragette Amendment, and young women were quick to develop a carefree, in-your-face attitude that probably took the movement beyond anything the suffragettes had imagined. "Flappers"[16] outraged generations of tradition-encumbered Americans who regarded as sinful their short hair, revealing skirts, and hedonistic public behavior. Another world war would come and go before women were further liberated, but now all the pieces were in place for Bessie to step into the big spotlight. And if the decade needed a musical score, it found the perfect one in the frenetic syncopation and liberated sound of jazz. An embryonic record industry found jazz, too, realized the high marketability of African-American music, and inadvertently launched a blues boom that seemed tailor-made for Bessie.

2

It's a long old road, but I know I'm gonna find the end.
"*Long Old Road*"

Bessie was now moving at a fairly fast clip down that long old road—at least the first, hard stretch of it. While she worked in the cabarets of Atlantic City and Philadelphia, record company executives in New York were making decisions that would significantly affect her future. The twenty-year-old record industry was at last beginning to realize the commercial potential of African-American talent, but it had been a long time coming.

For several years, black people had entertained white audiences in cabarets, theaters, and traveling shows, and it was not unusual to see headlining white performers catching these shows. They were certainly there to be entertained, but their patronage also had another purpose: business. White performers recognized their black counterparts as valuable sources of "inspiration" and material. "They studied us so hard that you'd think they were in class," said Alberta Hunter, who performed in several less reputable Chicago dives before enjoying great success at the city's most elegant club, Dreamland. "The white shows used to come in from New York and everybody was down there to see us work, the stars, the chorus girls, Al Jolson, Sophie Tucker, everybody. One night I was doing 'A Good Man Is Hard to Find' and they handed me a little note from Sophie Tucker. She wanted that song, and that's how they were, always trying to get something out of us, always trying to pick up on our little tricks. And what could *we* do? Only thing we could do was to do those numbers even better—which we did."[1]

On January 30, 1917, Columbia became the first label to make a jazz record: two sides by the Original Dixieland Jazz Band, a white New Orleans group that had caused quite a stir at New York's Reisenweber's Café. There is certain irony in the fact that jazz, a decidedly African-American music, was first widely disseminated by a white band, but that is a reflection of the day's mindset. The ODJB, as the band is more conveniently referred to, offered imitative hokum that only faintly mirrored the real thing, that being the early black bands of New Orleans. But this was a music in its embryonic stage, and it would appear that even the black bands tended to sound somewhat crude at the beginning of the century. "They had a raw sound," band leader Peter Bocage recalled in a 1961 interview with the author, "it was gut-bucket blues. People like Buddy Bolden couldn't play anything else, but this is what those people liked—they were very dark and real primitive, if you know what I mean." Bocage, a man of light complexion, lowered his voice as he ended the sentence.

Regarded as a novelty band, the ODJB scored a tremendous hit with appearances in New York and London. Columbia seems to have had little faith in the band, but subsequent recordings, starting with a February 1917 coupling for the Victor Talking Machine Company, sold more than a million copies. These recordings make an interesting study, but their value today is more historical than musical. Still, the band served as an inspiration to a new generation of jazz musicians, black and white alike.

One reason record companies were so slow to recognize black talent might be attributed to poor marketing research. Many black artists performed material that had universal appeal, but there was also entertainment that specifically addressed black audiences. That, alone, should have brought black artists into the studios sooner, but record company decision-makers assumed that only upwardly mobile blacks could afford phonographs, and they reasoned that the relatively few who actually owned one belonged to the emerging black middle class. This group was believed to share their white counterparts' taste for refinement and "wholesome" entertainment. Thus, before 1920, record companies made no attempt to reach black consumers, assuming that this minority within a minority would be content with such regular catalog fare as barbershop ballads, studio orchestras grinding out Rossini overtures, Madame Ernestine Schumann-Heink singing a Donizetti aria, or white vaudeville artists combining English music hall traditions with traces of sounds borrowed from as-yet unrecorded black artists.

It was composer-pianist Perry Bradford whose persistence and faith in the marketability of blues brought about the first recordings of black music by black performers. That happened exactly three years after the Original Dixieland Jazz Band made jazz record history. A distinctly African-American musical form, blues was developed by generations of unknown black folk artists long before W. C. Handy, the so-called Father of the Blues, was born. In the early twentieth century, before the northern migration of New Orleans musicians began in earnest, and before the ODJB made its splash, orchestra leaders like Wilbur Sweatman and Joe Jordan brought to Chicago and other Northern cities a ragtime orchestral sound that heralded the arrival of jazz. The repertoires of these orchestras included instrumental blues, although they were not always labeled as such, but vocal blues was still very much rural poetry, even as late as 1920. It was a musical form relegated to the South and performed by ordinary people and local artists who sought no spotlight. The words were often raw and at times salacious, but even when performed without words, blues was often regarded as the devil's music by older generations of Southern blacks. Lil Hardin Armstrong recalled being intrigued by a tune her Uncle Josh often entertained her with when she was a little girl growing up in Memphis. One day her mother, a deeply religious woman, caught Lil and her cousin listening intently as Josh sang this song, accompanying himself on a guitar. "She said the music he played wasn't fit to listen to, and threatened to break up the guitar if ever again she caught him playing such trashy music for us. John and I didn't know or understand why she made such a fuss about it, we didn't understand what the words meant. Later, I found out that 'Stinky Butt' was the Memphis version of 'Buddy Bolden Blues,' commonly known as 'Funky Butt' in New Orleans."[2] When Lil's mother later caught her playing the tune on the piano, without words, she was just as upset. Northern blacks who had acquired a degree of urban sophistication were not likely to object to blues on religious grounds, but they tended to distance themselves from anything that might link them to their past. Blues was the primitive expression of country people—it was slow, it had about it an embarrassing earthiness, and it lacked "metropolitan polish."

Bradford had no such hang-ups. A Southerner who spent his early years traveling with minstrel shows, he was an experienced if unimaginative performer with an ear for trends and the business acumen to take advantage of them. Steeped in the blues tradition, he viewed the genre as a gem in the rough; give it a slight polish, he felt, and even Northerners would recognize its true beauty. As he armed himself with blues material and aggressively made the rounds of New York record companies, Bradford became a man on a mission, a visionary determined to open the ears of the music industry's decision-makers. But his main objective was to peddle his own songs (or songs he had published as his own) and to secure a recording agreement for Mamie Smith, a black vaudeville singer from Cincinnati, Ohio, whom he represented.

After suffering the rejection of his package deal by the major labels, Victor[3] and Columbia, his persistence finally convinced Fred Hager—director of the General Phonograph Corporation's Okeh label—that it would be to his company's advantage to record two of his songs: "That Thing Called Love" and "You Can't Keep a Good Man Down." Hager liked the songs but seemed unwilling to take a chance on Mamie Smith—he wanted Sophie Tucker. As luck would have it, Miss Tucker—whose style (and, sometimes, material) was, as we have seen, on loan from Alberta Hunter—had contractual obligations to another company, so Bradford prevailed and Mamie Smith became the first African-American singer to be recorded in solo performance.[4]

Indistinguishable from white pop music fare of that period, "That Thing Called Love" registered only moderate sales, but it did prove to skeptical record company executives that a black singer could be as marketable as a white one. Though disappointing, the sales figures were sufficiently encouraging to warrant a second Mamie Smith session six months later. This time Bradford took his quest a step further: he talked Hager into using a black band to accompany Mamie and to have her record "Harlem Blues," a number from her current Lafayette Theater show, *Maid of Harlem*. It has been said that the song's title was changed to "Crazy Blues" because Hager wished to obscure the racial identity of its performers, but Bradford claimed to have made the decision himself in order to make the song appear new. Either way, the general attitude toward "coloreds" was such that Hager's nervous approval represented a gamble of sorts: the result was likely to be a distinctly black sound, which dealers and the public might not welcome.

If "Crazy Blues," cut on August 10, 1920, had not been the first vocal blues record issued, it would probably be long forgotten, for it is an undistinguished blues composition rendered by a singer whose métier was the so-called sweet song. The record nevertheless struck a responsive chord, sold more than a hundred thousand copies during the month of its release, and opened the eyes of the record industry to a totally new market. "You couldn't walk down the street in a colored neighborhood and not hear that record," recalled Alberta Hunter. "It was everywhere." So much for African Americans not having phonographs. Before long, several record companies dispatched talent scouts to black-populated parts of the country in search of women who sang the blues, and suddenly there appeared to be an abundance of such women. Most of them, as it turned out, were overnight converts from pop music who learned the form but lacked the feel of the blues idiom.

While Bradford was busy collecting his royalties and fighting lawsuits brought on by his having sold "Crazy Blues" to various publishers under different titles, his pioneering effort was giving birth to a new phenomenon, the "race" record. This term was now applied to all recordings by black performers, and the major companies — assuming incorrectly that such records would be of no interest to their white customers — began issuing dedicated "race" catalogs. To avoid a mix-up, Victor even went so far as to have its engineers scratch the word *colored* in the recording wax.[5]

Segregated marketing strategies had companies limited their advertising of race records to the black press; and their distribution to record outlets in black-populated areas. Thus, a white person residing in the North could conceivably live through the 1920s without ever knowing that black music existed on records. White Southerners, on the other hand, readily identified with the music and became a part of the race market.

The success of "Crazy Blues" inspired other companies to enter the field, causing what might be termed a blues gold rush. Among several new labels that specialized in black music was Black Swan, founded in 1921 by composer W. C. Handy and his partner in the music-publishing business, Harry Pace. It was the first black-owned record company, a fact Handy and Pace played up in their advertising: "The Only Genuine Colored Record, Others Are Only Passing for Colored." Ethnic pride notwithstanding, Black Swan rejected the very black sound of Bessie Smith when she auditioned for the label in 1921 but recorded the "whiter" sound of Ethel Waters extensively.

The Paramount[6] label, though located in Port Washington, Wisconsin, was a part of the New York Recording Laboratories, a division of the Wisconsin Chair Company. The company introduced its first releases in 1917 and entered the race records market with its 12000 series in 1922. It was not unusual for furniture manufacturers to offer recordings along with their phonograph cabinets; even the major labels made and sold the hardware: Columbia had its Grafonolas and Victor its Victrolas. Phonographs were fast replacing the parlor piano as a source of music in homes — records were the lucrative software. Thanks to blues artists like Alberta Hunter, Ida Cox, and the great Ma Rainey, Paramount soon gave the full-time record companies competition in the race market. Its recording activity centered around Chicago, which put Bessie out of its geographical range, but for Bessie, that was a blessing in disguise — Paramount's poor technical quality would not have done her voice justice.

With all this interest in the blues, with the hopeful and the hopeless being hustled into recording studios, it seems strange that Bessie — already widely known as a blues singer with extraordinary drawing power — had to wait two

The author goes over lyrics with Ida Cox at her 1961 Riverside recording session. Photo by Steve Shapiro, from the Valerie Wilmer Collection, London.

years to make her recording debut. If she did record before 1923, as some collectors have suggested, none of the discs has been found, but a couple of newspaper items keep alive speculation that there might be some pre-Columbia Bessies collecting dust somewhere.

One such clue is an intriguing item buried in the entertainment pages of the February 12, 1921, issue of the *Chicago Defender,* under the heading "New Star": "One of the greatest of all 'blues' singers is Miss Bessie Smith, who is at present making records, with the aid of six jazz musicians, for the Emerson Record company. The first release will be made about Mar. 10. Bessie Smith is a native of Chattanooga, Tennessee."

Although the records referred to apparently were never released, and there is a good chance that they were never made, record collectors have not given up the search. Some—the late John Hammond among them—have attributed two Rosa Henderson sides to Bessie, but careful analysis does not support such speculation. More tangible is the billing given Bessie in a May 14, 1921, advertisement for an appearance at the Philadelphia's Standard Theater:

BESSIE SMITH
Hits on Columbia Records and her 5 Jazzoway Dandies

This advertisement for Gibson's New Standard Thetare [sic] appeared in the *Philadelphia Tribune,* May 14, 1921. The reference to Columbia Records was a false but prophetic claim; Bessie would join the label twenty months later. Notice that ticket prices included a "war tax." From the author's collection.

By the time this advertisement appeared in the *Philadelphia Tribune,* Columbia had entered the blues field with its own version of "Crazy Blues," sung by Mary Stafford, a singer who appeared with Bessie at the Paradise in Atlantic City. It is conceivable that Bessie auditioned for Columbia as early as 1921 and that the reference was an anticipatory one, but the earliest mention of Bessie in the company's files dates from February 1923.

If Bessie did not record commercially before her first Columbia session, she at least made attempts to do so. An oft-told story, attributed to pianist-composer Clarence Williams, has Bessie auditioning for Okeh in January 1923. She sang "I Wish I Could Shimmy Like My Sister Kate," but the resulting test record failed to please Fred Hager, who found her voice "too rough." New Orleans musician Sidney Bechet[7] lends credence to the story with a reference in his autobiography, *Treat It Gentle.*[8] He claims to have arranged the audition around the time when he and Bessie appeared together in *How Come?*[9] a musical comedy that was trying out at the Dunbar Theater in Philadelphia. In his book, Bechet takes credit for bringing Bessie to the show as a replacement for singer Gloria Harven, but comedian Eddie Hunter, the show's writer and producer, disputed that when interviewed for this book.

Hunter confirmed that Bessie joined the *How Come?* company in January 1923, at which time five of the show's twenty-three songs were blues. She was not cast in a character role, he said, but rather was to sing after each act, serving as a transition between what essentially was a series of skits. Bessie sang under her real name, but the songs were not from her own repertoire. Although this was an easy engagement that required her only to do what she did best, her stay with *How Come?* ended a week after it began. The abrupt dismissal was the result of a run-in with Eddie Hunter.

The way Hunter recalled the incident almost fifty years later, he had just come offstage and was rushing up a narrow stairway for a costume change. At the same time, Bessie, her cue imminent, flew down the same stairway and they collided. Ignoring the fact that Hunter was her boss, and that it was as much her fault as his, Bessie erupted. According to Hunter, there was a heated exchange of words, which went something like this:

Bessie yelled, "What the fuck do you think you're doin'?" and followed up with a barrage of curses that rang through the backstage area. When Hunter tried to respond, Bessie's voice grew louder and her language became increasingly abusive, further fueled by the sight of curious cast members, who stuck their heads out of dressing rooms to see what was going on. Embarrassed by Bessie's lack of respect, and unable to get a word through to her, Hunter summoned the stage manager and instructed him to "Pay this woman off and let her out."

Shortly after Bessie's departure, but for unrelated reasons, *How Come?* closed for "reorganization." The new production opened on April 16, 1923, in the heart of New York's theater district, at George White's Forty-second Street Apollo Theater. Bechet still held the title role as a Chinese laundryman, but now a new singer, Alberta Hunter, provided the transition between acts. With fifteen Paramount releases already on the market, Hunter proved to be a bigger draw than Bessie had been, but this was not something she attributed solely to her vocal talent. "Nobody could sing the blues like Bessie," she recalled in 1976, "but I gave them something else they weren't used to, beautiful dresses. They weren't used to seeing that, but I had me a slew of them, and I changed several times during the show—the audience loved it."[10]

After thirty-two performances in New York, the show embarked on a tour that included Cleveland, Cincinnati, and Chicago. In his autobiography (which was transcribed and edited from tapes), Bechet claimed that Bessie was on this tour, but Hunter had a different recollection: "No, no, no, Bessie wasn't on the tour. She had left the show, she was only there in Philadelphia, for a very short time."

Bechet also speaks of having carried on a love affair with Bessie during their

Looking a lot like Jack Benny, Jack Gee had this photo taken while still living in Yonkers, New York. From the author's collection.

shared time in *How Come?* If so, their amorous liaison had to have been little more than a fling, but she is not likely to have involved herself with Bechet in 1923, for by then she was deeply involved in a love affair with John Gee, a semi-illiterate night watchman whom she would marry.

John (better known as Jack), moved with his sister to Yonkers, New York, from their family home in Virginia. In Yonkers, he and a partner operated a bar, but business was not good, so when he learned that the Philadelphia Police Department was recruiting blacks, he sold his share and moved there only to have the police department turn down his application. Jack nevertheless decided to stay in Philadelphia and was soon working as night watchman. In later years, he often flashed a photo of himself in a policeman's uniform, claiming to have been on the force. Jack had seen Bessie perform in Atlantic City, but they did not meet until 1922, when she was appearing at Horan's cabaret in Philadelphia. Jack was hooked at first sight. "I was living in New York with my grandmother when Jack first told her about Bessie," recalled Ruby. "You would think he had met Miss America, he was crazy about Bessie, and we got sick and tired of hearing him talk about her."

Their first date got off to a bad, almost fatal start when Jack asked Bessie out to dinner and they happened upon a street robbery. Details vary, but it appears that Jack—possibly showing off in front of his new girlfriend—chased the armed robber down the street and suffered a serious bullet wound that landed him in the hospital. Over the next five weeks, Bessie made daily visits to Jack's hospital bed, and a close relationship developed. Infatuation is said to have blossomed into love, and Bessie moved in with Jack soon after his release. That is probably a very simplified account of the courtship, but details have been lost with time. It is easy to view Jack critically and label him an opportunist, but although it is true that opportunism marked his actions after Bessie's death, and that their relationship put him in the money for the first time in his life, it is also true that his interest in Bessie preceded her "discovery."

Throughout the history of jazz—and, for that matter, modern show business—critics, agents, and recording executives have taken credit for the "discovery" of artists like Bessie. Artists, of course, are neither discovered nor rediscovered; they are simply recognized and given an opportunity to exhibit their talent. As a rule such opportunities are offered by people who see in an artist a means of making money and are in a position to exploit the prospects. Many hard years of performing honed Bessie's artistry to perfection long before she achieved any measure of fame. By 1923, when she made her first known recordings, she had already been discovered by the thousands of people who paid to hear her sing throughout the South and Northeast. It was just a matter of time before someone recognized what she could do for him and gave her that sought-after "first big break."

Frank Walker, the man Columbia put in charge of its "race" records division, claimed to have heard Bessie sing in a "low-down dive" in Selma, Alabama, as early as 1917. "She was just a kid of 17, maybe 18," he told George Avakian. "I had never heard anything like the torture and torment she put into the music of her people. It was the blues, and she meant it." She made such an impression on him, the story goes, that he in 1923 sent Clarence Williams, his "race record judge," to bring her up from the South: "I told Clarence about the Smith girl and said, 'This is what you've got to do. Go down there and find her and bring her back up here.' "

Williams—a pedestrian pianist who seemed to have made a close study of Tin Pan Alley's unscrupulous business habits—knew that he didn't have to go farther than South Philadelphia, for he had brought Bessie to New York for the Okeh audition a couple of weeks earlier. His account is slightly different:

Frank Walker, who supervised all of Bessie's Columbia recordings, was said to be the only white man she trusted. Photo courtesy of Sol Handwerger.

"When Mr. Walker came into Columbia," he told a *Down Beat* interviewer, "he asked me to get that Bessie Smith I had been talking about. I said that those others had said that her voice was too rough. 'You just get her here,' he told me."

So one might ask, who told whom about Bessie Smith? Perhaps it was neither Walker nor Williams; the credit probably should go to Charlie Carson, the owner of a record shop at 518 South Street in Philadelphia. Jack Gee recalled that it was Carson who got in touch with Clarence Williams in February 1923 and persuaded him to take Bessie to Frank Walker. According to Gee, Williams took her to Columbia, there was a successful audition, and a deal was made. The truth is probably in there, somewhere, for Jack's story makes no mention of the Okeh audition, which may have been where Williams first took Bessie.

Jack Gee pawned his watchman's uniform and a pocket watch to buy Bessie a dress for her recording debut; this was, in view of his later behavior, an act of uncharacteristic generosity for which Bessie rewarded him well. A few months later, Ruby noticed a clear change in her uncle's demeanor: Bessie's financial and artistic success had clearly gone to his head; he began to step out of character and put on airs as he showed off his two- and three-hundred-dollar suits and flashed new jewelry. The harder he tried to assume an air of importance, the more foolish he appeared, and all he accomplished was to make himself the show's laughingstock. "We giggled behind his back," Ruby said, "but not in front of Bessie—she would knock you down if you made fun of Jack, at least when she wasn't drinking."

From this point on, the story of Bessie Smith loses much of its vagueness and some of its mythical embroidery. People find it much easier to remember the famous, and Bessie was about to achieve that status.

During the first week of February 1923, Bessie and Jack went to New York in preparation for her initial Columbia recording session. They stayed at his mother's house, between Fifth and Lenox Avenues on 132d Street, just north of what was then a loosely defined border between black and white Harlem. The area below 132d Street was still largely white, but north of that, the streets teemed with black people—Harlem's demographics were changing and the nightlife had begun to sizzle. "The world's most glamorous atmosphere," young Duke Ellington said of black Harlem when he first saw it that same year. "Why, it's just like the Arabian Nights!"

The frenetic, pulsating beat that characterized much of Harlem's music at the time starkly contrasted the slow, drawn-out blues sung by Bessie and her colleagues. "This is one reason she didn't go over too big with New York musicians," suggested Sam Wooding,[11] whose band was featured at the Nest Club in 1923. "I remember her singing at the Nest one night, accompanied by my guitarist, John Mitchell, who liked her. She would sing something like 'Baby I love you, love you mo' and mo'.' I'd go to the bathroom, come back and catch the rest of the verse, 'I hope you never leave me, 'cause I don't wanna see you go.' She had dragged out each word so that I hadn't missed a thing."

Even after she enjoyed wider celebrity, it was not unusual for Bessie to give an impromptu performance when the mood hit her. Having enjoyed the nightlife on previous trips to New York, she was eager to share it with Jack; Ruby recalled that they spent the first few evenings of this visit out on the town but that Bessie was strictly business during the day. Rehearsals for the recording session took place in the Victorian surroundings of the Gees' foyer, with Clarence Williams at the family upright, and Ruby, then about twenty, taking it all in as she stood, mesmerized, in the doorway. Ruby originally met Bessie when she accompanied her mother on a hospital visit to Philadelphia, but this was the first time she heard her sing. "I just stood there and watched her, and my whole life changed," she recalled. "Of course I didn't know it then, but that's what happened." As she took in the rehearsals, Ruby quickly learned Bessie's songs, and she remembers standing in the adjoining living room, out of sight, emulating Bessie's movements and mouthing the words to her songs—it was the start of a fascination that would remain with Ruby for the rest of her life.

Bessie rehearsed four songs, including Williams's own "Gulf Coast Blues" and "Down Hearted Blues," a number written by pianist Lovie Austin and Alberta Hunter,[12] Bessie's replacement in *How Come?* Unlike so many of her peers, Alberta Hunter had a keen business mind, which prompted her to send the sheet music for "Down Hearted Blues" to Frank Walker. Since she was under contract to Paramount Records and had already recorded the tune for that label, she suggested that he have a Columbia artist record it. In a previous exchange, Walker had mentioned King Oliver's band (which had yet to record) and Hunter indicated that she thought it a good idea to have Oliver do the song. As Walker's reply, dated January 19, 1923, indicates, he was more interested in bringing Alberta Hunter into his Columbia fold:

> Miss Alberta Hunter
> #64 East 36th Place
> Chicago, Illinois
>
> Dear Miss Hunter:-
>
> Replying to your letter of the 15th instant, won't you please advise me at your earliest convenience just how long your exclusive contract with Paramount Company runs. No doubt you know that the Paramount Company is very small indeed and the prestige which you gain from singing for them is very limited.
>
> Regarding Joe Oliver's Band, my only idea in this respect was to use them as an accompaniment for you in case you did work for us. It will therefore be necessary for us to forget them until such time as you will be ready to put through a test record for us.
>
> We will try to see what can be worked out of the "Down Hearted Blues" for you but in the meantime would ask that you let us know about the Paramount contract as soon as possible so that we can make our plans accordingly.
>
> With kind regards, we remain,
> Very truly yours,
> COLUMBIA GRAPHOPHONE COMPANY
> (signed) Frank B. Walker

Walker failed to lure Alberta over to Columbia, and he probably lived to regret not having signed the King Oliver band, which, only three months later, would create history with nine classic Gennett sides that marked Louis Armstrong's recording debut. Walker did, however, do something about "Down Hearted Blues"—he gave it to Bessie and thus ensured its longevity.

Although she was already a seasoned stage performer, Bessie was nervous on February 15, 1923, when she entered Columbia's Columbus Circle studio for her initial session. Some twenty-five years later, Frank Walker gave George Avakian his first impression of Bessie. She was, he said, "so gosh-darn country—real southern. She looked like anything *but* a singer, she looked about seventeen, tall and fat and scared to death—just awful!" Ruby was not present, her request to be taken along having been denied, but she adamantly refused to accept Walker's observations as true. "I don't believe anything that

COLUMBIA GRAPHOPHONE COMPANY

SOLE DISTRIBUTORS FOR

COLUMBIA GRAPHOPHONE MANUFACTURING COMPANY

MANUFACTURERS OF

COLUMBIA GRAFONOLAS, COLUMBIA RECORDS AND THE DICTAPHONE REG. U. S. PAT. OFF.

RECORDING STUDIOS

1819 BROADWAY
NEW YORK CITY

January 19, 1923.

Miss Alberta Hunter,
#64 East 36th Place,
Chicago, Illinois.

Dear Miss Hunter:-

Replying to your letter of the 15th instant, won't you please advise me at your earliest convenience just how long your exclusive contract with Paramount Company runs. No doubt you know that the Paramount Company is very small indeed and the prestige which you gain from singing for them is very limited.

Regarding Joe Oliver's Band, my only idea in this respect was to use them as an accompaniment for you in case you did work for us. It will therefore be necessary for us to forget them until such time as you will be ready to put through a test record for us.

We will try to see what can be worked out of the "Down Hearted Blues" for you but in the meantime would ask that you let us know about the Paramount contract as soon as possible so that we can make our plans accordingly.

With kind regards, we remain,

Very truly yours,
COLUMBIA GRAPHOPHONE COMPANY.
Frank B. Walker

FBW:CGB

As Bessie prepared to make her first recording, Frank Walker sought to lure Alberta Hunter away from Paramount. She had suggested that he give her "Down Hearted Blues" to King Oliver, but Walker did better than that—he gave it to Bessie. From the author's collection.

had to do with singing could make that woman nervous or scared," she said. "In fact, it took an awful lot, period, to make Bessie scared, and singing was one thing she knew no one could beat her at."

Bessie's performance supports Ruby's contention; she sounds self-assured, the strong sustained notes that would become her hallmark are in full evidence. From the first note of the word "trouble," in the opening chorus, her delivery is clarion clear, absolutely steady, and rock hard. Also audible here are other characteristics of the mature Bessie. There is a wonderful bent note in the opening verse, just as she reaches the end of the sixth bar ("heartbroken too-oo") and a little later she stretches out and pronounces in her own prepossessing way the word "blues." Her enunciation is remarkably clear when she wants it to be, and so are the liberties she takes with the language: "disgustit," "three mens," and so on. But what really grabs the listener's attention is that full-throated, resonant voice that won Bessie new followers at every appearance.

Although Bessie's performance belies the trepidation Walker described, it would not be unreasonable to imagine that she was daunted by the task ahead. True, she had previously recorded an audition session, but this was the real thing, and Columbia was a label that attracted some of the biggest stars of the day. Today's recording technology is a digital process—performances are played back immediately and flawed passages can be done over to fit seamlessly into the whole—but recording was done acoustically in 1923, which meant that Bessie sang into the gaping mouth of a large conical horn through which her voice was transported and etched into the groove of a waxlike disc. Because the technology allowed only one playback in the studio, the first recordings were balance tests. Once an acceptable sound was achieved, the actual session could proceed, but the result was not known for a few days, not until test pressings were received from the factory. For this reason, artists performed a number over and over until it sounded right in the studio, and even when it did, they made a spare take, just in case.

Something obviously went wrong at the first session. It may have been a case of jangled nerves, equipment failure, or perhaps a little of both, but after nine takes of a tune called " 'Tain't Nobody's Bizness If I Do" and two of "Down Hearted Blues," the session was called off and a full day's work rejected. On the following day, February 16, things went a little better. Although five takes of "Keeps on A-Rainin' " proved unsatisfactory, it took only three tries each to come up with two usable selections: "Down Hearted Blues" and "Gulf Coast Blues." Columbia now had its first Bessie Smith coupling, and as trying as the experience had been, Bessie had given the most important performance of her career.

The history of American show business is rife with instances of whites exploiting black performers, but exploitation and skulduggery know no color bar. Perry Bradford and Clarence Williams were among the most notorious black exploiters of the 1920s, and they often schemed together. Acclaimed for their prolific output of songs, they were known to put their names to compositions they didn't write, a common practice in an era of song rustlers. Bradford and Williams were masters at stealing material outright or purchasing it for a token sum from a composer who did not know its real value.

In the spring of 1923—while Bradford was serving out a jail sentence for subornation of perjury in a copyright suit and Williams, acting as Bessie's

Clarence Williams often accompanied Bessie, but his bookkeeping was more creative than was his piano playing. From the author's collection.

manager, was getting her ready for a Southern tour—Jack began looking into his future wife's business affairs. When he discovered that Bessie's recording contract was drawn up between her and Williams rather than Columbia Records, he thought nothing of it, but when he learned further that Williams was pocketing half of Bessie's $125-per-selection fee, he decided to do something about it. It was mid-April and Bessie had made four more recordings, for which she should have received $750—more money than she or Jack had ever seen at one time—but only netted $375. A $5 discrepancy would have brought Jack's dander up, but $375 spelled doom for Clarence Williams's association with Bessie.

As Ruby and Maud heard the story, Jack stormed into Williams's midtown Manhattan office with clenched fists and Bessie at his heels. The ferocity of their sudden entrance and the sight of Jack's persuasive physique sent Williams crawling underneath his desk.

As Bessie relayed the incident, Jack pounded his fist on the desk and yelled to Williams, "Come on out of there, you dirty no-good cheatin' bastard!"

Williams was said to have emerged slowly, shaking at the sight of two huge, hot-tempered, angry people standing over him, and just as he straightened up, Bessie jumped him and pounded him to the floor with her clenched fists. She allegedly kept pounding until she and Jack got what they were after: a release from all contractual obligations to Clarence Williams.

The next stop was Frank Walker's office. Walker, who apparently had been unaware of Williams's private arrangements, signed Bessie to an exclusive

EXCLUSIVE ARTIST

CONTRACT-DATED	Apr,20-23
YEARS	1
COMMENCING	Apr.20-23
ENDING	Apr.21-24
RECORDINGS	12
ROYALTY	-
ADV.-ON-ACCT.	-
FLAT PAYMENT	$125.00
RENEWAL-OPTION	1 yr.
RENEWAL-NOTICE	Mar.21-24

REMARKS:
Guarantee - $1,500.00
Additional term of 1 yr.
$150.00 per selection
Guarantee - $1,800.

DATE MADE 1923	MATRIX NO.	TITLE	DATE O.K'd 1923	DATE PAID 1923	AM'T PAID	MONTH
Apr.1	80949	Aggravatin' Papa (with Trio)	4-21	May 2	$125.	Spec
Apr.1	80950	Beale Street Mama (with trio)	4-21	May 2	125.	"
[illegible]	[illegible]	Baby Won't You Come Home-Blues	4-25	May 2	125.	Jly/
Apr.2	80953	Oh Daddy-Blues	[illegible]	[illegible]	125.	"
Apr.26	80862	Tain't Nobody's Bizness if I Do	5-5	May 9	125.	Spec
Apr.26	80865	Keeps On a-Rainin'	5-5	May 9	125.	"
Apr.28	80995	Mama's Got the Blues	5-7	May 9	125.	Aug.
Apr.28	80996	Outside of That He's Alright With Me	5-7	May 9	125.	Aug.

This page from a Columbia Records ledger lists only issued (that is, acceptable) selections and covers Bessie's first contract with the label. Owing to a bit of skulduggery on Clarence Williams's part, there are no entries for the first two sessions. Notice also the absence of a royalty fee. From the author's collection.

one-year Columbia contract commencing April 20, 1923. It obligated her to record a minimum of twelve selections, at $125 per usable side,[13] guaranteed her $1,500, and contained a one-year renewal option for twelve sides at $150. Furthermore, since Clarence Williams had not yet received her fee for four sides made during the first week of April, Walker handed Bessie a check for $500. It was more than Bessie and Jack had bargained for but not quite as generous as they thought; by striking out the royalty clause Walker made a deal that decidedly favored Columbia. Since neither Bessie nor Jack knew anything about royalties, they saw Walker as a true friend, and Bessie was so impressed that she asked him to become her manager. An honest man would have pointed out the conflict of interest inherent in such an arrangement, but Walker said nothing.

Because Alberta Hunter's recording of "Down Hearted Blues" had generated impressive sales in 1922, and other artists had subsequently recorded it, the song was considered to have run its course by the time Bessie got to it.

But, to everyone's surprise, sales of Bessie's version soared to an impressive 780,000 copies in less than six months. At first, the high volume was attributed to the flip side, "Gulf Coast Blues," but audiences soon made known their preference for "Down Hearted," whose lyrics Bessie delivered with an honesty no other singer had matched. Many years later, Walker confirmed that he had simply assumed that "Down Hearted Blues" would be the secondary side but that the record-buying public thought otherwise. "There was one line in the blues that did it," he said. "It was the first time that it was used and it made that record a hit. It was 'Got the world in a jug, got the stopper in my hand.'" It didn't matter that Williams's accompaniment came straight from the published sheet music, Bessie's masterful blend of pathos and defiance overshadowed his unimaginative work. Nor did it make a difference to his wallet that people preferred Alberta Hunter's tune over "Gulf Coast Blues," for which he was the copyright owner; one side of a record sells exactly as many copies as the other. Because Bessie received neither performance nor composer royalties, Clarence Williams actually made more money on the release than she did.

As "Down Hearted Blues" hit the market and Frank Walker made preparations for Bessie's promotional tour, Jack took care of a slight formality: on June 7, he and Bessie stood before a clerk of the Orphan's Court of Philadelphia County and applied for a marriage license. With papers in hand, they proceeded to the home of the Reverend C. A. Tindley[14] on Christian Street, where they were quietly pronounced husband and wife.

In the meantime Bessie earned another five hundred dollars under her new Columbia contract, which would have been enough money to give the newlyweds a honeymoon, but the brisk sales of Bessie's debut release made Walker decide to seize the momentum and schedule another session for a week after the wedding.

Between June 14 and 22, Bessie recorded seven more songs, thus exceeding her annual contractual obligation in only half a year. Columbia valued her as an artist and decided to invest more money in her recordings, as well as promotion. With Clarence Williams out of the picture, she would now be accompanied by Fletcher Henderson, a soft-spoken, well-educated man whose gentle personality sharply contrasted hers and whose musical skills far outweighed those of Williams. Henderson was born in Cuthbert, a small Georgia town, and grew up in a fairly affluent family. Although he had a strong interest in music and had played piano since childhood, it was not the glitter of show business that brought him to New York in 1920. He had come to do postgraduate research in chemistry at Columbia University, but the closest he came to that was a part-time job with a chemical company as a laboratory assistant. The music jobs Henderson took to supplement his income soon proved more

As Bessie embarks on her successful recording career, she strikes a regal pose for Columbia's publicity photographer in 1923. Photo courtesy of Svend Holsoe.

rewarding, so he decided to stay in that field. It has been suggested that race entered into Henderson's decision to put aside his scientific ambitions, but he is not known to have confirmed this. Had he followed his original course, American music would have been all the poorer for it.

Bessie developed a good working relationship with Henderson from the start. There was a mutual recognition of talent, and Henderson knew how to dress up and frame Bessie's vocals in a way that Clarence Williams never had. Ruby recalled that Bessie was as impressed with Henderson's quiet personality and good manners as she was with his musical ability. He was, she told Ruby, "a real gentleman." Like Bessie, Fletcher Henderson stood on the brink of success, destined to become a pioneering arranger-composer in the big band field and—ironically—to create sounds that eventually made many view Bessie as an anachronism.

Publicity photo taken in 1923, shortly after Bessie signed with Columbia Records. Photo by Edward Elcha, New York, from the author's collection.

Just married, Bessie and Jack are all smiles and a picture of elegance. Their roller-coaster ride was about to begin. From the author's collection.

Soon after finishing her recording sessions with Henderson, Bessie embarked on her Southern tour. Henderson's commitments in New York prevented him from joining Bessie on the road, so she hired pianist Irvin Johns as her new musical director. Arranged by Frank Walker, this was as much a promotional tour for her recordings as anything else. It marked Bessie's first Southern trek as a recording star, and the anticipation was high when she opened at the "81," her old Atlanta stomping ground, on Monday, June 25, 1923. If Bessie was worried, she need not have been, for the "81" engagement proved to be a triumphant return, and it set the tone for the rest of the tour. The first show was such a box office and artistic success that radio station WSB broadcast the following night's performance in its entirety. Still in its infancy, radio had a limited, mostly white, audience, but Bessie's appeal crossed racial lines, especially in the South, and she soon became a seasoned broadcaster. Recordings were not aired in the early years of commercial radio, but live broadcasts boosted their sales and increased box office traffic. Bessie was quick to recognize that Frank Walker was steering her in the right direction; the promotional value of radio and the wisdom of linking her broadcasts to her record affiliation paid off, she was now billed and introduced as "the famous Columbia recording artist."

Bessie would soon become known for her extravagant productions, but Walker was testing the waters with this tour, so it was a relatively modest one. Bessie was the headline act of what essentially was a vaudeville show, the star attraction for whose appearance everything else was a prelude. The handful of performers who shared the bill with her had mostly been drawn from local talent, and even Bessie put the glitter on hold. Her one prop was a backdrop with the silhouette of magnolia trees set against an orange sky and a bright full moon. Costumed in an unadorned style, she wore a plain dress with beaded fringes, a Spanish shawl loosely draped around her shoulders, a simple necklace, a skullcap covered with beads and pearls, and a wig of shiny black hair that ran down to her shoulders. As some who heard her have said, Bessie could have come out in her street clothes and just stood there, casting her glorious voice into the far corners of the theater, but she always gave her audience more than they might have expected. Maud recalled people screaming with delight as she accompanied her vocal tales with suggestive movements and subtle dance steps.

No one had a voice as powerful and compelling as Bessie's, and no other singer of her day could tell a story as convincingly. Bessie's songs, whether she wrote them or not, became shared personal experiences. While contemporary pop singers built a "Stairway to Paradise" or made love "'Neath the South Seas Moon," Bessie sang with tragicomic optimism of mean mistreaters and two-timing husbands; she offered advice to the dejected and made it quite clear that she herself was not immune to such problems. She occasionally borrowed a song from Tin Pan Alley, but only if it had lyrics she could identify with, and then she often gave the lines a subtle nudge and deeper meaning. Audiences also liked Bessie's defiance, which came through in many of her songs, but perhaps nowhere as forcefully as on "'Tain't Nobody's Bizness If I Do." We can only speculate why it took ten attempts, spread over four sessions, to arrive at an acceptable take of this song, but the result is masterful. "That was Bessie's song all the way," said Ruby. "Clarence[15] must have had her in mind when he wrote it, because nobody got into Bessie's business without getting into trouble. She never gave a damn what anybody else thought." Bessie's timing is shamelessly unorthodox, and she breathes in the wrong places, but "wrong" sounds gloriously right as everything falls into place. To be sure, "criticize" is not three words, but when Bessie splits it up that way, the result sounds perfectly natural. Later, she adds her own "do do do's" at the end of a chorus, turning out a melody tag of her own. There is not a hint of hesitation in her voice as she sails it past Williams's robotic piano and into the horn that would capture it forever. This became one of Bessie's most popular numbers on the road, one that Ruby remembered as having had a particularly mesmerizing effect on the audience, but record sales were less spectacular.

Although Bessie sang with commanding authority, and surely never questioned her own talent, she was adamant in her refusal to share a bill with another female blues singer. So-called sweet singers were another matter, these were essentially pop artists who rendered the Tin Pan Alley songs of the day,[16] and Bessie often included one in her own show. She also felt quite comfortable sharing a bill with a nonsinging act, even one whose popularity rivaled her own. One such artist was Charles Anderson, a yodeler from Birmingham who received second billing to Bessie at the "81," and drew as much applause; the two headliners got along fine, and Bessie went out of her way to help Anderson obtain further bookings on her tour. "She did that all the time," said Ruby, "helping other show people."

By June 1923, when Bessie's first record hit the street, she had recorded nine additional sides under her new Columbia agreement. Although it seemed a misfit in New York, blues was turning out to be good business around the country, so Walker signed another of its new exponents to the label, Clara Smith. She was an attractive woman of Bessie's age, but she had a slimmer build and a thinner voice. Born in Spartanburg, South Carolina, Clara had spent more than ten years performing pop songs on small Southern vaudeville circuits. She was not related to Bessie, nor did she ever pose a real threat to her popularity, but—with a new repertoire and stylistic direction by Walker and Clarence Williams—she became Columbia's second most important female blues singer. Columbia's publicity department promoted Bessie as "Queen of the Blues," so they dubbed Clara "Queen of the Moaners." Surprisingly, a good relationship developed between the two singers, who occasionally confused people by pretending to be sisters.

As Walker prepared to launch Clara's Columbia career, Bessie continued to expand her flock of followers in the South. After closing in Atlanta with a special midnight performance for whites only,[17] she moved on to the Frolic Theater in Birmingham, Alabama, again breaking all previous attendance records. Carried by most of the black press, Billy Chambers's review may have been slightly exaggerated, but if attendance was not quite as spectacular as he reported it to be, such publicity would soon make it so: "Streets blocked, hundreds and hundreds and hundreds were unable to gain entrance to this performance . . . Bessie Smith with Irvin Johns at the piano before their own special drop opened full stage with 'Nobody's Bizness if I Do,' with the 'Gulf Coast Blues' following, which received heavy applause, leaving the house in a riot." Chambers, however, did not condone the commercial exploitation that went on between acts: " 'Buzzing' Harris [one of the performers] announced the 'Gulf Coast Blues' for sale and went down into the audience to sell copies. This, we think, is nonprofessional at this or any other performance, as the lady's reputation should sell the songs at every music house in the city."

They were selling sheet music, not recordings, in the aisles, but record shops always reported increased sales when Bessie was in town. People listened to their favorite artists on their Victrolas, then performed the same songs on the parlor piano, and just as live performances boosted record sales, so theater attendance went up with each successful record release. Columbia wasted little time issuing Bessie's recordings, and soon the catalog contained five of her releases. The way people flocked to hear her in person left no doubt in Bessie's mind as to their promotional value. It had all happened so fast, the sudden surge in popularity, the radically increased income, and the respect that came with being an "Exclusive Columbia Artist." Such acclaim and elevation had been known to inflate egos beyond the bearable, but Bessie took it in stride. One thing, however, was missing in her life: someone to share the success with. That would normally have been Jack, but he was still shaking doors in Philadelphia, and she was now spending much of her time on the road. They had seen little of each other since their marriage, but that was about to change.

Because he kept in touch with Frank Walker, Jack was well aware of Bessie's success, not to mention the $350 she pocketed each week while on tour. It would have seemed a staggering amount of money to him, enough to warrant quitting his job, which is what he did in August 1923. He didn't inform Bessie of his decision, nor had he any idea how she would react to it, but he rationalized that he could serve as her road manager. It was a naive decision considering that Jack had no experience in that field, that his backstage experience was limited to that of an onlooker, and that he even had difficulty understanding show business mentality. "He could have told her up front," said Ruby, "she probably would have said, 'come one down,' because, she still loved Jack to death, back *then*."

Jack decided to surprise Bessie when the tour took her back to Atlanta. Ruby's hindsight was twenty-twenty, for Bessie was delighted to find her husband waiting on the platform as she stepped off the train. They probably embraced madly, but neither of them could have foreseen that this would be the start of a wild roller-coaster ride, a love-hate relationship that that could serve as a textbook on mutual spousal abuse.

If Jack had entertained any doubts about Bessie's moneymaking potential, they were wiped away by what he saw at the theater in Atlanta: three lines of people fighting to get in for the next performance, creating a mob scene that ten policemen could barely control. Jack saw this scene replayed at Bessie's next three stops: Birmingham's Frolic Theater, the Bijou in Nashville, and the Beale Street Palace in Memphis. When Memphis radio station WMC carried one of Bessie's Beale Street Palace shows live, the *Chicago Defender*'s correspondent in Atlanta filed a typical review:

> The spirit of the Old South came up from Beale Street at 11 o'clock last night to give the world a concert of Negro folk songs that will be remembered by WMC as long as a midnight frolic is broadcast from the roof of the Commercial Appeal. Bessie Smith, known from coast to coast as a singer of blues that are really blue, gave the air some currents that it will not forget as long as a cloud is left in the sky, and Memphis has its Beale Street . . .
>
> The star of the frolic greeted the atmosphere with " 'T'ain't Nobody's Business but My Own," which she gave with unction and a rich Negro accent. Accompanied by Irvin Johns, her pianist, she followed with "Beale Street Mama." Singers have come and gone with that number, but it remained for Bessie to sing it before its possibilities were fathomed.
>
> Perhaps the greatest hit Bessie registered last night for WMC was "Outside of That He's All Right with Me." She repeated the number upon the request of a large number, who telephoned to the studio and wired from the Memphis territory . . . While the orchestra built up an excellent background for the entertainment, Bessie carried the evening with her "blues."

In radio's early years, there were no stations dedicated to black listeners. WMC was owned and operated by the Memphis *Commercial Appeal*, and its listeners were mainly white Southerners.[18] The *Defender*'s "Atlanta correspondent" may well have been a white reporter working for the *Commercial Appeal*. Paradoxically, it was only in the South that Bessie had a substantial following of whites, but the enthusiasm they had for her as an artist rarely followed her offstage. Still, because she was who she was, Bessie received surprisingly considerate treatment from some Southern establishments—"they treated her well for a black person," said Ruby. One of the show's chorines, Bucher Swan (also known as "Bootsy"), agreed with Ruby's qualifying remark, "Bessie knew this, of course," she added, "but she went along with the game—unless somebody gave her trouble. Then, it didn't make any difference whether they were white, black, Southern, or Northern, she'd give them a tongue-beating or she'd beat up on them with her fists."

As Bessie basked in her newfound fame and Jack more or less posed as her manager, the couple came as close to having a honeymoon as circumstances allowed. Bessie had vowed to bring Viola and the rest of the family up from Chattanooga as soon as she could afford it, and it was a promise she intended to keep. Whether she had mentioned this to Jack at this point is unknown, but

Ruby and Maud were inclined to think not. "Jack didn't want nobody around Bessie who wasn't helping her make money," said Ruby. "I know he was definitely jealous of Viola and that bunch later on, but I don't even think he liked them back then when everything was going well between them."

Perhaps to prepare him for the inevitable, Bessie pressed to have Jack meet her family. Taking advantage of their proximity to Chattanooga, she arranged to make a stopover there as they headed home to Philadelphia, in mid-September. They stayed with Viola, who may not have shared Bessie's excitement over the reunion and, from all accounts, took an immediate dislike to Jack. The feeling was mutual. The years had not mellowed Viola's disposition; on the contrary, she had become a bitter old maid and chronic complainer. Whatever pride she may have felt because of her little sister's success seemed tempered by feelings that life had dealt her a losing hand. Hard work and a lost childhood had aged Viola far beyond her years and driven her into alcoholism. Jack, who never touched a drink, probably took a dim view of Viola's chronic state of drunkenness, but he appears to have been far more troubled by the generosity Bessie showed her family.

During their stay with Viola, Bessie was contacted by Sam Reevin, a TOBA officer who owned Chattanooga's Liberty Theater. He offered her a ten-week TOBA contract at $350 a week. It was an amount she already commanded, but the length of the contract made Reevin's bid attractive. Driven more by greed than by any genuine desire to become a part of show business, Jack seized the opportunity to turn into practice a notion that had been little more than a pipe dream. Having witnessed Bessie's drawing power and done the math, he regarded the offer with suspicion, urged her to hold out for more money, and suggested that she let him handle the negotiations. Bessie agreed.

In years to come, Jack would make a serious attempt to assume the role of Bessie's manager, but he remained ill suited for the task. "Jack couldn't even manage himself," said Maud Smith. "He would always have signs saying 'Jack Gee presents Bessie Smith,' and he would call himself a manager, but he couldn't even sell a ticket. He could count money, and he could ask for money, but that's about it." As her career progressed, Frank Walker continued to set up Bessie's tours and manage her recording affairs, but business on the road was turned over to her brother, Clarence, and her nephew, T. J. Hill (better known as Teejay). Bessie rarely involved herself in direct money negotiations, but she liked to keep it in the family and allowed no major decision to be made without her approval. Neither Clarence nor Teejay had joined Bessie's entourage at this point, so she readily placed Reevin's proposal in Jack's hands. Given his limited knowledge of such matters as contracts, and his total lack of diplomacy, handing the matter over to Jack could easily have killed the deal, but he did remarkably well and persuaded Reevin to reconsider and come back with a far more generous offer.

The Gees now had an apartment at 1236 Webster Street in Philadelphia, but it was little more than a place to stay between working engagements. Visitors recalled that it lacked the atmosphere of a home. "There was nothing special about it," Ruby said, "no fancy furniture or anything like that, just big easy chairs, a sofa, and lamps and tables with pictures and statues and things. Bessie never went in for no fancy stuff around the house, even when she made all that money, because she just wasn't there that much." Home or no home, Bessie seemed happy for any opportunity to stay there during the early months of her marriage—Jack was attentive, and her career was proceeding at an encouraging pace.

When they arrived home from Chattanooga, the Gees found several telegraphed booking offers, and more are said to have arrived each day, but Bessie could now afford to be selective. In spite of Jack's beginner's luck, she wisely turned the new offers over to Frank Walker, who seemed bent on recording Bessie at every opportunity. Two days after her return to Philadelphia, he had her on a train bound for New York. She didn't mind having to work so hard, said Ruby, because she had great faith in Walker, nor was it difficult to persuade her to visit New York, a city she seemed increasingly fond of. In 1923, Harlem's black population was growing rapidly, and as the nightlife recovered from a postwar doldrums, it was being reshaped by Prohibition; clubs and basement dives were breeding grounds for jazz, and bootleg liquor flowed freely at rent parties—in many ways, Harlem was livelier than ever.

As the often frantic, syncopated sounds of jazz caught the fancy of young people, its liberating qualities raised concern among generations brought up in a less permissive atmosphere. It is a pattern history repeats with regularity as new musical forms capture the imagination of young people and feed radical trends. Just as bebop, rock, and rap would affect our culture in future decades, so jazz became the leitmotif for what some in the 1920s perceived as a nationwide moral decadence. Many black newspapers carried a warning from Dr. Elliot Rawlings, a "noted physician" whose research showed that "jazz music intoxicates like whisky and releases stronger animal passions." The doctor told of an experiment in which he left a young couple alone in a room with a jazz recording on the Victrola. Before long, he said, the couple was dancing and even kissing. However, when left alone with a waltz, the same couple treated each other with utmost civility. This prompted Dr. Rawlings to issue a "just-say-no" message to young people and a warning to parents.

The doctor's admonition, of course, was ignored, and he soon saw the Charleston—a dance introduced by Cecil Mack and Johnny Johnston in the revue *Runnin' Wild*[19]—become a veritable social epidemic.

In the 1920s, black America's cultural contribution was becoming increasingly evident to Harlem intellectuals, but white America was largely unaware of the creative individuals whose collective efforts came to be known as the Harlem Renaissance. Paradoxically, with only one or two exceptions, those who spearheaded this cultural flowering paid little attention to jazz and blues. To be sure, it was the beat to which the painters, sculptors, writers, and poets stomped and percolated, but they seemed to overlook its artistic value and cultural significance. The real irony is that they were treating as a backdrop black America's most vital and original contribution to the arts. By the end of the twentieth century, few Americans, regardless of their ethnic background, were not each day affected in some way by the creative thinking of African Americans. Today, black talent fuels a multibillion-dollar industry that shapes our schedules, tug at our emotions, and influences our thoughts. It is hard to imagine life without the arts, and it is equally difficult to imagine the arts without the creative input of African Americans. We would still have shelves of great books and there would be Shakespeare plays and works by Bach, Wagner, and Chopin, but the music of such composers as Ravel, Stravinsky, and Shostakovich would be different, as would the paintings of Picasso and Braque; Broadway musicals would almost certainly be less vibrant, and there would be no jazz nor blues, which means no rock and roll, no George and Ira Gershwin, no Cole Porter. And dance? Let's not even go there. Show business begins to affect us at an early age, and although it is a wonderful mélange, shaped by virtually every ethnic group on the globe, the African-American contribution to it is so immense as to be immeasurable.

Bessie's sudden departure was premature, but her arrival on the entertainment scene could not have been better timed. As the entertainment industry grew, the dances, music, and humor of black people increasingly became a source of fame and money for white imitators. By 1923, when Bessie's first recordings spread her fame, the standard-gauge minstrel shows with top hats, tails, coon songs, and painted thick-lipped grins were gone, but the racist, satirical embellishments they had introduced lingered on. Minstrel show stereotypes so distorted white America's image of blacks that, in order to be "believable," lighter-complexioned black artists found it necessary to work under burnt cork and thus mock themselves.

While Bessie and Irvin Johns rehearsed in the foyer of the house on 132d Street, Jack—following up on his success with Reevin—was on the phone with Sherman H. Dudley, another TOBA officer, who offered to pay Bessie the staggering sum of $1,100 for a week's engagement at his Koppin Theater in Detroit. Jack may never really have learned the ins and outs of show business, but he was in his element when it came to asking for more money—he held out until Dudley agreed to $1,500. In return for that substantial fee, Bessie was expected to deliver a revue rather than a solo act and to pay all production costs, including salaries. Still, $1,500 was an impressive amount, and—nonunion salaries being as low as she wanted them to be—Bessie got to keep most of it, but she had plans. Now that Jack had met her family, she thought it prudent to let him in on her old promise to Viola. She told Ruby that she had broken the news to Jack gradually, at first telling him how Viola had raised her and the other siblings, then suggesting that she owed them all something. "I know she gave him gifts just to butter him up," said Ruby, "because that's the only way she could get him to listen, and Jack had met Viola and that bunch down in Chattanooga, but they didn't get along. I guess he would go along with anything Bessie wanted, as long she gave him fancy things—and she did, all the time."

When Bessie finally told Jack that she was going to relocate the whole family to Philadelphia, the news fueled his growing resentment for Viola. It was Ruby's opinion that Bessie was deliberately pitting Jack and Viola against each other. "I knew about Viola locking Bessie up in the outhouse when she was mad at her," said Ruby, "so I thought maybe Bessie was getting even by making her deal with Jack." Ruby's reasoning may have been off the mark, but Bessie clearly was not going out of her way to mend the tattered relationship between her sister and husband. She knew that Jack begrudged Viola anything she gave her, yet when money had to be wired to Chattanooga, he was often the one she sent to Western Union. Thus Jack was well aware of the southward flow of cash, and having been apprised of Bessie's further intentions, he must have known that it was only a matter of time before he would be told to order train tickets, too.

Although Jack had handled his negotiation with Sherman Dudley successfully, Bessie eventually decided that her business affairs were better left in the hands of Frank Walker, the only white man she trusted. Given Jack's successful start, it seems odd that Bessie did not turn the job over to him, especially considering how well the marriage was going. Ruby thought that it had probably been Frank Walker's idea and that Bessie went along with it because she so implicitly trusted his judgment. Maud took that theory further, suggesting that Reevin and Dudley may have complained to Walker—after all, Jack lacked polish and may have made them uncomfortable.

Walker was still recording Bessie at every opportunity, scheduling her for seven sessions between September 21 and October 16. Forty-nine takes yielded ten acceptable sides, the first of which was "Jail House Blues," a tune that is always credited to Bessie and Clarence Williams but that Ruby claimed to have been written by her brother, Leroy:

"My brother hung out on 133rd Street, between Fifth and Lenox Avenues. In them days, only dope and liquor heads, and what-have-you hung out there—pickpockets and, you know, the run-of-the-mill. The cops were always after him. The bunch Leroy hung out with never worked, they stole for a living. The whole gang hung out in an old railroad apartment and left their guns with a woman who got her cut of the loot that was stolen. Whenever there was a holdup or murder, the cops would run into that apartment and look in every crook and hole.

"One day Leroy stole something and he hid from the police in the basement, behind the coal. When the cop got close to him, he shot and killed the cop, but no one ever found out who did it. Once my brother went to Boston and robbed and killed a woman and her husband. This time he was caught and put away from ten to twenty years. My mother, who used to go see him every visiting day, had the nerve to say, 'He was a good boy, he just got in with the wrong crowd.' The usual saying of all mothers, regardless of how bad the child is. Anyway, while my no-good brother was in jail, he wrote the song 'The Jail House Blues' and sent it to my aunt Bessie. She made it popular and with the money that she made on it, she got my brother a good lawyer, and he got out of jail in ten years."

In an interview for this book, dancer-singer Mae Barnes, who married Leroy Walker shortly after his release from jail, could not confirm that her husband had written "Jail House Blues," but she acknowledged it as a possibility, adding that Bessie had indeed facilitated his release.

Ruby's brother had obviously not learned his lesson, for soon after his release and marriage to Mae Barnes, he took on a business partner and embarked on a new career as a drug dealer. The drug partnership lasted only a short while, then came to an abrupt, dramatic end when Leroy learned that Mae had become romantically involved with his partner. The news sent him rushing off to his partner's apartment at 129th Street and Eighth Avenue, and when his own wife greeted him there, he pushed her aside and barged into the apartment. There he found his partner, having dinner at the kitchen table. Leroy took aim and killed him with one well-directed shot. Mae had fled the house and her hysterical screams attracted the cop on the beat. "I couldn't even talk," she recalled, "because I was a wreck, so I just pointed to my house." When the policeman got there, Leroy was no longer in the apartment, but he had not been seen leaving the house, so the police officer headed for the roof, where he found him and shot him dead.

The policeman, a West Indian who had been assigned to the neighborhood beat for a few years, was no stranger to Leroy. He was known to be on the take and to have benefited from Leroy's drug dealings. The two had a history of business-related run-ins, which may account for the swift justice carried out on the rooftop. "I think he did that so my brother wouldn't blab on him," said Ruby, and Mae Barnes concurred, unable to think of another reason why her husband was killed rather than taken in.

Bessie's October 4 studio date was unlike any of her other sessions up to that point. For the first time, another singer joined her in the studio, and the remarkable thing about this pairing was that Bessie's vocal partner was Clara Smith. a rival Columbia blues queen. Considering Bessie's adamant refusal to share a stage with another blues singer, the joint session may be taken as a measure of the trust she put in Frank Walker. Clara and Bessie had much in common: they were about the same age; both were dedicated blues singers; both recorded under Walker's supervision, often employed the same accompanists, and aimed at the same market. Their material was also quite similar, but Walker saw to it that one never duplicated the other's song.

Now, of course, they would share songs, but perhaps not on equal footing, for in spite of the similarities, there were significant differences between the divas. Bessie's recordings consistently outsold Clara's, her fee was twice the amount, she received preferential treatment on advertising and promotion, and when it came to command of the blues, there simply was no comparison — Clara had a good voice but she lacked Bessie's power and intuitive sense of timing. "I think Bessie knew she didn't have anything to worry about as long as they were together on a record. But I guess she wouldn't have been too happy about being seen with her onstage, because Clara was much thinner and prettier than Bessie," Ruby observed.

A friendly rivalry existed between Bessie and Clara, though jazz historians have often given an opposite impression. There is no evidence to support stories of enmity, at least not at the time of their joint recordings. If any bitterness existed between the two stars, it would probably have been on Clara's part, but those who knew both singers recalled that they seemed to have enjoyed a personal, friendly mutual relationship.

Ethel Waters was among the few singers who might have made Bessie uneasy. She had an equally engaging but dissimilar vocal style, but her appeal was broader. Waters — who became an extraordinary stage and film actress[20] — triumphed on Broadway and in Hollywood, but her early years were spent with struggling road companies and in TOBA theaters, sometimes on the same bill as Bessie. In her autobiography, *His Eye Is on the Sparrow,*[21] Waters recalled an incident at the "91" Theater in Atlanta before 1920:

Ethel Waters, whom Bessie called "one of them Northern bitches," looks into Carl Van Vechten's camera. Photo by Carl Van Vechten, 1938.

"Bessie was in a pretty good position to dictate to the managers. She had me put on my act for her and said I was a long goody. But she also told the men who ran No. 91 that she didn't want anyone else on the bill to sing the blues.

"I agreed to this, I could depend a lot on my shaking, though I never shimmied vulgarly and only to express myself. And when I went on I sang 'I Want to Be Somebody's Baby Doll So I Can Get My Lovin' All the Time.' But before I could finish this number the people out front started howling, 'Blues! Blues! Come on, Stringbean, we want your blues!'

"Before the second show the manager went to Bessie's dressing room and told her he was going to revoke the order forbidding me to sing any blues. He said he couldn't have another such rumpus. There was quite a stormy discussion about this, and you could hear Bessie yelling things about 'these Northern bitches.' Now nobody could have taken the place of Bessie Smith. People everywhere loved her shouting with all their hearts and were loyal to her. But they wanted me too.

"When I closed my engagement in the theatre Miss Bessie called me to her. 'Come here, long goody,' she said. 'You ain't so bad. It's only that I never dreamed that anyone would be able to do this to me in my own territory and with my own people. And you damn well know you can't sing worth a fuck.' "

Bessie's October 29, opening at the Koppin in Detroit caused a near-riot on Gratiot Avenue. With $1,500 invested in her show, Sherman Dudley reputedly made it the most heavily promoted in Detroit's history. However, he probably could have spared himself the expense, for in 1923, Detroit's auto industry attracted large numbers of African Americans, Southerners who would have flocked to hear the Queen of the Blues anyway. "You should have seen the crowds that Bessie would draw out on the road—standing room only," said Ruby. "They would be out on the sidewalk waiting for the first show to be over so that they could get in to see the next one."

The story was the same at the Globe Theater in Cleveland. Higher-than-usual prices notwithstanding, there weren't enough seats in the theater to hold Bessie's new fans. With Bessie headlining eight acts, and the pit band—Cheatham's Jazz Syncopators—playing in between, the show ran long. That translated into less revenue for the theater, so the Globe's management pulled an old trick: Bessie was told to cut the show. Shortening the duration of each show allowed the theater to increase the number of daily performances, which ultimately meant more work for Bessie and her performers, but it enabled the theater owner to meet her new asking price and also make a handsome profit.

The reality of black stars was a relatively new phenomenon in the entertainment world, and the relationship that existed between them and their followers was quite different from that which white stars shared with their fans. When the Valentinos, Swansons, and Negris were courted by heads of state and embraced by high society, it immediately set them apart from ordinary people. It didn't matter that most of them had come from humble backgrounds, only that they now were among the wealthy and the widely adored. Black entertainers, in contrast, continued to face closed doors in the United States, no matter how bright their spotlight had become. Artists like Josephine Baker, Alberta Hunter, and Ethel Waters were embraced by European high society, but at home—regardless of their income or the magnitude of their artistic talent—neither Warren Harding nor Calvin Coolidge ever placed their name on a guest list. Of course African Americans had their internecine problems, but there was a bond—a feeling of shared pain—that almost made it impossible for black artists to rise so far above the flock as to become deified in the eyes of their own people. Blacks knew all too well that there was only one reason why even their biggest stars were unlikely to find a seat at White House dinners: ancestry.

To be sure, a certain amount of snobbery existed among black stars, but there was little or no mystique. Hollywood created its gods and goddesses out of ordinary people by distancing them from the public. With fanciful press releases, clever spins, and well-organized gossip, stars of the silver screen became blurred, mythical images who rarely if ever did anything mundane—

While Bessie continued to tour the TOBA and play small hamlets with her tent show, Alberta Hunter hobnobbed with the chic crowd in Europe. This 1928 photo shows her in Paris with a gathering of friends, including Mabel Mercer and Bricktop. From the author's collection.

at least that was the projected image. In contrast, black entertainers tended to be highly accessible. What fans knew about their private lives was often something they experienced firsthand and could identify with.

There were no special watering holes for black celebrities, nor would people like Bessie have been comfortable in such exclusive surroundings. It was, in fact, one of Bessie's most prepossessing traits that she kept her mind at street level—it is what made it so easy for her audiences to recognize themselves in her songs. Of course, not everybody had an opportunity to rub elbows with a star, but there was the grapevine, and almost anything a well-known black performer did was eventually heard through it. No fan magazine's written report could match the verbal communication that had flowed so eloquently between black people since the days of slavery. Even though newspapers like the *Chicago Defender* kept rural and Southern blacks apprised of happenings in the North, the spoken word was often more effective; what you heard, no matter how it had been embellished, was more believable than what you read. Stories circulated throughout black communities and subcommunities with the swiftness of small-town gossip. By way of touring entertainers and Pullman porters, word spread from Atlanta's Fourth Ward to Chicago's South Side to Harlem and even to the West Coast.

People's knowledge of Bessie went beyond what they saw on stage or read in the papers. They knew that she had a fiery temper; that she would engage man or woman, regardless of size, in physical combat at the drop of the wrong word; that she had periods when she drank up a storm; that she carried an impressive quantity of corn liquor in her purse during such spells; and that some of her people's servile behavior toward whites filled her with disgust and pain.

They also knew that Bessie was a staunchly independent sort who disregarded political correctness when it suited her to do so. Such forthright behavior was envied by some and damned by others, including the emerging, "dicty" black bourgeoisie, who found her lack of grace and tact abhorrent. "The thing about Bessie," said Alberta Hunter, "is that she was always herself. Some of us were always trying to be little stars, but not Bessie." To illustrate her remark, Hunter told how she used to send letters from Europe to the *Defender*, implying that she had been swept off her feet by a count. "There was no Count," she said, laughing at her deceptiveness, "but people were so impressed with royalty, you know. I sang for the Prince of Wales, but that wasn't half as impressive as having a love affair with a Count." The "Count," she later revealed, was actually a lesbian lover.

Bessie might throw an ermine coat over her shoulders, but she never put on airs, she was at her happiest when mingling with the folks in the street and being one of the gang. Still, her presence was so imposing that even when she let her hair down, most people addressed her as "Miss Bessie." Over the years, much has been written about Bessie's personality. Early writers tended to stereotype her as a big fat mama who drank a lot, fought like a dog, and sang like an angel. Perhaps because there is a tendency to judge her by her many recordings, one is sometimes left with the impression that Bessie's only redeeming quality was her glorious voice. The truth is that her artistry and personality reached far deeper than that implies. She was a well-rounded entertainer in the vaudeville tradition, an artist who gave her audiences drama and humor with equal skill. True, Bessie had a tough-as-nails side to her, but she was no hard-hearted Hannah, as many who worked with her found out. In fact, Bessie had a backstage reputation for being a soft touch, but she did not always have to be asked. During her run at the Globe Theater, she learned that Buster Porter, a performer with whom she had worked in leaner days, was hospitalized in Cleveland and unable to pay his doctor's bill. That afternoon, between shows, Bessie grabbed a cab and visited the man in his hospital bed, giving him the fifty dollars he needed. This was not an uncommon gesture for

Bessie, who often bailed friends out of jail, responded favorably to a less fortunate stranger's outstretched hand, lavished friends and family with gifts, and developed a reputation for leaving exceedingly generous tips. She liked good jewelry and well-made fur coats, but she otherwise spent relatively little on herself, feeling little need to impress others. Yet even though it seemed that the more she made, the more she doled out, Bessie was generally frugal and sometimes downright stingy when it came to paying her performers and crew.

By all indications, the fall 1923 tour was going well when Bessie, on November 17, suddenly canceled two Nashville dates.[22] There were conflicting reports as to the reason for the abrupt change in schedule, one of which was given as an unspecified illness—very likely, exhaustion. The Gees headed back to Philadelphia, and again, Frank Walker set up a recording date, December 4. The tunes she recorded were "Chicago-bound Blues" and "Mistreatin' Daddy," Bessie's final coupling for what had been a banner year. She now had twenty-nine usable sides to her credit, more than twice the number her contract had called for. Adding in the unused takes, Bessie had actually recorded close to 140 performances, a total that few singers could match in 1923. All this studio work was also having a positive effect on her delivery, for she was now able to face the recording horn with the kind of self-assurance she always had on stage.

Columbia Records had good reason to be grateful to Bessie. The label had been experiencing financial difficulties when Frank Walker signed her, and the situation was so dire that the company had applied for receivership in February 1922, selling out to the Constructive Finance Company, a British holding company, just two months before Bessie's first session. The situation had begun to improve by October 1923, when Judge Learned Hand appointed two receivers for the American Columbia company, and Frank Walker launched the label's official "race" series (the 14000 series) with a Bessie Smith release.

The oft-told story that Bessie saved Columbia Records from bankruptcy is an overstatement and is unfair to such Columbia artists as Eddie Cantor, Ted Lewis, comedian Bert Williams (who died eight days after Bessie's recording debut), and the outrageously racist but popular and highly marketable comedy team known as the Two Black Crows.[23] Nevertheless Bessie was Columbia's hottest artist at the time, and her contribution to the company's welfare was incalculable.

As she neared the end of an exhausting year, Bessie seemed tireless to all but close friends, who marveled at her ability to keep going but noticed subtle signs of fatigue. Four years had passed since the team of Green and Smith appeared at the Douglas Theater on Baltimore's Gilmor Street, and it was under strikingly different circumstances that Bessie, on December 17, 1923, returned to fulfill a week's engagement as a headliner at the same theater. Being signed to a major label gave Bessie an imprimatur that registered dramatically at the box office: the Douglas's manager declared the engagement the most successful in the theater's history.

Ruby recalled an incident that took place during the Baltimore engagement:

"To me, this was a disastrous town. After the last show on the third day in town, we went to a little nightclub on Pennsylvania Avenue called the Wagon Wheel, it was really rocking and crowded. They did not have any empty tables, but when they saw Bessie and her girls, they made a bunch of beer drinkers get up. They gave us their table. Of course they resented it, but the proprietor, if they had their way, would throw out all beer drinkers, because they crowd up the place and after one or two rounds, they make more noise than anyone. In other words, they are cheap drunks. When the crowd realized that Bessie Smith and her chorus girls was there in the club, they started clapping and whistling for Bessie to do a song. A lot of them had seen her at the theater.

"Bessie told me to sing in her place, because she did not feel like it. As I started up on the bandstand, some tall black gal with a disgusting afro and great big ear rings jumped in front of me with a brand new switchblade knife. She was so tall that she was standing over me. Boy, did she look tough. She said, 'You and the rest of them bitches over there at the table, took our table and I'll see to it, that you never do it again to anyone else.' How Bessie got there so fast and knocked the woman down, I don't know, but when it come to fighting, she is the best. She grabbed the woman's arm that had the knife in her hand and twisted until the knife flew out of her hand. I grabbed the knife. Bessie started fist-punching. She knocked the woman's wig off and Uncle Sam's eagle was not as bald headed as that bitch. After she had pushed the woman aside and the bodyguard came and took the woman outside somewhere, the people in the audience was so pleased, that they still wanted Bessie to sing. So Bessie said to me, 'Go on up on the bandstand and finish what you started.'

"I went up on the bandstand and told the band to play 'St. Louis Blues' in B-flat. They made the introduction and I opened my mouth to sing and not a sound came out. They played the introduction again, the same thing happened. I had never had a person draw a knife on me before and I was in shock. There I stood on the bandstand with my mouth open, still holding the woman's knife. So Bessie made me sit down and she sang one chorus and came back to the table. We all left to go to the hotel, with the crowd still clapping and whistling. Just as we got to the door of the club, I heard a shot ring out and I felt as if someone had grabbed my right foot and tore it off. It felt like I had got hit with a heavy iron. I blacked out and when I came to I was in the hospital. I started yelling and the nurse came in, then the doctor. I was saying, 'What happened to my foot?' because it was paining so bad. They told me that I had got shot in the foot, but it was not serious, because the bullet went through and it also did not break any bones. I stayed there three days and Bessie and some of the girls came and got me. I left town with the show."

In spite of her vastly increased income, Bessie made no significant changes to her lifestyle. She now had to spend more money on costumes and props, and hire more people to keep her touring companies running, but—except for the fact that her gifts were now more expensive—the only noticeable change was, as noted, in her clothes. "Bessie liked to dress well," Ruby Walker recalled, "and she liked for her men to dress well, so she'd buy expensive suits for Jack and she got herself some fur coats and jewelry—real diamonds. At home she was still the same old Bessie, slopping around in her slippers, her hair flying all over the place, and cooking up a lot of greasy food.

"Jack thought he was a big shot, because he married Bessie. When she married him, he didn't have a pot to piss in, or a window to throw it out. She bought him a five-carat diamond ring, and a watch. At that time, it was the style for men to wear their watches in their vest pocket, with a gold chain hanging down, and on this chain was a lion's head with its mouth open, and a three-carat diamond in his mouth. She bought him suits, costing two hundred and fifty to three hundred dollars. Boy, you couldn't tell him nothing then. She even had shirts made up for him by the dozen, Japanese silk and his initials. He would stand on every corner and show his diamond ring, pull his chest out. Bessie Smith's big-time husband. When we played Atlanta, they grabbed his black ass and stole everything. Bessie warned him to stop showing off, they took his suit, his shirts, his ring, his watch. He came backstage in his shorts. When I saw him, I ran to Bessie's dressing room, I said, 'There's a race runner out here looking for you.' He was so mad he slapped me down. The cops got all of his stuff back, but that learned him a lesson. After that, he didn't flash his diamonds anymore. He took it out on all of the whole show. He sat all over the audience. We never knew where he would be and if we made one mistake or didn't smile, he would fine us all five dollars. The girls would he whispering to each other, 'Where's old dragon head? Do you see him?' We was afraid to laugh too soon, because he could fine us for that."

If Bessie and Jack had wanted to enjoy their new prosperity, they would hardly have found the time; she now had more offers for well-paying engagements than she could possibly accept.

On December 22, 1923, four months before her first contract with Columbia was to expire, the company—overwhelmed by the success of her records—signed Bessie to a new and better contract. Again, she was to record a minimum of twelve sides, but she was to receive $200 per side rather than the $150 called for in the option. Bessie was guaranteed $2,400 for the year, but it was clear that, even with the royalty clause struck from her new contract, she would make much more.[24]

Bessie concluded her week at the Douglas on the following day, and opened Christmas Eve at the Dunbar in Philadelphia—the same theater she had been fired from when she appeared in *How Come?* earlier in the year. Now she was the boss, heading a cast of sixty performers for a two-week run of John T. Gibson's musical comedy extravaganza *Tunes and Topics*. When she found the time to rehearse for this show is hard to imagine, but Bessie's name alone was a big drawing card at this point, and she may simply have incorporated her own regular songs and routines into Gibson's show. Most of these shows lacked a theme, anyway—often the major change consisted of a new title.

At the onset of 1924, Bessie could look back on a wildly eventful and successful year, but the future looked more interesting. She was enjoying a happy relationship with Jack, her career had taken a dramatic upward swing, and she relished the prospect of soon being able to move her family to Philadelphia. Jack was still grumbling whenever the subject of relocating Bessie's family came up, but he could do little about it beyond hoping that Bessie would change her mind. At this point, he was still dazzled by his wife's meteoric rise to fame and all that came with that; he had not grown accustomed to the show business lifestyle, but he certainly must have seen it as a welcomed change of pace from his lonesome nights as a "door shaker." Bessie had to make less of an adjustment. She had worked long and hard to prepare for this recognition of her talent, and having a husband to share it with made the reward even greater. All of this gave her the energy to maintain a schedule that few could endure, and if Jack noticed that his wife was literally wearing herself out to satisfy the appetite of others, he made no attempt to slow her down. "Jack didn't care," said Ruby, "all he was interested in was the money and all those things Bessie gave him. Baby, she was crazy about him." That would change.

3

From now on, small change I refuse;
Mama's got them one and two blues.
"One and Two Blues"

Bessie began to feel the one and two blues in 1924, as her work schedule grew tighter: money solved old worries, but it also brought new ones. It probably lessened the pain somewhat that she had the one- and two-thousand-dollar-a-week blues, but Bessie was driving herself too hard, and the more she made, the less time she found to spend with Jack. In fact, she had little time for anything but work, and would probably have been content making less money if it meant having more leisure time. However, Jack and Frank Walker had in common a desire to cash in while the going was good.

On January 6, two days after closing at Philadelphia's Dunbar Theater, Bessie returned to the recording studio for yet another three-day session. The first day's result indicates that her hectic schedule was taking its toll—Bessie sounds tired and spiritless on "Frosty Mornin' Blues" and "Easy Come, Easy Go."[1] This has prompted some blues scholars to suggest that these sides belong to another singer, but although the voice is unusually high-pitched and the singer seems unable to sustain a note, the phrasing is unmistakably Bessie's. A third selection, "Blue Bessie (The Bluest Gal in Tennessee)" — a song she had previously recorded without success — was again rejected.

The next two days' sessions produced only slightly better results. Fletcher Henderson, who had first recorded with Bessie the previous summer, brought to the studio a small group of outstanding musicians from his big band. For future sessions, the Henderson orchestra would become a source for some of Bessie's most memorable accompaniments, but even the best of musicians have bad days. January 9 was such a day for Don Redman, who later achieved fame as an arranger and bandleader; his clarinet playing on "Haunted House Blues" and "Eavesdropper's Blues" is marred by novelty effects and perhaps handicapped by Bessie's performance, which again is listless.

Things apparently went from bad to worse at the January 10 session. Accompanied by an unidentified group labeled as "her jazz band," Bessie recorded "Rampart Street Blues" and "Lawdy, Lawdy Blues." The songs, written and previously recorded for the Paramount label by Ida Cox, were probably chosen by Walker based on their proven appeal, but Bessie's versions were never released.

Four days after the session, Bessie made good her Nashville obligations and opened at the Bijou Theater. As fate would have it, the Bijou's outgoing production was headed by Ida Cox, which gave the two blues ladies a opportunity to meet. "I had seen Bessie before, in Atlanta," recalled Cox, "but this was the first time I actually spoke to her. She was as sweet as she could be — she told me she had recorded some of my songs, and she paid me a compliment on them. I heard later that she never said anything nice about other blues singers, so it just thrills me when I think about it."

Maud recalled that Bessie seldom discussed the work of other star performers, attributing that to the fact that she rarely had the time or inclination to catch someone else's show. "When Bessie wasn't performing," said Ruby, "she was either drinking and having her fun or spending her time with Jack. You didn't see her going to other theaters except maybe to say hello to a friend. Bessie had been in show business a long time, so she had a lot of friends that was working in other shows." Another factor was sheer physical exhaustion; on the road, Bessie's workdays were long, leaving her with little in the way of energy and no desire for a busman's holiday, but she had remarkable resilience. As tired as she sounded on her last recording sessions, there apparently was no sign of fatigue during her stage performances. *Billboard* magazine wrote that her show at the Bijou was "drawing heavier than on previous appearances,"[2] and noted that she and Ida Cox had each made a special appearance at Nashville's all-white Orpheum Theater on January 15 and 16, respectively. About the latter shows, *Billboard* wrote: "Miss Smith made special appearances at the Orpheum theater, a house catering to white patronage. A local correspondent comments favorably upon the improved character of the songs offered. Miss Smith and Miss Cox were elaborately gowned and had special settings."

Contrary to reasonable assumption, white Southerners took to Bessie long before their Northern counterparts did. Her performances for whites were labeled "special" only because the audience was Caucasian. She did not alter her material to suit their taste, nor would she have wanted to, but there was a line to be drawn: black performers knew that acceptance by white audiences hinged on their conforming to a certain image. A mammy costume never failed to please Southern white audiences, but Bessie wearing a glamorous gown would have been upsetting to them. Ethel Waters would never have made it before a white Southern audience singing "Supper Time" or "Harlem on My Mind," but Stepin Fetchit's rolling eyes and "Yawsuhs" were fully in keeping with the stereotype of blacks as simpleminded, obsequious Toms.

Perhaps it was the power of her singing voice or her commanding presence, or a combination of the two, but Southern whites were less discriminatory than usual when it came to Bessie. They liked her comedy, her suggestive movements, her wild costumes, enormous ostrich-plume headgear, and glittering costume jewelry, but above all, they liked her songs.

Wherever in the South Bessie appeared, her songs and humor registered as well with whites as they did with her own people. Her shows were considered pure entertainment, and—except for the occasional veiled allusion—she never touched directly on racial issues. She sang of love, sex, and misery, and balanced the pain with slapstick hokum and hilarity. Another reason why Bessie's repertoire appealed more to white Southerners than even to black Northerners is that people in the South grew up hearing blues, and they felt at home with it. Acceptance, however, should not be viewed as absence of racism. In Louisiana, one record vendor—with a little help from Columbia's local representative—came up with a novel, decidedly racist promotional gimmick that oddly teamed Bessie up with America's most celebrated blackface performer, Al Jolson. It was written up in the January 26, 1924, issue of the *Music Trades:*

> DRAMATIC ACTION IN WINDOW NETS BIG SALE IN RECORDS
> "Jail House Blues" Advertised by Live Boy in Striped Uniform in Window of Kaplan Furniture Co., Alexandria, La.
>
> ALEXANDRIA, LA., Jan. 21.—The Kaplan Furniture Co., Inc., this city, has demonstrated that merchandise backed by a live, attractive window trim will move a substantial quantity of records.

When Columbia records of "Jail House Blues," by Bessie Smith, and "Waitin' for the Evening Mail," by Al Jolson, were released, the Kaplan executives decided to experiment with the pulling power of their window. The window in the attached illustration cost less than $20, including the union rate of the impersonator. The favorable publicity was worth at least $750. It cleaned out the stock of the above records. At the same time it stimulated record business generally and increased sales in the other departments of the store.

Henry H. Irwin, Columbia field representative in the district, worked in connection with the Kaplan Furniture Co. in designing the window. Mr. Irwin understands the colored trade. He is the author of "Those Painful Blues" and "Strut Your Stuff and Do It Right."

Mr. Irwin states that the colored boy selected for the living subject wanted to be released at the last minute. He was afraid his girl would come along and see him in his new suit. When the firm promised to send a couple of the records to the dusky lady he soon changed his mind.

What remained a tradition in the South was already by 1924 becoming a fading novelty in the North. New York was never a serious market for male, rural blues, and its half-hearted embrace of the so-called classic blues, which Bessie, Clara, and Ida exemplified, only went out to its handful of major artists. Even that limited acceptance was relegated to bookings in black theaters. Such news as W. C. Handy's Black Swan label—which boasted receipts totaling $104,628 in 1922—having sold out to Paramount Records was misconstrued as a sign of sagging blues interest, and there were other signs if one did not take into consideration the broader picture. Bessie and her blues-singing colleagues paid little attention to such predictions; if blues was on the wane in New York City, there was no measurable decline in its popularity elsewhere. Many of the classic blues singers, including Ma Rainey, rarely if ever appeared in New York, and those who did continued to attract sizeable crowds of transplanted Southerners. The *New York Clipper,* noting that sales had leveled off, took it as a death knell:

"RACE" SONGS ON THE WANE

Discs Not Selling—Passing Craze Back to Normalcy

The "swan song" of "race" phonograph discs seems to have been sung. Only two of the larger companies, Columbia and Okeh, are going after their "race" catalogs with anything approaching the energy spent last year.

The February 16, 1924, issue of *Music Trades* used Bessie's Columbia contract renewal to express a more optimistic outlook for blues, failing to mention that she had been a highly successful Columbia artist for a year:

DEALERS EXPECT BIG SALE OF BLUES RECORDS
BY BESSIE SMITH, WHO HAS JOINED
COLUMBIA ARTISTS

Bessie Smith has signed a contract to record for Columbia new process records. Her singing of "Gulf Coast Blues" has made that selection deservedly popular among the younger set of her race in nearly every city.

Miss Smith draws capacity houses in every city where she appears in vaudeville. North or South, it makes no difference, for wherever there are colored folks, there is a strong demand for Bessie Smith's blues. The size of the crowds that hear her seems to be limited only by the sitting and standing room of the houses in which she appears.

The sale of negro records is becoming more and more of a volume proposition for phonograph dealers all over the country. Dealers who can offer the latest blues by the most important of all colored singers of blues selections, are in a strategic position to dominate in the sale of records to the colored population of their locality. That is just what Bessie Smith's Columbia new process records mean to Columbia dealers.

It is interesting to note that although Bessie Smith sings selections written especially for the colored trade and generally written by colored composers, her records enjoy a considerable demand among white people. This has been especially noted among professional white entertainers, all of whom seem to recognize and appreciate her unique artistry.

Bessie Smith possesses a voice of that peculiarly desirable quality for which the old fashioned colored folks of the South were so noted. She recognizes the value of this gift—and strives constantly to retain those qualities which many a colored entertainer has lost beyond recall through a mistaken desire to take on a so-called metropolitan polish.

A consummate actress, Bessie Smith throws her whole personality into the characters of her songs. To hear the records is to realize this. Columbia dealers all over the country have learned, to their profit, the value of Bessie Smith's records as a drawing card.

The same issue of the *Music Trades* described another vendor-inspired promotional effort:

BRINGS CEMETERY TO STORE TO INCREASE RECORD SALES
Leo Kahn Uses Unique Window Display in Memphis, Tenn., to Boost Sale of Bessie Smith's Columbia Disk

MEMPHIS, TENN., Jan 30.—Selling Columbia records in a graveyard is not exactly a happy business prospect. In fact the idea of reproducing a cemetery in a store window would discourage most dealers, despite prospects of immediate sales. Not so with Leo Kahn, recently elected president of the Memphis Exchange Club, who has enough live business ideas to wake the dead.

As a matter of fact, the graveyard in the accompanying picture has been lulled to sleep by the soothing minor voice of Bessie Smith, comedian and Columbia artist. Mr. Kahn believes that when Bessie sings the public will be perfectly willing to follow her anywhere, even if it leads to a couple of daisies and a nice white stone.

This display in the roomy window of the Leo Kahn Furniture Co. is celebrating "Cemetery Blues"—a Columbia record. "It's the spirit of the thing," says Mr. Kahn, "that we have reproduced." And the satisfied customers answer by buying more Columbia records.

At the end of January 1924 Bessie returned to the Beale Street Palace in Memphis. When she made another a broadcast over station WMC on February 1, the *Memphis Commercial Appeal* had a reviewer on hand:

Bessie Smith, colored singer of deep indigo blues, gave WMC listeners a treat with a score of her latest successes as she led the midnight frolic at 11 o'clock last night, with Yancey and Booker's orchestra and the Beale Ave. Palace theater orchestra playing accompaniments in slow Negroid rhythm.

"Sam Jones Blues," "Chicago Bound," "St. Louis Gal," and "Mistreatin' Papa" led the way for a score of others. Bessie has a voice that will never be mistaken for another's. She is in a class by herself in the field of "blues."

The two orchestras, splitting the midnight frolic, were delightful in their original handling of the popular numbers of today. They took back the numbers written from the old Negro folk songs and put that Negro touch to them that the authors missed. The boys put Beale Ave. into the air, with the result that WMC was flooded with requests from the territory and was the recipient of wires from East, West, North, and South.

Bessie Smith will give a special performance for white people only at the Beale Ave. Palace theater in Thursday night at 11 o'clock.[3]

Few black shows were asked to give a command performance for white audiences, but it was a desirable call because ticket prices were raised, and that translated into higher performance fees. On Friday, February 13, 1924, Bessie again appeared before white audiences—this time at her former home base, Atlanta's "81" theater. Reviewing this performance in the *Pittsburgh Courier,* the paper's Atlanta correspondent pointed out that Southern whites also liked Bessie's recordings:

The program was greatly enjoyed by the white people who filled the house after the regular performance. According to the management, practically all seats in the house were taken for this special performance as early as Thursday morning. Miss Smith is a great favorite in Atlanta. Few white homes here

> are without her records made by the Columbia Phonograph Company. A prominent white music dealer told a reporter of the *Preston News* that Bessie Smith's records actually outsell everything else in the catalog.[4]

So they listened to her recordings, enjoyed her broadcasts, and eventually filled black theaters for special whites-only performances, but Southerners were not prepared to book Bessie into their mainstream theaters. The two performances at Nashville's Orpheum represent the only known exceptions. "Bessie wasn't fooled by those Southern crackers smiling at her," said Ruby. "She wasn't scared of any of those white people down there. Not Bessie—she would tell anybody to kiss her ass. Nobody messed with Bessie, black or white, it didn't make no difference." In the North, Bessie's show was relegated to bookings in predominantly black theaters, but that was due more to her material than to her complexion. Bessie's stage presentations and blues were considered too crude and simplistic for sophisticated Northern white audiences.

There were several attempts to form black theater circuits, but none as successful as the Theater Owners' Booking Association. "Toby Time," as it was popularly called, was the largest, most prestigious, and longest surviving of such organizations, but compared to white counterparts like the Keith Circuit, its operation was substandard. Founded around 1911, the TOBA was managed by an interracial group of theater owners. Performers, unhappy with contracts that gave light recompense for a heavy work schedule, half-jokingly claimed that the initials more appropriately stood for Tough on Black Asses, but not everybody felt cheated by the TOBA. Headliners like Bessie, because they set the salaries of their supporting cast and paid them out of their own money, more or less set their own fees, which were usually considerably above anyone else's in the show. This often created legitimate grievances from chorines and bottom-of-the-bill acts, who were among the lowest-paid performers, but walkouts were rare because the alternative could be far less glamorous and exciting. Bessie had a reputation for paying minimal wages, but there was certain compensation in the high production values that characterized her shows and in the knowledge that one would be performing to capacity audiences.

Most TOBA venues were run-down and poorly maintained, but there were a few exceptions, and Cincinnati's Roosevelt Theater was among them—it even offered decent backstage surroundings. Newly built when Bessie first appeared there, it boasted ten large, well-lit dressing rooms, each with a sink, running water, electric call bells, and mirrors: real luxury. When Bessie opened there on February 25, 1924, she brought a show that was worthy of the theater's splendid interior, including a variety of highly imaginative, dazzling costumes and headgear. Her personal favorite, said Ruby, was a white and blue satin dress with a moderate hoop skirt, adorned with strands of pearls and imitation rubies. To complement that, she wore headgear that resembled a cross between a football helmet and a tasseled lampshade. The flashy outfits offered fans a momentary escape from everyday reality, but the lyrics to Bessie's songs soon brought them back down to earth, and they seem to have loved the contrast.

On this, her second visit to Cincinnati since her pre-stardom days, fellow performer Gang Jines—who also happened to be the *Defender's* Cincinnati correspondent—proclaimed her unspoiled by success:

> Bessie Smith has always been a headliner, even when the salaries were absolutely nothing. Of course, her recording has made her prestige rise higher, but glad to say, she is the same Bessie, wearing the same size shoes, where a few have let prosperity almost kill their drawing power, and without a doubt, regardless of other reports, Bessie Smith is "Queen of the Blues," and some more, and is positively the biggest attraction of her kind on the T.O.B.A. The act carries special settings and is attractive and immaculate. Twenty minutes in full ovation and bows.

From Cincinnati, Bessie and her company proceeded to Detroit for a return engagement at the Koppin. In the year that they had been married, the Gees had not had much time to themselves, so Bessie acted on an impulse when the train reached Springfield. Taking everybody completely by surprise, she announced that she and Jack were disembarking and would meet up with the show in Detroit. With that, she grabbed her bewildered husband by the arm and they left the train. Bessie headed straight for a cab and ordered the driver to take them to the nearest car dealer. When she saw that a 1924 Nash caught Jack's fancy, Bessie surprised the salesman by lifting up the front of her skirt and revealing a carpenter's apron behind it. Dipping into the apron's pocket, she extracted enough cash to pay for the car in full. Then it was off to Detroit, with a very happy Jack Gee at the wheel. "When Bessie went out, she usually carried a few thousand dollars in that apron," said Ruby, "because she never wanted to get caught needing it, and you never knew what she could think up—like taking a cab, from one city to the other; Bessie used to do things like that."

Previously, Bessie had broken all attendance records at the Koppin, and she didn't disappoint the theater's management on this visit. Even bigger crowds awaited her at the next stop, Pittsburgh, where advance publicity hailed her as "the most popular singer ever to appear in the city." On opening night,

March 17, scores of policemen were called to the front of the Lincoln Theater, where a scene played out that would become familiar over the next two weeks. The *Pittsburgh Courier* described it vividly: "Early in the evening, crowds started to gather, and by 7 o'clock in the evening the street car traffic was blocked. Thousands of people were turned away and those who did attend stormed the theater . . . Hundreds of letters, both out-of-town and local, have poured into the theater asking the management to hold Bessie Smith another week."

Originally booked for a week, Bessie was such an overwhelming success in Pittsburgh that a neighboring theater, the Star, offered to extend her stay by another week. This meant having to postpone the following Monday's Philadelphia opening, but Bessie's drawing power was such that the Standard Theater accepted the last-minute schedule change. Even with the extra booking, and even though the Star's management shortened the show to accommodate more patrons, Bessie's two-week visit left her Pittsburgh fans wanting. To meet the demand for Bessie, and sell more of her records, the city's largest "race" record dealer sponsored a half-hour broadcast featuring her and pianist Irvin Johns over radio station WCAE[5] on Friday night, March 28.

Four days later, when Bessie and Jack returned to Philadelphia, they barely had time to relax before she was off to New York: undaunted by the alleged deflation of the blues craze, Frank Walker had booked yet another series of recording dates for Bessie between April 4 and 9. Perhaps inspired by the positive reception given John Snow's violin accompaniments on the tour, Bessie's musical director, Irvin Johns, hired a New York violinist, Robert Robbins, for some of the sessions. The result was interesting.

The violin was not new to jazz. It was used regularly in early New Orleans jazz and ragtime bands, as well as in black and white country music, but the period's three pioneering jazz violin virtuosi—Stuff Smith, Eddie South, and Joe Venuti—were relatively unknown in 1924, and obviously not models for Robbins's style. His approach was closer to that of the Southern country fiddlers, which gave Bessie's recordings a folk flavor unlike anything heard on her previous recordings. At the April 4 session Bessie performed "Boweavil Blues" and "Moonshine Blues"[6]—the only Ma Rainey tunes she ever recorded—and three of her own compositions: "Sorrowful Blues," "Pinchbacks—Take 'Em Away," and "Rocking Chair Blues." These are not among Bessie's better-known recordings, but they capture her in splendid form.

Bessie was a good, if not wholly original, lyricist; when inspired by a personal experience or a story she heard, it didn't take her long to turn out a lyric, but she usually left the music to her pianist. "Rocking Chair Blues" and "Sorrowful Blues" were collaborations with Irvin Johns. Columbia Records' pub-

With a boost in Bessie's career came new costumes, including this unusual 1924 lampshade style by a designer named Palamida. From the author's collection.

licity release described the latter as "despairing"; actually it is quite humorous, right from the unusual vocal opening, a sort of scat. It sounds as if Bessie is mocking Robbins's sobbing violin, but the birdlike line is actually something she—ironically, as it turned out—borrowed from Gertrude Saunders:

> Twee twee twah twah twah,
> Twee twah twah twah twah twee.
>
> If you catch me stealin', I don't mean no harm,
> If you catch me stealin', I don't mean no harm;
> It's a mark in my family and it must be carried on.
>
> I got nineteen men and I want one mo'
> I got nineteen men and I want one mo';
> I'll get that one more, I'll let that nineteen go.

I'm goin' to tell you, daddy, like the Chinaman told the Jew,
I'm goin' to tell you, daddy, like the Chinaman told the Jew,
If you don't like-a me, me sure don't like-a you.

It's hard to love another woman's man,
It's hard to love another woman's man;
You can't git him when you want him, you got to catch him when you can.

Have you ever seen peaches grow on sweet potato vine,
Have you ever seen peaches grow on sweet potato vine;
Yes, step in my backyard and take a peep at mine.

While it is hyperbole to suggest that there is no such thing as an original blues lyric, it has, historically, been common practice to "borrow" lines and virtually create songs through a cut-and-paste process. The very nature of folk music is that it passes from one performer to another and picks up embellishments in the process; this makes it virtually impossible to establish true authorship, so no one seemed to mind the not-so-coincidental repetition. The blues ladies drew their material from commercial sources rather than street corners, but even Tin Pan Alley tunesmiths occasionally scooped a line or two from Southern soil. Sometimes whole songs were picked up by hucksters like Clarence Williams, W. C. Handy, and Perry Bradford, who made a change or two and published them under their own name.

In her "Sorrowful Blues" Bessie borrowed more than twees and twahs. Two verses are almost identical to ones sung by Ida Cox on her "Chicago Monkey Man Blues," as recorded for Paramount a month or so earlier. Bessie could not possibly have heard Ida's recording before making her own, but either singer could have heard the other perform it in person. Yet the most likely explanation is that these were borrowed, circulating verses.

When it came to lyrics, political correctness was not a consideration in Bessie's day. Country singers and groups seemed quite comfortable with such racist words as "coon" and "nigger," and nobody complained when Bessie or Ida sang: "I'm gonna tell you like the Chinaman told the Jew, / If you don't like-a me, I sure don't like-a you." Even record companies seemed blind to racism; their catalogs and advertisement in the black press routinely depicted black people as sobbing or grinning Sambos. Even more remarkable is that such blatant racism met the tacit approval of African-American newspaper editors—it was a time when society showed an extraordinary tolerance for ethnic insults. As exemplified by a Columbia publicity release for "Ticket Agent, Ease Your Window Down," copywriters were right in tune with the graphic artists as they clearly aimed their condescending prose at simple-minded consumers:

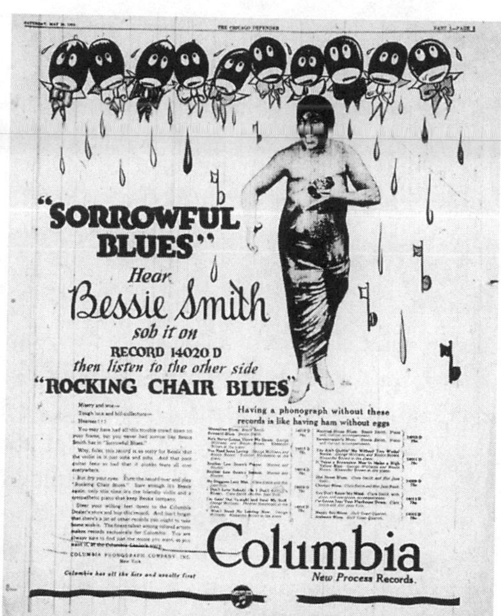

Sobbing "Sambos" and a patronizing text characterize a typical advertisement for Bessie's latest 1924 Columbia release. From the May 24, 1924, issue of the *Chicago Defender*.

> Bessie Smith certainly turned loose a red hot one when she made No. 14025-D. The title is "Ticket Agent, Ease Your Window Down." Here is a gazook who is about to hand his lady an arm full of adios. She knows that if he is refused the purchase of a ticket he will have to stick around a bit and she figures, with the past in mind, that if that happens, she will be able to "square" things for a real reconciliation. So she hies to the ticket man, and if you ever heard a plea that came from the bottom of an apprehensive heart you have a very slight idea of how the "gal" put her stuff over. It's a bear.

Much to Ruby Walker's delight, Bessie and her Uncle Jack stayed at his mother's home on West 132d Street throughout April 1924. More than a year had passed since Ruby stood in the living room doorway and listened to Clarence Williams and Bessie rehearse for her first recordings. She had fantasized about being in show business ever since, and now that her aunt Bessie was a real star, she saw an opportunity to realize her dream. Ruby made no secret of being stagestruck, but the idea of Bessie taking her under her wing went against Jack's grain; every time the subject came up, he expressed his disapproval, but the more he protested, the more Bessie seemed to like the idea. Her own situation had borne no resemblance to the dire circumstances that drove her to leave Chattanooga, but she understood the urge to get away. Considering that an age gap of almost twenty years separated them, Bessie and Ruby had developed a remarkable mutual rapport. Each had a need that could be fulfilled by the other: Bessie was both an inspiration and a key to Ruby's show business career; Ruby was family and therefore—as Bessie saw it—someone who could be trusted, a confidante for life on the road. It all added up to Jack being overruled.

In spite of her phenomenal success in Northern cities like Pittsburgh and Detroit, Bessie approached her next tour with apprehension. It was to start with her first appearance in Chicago, a city that was fast developing a reputation for attracting good blues performers. Adding to Bessie's concerns was that she would be appearing as a single and that Jack would not accompany her on the trip. None of this escaped Ruby, who quickly seized the opportunity and offered herself as a companion: "I started putting ideas into her head, but Bessie didn't seem too interested, so I practically begged her to take me along, and when Jack saw what I was doing, he tried to talk Bessie out of it, but he didn't know that she hadn't made a decision yet. Bessie just played along until she finally said I could go." To justify her decision, she explained to Jack and the family that Ruby could serve as a wardrobe mistress and that she might even teach her a few dance steps. Bessie was anxious to show them off her new costumes and headgear, including elaborate getups that weighed as much as fifty pounds.

Herself an experienced dancer, Bessie taught Ruby a few routines, and she may have marveled at how fast she caught on; the truth was that Ruby had been practicing for months, waiting for just such an opportunity. On May 5, the *Chicago Defender*'s entertainment editor, Tony Langston, attended the premiere show and gave Ruby her first press mention:

> Bessie Smith, "Empress of Blues Singers," opened her first Chicago engagement at the Avenue on Monday night to a capacity audience. So much has been said of Bessie that Chicagoans were looking for something far above the average in her line, and that's just what the famous artist handed them. Her routine of songs are new and well selected and she put each and every one of them over with the well-known "Bang." In fact, Bessie tied up her own show and it is a safe prediction that she has earned a standing welcome with "Blues" fans. She is aided at the piano by Irving [sic] Johns and a bit of speedy dancing between the changing of several gorgeous gowns is done by Ruby Walker.

Bessie shared the bill with a roster of acts that, as Langston described them, reads like a vintage Ed Sullivan show and is typical of the day's variety theater offerings:

> The curtain raiser is the act of Rastus and Jones, a mixed team working under cork, who have a more than ordinary offering. They are followed by Margaret Scott, a prima donna, who has been with us for some time but who never fails to "get hers" along the vocal line. Then comes the rightly named

> "Three Baby Vamps," whose dancing abilities have been developed by Hazel Thompson Davis to such an extent that the youngsters actually stopped the show. Robinson and Mack were fourth and on their "The Bootlegger" offering coupled with several nifty songs and a bit of dancing, went over in great shape. They preceded Jolly Saunders, one of the greatest of all comedy jugglers, and the Baby Ali Co., a singing and dancing trio of fine caliber. Tim[7] and Gerty Moore, in new songs and dialogue, led up to the big noise [Bessie], and proved by their popularity that they have not grown too old for high-speed competition. It is some bill.

Bessie decided to make Ruby a regular member of her chorus line. "On my first tour with the full show, Bessie put me in the dressing room with three other chorus girls," Ruby recalled. "My mother was forty-seven when I was born, and I was raised by older people who made me wear long underwear, which was the style for kids and adults in those days, we called them long johns when I was a kid. When I got older, we called them 'funky busters,' because after you kept them on a week they could stand on their own. Imagine what an adult smelled like. Well, I had on a pair of these funky busters when I walked into the dressing room. All three of the girls was chatting and chatting about the men they had gone out with and how much they had spent on them, and how much they had gave them. While they was talking, they were undressing. When they got down to their underwear, it was beautiful, whoo-wee, silk and chiffon panties, with bra to match. The room was smelling of very expensive perfume. Their hair looked as if they lived in the hairdresser's—sharp chicks. No wonder the men spent so much on them. I was ashamed to take off my clothes. I was afraid they would see me. Only one looked around at me and said, 'You had better hurry up they have already called thirty minutes.' They all went back, talking to each other. They did not look around again. I slipped off all my things and took the bull woolies with it. Then I threw the bull woolies over in the corner and put on my opening costume, which looked like a bikini. I was shaking all over from fear and feeling chilly. I had never had all of my clothes off before in front of anyone, except my mother and grandmother. But I soon got over that. It was nothing for the girls to go from dressing room to dressing room naked. That was why no one was allowed backstage or in the dressing rooms. Nothing but the show or any one connected with the show. Between the shows, the boys in the band, would come down to rehearsal outside of the dressing rooms, and it was nothing for the girls to come out naked to get something from one of the girls in another dressing room. They would pay the band no mind and they would pay her no mind. That is true that a musician and a showman don't pay a naked woman no mind, they have seen too many of them. We would wear patent leather shoes with holes on both sides, to put ribbon in. We wore all colors of ribbon to match our costumes. If we did not have the ribbon clean and starched, we was fined. Sometime we wore opera-length stockings, which was white. We had to keep them snow white and not dingy. Then sometimes we went bare-legged, that meant a lot of Max Factor makeup.

"We was experts at making up. That is because we had a good teacher, Bessie herself. When I threw my bull woolies in the corner, I never went near them again. One of the girls found them the next day. She held them up and said, 'What old dilapidated woman has been in here and lost or dropped her funky busters?' I had been to the store and now I had on sharp underwear, too, so I could afford to laugh with them. It was a wonder that I did not get pneumonia, because I went home that night, that I took off my bull woolies, with nothing on but my dress and coat. The snow on the ground was a few inches deep. I hurried home and I got into a hot bath and rubbed down in alcohol and took two aspirins and got in bed. The next morning I felt great, I think the whole trouble with me before was too much old-fashioned living. I did not let my mother know about this. She would have pitched a bitch.

"Bessie was the only one who hired the black gals, and they appreciated that, so they really worked the show. When we got on stage, all our heads moved together, and our lines was as straight as a ruler. We all smiled, whether we felt like it or not. I was not as black as the other gals, but I was still not yaller, so that put me in between—I was light enough for the yaller chorus girls and I was too light for the black gals, but—Bessie being my aunt—I got away with it."

Chicago was becoming a melting pot for jazz and blues artists who brought their disparate styles to the city from different parts of the South and Midwest and gave it a nightlife few other urban centers could match. This was home base for some of the finest black performers of the day, budding talent that soon would achieve national and international fame. This was where many of them fine-tuned their art, made their recordings, and planned their tours. By 1924, Chicago also had its reigning queens, so Bessie knew that she was up against established competition and would have to work hard to win over the audiences of such local divas like Ida Cox, Alberta Hunter, and her old friend Ma Rainey. These women had come to Chicago when there was no local competition, and all had built up a loyal following. But Bessie could have spared herself any anxiety, because, fine as they were, none of Chicago's resident singers had Bessie's command of the blues. There were no objections when the *Defender* printed Tony Langston's proclamation: Bessie was no longer the Queen of the Blues—she was the Empress.

Chicago's nightlife rivaled Harlem's and had much in common with it.

Gangsters and racketeers controlled the cabarets and speakeasies, along with the liquor that fueled them. They also had a tight grip on the entertainment industry, including management of some of the country's finest jazz musicians and singers.[8] But New Yorkers liked their jazz fast, brassy, and furiously rhythmic, while Chicagoans danced to a slightly different beat. A Chicago style was emerging as a result of a post-1917 influx of New Orleans players, whose approach to jazz blended in with Southern blues traditions. Added to that was the distinct sound of white musicians who now sought to emulate their black colleagues but ended up creating something slightly different.

Louis Armstrong's second wife, Lil Hardin Armstrong, hailed from Memphis, but she became an important part of Chicago's jazz scene when she worked with King Oliver and other New Orleans bandleaders. In an unpublished autobiography, she described the music at the Deluxe Café, where she worked with the New Orleans Creole Jazz Band: "There was no dancing there, but the people ate up the music, just listening and being 'sent.' I didn't take any serious interest in the music we were playing then, but I did find it exciting. The cornet player, Freddie Keppard, made funny noises with glasses, cups, and old hats in front of his horn. Lawrence Dewey's clarinet squeaked and rasped with uneven scales and trills, Roy Palmer's trombone was sliding back and forth, Jimmie Palao's violin sighed and wheezed, and, to top this all off, we in the rhythm section beat out a rhythm that would have put the Beehuana tribe to shame."

In the spring of 1924, South Side Chicago's biggest musical attraction was King Oliver's Creole Jazz Band, which appeared nightly at the Lincoln Gardens Café. Musicians came from miles around to hear this great New Orleans band and its main attraction: twenty-two-year-old second cornetist Louis Armstrong.

Armstrong would arguably become the most famous of all jazz musicians, and even in the early 1920s he inspired just about every musician who heard him. His idolaters included Muggsy Spanier, Frank Teschmacher, Jimmy McPartland, and Bud Freeman, white kids who absorbed what they heard and later turned it into a style of their own, the so-called Chicago style. Some of these musicians—a small group collectively known as the Austin High School Gang—recalled hearing Bessie sing in a cabaret while legendary cornetist Bix Beiderbecke threw a week's pay at her feet. If the story is true, the incident may well have occurred at an after-hours joint run by Richard Morgan, an old friend whom Bessie met in Birmingham, Alabama, during the early stages of her career.

A flamboyant dresser, Richard combined good looks and great charm with considerable entrepreneurial skill. In Birmingham, he was employed by a local foundry, but—like Bessie—he had his sights set on higher ground. Richard had expensive taste and his salary at the foundry was insufficient to meet his requirements, so he diversified and supplemented his income in as many ways as he could. One early scheme was to grant shoeshine concessions to neighborhood kids, and Lionel Hampton, Richard's nephew, recalled that his uncle also had a business composing letters for illiterate people; his specialty, said Hampton, was writing love letters, whose text he largely copied from books. The charge was twenty cents per letter, with a nickel added for illustrations.

Morgan was among the many Southern blacks who, shortly after World War I, migrated to Chicago in search of work. He was first employed in the stockyards, where jobs were plentiful, but his resourcefulness—and the Eighteenth Amendment—soon led him to the more lucrative field of bootlegging. Here his winning personality and take-charge attitude stood him in good stead as he made friends with upper-echelon underworld figures—including, it is said, Al Capone—built up a liquor concession, and became the South Side's most successful purveyor of bathtub gin. Morgan shared Bessie's penchant for getting down and having a good time, and he was—in his own way—a patron of the arts. Diversification had served him well in the past, so he supplemented his income from liquor distribution by operating a popular after-hours club in his South Side brownstone. Catering mostly to entertainers, it was a place where they could let their hair down and spend the remainder of a night socializing with colleagues in a leisurely atmosphere. Here, in smoke-filled rooms, they renewed old acquaintances, gossiped, and even performed when they felt like it.

It was not unusual to find Ma Rainey at Richard's place, singing to the accompaniment of pianist Jelly Roll Morton, or Louis Armstrong cutting through the smoke-filled air in royal musical battle with violinist Eddie South while the rest of Jimmy Wade's Syncopators—who were almost nightly guests—joined in.

And more often than not, one would find teenager Lionel Hampton seated in a corner, absorbing it all. "My uncle bought me everything," he recalled. "Silk shirts, the finest clothes, my first marimba, my first set of drums—it had a light in it. Yeah, my uncle was a real cool dude, and he used to take me everyplace with him—he furnished whiskey and bathtub gin for almost all the dives on the South Side. He was crazy about piano players, but all the musicians used to love to come to his place because they could meet all the chicks there, and my uncle would give them all the whiskey they could drink, and all the chitterlings they could eat. I used to dream of joining Ma Rainey's band because she treated her musicians so wonderfully, and she always bought them an instrument, but my uncle always said that Bessie was the greatest singer—he was always very fond of her."[9]

In a 1969 interview with the author, Lil Armstrong was almost certainly referring to Morgan's place when she described hearing Bessie at a party: "There was some big-time bootlegger on the South Side who always had these parties going. Louis took me there a couple of times and everybody got up and played. The music was always very loud, but one time Bessie Smith got up to sing, and the man who ran the place wouldn't let her start until everybody stopped laughing, talking, and carrying on. He didn't do that for us, but I guess maybe he was afraid of Bessie; she had a reputation for having a bad temper." Ruby sized up Bessie's reunion with Richard Morgan as nothing more than two old friends happy to see each other after a long separation, which is probably all it was. Her first impression was that of a "handsome" man who treated Bessie like a star and "worshipped the ground she walked on."

Ruby was having a grand time in Chicago. This trip offered her the first opportunity to get close to Bessie, and it was clear to Ruby that Bessie also enjoyed the companionship. "We were like sisters," she said, "and Bessie treated me so nice when she took me shopping." Ruby remembered hearing Bessie's new release, "Sorrowful Blues," coming from a record shop. "I said, 'Bessie, that's your recording, let's go in there,' but she didn't want to do that. Bessie didn't want strangers making no fuss over her. Of course I was thinking that way, I wanted her to go in there and be a star." As it was, people were recognizing Bessie in the street; many had seen her picture in the *Defender,* others had attended her performance at the Avenue the day before, and still others remembered her from the South. She could hardly walk a block without being spotted by a fan, and she always responded graciously when people stopped her, even when they asked for a handout. "Bessie bought a pair of dark glasses to hide her face, but it didn't work," said Ruby, "She said she didn't like people treating her special, but I think she was enjoying it—I know *I* was."

Chicago's nightlife was thriving on the South Side. In nocturnal gathering places like the Dreamland and Pekin Inn, clubs that have since become legendary, people performed grinds and stomps on small dance floors as musicians tested the boundaries of creativity, and some etched their names into music history. Bessie avoided the clubs on this trip, possibly because she had promised Jack to keep Ruby out of trouble, but what she heard at Richard Morgan's informal gatherings would have been a sampling of Chicago's nighttime offerings.

Indianapolis was Bessie's next stop on the tour, but she cut the engagement short, and when she didn't show up for her scheduled June 9 opening at New

Orleans's Lyric Theater, the papers offered no details other than that she had been "called back to New York." As we shall see, Bessie's abrupt departure was both dramatic and traumatic, but she was also just plain tired; her success as an artist was placing enormous demands on her time, and a year of almost constant work was catching up with her. One consolation was that it had been a lucrative year, one in which she made more money than she had in all the others put together. She could also find comfort knowing that, by all indications, her popularity was not fleeting.

With generous offers still pouring in, Bessie could well afford to take a vacation without impairing her career, but she chose instead to relax her schedule. A hectic touring commitment was draining, especially when accompanied by such heavy drinking and sleepless nights as Bessie's lifestyle increasingly seemed to demand. Ruby would later conclude that Bessie knew and was known in every drinking joint from New Orleans to Detroit, and she was drawn to them whenever Jack was absent. The "honeymoon" had been brief; already by 1924 Jack and Bessie were having arguments with unhealthy regularity. "She was afraid of Jack," Ruby recalled, "because he'd beat her up so. If he was around she didn't allow you to talk to her about nothing except maybe the show—she didn't want to be bothered, she'd go into her room, afraid you might whisper something and Jack would think she was planning something terrible."

Jack had good reason to be suspicious, for not only was Bessie drinking excessively, she was also feeding her remarkably uninhibited sexual appetite in his absence. Of course she made every effort to conceal her exploits, but she couldn't keep indiscretions from her fellow troupers; in the intimate environment of a traveling show, there were few secrets, but—fearing the wrath of Bessie—they remained relatively well kept. Still, rumors eventually reached Jack, and some of them had a ring of truth. Ruby felt that her uncle may have suspected infidelity on Bessie's part, but that he couldn't be sure, so he focused his anger on her more evident weaknesses: alcohol abuse and gift-giving, neither of which he condoned.

Within Bessie's show, the gossip mill was well oiled, and in 1924 the main topic was her heated affair with Arthur Pitts, a handsome young dancer from Detroit whose shaved head earned him the nickname "Eggie." Primarily a tap dancer, Pitts also did some fancy juggling and headed up the Dancing Sheiks, a tightly choreographed song and dance trio that had become a popular feature of the show.

"He was built like a bronze statue," said Ruby. "Bessie took him, dressed him up and made him her man. She was old enough to be his mother—when you got money you can buy anything. Some way or another Bessie fell for that boy, and he *was* a boy compared to her." Almost ten years younger than Bessie, Eggie was flirtatious, especially around the chorines, who responded in kind. Ruby developed quite a crush on Eggie, but as Maud put it, "no one dared mess with the boss's squeeze." Still, Ruby came close to doing that on one occasion: the incident that cut short the show's Indianapolis engagement.

Ruby knew that her good relationship with Bessie was not worth sacrificing for a mere fling, so she tried to distance herself from Eggie, but temptation got the best of her one night at the Indianapolis Theater. Ruby and Eggie were not doing anything eyebrow-raising that night, just some youthful fooling around and giggling in one of the dressing rooms. Suddenly the door flew open and Bessie entered the room, fuming.

"Everything I like, you like," Ruby remembered her shouting, "and I'm going to break you out of the habit of trying to be Bessie Smith—I'm gonna let you *know* you ain't Bessie Smith." With that, she jumped Ruby and beat her up. Eggie fled the room as the two women grappled, and Ruby's screams intensified. Just as she finally managed to wrestle herself out of Bessie's grip, the police arrived. "I kept on hollerin' even when I saw the cops coming, I was that mad. They asked what had happened and I said, 'That woman beat me,' I acted like I didn't know Bessie. They took Bessie, me, and Eggie in, and put us all in jail. Bessie was drunk, I was half drunk, and they locked Eggie up because we were fighting over him. I wasn't fighting, it was Bessie, she was so jealous."

On the following day, someone paid the fine and the three were released. "I beat you up this time in this town," Bessie told Ruby, "and you'd better get ready to be beat up in the next town if you don't stop messin' aroun' with *my* men." She meant it, but as usual the two women quickly resolved their discord and the bonding continued.

From Indianapolis, Bessie went home to Philadelphia for a few quiet days with Jack before going to New York for more recording sessions. Perhaps driven by guilt, she spent over two thousand dollars on a diamond ring for Jack; such costly generosity seriously bothered him only when the beneficiary was someone else, but he found it perfectly acceptable when he was on the receiving end. "So that's how crazy two young people with money was who never had anything," he later recalled in a *Down Beat* story. "We never, neither of us, really knew the value of money."

Between July 22 and August 8, 1924, Bessie did five recording sessions with Fletcher Henderson. Perhaps success had given her more confidence, or time may have seasoned her voice, but it was a more mature singer who now overcame appallingly unimaginative accompaniments on "Lou'siana Low Down Blues" and "Mountain Top Blues," her voice rising majestically above Don

Redman's painfully corny alto saxophone. She performed even better on the following day when Henderson brought in trombonist Charlie Green, a new member of the Henderson band, who had recently come to New York from Omaha, Nebraska.

"Work House Blues" and "House Rent Blues" mark the beginning a long and fruitful collaboration with Green, whom Bessie soon named as one of her favorite musicians. On the close to fifty recordings she had made so far, her backing had been pedestrian at best, but Green changed that. He gave her more than mere accompaniment, his horn became a second voice, commenting on her lyrics and interacting with every subtlety in her phrasing.

Following the sessions, Bessie returned to Philadelphia to spend the remainder of August and the first two weeks of September at home. In the meantime, Frank Walker negotiated with the TOBA and planned her fall tour. The TOBA had been under much criticism for what one reviewer described as a "steady decline" in production values; it needed to create a better image, and Bessie was just the ticket. So the organization booked her for another season: a twenty-week nonconsecutive tour that allowed for side trips to relax in Philadelphia and record in New York. Bessie's phenomenal success and the TOBA's need to put on a better face put Walker in a good bargaining position. Bessie would no longer have to drive herself as hard as she had during the previous year, and the terms of the new contract were the most generous in the TOBA's thirteen-year history. A press release, dated September 9, noted that Bessie had been signed "to improve the quality of the circuit." Considering that she was already a familiar figure on the TOBA trail, one whose shows regularly lit up the SRO sign, Bessie's presence alone would not have made a difference at the box office, but she was now being paid a higher fee and, in turn, was being asked to spend more money on production. The logic, as TOBA officials figured it, was that a truly dazzling production compensated for the shortness of each show, and squeezing more shows into each day created a profitable audience turnover. The new contract made Bessie the country's highest-paid black performer and seemed to fit her titular elevation to Empress, even though the upgrade had come from a promotion-minded journalist.

Her relatively light summer schedule gave Bessie renewed energy as she prepared for her 1924 fall tour. She spent the last two weeks of September in New York, rehearsing, making more recordings, and fulfilling a four-day engagement as an "extra attraction" and headliner at the Lafayette Theater on 132d Street. In a brief mention of Bessie's Lafayette appearance, *Billboard* reported that a severe cold "prevented her from doing her usual stuff" that week, but that belies what we hear on her September 26 recordings. In fact, Bessie is in fine voice on "The Bye Bye Blues" and "Weeping Willow Blues,"

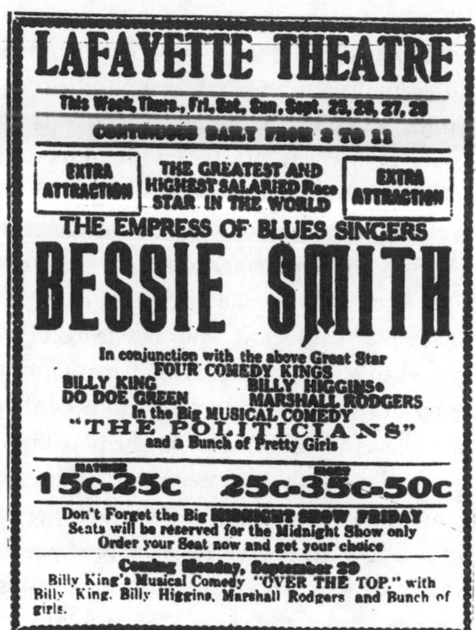

During this engagement at the Lafayette, Bessie spent one morning recording with Fletcher Henderson, Charlie Green, and, for the first time, Joe Smith. He became her favorite trumpeter. From the September 27, 1924, issue of *New York Age*.

two outstanding performances that rank among her best. With its story of a woman abandoned by an ungrateful lover, the lyrics to "Weeping Willow Blues" might have sprung from personal experience, but Bessie did not write the song—Paul Carter did. Originally recorded in 1919 by the Louisiana Five, there is good reason to believe that its 1924 revival was the work of an aggressive song plugger. Within two months of Bessie's recording it was also to be found on releases by Monette Moore and Virginia Liston (accompanied by Clarence Williams), but neither performance proved to be as enduring as Bessie's. Backed by a small ensemble, she casts herself as the lead instrument; stepping forward and unabashedly showing the way, she effortlessly but firmly moves her voice to a place somewhere between the horns and heaven.

No sneezes and sniffles here. Bessie sounds inspired and her performance is fully complemented by Henderson's subtle piano and the horns of cornetist Joe Smith and trombonist Charlie Green. It is as if Henderson suddenly realized the full magnificence of Bessie's artistry, for this accompaniment—also drawn from his orchestra—is far superior to the ones he previously provided her with. Here, the rapport between singer and accompanists reaches perfection. Joe Smith's work on these sides illustrates well the qualities that attracted Bessie to his playing: a pungent, blues-drenched style that fit her own like a well-cut dress. Smith could make his horn sob while also injecting a tinge of humor, and — like pianist James P. Johnson, another Bessie favorite — he had a prepossessing flair for imaginatively embellishing a vocal without intruding upon it. Further enhancing these performances is the extraordinary mutual rapport that existed between Joe Smith and Charlie Green. Smith was an experienced vocal accompanist, having previously worked with numerous vocalists, including Ethel Waters and Mamie Smith. Bessie rarely showed enthusiasm for the work of other performers, but after listening a few minutes to Joe Smith she walked over to Frank Walker and pronounced him her favorite cornet player. "You got the best boys here today," she added, pointing to Smith and Green. "You may not believe this," said Ruby, "but Bessie liked Joe better than Louis [Armstrong]. Bessie wasn't much for playing her own records, but I remember her using them to show the boys on the road how they should play — especially Joe Smith; she was crazy about the way he played for her." Bessie's admiration for both horn players showed excellent judgment, which makes it all the more regrettable that Columbia did not allow her to choose her accompanists. Neither did Frank Walker give Bessie a free hand in selecting her recording repertoire, though he was always open to suggestions.

After three choruses of the song's rather sentimental story, the band shifts to a stop-time riff pattern as Bessie — with little more than a singsong figure to go on — steps away from the blues to address the listener directly with her own cynical take on the situation. "The way he treats me, girls," she declares before returning to the closing bars of the blues, "he'll do the same thing to you." Bessie often incorporated such patter section into her recordings, providing a well-timed change of pace and giving her an opportunity to make the kinds of humorous asides her theater audiences loved. Though this was a common vaudeville approach, it was not always easy to bring off: the performer had to possess a strong voice, a forceful personality, and — above all — good timing. Bessie had all three.

Bessie's live performance accompaniments seemed to improve systematically as her career moved forward. Irvin Johns had been an improvement over Clarence Williams and Fletcher Henderson, and now she found an excellent pianist in Fred Longshaw, whom she worked with during the four-day Lafayette engagement. Her original intention had been to pick up a band — leader and all — in Birmingham, Alabama, where her fall tour kicked off the following week, but Longshaw so impressed her that she hired him as musical director. On arriving in Birmingham, he formed a seven-piece band of local musicians that included trumpeter Shelton Hemphill, who was later to record with Bessie in New York, and saxophonist Teddy Hill, in whose band Dizzy Gillespie would work in the late 1930s. As manager of Minton's Playhouse during the early 1940s, Hill would play midwife to an emerging jazz style known as bebop.

From Birmingham the tour took Bessie to Kansas City, then on to an October 27 opening at the TOBA's Grand Theater in Chicago. Again Tony Langston offered his *Defender* readers a glowing review:

> Bessie Smith, the famous blues singer and Columbia record star, is the "piece de resistance" on an excellent show at the Grand this week. Bessie, whose reputation is world wide, had them howling long before her first number was half finished. Bessie, to say the least, is a bundle of personality and when we use the word bundle we are not casting disparagement at Bessie's generous shape. It takes personality to send over "blues" material. In a proper rendition of blues, art is a secondary consideration. Bessie has a routine which fits her like the well-known glove. There are four numbers offered and all of them made the bullseye. Following Bessie's first song, "Work House Blues," her pianist, Fred Longshaw, turned loose a thrilling solo that had everybody in the place pantomiming. Fred is there like a duck on the ivories and is in direct contrast to some of the freight carried by "blues queens" we have been pestered with from time to time. Bessie essayed a bit of monologue preceding her second song, and this writer is of the opinion that Bessie and the world at large would get along just as well without it . . . A "sold out" sign showed for all three performances on Monday night, which indicates that the Grand patrons want what Bessie carries.

The next tour stop was the Howard Theater in Washington, D.C., for Thanksgiving week. Again Bessie was an "added attraction," this time sharing top billing with the touring company of Sissle and Blake's *Shuffle Along*, Broadway's first successful black musical.

It was quite an eventful holiday weekend in the nation's capital. A football game had attracted twenty-eight thousand visitors, many of whom were anxious to also catch the show at the Howard. The result was a near-riot in the streets outside the theater. "It was almost disastrous," reported a *Journal and Guide* correspondent. "The 'Shuffle Along' gang attracted many of the sports enthusiasts, but if Miss Smith had appeared alone, it would hardly have made things easier for the police. The race never had a more popular star."

Returning to Philadelphia, Bessie had little more than a week's rest before going to New York for more recordings. Her tour had been successful, not nearly as hectic as previous ones, and—because Jack's constant presence squelched any opportunity for carousing—relatively uneventful. Married life still seemed to agree with Bessie, but Jack obviously did not fulfill all her needs. Ruby recalled that Bessie could sometimes go for weeks without touching liquor, "but when she went on one of those benders, she would stay on for weeks without letting up. When her and Jack were on good terms, you couldn't pay her to touch a drop, but when they had their fights she really carried on—she would drink like mad. You see, Jack was so conservative that you couldn't ball with him. He was so strict and he wasn't in Bessie's life at all—he was all right for her when she felt like being quiet, and no drinking, just a wife, a homebody. But when it came to a good time, and she got those spells and wanted to go off, Jack wasn't the one for her. That's why she always had to go and mess with the young people, those who were of her breed, those who could keep up with her.

"She was a strong woman with a beautiful strong constitution, and she *loved* a good time. She was strictly show business: sitting around was all right for a month or so, but that's as far as she could go without going out and clowning. She would go out, stay two or three weeks, ball, and then be ready to keep quiet for a month or so. Then Jack would come in handy, but Jack couldn't see it that way, that's why every time you looked he was knocking her down, or catching her going out of a place or coming into a place."

While on the road, Bessie began an affair with her musical director, Fred Longshaw. Wishing to continue their romantic liaison after the tour, she rented a small apartment in New York, specifically for that purpose. It would later serve her just as well for other affairs of the heart and as a good place to hide after a fight with Jack. Of course, Jack was not the only love interest Bessie had problems with; Ruby recalled a stormy moment involving Longshaw:

"We got back to New York in time to go to the faggots ball. It was a big ballroom in Harlem, named the Rockland Palace. And all the faggots was there showing their glamour, some women wished they could look as good, with their false titties, and wigs, high heel shoes, evening gowns and jewelry, they were beautiful sights to see. To see them, dancing with a man, you would say, 'Look at that man dancing with that beautiful woman, and he had his dick strapped down so tight, that it looked like a fat pussy instead of a dick.' The way they switched was so graceful, like a swan. How many women wished they could walk like that? Because I know of a few gals that walked like they were behind a plow. Only the horse should be in the back and they should be in the front pulling the plow.

"Bessie at that time was going with Fred, her piano player. He went to the dance without us, because he knew Bessie was drinking and she is very nasty at the least thing. She would blow off and he did not want to be embarrassed. So Bessie and I started to the dance alone. We met some of the musicians outside of the dance. They told Bessie that Fred had just went in ahead of us. Did Bessie get mad? She started cursing aloud. She said, 'That motherless bastard could have waited for us, wait until I find his black ass, I will kick his black ass until he menstruates and swears that he is a bleeding bitch.' I got scared and hoped that we would not find the piano player. The place was so crowded with performers, movie stars and celebrities. I was trying to hang in back. She grabbed a hold of me and she was dragging me all over the place. She was looking in all the box seats. We ran into some special celebrities that knew Bessie personally. They asked her to come in and have a drink with them. They had a set up of ice, lemons and oranges and cherries and seltzer water.

"They had drinks, such as Johnny Walker, red and black label. The best of gin, champagne. Bessie said, 'What y'all drinking?' They pointed to what was there. Bessie said, 'Oh no, y'all will never make me sick, give me some ice in a glass.' She pulled out her bad liquor, poured it in the glass and said, 'Here's to all ass holes and dicks, hope you always get a pleasant feeling.' Bowed her head and said, 'Amen,' grabbed me and said, 'Let's go.' We started looking again for her boyfriend, Freddie, which was not important to me, because I was sick of her pulling me all over the place. She finally found him on the dance floor, dancing with a fine looking chick and I didn't know if it was a faggot or a girl. There was so much of everything that night. Bessie made such a scene that she was asked by the guards to leave. Here we go again, thrown out of another place. Bessie was still holding on to Freddie Longshaw. I dragged along behind them. They went to her apartment, the one she had rented to get away from Jack, and I was put in a cab and sent home. That was not unusual. She often wanted to ball with some of them fine looking cats on the show. It depended on what the liquor told her. Oh, you would never think she was the same woman when Jack was there. She wouldn't drink a drop of liquor and acted like she should act—strictly business, you know, but no sooner than he would go away. She would get back into the bottle and the ball again."

On December 6, Bessie and Longshaw recorded a Porter Grainger tune, "Sing Sing Prison Blues," and five other selections that were rejected but were successfully remade the following week. On one of these, "Sinful Blues," Bessie not only sings but plays an instrument: a comb and tissue-paper kazoo. "She always liked to take a comb and paper and pretend she played an instrument," said Ruby. "Jack used to think that was too low-life, but she paid him no mind, because she always got a big laugh from the audience when she played that way." After a tale about a woman driven to murderous, suicidal thoughts by her philandering husband, Bessie throws off her vocal shackles and engages in a bit of jazz improvising, her crude instrument adding marvelous comic relief. As an instrumentalist, she was no match for Louis Armstrong—or, for that matter, fellow kazoo-ist Red McKenzie—but she delivers a loose-limbed, relaxed solo, and obviously has fun doing it. Then she underlines her juxtaposition of morbidity and humor with a joyful outburst, "ha ha," and someone, perhaps Bessie herself, strikes a cymbal with unmistakable finality. The following day—accompanied by Fred Longshaw and

Charlie Green—she put a cap on her 1924 recording activity with "Dying Gambler's Blues," a tune she wrote and, in a conciliatory gesture, credited to Jack.

Although hard work and box office triumphs characterized Bessie's career in 1924, this was also a year in which she took more leisure time than before. Her popularity and income had topped anything she could possibly have imagined, yet this was not a happy year, for Bessie's marriage was beginning to take some wrong turns. She and Jack still enjoyed harmonious moments together, but he was more often absent from the show and less apt to jump when Bessie dangled material rewards. Ruby now sensed that her aunt was beginning to experience periods of loneliness and that she "covered it up from the rest of the show."

4

I've got the world in a jug;
The stopper's in my hand.
"Down Hearted Blues"

When Bessie sang those words on her first recording date in 1923, her future looked promising, but by the onset of 1925, there was no longer any doubt—Bessie had "arrived." She could look back on a year and a half of prominence and prosperity; her billing as "The Greatest and Highest Salaried Race Star in the World" was accurate; dreams of supporting her family had come true; and she did, indeed, seem to have the stopper in her hand.

On Wednesday, January 14, Bessie began her 1925 musical journey on a note of artistic triumph, at Columbia's Columbus Circle studios. Fletcher Henderson had introduced Frank Walker to his most talked-about player, twenty-three-year-old Louis Armstrong, and Walker was apparently impressed, for this was just one of several sessions for which he hired the young, budding genius. Born in New Orleans, Armstrong joined Henderson's orchestra in October 1923, having first lived almost a year and a half in Chicago, playing second cornet to King Oliver. He was still relatively unknown to the public at large, but his reputation among musicians was well established and a series of recordings would soon bring him worldwide fame, not to mention immortality.

At the time of this historic recording session, Henderson's orchestra had a running engagement at the Roseland Ballroom, in midtown Manhattan, but it also appeared in such Harlem spots as the Renaissance Casino, the Newspaper Club, and Happy Rhone's Orchestra Club. Armstrong had further kept busy on his own, participating on several recordings with groups like the Red Onion Jazz Babies and Clarence Williams's Blue Five. His previous Columbia sides had been accompaniments for Maggie Jones and Clara Smith, but he finally found his artistic counterpart in Bessie Smith, and a more perfect team can hardly be imagined. The third participant was Fred Longshaw, but Armstrong's cornet complements Bessie's voice so thoroughly that the result sounds more like a series of duets with keyboard accompaniment. On the first two sides, that keyboard was a harmonium, an undersized, wheezy, foot-pedaled reed organ often found in small Southern country churches. The session started with "St. Louis Blues." Jelly Roll Morton recalled that W. C. Handy—its publisher and composer of record—first published the tune in 1913 as "Jogo Blues" and credited it to his guitarist, Guy Williams. Morton claimed that Handy added some personal touches the following year and brought the tune out as "St. Louis Blues," the title under which it became the most widely recorded of all blues. Others believe that Handy simply added his own refinements to a circulating folk tune and published it. Armstrong's 1929 instrumental recording of the song is a classic, but many consider his collaboration with Bessie to be definitive.

"Bessie Smith, I think she's one of the greatest, the madam of the blues, that we are going to get for generations to come," said Armstrong in an October 1952 radio interview for Armed Forces Radio Service (AFRS), Frankfurt. "It's too bad that she didn't live a little longer so that the younger generation could at least have heard her in person, you know. But her records will stand up forever, and the 'St. Louis Blues' I think is very beautiful, I think I'm playing it muted on here." He is, and with Longshaw's harmonium lending a delightful country church air to the proceedings, the two voices—Bessie and Louis—blend so effectively that one might mistake this effort for the fruit of a long and happy association rather than a first meeting. Undoubtedly inspired by young Louis's mastery, Bessie gives a stellar performance; her steel-blue tones—punctuated by Armstrong's crisp attack—drive the familiar lyrics into the listener's very marrow. Her pacing is marvelous. At first mournful, she gradually builds up the emotional intensity, not unleashing her full power until she reaches the very last word, "nowhere," just before the final strain, which she delivers with an impassioned growl.

On "Reckless Blues," Longshaw's puffing but gloriously effective harmonium trudges felicitously around and under Bessie's plaintive vocal as Armstrong's cornet injects keen comments on her every phrase. Characteristically, Bessie sounds as though she is expressing her own thoughts, singing of her own experiences, delivering her own lyrics. In this case, she may well have written the words. No one can say for sure just how much material she actually contributed to songs that were credited to her or how many of the two dozen or so songs registered in her name actually originated with her. Like all blues singers who wrote songs, Bessie picked up ideas and lines wherever she could find them. Columbia's early session logs gave few details; no one paid much attention to the source of the material being recorded, and some songs were not registered for copyright until months later. Bessie and Fred Longshaw have both been listed as sole composer of "Reckless Blues," but ASCAP lists the writers as Bessie Smith and Jack Gee. Chances are that Longshaw wrote the music and Bessie the words. She was known to give her marriage a boost by having Jack listed as co-composer. Like Maud said, tongue in cheek, "Jack couldn't even compose himself, much less a song. He wasn't creative at all."

Longshaw switched to the more conventional piano for the rest of the session, which went equally well: "Cold in Hand Blues," "Sobbin' Hearted Blues," and "You've Been a Good Ole Wagon"—song after song became a classic.

The slow tempo at which Bessie delivers Perry Bradford's "Sobbin' Hearted Blues" supports Sam Wooding's claim that one could go to the bathroom in the middle of a blues and return without missing anything. "That type of blues was like a soap opera," he said in a 1971 interview for this book. "The stories were all the same, and it took forever to tell them." One could easily give Wooding an argument on that claim, but he was right about the tempo. Armstrong's soulful open horn and Longshaw's mournful piano set the mood with a laconic introduction, then Bessie's story unfolds, enhanced exquisitely by a filigree weave from the cornet. The effect is breathtaking from beginning to end. Bessie's generous pauses give Armstrong ample room to fill the spaces with glorious cornet comments. And he returns the generosity by leaving Bessie time to linger over a single note as long as she wishes, bending her way around it without feeling the need to rush on to the next phrase. Bessie's rendering is a deep shade of blue, but far more relaxed than on previous collaborations with Armstrong. His coda is a memorable statement in itself, and when the results are as satisfying as this, who can quibble about tempo? That night, having recorded so gloriously with Bessie, Armstrong was back with the Henderson orchestra, playing for the Harlem YMCA's annual dinner; the band was seated in the center of the gym, surrounded by tables of elegantly dressed guests. One wonders if there was much dinner conversation.

During Armstrong's 1952 interview for AFRS, Frankfurt, a German fan mentioned that "Sobbin' Hearted Blues" was his favorite. "Yeah!" exclaimed Louis. "What about 'Good Ole Wagon' . . . 'St. Louis' . . . In fact, everything I made with Bessie Smith. And it's wonderful how she'd stand there all day and make the blues, and give them titles. It's a wonderful thing, you know. We'd meet about nine o'clock in the morning and when she finished a blues, I'd say, 'What's that one, Bessie?' and they were all different and pretty. So you know she's a creator."

Bessie and Louis ended their first studio encounter with one of Bessie's own compositions, "You've Been a Good Ole Wagon," a recording that has become a classic in the traditional jazz repertoire. With its burned-out-lover theme, it typifies Bessie's brand of humor and is the kind of song her live audiences loved. Even her male audiences were amused by the image of a woman putting her man out to graze. "Bessie used to get them all choked up with those sad blues," recalled drummer Zutty Singleton, who often observed her from the orchestra pit of the Lyric Theater in New Orleans, "but just as they were all ready to tell the world goodbye, she'd snap them out of it by calling for something she could work for laughs—it could be a sad story, but Bessie could tickle your funny bone with anything, if she set her mind to it."

As Longshaw's appropriately ambling piano marks out the path, Armstrong delivers a commanding performance, moving furtively with Bessie and providing brief, stunning, and sometimes humorous asides along the way. He is less prominent though equally effective here. From a purely artistic standpoint, this was a remarkably satisfying set of performances, a reminder of how fortunate it is that Bessie and Louis, unchallenged masters of their individual genres, were captured together at their artistic zenith.

Armstrong, who kept and meticulously cataloged copies of all his recordings, counted this session with Bessie among his favorites, but it wasn't the music alone that made it so memorable. "I'll never forget this date," he told a Voice of America interviewer, "because one day I wanted to get change for a hundred dollars—it was the first hundred dollar bill I had, and nobody had it in the band, quite naturally, so I said, 'I wonder if Bessie Smith got change for a hundred dollars?' I said, 'Bessie, you got change for a hundred?' She said, 'Sure,' and, man, she just raised up her dress and, like where a carpenter keeps his nails, she had so much money, it killed me." Armstrong also mentioned Bessie's remarkable apron in his 1952 Frankfurt interview: "What knocked me out was that she always had thousands of dollars right under that dress, there. You ask for change for a thousand dollars, she'd raise up her dress and snap one of those bad chickens, like a carpenter carries his nails—'Louie, I'll give you change for a thousand dollars.' Yeah, I liked that part, too."

In February, as her latest recordings shipped to dealers, Bessie embarked on a theater tour that held special significance for her—this time the itinerary included a week at the Liberty Theater in Chattanooga. Bessie had not returned to her hometown since 1912, when she ran away with her brother Clarence and the Moses Stokes company. A local paper mentioned that she had started her career as a child, performing on the streets of Chattanooga, and just about everyone in the city's black community knew that she had "gone north" and become a star. The Liberty Theater made the most of this homecoming event, selling out tickets far in advance, but nobody was as excited as Bessie herself.

Throngs of people milled about in the streets as lucky ticket holders lined up at the theater entrance and others waited patiently at the stage entrance, hoping to catch a glimpse of the hometown girl who made good. "If they really knew Bessie," said Ruby, "they would know that you didn't have to stand out there in the crowd to see her. Everybody who knew Bessie knew that she was regular and they could probably find her after the show drinking in a bar—or speakeasy, or some place not too fancy. Like everybody else." Ruby recalled that people who remembered Bessie as a child—or thought they did—came to her dressing room all day long to say hello. She was also handed more invitations than she could possibly accept, but there was one that seemed to catch her fancy: a pig-foot party following the last show on Friday night.

Despite Jack's absence, Bessie had managed to remain sober throughout the engagement, but the time to unwind had come. Ruby remembered the evening well: "The hustlers down at the pool parlor, the whores, and anyone that had any kind of racket got together and made a big party for Bessie. They came to the theater and got all of us one night after the show. This lady came and got all of us, the girls and some of the boys, and took us to this shaky old house that sat in the middle of a bunch of weeds."

Located in a fairly isolated part of town, the house was built in days when nobody thought of streets, and ignored when somebody did. The new concrete sidewalk was over a block away, so the only approach to the house was over bare ground, which a downpour earlier in the evening had turned into a muddy mess.

A small group of her cast members followed behind Bessie and their escort, the girls stepping gingerly to avoid splashing mud on their Sunday-best dresses. It was a dark, moonless night, but the party was already well under way as they approached the house, taking direction from its lights and noise. By the time they reached the sagging wooden front porch, some of them were already having second thoughts. "Most of them didn't stay long," Ruby recalled. "The house was packed with some seedy-looking characters, and they lost interest, so it was just Bessie, three girls, and I—we were the old standbys, regardless of what happened, we were there."

The girls stayed close to Bessie as she maneuvered through the tightly packed crowd, stopping occasionally to greet a well-wisher or an old friend. "She went straight for the kitchen and we followed—we were afraid not to, because we didn't know these people and she did. Later on, somebody started to play the piano, which was as old as the house. It swayed with the piano player and half of the keys didn't move, but he got a tune out of it anyway—or it seemed like that to us, because we weren't feeling no pain. Bessie said, 'The funk is flyin',' and she was right, because the whole house smelled of food, bad liquor, smoke, and sweat."

The group withdrew to a corner of the kitchen, where the girls looked on as Bessie raided the steaming pots of pigs' feet, collard greens, black-eyed peas, and scallions. She sat down at the large kitchen table and began eating, washing the food down with gulps of homemade liquor.

"Some of those smelly cats came over and asked us to dance with them," said Ruby. "Naturally, we refused, so they got mad and called us all kinds of names, 'You black bitches, who do you think you are?' If you wanted to get knocked down and cursed out, let anyone bother Bessie's girls, but Jack did not care as long as the girls was making money. He said to Bessie, 'If she is all that delicate, let her go home, the men can't hurt her giving her a little pat or whispering something in her ear, that is human nature for a man. When a man sees a half-naked woman, he gets excited.' That's why the girls loved Bessie so. She was so much for the right. Jack would also say, 'Who would hurt that black gal? If anything, they would hurt theirselves, getting out of the way, afraid she would bite them.' He loved yaller gals."

That night at the party, one man was particularly aggressive. He had been dancing, perspiration had stained his loose-fitting, shiny dark blue suit, and he reeked of liquor. When he asked Ruby to dance, she shook her head. "He stood there, grinning with his gold teeth," said Ruby, "and then he grabbed my arm and was going to make me dance anyway. Bessie just kept on eating, but I know she had an eye on this cat."

The man pulled Ruby towards him, "C'mon, baby, let's dance," he suggested, but it sounded more like an order than an invitation, and the other girls retreated farther into their corner, cowering behind Bessie. Ruby tried to pull away, but the man stubbornly maintained his grip on her until he saw Bessie slowly rise from her seat. Now he let go, and Ruby ran over to the other girls.

"We don't want to be bothered," said Bessie, striking a characteristic hands-on-hips pose and defiantly spitting a small bone in the man's direction, "so you just get back in there and let them alone."

"Who in the hell are *you?*"

Bessie's calm was deliberate and effective. "Did that fucker say something to me?" she asked softly, but before anyone could respond, she jumped the intruder and brought her clenched fists down on his head. As stunned by surprise as by the blow itself, the man fell to the floor. Bessie turned back to the table, sat down, and calmly resumed eating. "This here sure is some delicious food, uhm, uhm, uhm," she said, as her victim got back on his feet and stumbled discreetly out of the kitchen.

Several hours later, as dawn broke, Bessie and the girls finally left the house. "We had partied until daylight," Ruby recalled, "because when we went to a party, Bessie never left until all the liquor was gone and she was drunk. So, all of us held onto Bessie and we started to sing and laugh our way home." The unpleasant incident was all but forgotten as Bessie and her coterie—no longer worried about their dresses—trudged through the mud to get back to the sidewalk. They had walked about half a block towards the pavement when the kitchen intruder suddenly stepped out of the darkness, wielding a long knife. "It looked like one of those Spanish daggers," Ruby recalled, "and he plunged it into Bessie's stomach. Then, just as quick as he came, he left, and by the time we got our wits together, Bessie had chased the man about three blocks and collapsed. When we finally caught up with her, she turned to me and begged: 'Baby, take this thing out of me.'"

Ruby gripped the handle protruding from Bessie's stomach, but she was too squeamish to pull the knife out. When one of the other girls stepped in and performed the unpleasant task, a spurt of blood stretched several feet.

Others had apparently witnessed the stabbing, for the police and ambulance soon arrived on the scene. Bessie was rushed to Erlanger Hospital, where doctors strongly recommended she stay for a couple of days, but she abhorred confinement and declared that she would not miss the last day of her theater engagement. When urged to reconsider, she made such a fuss that the hospital let her go a few hours later. The stabbing had taken place at about four o'clock in the morning; at two that afternoon, Bessie was on stage at the Liberty Theater for the scheduled Saturday matinee.

That was how Ruby Walker remembered the incident. A different story appeared under the heading BESSIE SMITH STABBED in the March 7, 1925, edition of the *Chicago Defender:*

> CHATTANOOGA, TENN.—Bessie Smith, popular Columbia record artist, was stabbed by a man said to be Buck Hodge, in what is believed to have been an attempt at robbery. Miss Smith was brought to Chattanooga from Chicago to sing at the Liberty Theatre. The robbery was brought on by her display of

> costly diamonds and gems. Nothing serious resulted, although she was rushed to Erlanger hospital for treatment.

Ruby also remembered hearing about an aftermath, which none of the papers reported: "They said some of the boys in the pool room got a hold of this man after he got out of jail, and that they beat him to death. I can believe it. This was Bessie's hometown—they loved her there." After completing the week at the Liberty Theater, Bessie and her show moved on to the Beale Street Palace in Memphis and the Bijou in Nashville.

One of the show's routines had Bessie dressed as a Southern mammy, complete with bandanna, a red dress with white polka dots, and an exaggerated posterior, which was actually a pillow. It opened with the girls doing a straight Russian dance for about three minutes before Bessie's entrance. Wearing the mammy getup and wielding a whiskbroom, Bessie proceeds to sweep the stage, paying little attention to the dancers other than an occasional annoyed look. Seemingly oblivious of Bessie's presence, the girls continue their dance, which is carefully choreographed to move them around her without getting in the way of her broom. Gradually the dancers begin, by design, to get in Bessie's way and, still choreographed, she sweeps them off the stage until only one remains. "That was my part," said Ruby, "the girl who wouldn't get off the stage. Bessie would do everything she could to sweep me off like the rest of them girls, but I was supposed to be stubborn. Finally, she would pick up her skirt and chase after me, hitting me with the broom—that always gave us a big laugh from the audience."

One afternoon at the Bijou, the audience roared louder than ever. Bessie, having had a bit too much to drink before doing this routine, staggered onto the stage and, remarkably, made it through her sweeping routine without a hitch. But when it came time to hit Ruby with the broom, she swung it harder than usual, causing her artificial behind to drop to the floor. The mishap convulsed the audience, but no one laughed harder than Ruby. Professional that she was, Bessie turned the potentially embarrassing situation to her own good: shaking the broom at Ruby, she turned to the audience and declared, "I'm gonna buy you a damn ticket and let you sit up front, bitch, 'cause you're my best customer."

Like most Southern theaters, the Bijou employed female ushers, one of whom caught the fancy of Eggie Pitts. One night, as she was about to go onstage for her final performance of the evening, Bessie saw Eggie making eyes at the young woman, who obviously had paid him a backstage visit. This enraged Bessie, but the show had to go on, and she managed to contain her jealousy until she had taken her final bow. Then she dashed off stage and began looking for Eggie. When someone mentioned that he had returned to the hotel, she grabbed Ruby by the arm. "C'mon, Ruby," she ordered, "don't worry about your costume, you're gonna help me find that no-good bastard." And out into the daylight they went, an obese, angry mammy stomping up the street with a frail Russian dancer tagging behind.

They were about a block from the hotel when they spotted Eggie and the girl, arm in arm. Bessie wasted no time making her presence known: "You motherless bastard," she shouted, waving her fist in the air. Then she turned to Ruby and warned, "If you can't keep up with me, you'd better get out of my way." With that, she tore down the street towards Eggie and the startled usherette, running as fast as her mammy costume would allow her.

Eggie immediately took off in the opposite direction, leaving the frightened young lady frozen in her steps. The girls still seemed unable to move as Bessie approached her, but rather than stop or even slow down, the racing mammy simply threw out her fist, knocked the poor usherette to the ground, and kept running. In the meantime, Eggie sought refuge in a building, dashing down its basement steps. Bessie saw that and rushed down after him but reemerged soon thereafter, at an accelerated clip. The basement, it turned out, belonged to a funeral parlor—Bessie had stumbled head on into a room full of caskets. She promptly gave up her pursuit.

Bessie and Eggie had reconciled by the time the troupe reached Macon, Georgia, for a week's run at the Douglass Theater. The booking included another exclusive performance for whites, which gave *Chicago Defender* columnist Tim Owsley an opportunity to engage in a bit of backslapping. The heading was interesting:

> BESSIE PLEASES OFAYS
>
> Bessie Smith, the famous Blues artist, while playing a week engagement at the Douglass Theater, Macon, Ga., gave a special night performance for "white only" and scored a complete knockout. C. H. Douglass, owner of the theater mentioned and other fine business and residential properties in the Georgia village has done more to break down racial prejudices than any other individual in that section. He is a wide awake and well-liked gentleman and the Old Roll Top Desk man is proud to be able to count him among his friends.[5]

Bessie had a special interest in Macon: a five-year-old boy whose mother was the niece of Margaret Warren, one of the show's chorines. The boy's father had been a stranger in the night, and the mother—who had other children—was having a difficult time making ends meet. Noting Bessie's obvious fondness for her child, the mother pledged to give the boy to her for adoption if ever she decided that she couldn't keep him. Since receiving that promise, Bessie maintained contact with the mother through Margaret, and every time the show played Macon, she spent time with the boy. She nicknamed him "Snooks," and showering him with gifts and affection. "Bessie loved that little boy," said Maud Smith, "and she went to a lot of trouble for him. Wasted, if you ask me."

Inexplicably, Bessie made the last leg of her tour with the show reduced to six people: herself, a pianist, Ruby, and Eggie and the other two Dancing Sheiks. They were appearing somewhere in Kentucky when Bessie and Eggie had their next big quarrel, a particularly heated exchange of insults that quickly developed into a physical fight. When Bessie knocked Eggie to the floor and it looked as if she was about to pummel him further with her fists, Ruby and the two dancers stepped in and restrained her until Eggie had fled the room. When Bessie managed to pry herself loose, she stomped angrily into her own dressing room and slammed the door behind her. "If you mess with me," she shouted through the closed door, "I'll leave the whole damn bunch of you."

Now it was Bessie against her youthful gang. They joined Eggie in the dressing room next to Bessie's. Through the thin wall they could hear Bessie moving things around, mumbling to herself, and occasionally raising her voice. "That did it, *that* did it," she said, repeatedly. When they heard her open the door, Eggie stuck his head out into the hall. "She's leavin' us, she's packed her stuff," he said. "I'd better go and get her back here." With that he chased after Bessie, who had exited the theater. Ruby and the dancing boys waited anxiously. They were certain that Bessie and Eggie would have a go at each other out in the street, but there was an eerie silence. Neither Bessie nor Eggie returned—they had not just settled their differences, they had taken off for New York together, leaving the others stranded and penniless.

Ruby's mother eventually came to the rescue, wiring enough money for the hapless trio of abandoned troupers to get to Atlanta, where a few nights of work earned them train fare to New York. Ruby had no idea what happened to Bessie's pianist, he had already left the theater when the incident took place. "It was nothing for Bessie just to get up and leave if something made her mad enough, and then she didn't care what happened to anybody," said Ruby. "But she always felt sorry for people who had been left by someone else and she used to often help a whole bunch of other people get home. She took a bunch of Ida Cox's girls out of Dallas once—she was funny that way."

Bessie had probably dismissed the whole incident from her mind by the time she and Eggie arrived in New York. There were other things to think about, such as explaining to Jack and Frank Walker her abrupt departure from the tour. And then there was show business news to catch up on, such as Columbia adding Ethel Waters to its growing roster of black singers. Bessie and Ethel had appeared on the same bill in the South, and both had spent a summer working at Horan's in Philadelphia as relatively unknown performers. Although Ethel hadn't made as many recordings as Bessie, she had been at it longer, cutting her first sides as early as 1921. Ethel could handle a blues quite effectively—she didn't have the same authority as Bessie, but she was a more versatile artist. And like Alberta Hunter, Waters crossed idiomatic borders as easily as a chameleon changed its color. With a charming sense of humor and smooth-as-silk delivery, Ethel Waters rendered well-turned Broadway material with the kind of sophistication that inspired lyricists, and she could render a down-home blues with as much grit as anyone. Although Waters's considerable acting talent would not be fully used until many years later, it came to the fore each time she delivered a naughty song with disarming, childlike innocence.

Born to a rape victim in the Philadelphia suburb of Chester, Pennsylvania, Ethel Waters did not lack Bessie's natural earthiness, but she covered it up: her songs were more literate, her diction was always perfect, and her humor was never too ethnic for whites to understand. Northern audiences found it easier to identify with Ethel than with Bessie, but the disparity was less noticeable offstage, where Ethel Waters's same-sex preference was almost a given. When she joined the label, Columbia clearly gave Waters a back seat to Bessie, signing her to a three-month contract that called for four sides at only one hundred dollars each. But the contract was renewed for a year during which her recording of "Dinah" catapulted her to fame and gave Bessie good reason to regard her as a rival. In the spring of 1925, however, Bessie had no more reason to feel threatened by Ethel Waters than by Clara Smith.

Signing Ethel Waters wasn't going to affect Bessie's career, but Frank Walker had other news that would make a difference: Columbia was about to radically change the way it made recordings. Audio technology was moving beyond the acoustic method of capturing sound through a cone—henceforth all recordings would be made electrically, employing carbon microphones.

Four of Bessie's acoustical recordings with Louis Armstrong were now in stores, and sales looked promising. Anxious to hear how well the new technique captured Bessie's voice, Frank Walker scheduled a May 25 session featuring her with a contingent from Fletcher Henderson's band. Earlier that day, Maggie Jones[1] became Columbia's first race artist to test the system; her session featured the same accompaniment and preceded Bessie's by only one hour. The microphone captured sound with more clarity, but the old mastering system remained unchanged—wax-like discs still had to be metal-plated and processed at the factory before a playback could be heard, so the results of Jones's session were not yet in when Bessie made her electrical recording debut. The backup band, which had also accompanied Jones, consisted of Fletcher Henderson and a choice group of musicians from his orchestra, including Buster Bailey, Coleman Hawkins, and Joe Smith. Bessie had not previously recorded with as many musicians and engineers. Past sessions had featured one to three musicians, and one engineer,[2] but now there were several Columbia technicians on hand, as well as engineers from Western Electric.

Several electrical recording systems were under development at the time, but Western Electric's had reached an advanced stage. Although there were subtle differences between the various systems, the benefits were basically the same: a superior sound with higher fidelity. Now, for the first time, recording engineers had the ability to manipulate volume from the control booth, and producers could employ larger orchestras for vocal sessions without fear of drowning out the singer's voice. Large orchestras were not new to the recording industry but the use of microphones meant that they could be recorded with what—for the times, at least—seemed like amazing clarity. Columbia, wanting a head start on the competition,[3] was eager to participate in what was essentially still an experiment. The previous day, when a test run yielded an unsatisfactory sound, one of Western's engineers suggested that a better result could be achieved if the studio were smaller. It was a matter of acoustics and the carbon microphone picking up too much of the room's ambiance. To solve the problem and obtain a more intimate sound, one of Western's engineers suggested shrinking the studio with the help of a monk's cloth tent. Hastily designed and sewn together, a conical tent of monk's cloth was suspended from the ceiling by a wire and spread to the corners of the studio. It was small compared to the tents Bessie worked under on the road, but large enough to cover her, seven musicians, Frank Walker, the engineers, and the recording equipment.

Kicking off the session with "Cake Walkin' Babies from Home," a lively tune Alberta Hunter had recorded for the Gennett label[4] some months earlier, Bessie managed to sound extraordinarily vibrant despite the claustrophobic atmosphere beneath the tent. Her exuberant delivery and Joe Smith's magnificent cornet break in the middle of the instrumental passage more than makes up for a slightly rough ensemble, but Bessie's version of the song was never given a chance to compete with Miss Hunter's; it remained unissued until 1940, when former Columbia executive George Avakian discovered the original metal master in the company's vault. It is not difficult to imagine the astonishment and delight with which jazz collectors greeted the discovery of this record in 1940. By that time, Bessie was recognized as one of the major stars of jazz—and here, three years after her death, was a whole new Bessie, completely unrestrained, singing in a way few people had heard her sing before. The reason for its rejection is not clear, but one not so plausible theory is that "Cake Walkin' Babies," being a Sophie Tucker–type vaudeville song, represented a radical departure for Bessie, which Frank Walker did not think would do well in the 1925 race market.

Actually, the song itself was the greatest departure. A raucous, freewheeling vaudeville number, it contrasted sharply with the slow blues that had so far made up the bulk of Bessie's recorded output, though it was not untypical of the kind of material she performed in public. Bessie subsequently recorded other lively numbers—such as "Jazzbo Brown from Memphis Town," but they are more polished. On "Cake Walkin' Babies," she dons her stage star persona, belting out a joyous footlight favorite with all the gusto of someone trying to reach a dozing patron in the dark shadows of the balcony. It is a boisterous, shouting, exuberant performance, still replete with bent notes and other tools of the jazz workshop, but adapted to a new purpose.

Behind her, seven first-rank musicians who rarely had an opportunity to jam on record seem to be having the time of their lives. Whatever Coleman Hawkins was playing that day nobody will ever know; the new electric equipment missed him completely. However, the other players are very much in evidence—especially Joe Smith, who demonstrates a new fire as he takes a lead role in a small band. He delivers a memorable break in the middle of the one long instrumental passage, and a little later, when the ensemble shows signs of coming apart at the seams, his brassy horn and iron hand bring them all back together for a blazing finish.

The session's second selection was the more conventional "Yellow Dog Blues," by W. C. Handy. Again Bessie's voice shows exuberance. She had a little trouble with the lyrics, mixing up words here and there, as she often did, but her delivery was as fine as it had ever been, and the session might have yielded additional sides had it not been brought to an unexpected end by the tent's collapse. It happened shortly after the group finished the second take of "Yellow Dog Blues," and it must have been a comical sight. "I'm telling you," said Walker, "it was the wildest scramble you ever saw."

As the musicians, the engineers, Frank Walker, and Bessie tried to get out from under the huge blanket, the Empress is said to have contributed her favorite expression: "I never *heard* of such shit!"

Neither had her tent mates. The session was cut short, and the monk's cloth was folded up for good, but the theory proved to be correct, so a more permanent acoustical solution was designed and installed. The architectural changes were in place for Bessie's the next session, a week and a half later. This time, the accompaniment was modest: Fletcher Henderson and trombonist Charlie Green. They cut two very similar takes of "Soft Pedal Blues," both of which were eventually released. Written by Bessie and delivered by her in an appropriately rowdy fashion, "Soft Pedal Blues" is about a woman who runs a "buffet flat," but its lyrics only hint at the goings on in such establishments. Preceding a cowboy yell that must have knocked the engineer out of his seat, Bessie shouts "I'm drunk and full of booze" with great conviction, but she was probably sober, for Walker would otherwise have called the session off.

Bessie's sobriety presumably carried over to the next day when she recorded four more selections,[6] but that sporadic restlessness was setting in again. On the day of the session, May 15, 1925, she left the house on 132d Street early in the morning, completed her session at the studio, and promptly disappeared. Bessie had pulled such disappearing acts before, so her failure to show up for dinner that evening angered Jack more than it worried him. When two or three days passed without a sign from his wife, he decided to notify the police, but the phone rang before he could make that call. A man on the other end asked to speak to Ruby, who took the receiver from Jack and found herself talking to a very nervous Bessie. Ruby was quick to catch on, so she pretended to be having a conversation with a boyfriend. Bessie told her that she had spent the last couple of days in a Harlem hotel room with one of Fletcher Henderson's musicians, and that she now was afraid to come home. She wanted Ruby to hurry over to the hotel, give her a report on Jack's mood, and help her get out of her predicament as gracefully as possible.

Jack did not seem totally convinced that this had been a call from one of Ruby's boyfriends, but she stuck by her story and soon was able to slip away. Knowing that Jack was suspicious enough to follow, and less agile, Ruby made detours to confuse him as she rushed to the address Bessie had given her.

Ruby and Bessie were old hands at putting one over on Jack, but this was a tricky situation. They weighed several possibilities before Ruby suggested a scenario Jack might believe: they would pretend that there had been an accident near the hotel. Hit by a car, Bessie had been knocked unconscious and taken to the hotel by good Samaritans. Unable to identify her, the hotel people had simply cared for Bessie until she regained consciousness. It was a far-fetched story, but Bessie liked it and, to give it a ring of truth, promptly threw herself down the stairs that connected the first floor to the lobby. Not being in on this unexpected finishing touch, Ruby was taken by surprise and at first thought Bessie had actually had a real accident, but then she realized that staging such a fall would not be out of character for Bessie. She rushed down the stairs and bent over the lifeless body. "I saw you did that on purpose," she began, but Bessie quickly hushed her up. "Shut up, baby," she whispered from her awkward position on the lobby floor. "I'm supposed to be real hurt," whereupon she let out an agonizing groan for the benefit of the approaching manager. It was a farcical script right out of Hollywood.

The frightened manager, who had seen the fall, called the hotel owner, and that triggered part two of Bessie's plan. Assuring the proprietor that she was in a good position to sue, she made a generous offer of a settlement: she would forget the whole matter if he agreed to corroborate the story she and Ruby had concocted. Remarkably, it worked—Bessie and Ruby had not underestimated Jack's gullibility.

Bessie spent the following week at home, "recuperating" and rehearsing for a two-day session with Fletcher Henderson, Charlie Green, and Louis Armstrong. On May 26 and 27, these stellar artists cut two memorable sides, "Nashville Women's Blues" and "Careless Love Blues." Bessie's little "accident" had not impaired her vocal ability, she is heard in superb form throughout, but Armstrong—perhaps somewhat inhibited by Green—is a more subtle presence this time around.

"Careless Love Blues" is one of a handful of Bessie Smith sides for which an alternate take also exists. Until digital technology all but made them unnecessary, alternate takes were commonplace in the record business, and while there is generally good reason for issuing some takes and holding back others, the improvisational nature of jazz tends to produce alternates that are sufficiently different to be regarded as another original. In Bessie's case, however, the difference is not readily discernable; working within the three-minute time limit left no little or no room for impromptu variations such as she was known to bring into live performances. "Bessie could work a song for fifteen to twenty minutes," Ruby recalled. "She didn't do a whole lot of improvising, but she'd talk to the audience in between—make little remarks, do some mugging, or a dance routine." W. C. Handy, who published "Careless Love Blues" with new lyrics, recalled hearing a variation on it in Bessemer, Alabama, as early as 1892. Bessie's lusty performance features the more powerful lyrics of Martha Koenig and Spencer Williams, and her delivery of "this song of hate," is convincing and without self-pity. Clearly, love in her lexicon is a matter for shouted discussion rather than secret whispering. Armstrong and Charlie Green create the proper milieu with marvelous snippets of countermelody and just enough lament in their horns to keep this tale of a broken heart on the intended track.

The following day marked the final collaboration between Bessie and Armstrong. They recorded "J. C. Holmes Blues," and "I Ain't Goin' to Play Second Fiddle." Again, the two giants complemented each other perfectly. The latter song, a defiant proclamation written—or, at least, published—by Perry

Bradford, bore a title with which both artists could identify; it became their parting duet. Bessie could be bittersweet and plaintive when she wanted to, but she also had a wonderful way of injecting contrasting huskiness when it seemed appropriate for her story. This technique, which she employed selectively, suits the message of "Second Fiddle" perfectly. Charlie Green's presence lacks the intimacy that made Bessie's first collaborations with Armstrong so compelling, but his trombone comments are quite effective and Bessie could chalk up another successful record date.

Bessie's eventful, unscheduled between-tours rest period had been anything but relaxing; now it was time to gear up for the 1925 summer tent shows. Renting a rehearsal room in Lafayette Hall, next to the theater at Seventh Avenue and 132d Street, she began preparations for a new production called *Harlem Frolics*. The Lafayette Theater was undergoing a complete renovation under new ownership headed by Frank Schiffman, who would later acquire the 125th Street Apollo. His first show, a musical extravaganza featuring Clara Smith, was scheduled to run through the summer. Rehearsing in adjoining buildings, the two Columbia stars frequently looked in on each other, and Ruby recalled that they even sang together once or twice.

Directed by comedian Dinah Scott, *Harlem Frolics* boasted a chorus of seven girls, music by James E. Jones and a seven-piece band, and a variety of acts, including Eggie Pitts and his fellow Dancing Sheiks. Hilarity was assured by the presence of Tolliver and Harris, a popular comedy team, and a trio of comedians comprising Scott himself, James T. Wilson, and Bessie's brother Clarence, who had the role of straight man. Clarence also assumed a backstage role as the troupe's business manager, an arrangement that did not please Jack. Ruby saw it as yet another move by Bessie to "put Jack in his place."

Rehearsals went well and *Harlem Frolics* was ready to head south by the end of June. In years past, Bessie had covered thousands of miles, barnstorming under the most primitive circumstances, but her tent shows were now elaborate, well-organized affairs, with an advance man traveling ahead of the company to secure the proper licenses, select an appropriate site, and herald the show's arrival. Thanks to its new business manager's initiative, the 1925 *Harlem Frolics* tent tour introduced a new, highly visible element to Bessie's show: her own railroad car. Custom-made in Atlanta by the Southern Iron and Equipment Company, it was a formidable sight, painted a bright yellow with green lettering that proudly informed anyone who saw it that the Empress was in town.

When Clarence suggested that Bessie buy her own railroad car for the tent tours, Jack balked at the expense, but he was quick to take credit for it when the deal was closed. "Jack was bragging about how he bought a train," said

Clara Smith recorded four sides with Bessie, but only three were released. Billed as the "Queen of the Moaners," Clara was the second most important blues singer on Columbia's "race records" roster.

Ruby, "but everybody knew how he didn't even like the idea of the show having the car. Bessie let him get away with it." Jack told the *Chicago Defender* that he was going to pick the car up in Atlanta, but Maud Smith, who had just joined Bessie's show, told a different story: "I'll never forget it. It was Clarence's idea to buy the car, and it was delivered to us in a small town near Atlanta on a sunny Monday. Everybody was so excited, and we laughed and carried on as we walked through the car and examined every corner. And what a difference it made—some of the towns we hit didn't have hotels for us so we used to have to spread out, one staying here, another one there. Now we could just live on the train."

Seventy-eight feet long, the car was large enough to transport the entire show. Each of its seven staterooms slept four people in comfort, while a lower level served as somewhat cramped quarters for up to thirty-five people. The kitchen and bathroom featured hot and cold running water, and Ruby recalled that a flush toilet was particularly welcomed in an area of the country that still relied on outhouses. Clarence had given the designers specifications to make the car as functional as possible. Thus the kitchen was large enough to feed a troupe of forty, the tent's big center pole rested easily along a corridor that ran the length of the car, and a rear room was designed to house the folded canvas and cases of soft drinks, Crackerjacks, peanuts, and souvenir items. That room also served as uncomfortable sleeping quarters for the prop boys (sometimes called "canvas boys"), young men who were picked up en route and hired to erect the tent and perform whatever manual labor was required. Displeased by their fondness for chorines and aversion to soap and water, Bessie went out of her way to discourage fraternization; she made it clear that it would be in their own best interest to keep to themselves.

Blues singer-guitarist Lonnie Johnson, who toured with Bessie in 1929, recalled an incident involving a prop boy whom Bessie had seen making eyes at one of her girls. Although her inclination was probably to fire him on the spot, Bessie conveniently suppressed her anger until payday. In a 1959 radio interview with the author, Johnson described what happened when Bessie slowly approached the youth, who was standing in line to get paid about five dollars for a week of hard work:

> She walks up to him, smiling and looking real friendly. So he starts smiling, too, thinkin' she's gonna say something nice, but he should have known better, Bessie never said anything nice to those boys. This one never knew what hit him; Bessie just stood there, looking at him and smiling, and then, *wham,* she punched him in the face and knocked him several feet away from the line. "You lowly bastards ain't messin' aroun' with *my* girls," she said—and then she told her nephew, Teejay, not to pay him. She left that poor kid there, somewhere in South Carolina, without any money.[6]

As this incident demonstrates, Bessie could be as hard-hearted as she was generous. The prop boy's punishment was obviously an overreaction, and it may have been motivated by Bessie's protective instincts; her chorines were usually quite young, most of them in their teens. Then, too, Bessie's maternal feelings may have been combined with a touch of jealousy. "She always liked them younger than she was," said Ruby, "and it didn't matter if they were men or women, as long as they could show her a good time—like I said, Bessie *loved* a good time."

Working on the road for Bessie didn't make anyone rich—the chorus girls and dancing boys received fifteen dollars a week spending money with free transportation, room, and board. Hard work and empty pockets were recompensed by the job's inherent freedom and prestige and by the possibilities of making it to the top of the bill. After a relatively short period in the Empress's training camp, many a greenhorn became a seasoned performer—in more ways than one. Yet the prestige of working with Bessie Smith was not enough for everyone. While touring with the *Harlem Frolics* show, Tolliver and Harris questioned the fairness of their contract's financial terms and suggested to Clarence that it be renegotiated. When he brought their complaint to Bessie's attention, she stepped in and attempted to settle the dispute by throwing a piano stool at Tolliver. She was winding up for an encore when Tolliver grabbed his partner's arm and the two high-tailed it out the door. The August 8, 1925, issue of the *Chicago Defender* left the dramatic details out of its report: "Tolliver & Harris have left the Bessie Smith unit. They are making a stand in Jacksonville, Florida. They state they were double-crossed in the securing of their act for Bessie Smith unit."

Although Bessie's overhead was reduced by the acquisition of the railroad car, she did not pass the savings on to her cast and crew, but nobody complained, because it made life on the road easier for everybody. During stops, the car was parked on a dead track, and it was not unusual to be awakened in the middle of the night as it jerked, squeaked, and thumped from being pulled and hitched to an outgoing train. "You got used to it," said Ruby, "and you better not be off the train messing around somewhere when it was time to go. That happened to a couple of the gang, but they caught the next thing smoking. Bessie was pretty good about that, as long as they didn't miss a show, but Jack would fine them—he'd use any excuse to get back the money Bessie paid us."

Food was prepared in the car's galley, often by Bessie and Ruby, with everybody pitching in—even the musicians were drafted to peel potatoes. A typical meal featured stew, pigs' feet, or some other Southern specialty, and the portions were generous. "Bessie didn't let anybody go hungry," said Maud, "not even the nasty prop boys—but they wouldn't eat with us, Bessie wouldn't allow it, because they were too dirty." When weather permitted and the railroad car was near a suitable place, food was consumed in the open air, alongside the track. "It was like a party," Ruby recalled, "or rather like a family picnic."

While living in such close quarters occasionally produced friction among the cast and crew, Maud and Ruby agreed that the railroad car on the whole had a positive effect on morale. Good stage performance was the crucial ingredient of a successful show, but there were other important tasks to be performed. At each stop, a well-choreographed routine was performed by everybody: as soon as the car came to a halt, the prop boys unloaded the poles, ropes, canvas components, wooden benches, and merchandise, transported all this to the pre-selected site, and proceeded to raise the tent. The rest of the cast made sure that costumes were aired and ready for the evening's performance, and following a lunch or early dinner, the band members donned their short red coats and prepared to march through town announcing the show. Playing such lively tunes as "St. Louis Blues," "Cake Walkin' Babies," or "There'll Be a Hot Time in the Old Town Tonight," the band led a parade of fellow troupers who waved at the potential audience and carried placards proclaiming real and imagined enticements: "A Hot Show Tonight," "Bessie Smith and Her Gang Are Here." Hand-painted by members of the troupe, the signs often featured the names of entertainers who weren't even with the show or promised such exotic imaginary acts as "Beulah, the Ball of Fire." By the time the show's pied pipers reached the tent, a large entourage of eager customers and children had formed to face Bessie's family of ticket vendors—usually Maud, Clarence, and Teejay. But there were other offerings, too. Bessie had members of the show aggressively hawking soft drinks, Crackerjacks, hot dogs, and cheap novelty items, including paper fans with the show's name on them. The latter were purchased in New York at a penny apiece and sold for ten cents to overheated audiences. "Once we sold hot dogs and corn on the cob." Ruby remembered. "We had a grill for the hot dogs, and each week, a girl would sell the hot dogs in a costume, but Bessie stopped that because the girls got too many insults."

The *Chicago Defender*'s August 7, 1925, issue carried an item about the show, presumable based on information from Jack, who, according to Ruby and Maud, is the only one who would have identified himself as general manager:

> Bessie Smith, Empress of the Blues and her Harlem Frolics are now touring the Sunny South, packing 'em in at every engagement. Miss Smith has gained untold fame with her record-making for the Columbia Phonograph company.
>
> The best talent obtainable composes her revue, and the dress of the vehicle is par excellent [sic]. The revue is working under tent for the summer season, and enough camp chairs are not available to seat the huge throngs that clamor nightly to hear and see The Empress and her gang strut.
>
> Dinah Scott is directing affairs of the stage. Jack Ghee [sic] is general manager of the company. Clarence Smith is the assistant to the advance manager, H. H. Phillips.
>
> The show will travel in a fine 78-foot Pullman, recently purchased from the Southern Iron and Equipment Company. Mr. Ghee left the show last week and went to Atlanta, Ga. to bring the car back.
>
> The line-up of the show: Chorus, Helen Hill, Guitrie Scott, Boula Lee, Beula Brown, Anna Moore, Pearl Taylor, Lillian Young; acts: the Graham Trio, Frank Grady, comedians Dinah Scott, James T. Wilson and Clarence

Smith: straight man. James E. Jones: orchestra. W. H. Woods, Buster Johnson, Alvin Moss, Mr. Wardell, Walter Graham and Little Joe Williams.

The huge round tent was divided into two sections: a fifty-cent admission secured patrons a seat on one of the long wooden folding benches that formed several rows in the back; a front bench with a back rest cost an additional quarter. Only members of the family—usually Maud, Clarence, or Teejay—were entrusted with ticket sales. All money was brought to Bessie's stateroom, poured out on a table, carefully counted, and secured in a small safe.

Jack was always eager to count the money; he was good with figures, but he did not know how to make up a payroll—that job was given to Clarence. Although Bessie's payroll was modest, Jack acted it as if it were the Federal Reserve. In his absence, Clarence handled the task, but Jack handled it himself whenever possible, always placing a gun on the table to discourage any would-be robber. "We used to laugh at him," said Ruby. "That little bit of money wasn't worth getting into trouble for." Still, after a few weeks of touring, a considerable sum of money had accumulated.

An expert craps shooter, Jack also liked to engage members of the show in a game, hoping to win back some of their pay. "He would start a crap game with any of the boys or girls if they were fool enough to play with him, and get all the money back after he won, cheating if necessary," said Ruby. "Naturally, he wouldn't give them their money back, so they would come to Bessie, crying. She sometimes gave them the money back and bawled Jack out—but not always." Occasionally, members of the troupe who had lost their salaries to Jack asked Bessie for a loan, but she had no sympathy for those who repeatedly allowed this to happen. "If you're dumb enough to let him take your money back, he *should* take it back," she would say, but Ruby sensed that Bessie adopted this hard attitude only to discourage them from gambling with *Jack,* because his greed annoyed her. Bessie herself was no dilettante when it came to playing card games, but on the few occasions when she indulged in a game with her performers, she was strictly in it for the fun of it. Sometimes she even refused to collect her winnings from people who could ill afford the loss.

Jack's attitude was the exact opposite. His respect for money bordered on obsession, which often keeping him up for hours, separating nickels from dimes, quarters from halves. "After everything was put away and everyone was in their stateroom asleep, Jack would be up with all of his bags, counting his money. He had a penny, five-cent bags, ten-cent bags, twenty-five-cent bags and fifty-cent bags. He even had a silver dollar bag at that time. There was a lot of silver dollars in existence. On through the night, even after we would feel another train hitch our car on and we could feel ourselves moving, Jack would be counting his money, with his .45 police revolver beside him. No one would dare go near his and Bessie's stateroom for fear of being shot. Jack would let no one come near that stateroom. Thinking someone was going to hold him up."

Ruby recalled that Jack did more than count the money; he also took inventory: "When we worked one night stands and the tent was taken down and put safely away in back of the railroad car, with all the benches folded and stacked, he would count all of the things that was not sold, such as potato chips, salted peanuts, coated peanuts—everything." Though she disapproved of his preoccupation with money, Bessie was somewhat amused by it, and she was known to entertain friends by mimicking the wide-eyed Jack, crouching greedily over imaginary piles of change.

During her tent tours, Bessie occasionally made a theater appearance. The *Harlem Frolics* show played a week each at the Columbia Theater, in Columbia, South Carolina, and the Liberty Theater in Columbus, Georgia. Although it appears that Frank Walker was recording her at every opportunity, it is unlikely that he would have Bessie interrupt her tour just to make two sides. Her mid-August trip was therefore probably not made solely for the purpose of recording, but neither Ruby nor Maud could suggest what might have made Bessie take off from a successful tour.

Frank Walker scheduled Bessie to record on August 18, but when she showed up drunk, he immediately postponed the session until the next day. The accompaniment was an odd one, a trio that included pianist Isadore Myers, reed player Bob Fuller, and Elmer Snowden, a banjo player and band leader whose small band, the Washingtonians, was taken over by its pianist two years earlier. It eventually became the Duke Ellington orchestra.

Snowden recalled how well Walker and Bessie seemed to get along, even when she caused the cancellation of a session. "We didn't play a note," he remembered, "because you could take one look at her and know that it was no use having her sing. Mr. Walker said something to her and she smiled. She took it very nicely and said to us, 'I'm sorry, boys, but Mr. Walker is the boss and I'll sing twice as good tomorrow.' Then she walked out, arm in arm with Mr. Walker." The following day, Bessie, sober and in good voice, recorded "Nobody's Blues but Mine" and "I Ain't Got Nobody," overcoming accompaniment that left much to be desired. Considering the caliber of musicians Walker had hired for Bessie's recent sessions, this was a definite downgrade, which leads to speculation that this was indeed not a session he had planned in advance.

Just before Labor Day, Bessie wound up her show in Atlanta, which became the last stop for all her tent tours and the winter home for her new railroad car.

The car had been expensive, but Clarence told Maud that it had paid for itself on the first tour. Normally, the troupe would make its way back to New York playing one- or two-week engagements on the TOBA circuit, but this time Bessie headed straight for New York and, not surprisingly, another record date on September 1.

It would be a follow-up duet session with Clara Smith, and the original intent was to cut two selections, but as Bessie and Clara went "Down Old Georgia Way," they obviously hit a few bumps—the tune was abandoned after three unsuccessful tries. This setback was more than compensated for by the second tune, "My Man Blues," which is credited to Bessie and outshines her previous duets with Clara. A typical stage number of the day, it features the blues queens in a cohesive, partly spoken dialogue in which both stake claims on the same man, Charlie Gray, whose brief role in this triangle is probably played by the date's pianist, Stanley Miller. Toward the end of the song, the women reach an amicable arrangement to "have him on the cooperation plan," and join their voices in a sweet, harmonious duet about "that rotten two-time man." With its generous use of dialogue, and a story line, "My Man Blues" sounds like a skit that Bessie might have written for her stage show; it is a comedic routine in which the exchange is evenly divided between the two singers, and oddly enough, Clara gets to deliver the best lines. Her voice has a warmth that was not evident on their earlier duets, and the pairing with Bessie's meatier, more richly textured sound is perhaps unfair, but the blend is a prepossessing one. It is interesting to note that Columbia seemingly regarded duet singing as half a job—Bessie was only paid half her normal fee.

Having interrupted her normal tour schedule, Bessie now headed back south to complete the TOBA leg of her tour. Her *Harlem Frolics* show was scheduled to open at the Frolic in Birmingham on September 7, but she had promised Charles Bailey, the owner of Atlanta's "81" Theater, that she would do a couple of performances there for all-white audiences. Although Bessie and Bailey had occasionally clashed, they were good friends and she felt indebted to him for giving her a launching platform in the early years.

Bessie's disagreements with Bailey were always quickly resolved, and Ruby recalled that Bessie usually got her way. One such incident occurred when Bessie broke one of Bailey's strictest rule. He was adamant about not allowing his performers to enter the theater by any other access than the stage door. It was, he believed, improper and unprofessional for the audience to get a glimpse of them before show time. But to access the stage entrance, one had to cross the yard that adjoined the theater. This was where a much younger Bessie had rehearsed a few years back, but it was now rat-infested and strewn with garbage. Rule or no rule, Bessie refused to pick her way through such filth, so one night she grabbed Ruby by the arm, led her past the box office, brushed the ticket taker aside, and was about to walk down the center aisle, toward the stage, when Bailey stepped in front of them.

"It's me, goddammit," said Bessie as he approached, "and I ain't goin' no other way."

"Take it easy, Bessie," Bailey whispered. "If they see you before the show, they won't find you as interesting."

"I don't give a fuck," she retorted, not bothering to lower her voice, "and if you don't like it, kiss my black ass and give me my drops." Then she strutted down the aisle, drawing stares from astonished patrons. Bailey shrugged his shoulders and let her go. "The theater was packed," Ruby explained, "and he would have had to give people their money back if Bessie had walked out, so he said to her, 'Alright, alright, have it your own way.' I knew he wasn't going to make a big thing out of it, because when she got mad or drunk, it was nothing for Bessie to jump up and pull those curtains. I've seen her pull those drops down—hanging on them. She'd pull them down anywhere if the theater owner said the wrong thing."

Ruby shared Bessie's fondness for Atlanta: "Of course you know we never drank liquor from the store. We all had to drink that bad liquor that Bessie drank. She would get mad at us if we didn't. She said liquor from the store made her sick. We called it 'walk a block and fall.' For seventy-five cents, we could get a half-pint. Sometimes my palate was so sore that we could not drink water for days. We always had a lot of fun in Atlanta, because Bessie had so many friends there, and the people loved her so. That's where the garbage man sold liquor in the streets, he'd push this big can on wheels through the alley near the theater, shouting 'Garbage man, garbage man,' and the people would run out there with their whiskey glasses and buy that bad liquor from his can. Bessie didn't buy from him—she had to have it by the half gallon, and she'd buy it from a man who lived under the viaduct, near the boardinghouse where we stayed. One time the police caught me getting some liquor for Bessie. I was runnin' with this half gallon, and to make it worse, it was after the twelve-o'clock curfew, so they put me in jail overnight—it was nothing for us to spend a night in jail."

One day, Bessie and Ruby went shopping in downtown Atlanta before going to the theater for the two o'clock matinee. As they walked leisurely down the street, they looked in every store window, and fancied themselves in this dress or that hat, but when they saw what one shoe store had on display, both had to let out a little scream. "Bessie and I fell in love with those shoes," said Ruby, "so we went in and got two pair, exactly alike. They were very expensive, but when Bessie saw something she wanted, price meant nothing to her. Whenever she bought anything for herself, she would get me the same thing."

When they got to the theater, Ruby wanted to show off Bessie's gift to the other young ladies, but not everyone was impressed. "There was one girl on the show that hated my guts and she was jealous of me. She hated me because I was Bessie's niece and one of the three Dancing Sheiks, who was very attractive, used to be her boyfriend, until I took him away. He was so attractive, he looked better than Eggie and he had a walk that made you feel like telling him, 'keep on walking.' "

When the girls went upstairs to perform, Ruby left her new shoes in the dressing room and didn't give them a thought until after the second show. "Bessie called me up to her dressing room, which was on the stage floor, and said she was ready to go for supper at a café next door to the theater. I went downstairs and when I picked up my shoes, they had been cut everywhere and in every way. They was cut so bad, they were practically falling out of my hands. I screamed of fright and ran back upstairs to Bessie's dressing room, with what was left of my shoes. I felt so terrible that I couldn't speak, I just threw them in Bessie's lap. She got up and took me in her arms until I calmed down, as she always did when things got too much for me. We didn't have to ask who did it, we knew, because Bessie knew this woman hated me.

"Bessie told me not to say anything. She wanted to let that black bitch think that she had got away with it, so I finished the week out in the same dressing room with her. I acted like nothing had happened and Bessie took me to the shoe store the next day and got me another pair, just like the pair that got cut. But I left them in Bessie's dressing room."

At the end of the week, everybody went to the hotel after the last show to get paid. Bessie paid all salaries in cash and always at the hotel or in her railroad car. "That's where Bessie always paid the show off, never at the theater, because there was always some outsider hanging around the stage." Since Jack was not there, Ruby stayed in the room with Bessie, calling the troupers in, one at a time. "She paid the whole show off first before she paid that black bitch, that cut my shoes, then she said to me, 'Well this is it, call that bitch in.' I went to the door and called her. She came in grumbling, saying, 'It's about time,' because Bessie had never took so long to call her before.

"Bessie paid her all of her money, except twenty dollars. When she counted it, she said, 'I am twenty dollars short.' Bessie said, 'I know, I took that for Ruby's shoes.' She said, 'What damn shoes?' Bessie said, 'You know and we know, and you don't go no further with this show—we don't need your kind on this show.' The gal had a Coke bottle in her hand, and before we realized what she was going to do, she hit Bessie on the head and started to run, but

Bessie caught hold of her and hit her so hard in the mouth that it knocked two of her front teeth out, then she dragged her to the door."

The woman ran out into the street, screaming for the police, who responded promptly and took the two combatants away—the chorine to a hospital and Bessie to the police station. "Before they put Bessie in the police car, she slipped me the money that was left from paying her show off, and told me to give it to Eggie so he could bail her out," said Ruby, who found Eggie sleeping in his room. "He had got drunk earlier and he had no idea what was going on. I had to wake him up and tell him what happened, so I gave him the money, which was fourteen hundred dollars, and told him that Bessie wanted him to come down and bail her out. It was about three o'clock in the morning, so I was tired and I figured I had done what Bessie wanted me to do, and I went to bed."

The following afternoon, Ruby was still sleeping when Bessie came barging into her room. "She was yelling 'Where is he? Where is he?'—scared me half to death. Then she told me that Eggie never showed up at the jail and that Mr. Bailey got her out. She asked me did I give Eggie the money and when I told her that I did, she said couldn't nobody find him."

Inquiring around, Bessie found somebody who had seen Eggie grab a cab at the stand in front of the theater. The driver's memory, bad at first, improved when Bessie's hand opened to reveal a few bills. He confirmed that he had driven Eggie, "bag and baggage," to the railroad station and that he had seemed rather edgy. When they got to the station, he said, Eggie had asked him to go in and buy a ticket for Detroit, while he remained in the cab. Returning with the ticket, the driver was handed a hundred dollars and told, 'You never saw me.' That story made sense to Bessie, because Detroit was Eggie's hometown.

Bessie immediately called Charles Bailey, told him the situation, and asked for his help. "Regardless of how much hell Bessie raised, the whites down there loved her," said Ruby. "I don't blame them, she made enough money for them. So Mr. Bailey called some big shot and had the train stopped, and they found Eggie and took him off the train and brought to Birmingham, which was our next stop. They kept him locked up until Bessie got there to appear against him in court." Thus ended another of Bessie's romances—Arthur "Eggie" Pitts was history.

On Sunday night, September 6, 1925, Ma Rainey's all-star review closed a run at Birmingham's Frolic Theater, with Bessie and her troupe—minus Eggie and the destructive chorine—due for a Labor Day opening the following afternoon. Mindful of the overwhelming reception given her by the Frolic's patrons in 1923, the theater owner made this a double booking: two weeks at the Birmingham Frolic, followed by another two at the Frolic in nearby Bessemer. A streetcar ride separated the two theaters, so Bessie and her gang found it prudent to stay at the Birmingham hotel for four weeks, commuting to Bessemer during the last two.

"When we got to town, we used to go to the hotel and put our personal things down and then we would go to the theater to do the usual thing, such as getting the dressing rooms, getting out the costumes from the wardrobe trunk, showing the prop men and the stage manager which trunks to look in for the scenery and the curtains. Then we did a dress rehearsal, and went out and find the nearest restaurant to the theater, eat, and get back in time for the first show. But that mess with Eggie made us go to Birmingham a day before we were supposed to open," Ruby recalled, "so Ma Rainey was still at the Frolic, and Bessie wanted me to go with her and catch the show. I guess she needed to relax after that mess in Atlanta." Ruby had heard Bessie and others talk about the already legendary Mother of the Blues, but she had never met her or heard her sing. If Bessie bothered to catch her act, she figured, Ma really had to be something special.

Ma had not yet made her appearance on stage, but the closing show was already in progress when Bessie and Ruby entered the packed theater. Whistling Rufus—one of Ma's top performers, who later made it on his own—was finishing off his act with some fancy knee drops, accompanied by a lady pianist when Bessie took Ruby to a box overlooking the stage and seated her. Then she disappeared through a small door.

Rufus finished his act and took a bow to thundering approval. As the ovation faded, he exited and the curtain came down. Ma Rainey's five-piece Georgia Jazz Band was now assembled in the pit and tuning up. Anticipation filled the air, but Ruby was used to a livelier audience; this one seemed strangely sedated. Suddenly, the eerie calm was broken by a shout from the balcony: "The Phaaantuhm!" As if taking a cue, others joined in, and soon a growing chorus of voices from all parts of the theater was chanting: "The Phaaantuhm! The Phaaantuhm!"

Lon Chaney's silent movie *The Phantom of the Opera* had recently been a hot Hollywood attraction, and Ruby assumed the shouts to be a sign of its popularity, but when the Georgia Jazz Band struck up a blues, the shouts continued, growing louder until they reached a deafening volume and the curtain slowly rose—then all was quiet again. On the darkened stage, bathed in a dramatic bluish hue, stood a giant replica of a phonograph, and from inside its oversized cabinet there now rose the gravelly voice of Ma Rainey. She was not visible until the cabinet's huge doors swung open. There she stood, bathed in light, and the audience gasped. Ruby now understood that

Ma Rainey, not Lon Chaney, was the phantom of the Frolic—"The people screamed, she was *that* ugly."

Thomas A. Dorsey, Ma Rainey's pianist, gave a more detailed description of this presentation:[7]

> Ma Rainey's act came on as a last number or at the end of the show. I shall never forget the excited feeling when the orchestra in the pit struck up her opening theme, music which I had written especially for the show. The curtain rose slowly and those soft lights on the band as we picked up the introduction to Ma's first song. We looked and felt like a million. Ma was hidden in a big box-like affair built like an old Victrola of long ago. This stood on the other side of the stage. A girl would come out and put a big record on it. Then the band picked up the "Moonshine Blues." Ma would sing a few bars inside the Victrola. Then she would open the door and step out into the spotlight with her glittering gown that weighed twenty pounds and wearing a necklace of five, ten and twenty dollar gold pieces. The house went wild. It was as if the show had started all over again. Ma had the audience in the palm of her hand. Her diamonds flashed like sparks of fire falling from her fingers. The gold-piece necklace lay like a golden armor covering her chest. They called her the lady with the golden throat.

We get further details of Ma Rainey's show from a review filed by Bob Hayes, who caught it in Louisville, Kentucky, seven months before Ruby saw it.[8] The "dramatic sketches of real life" is an interesting feature that Bessie never included in her productions:

> LOUISVILLE, KY.—Ma Rainey, with her Georgia jazz band and all-star vaudeville revue, opened here Monday night, week of Feb. 2, with one of the hottest shows that ever played here, and long be it remembered for the first show the S.R.O. sign had to be hung out. "Blues" singers come and they go, but the way Ma draws them in she should be called the "mother of packin' 'em in" along with her title of being the mother of the "blues."
>
> The show is opened by Jolly Saunders who needs no introduction. He is well known as one of the Race's foremost novelty artists and never fails to more than please as well as thrill them. Next comes Broadway Walker and Happy Bolton, and when they get through with their clean, classy cross-fire chatter and dancing and singing, they always have to beg off. Next we are introduced to one of the best acted dramatic sketches of real life, by Glasco and Glasco, ever reviewed here. It's different, clean and a real treat and went over big. Bring on some more like it. Then comes another real treat, Whistling Rufus, and when he gets through with a little of everything and closes with his honest-to-goodness bare knee-drops, more—more, that's all.
>
> Now the show starts all over again, for in a beautiful setting, Ma Rainey is introduced. She is heard singing as only the mother of the "blues" can sing,

> but unseen until she steps from a big Paramount talking machine. Oh, boy! What a flash Ma does make in her gorgeous gowns, backed up by her Georgia jazz band, one of the best five-piece bands heard here in a long time. The personnel of the band follows: Piano, Mrs. Lil Henderson; cornet, Kid Henderson; sax and clarinet, Lucien Brown; banjo, George Williams, and drums, Happy Bolton, formerly Lyric Theater drummer, New Orleans.
>
> Ma does three numbers that burn 'em up, then comes little Danny Rainey, world's greatest juvenile stepper. He's a regular show stopper. Ma comes back with another number, joined by the entire company, in red hot dancing finish that sends them out screaming for more.

Looking closer to fifty than her real age of thirty-nine, Ma Rainey was no beauty by anyone's standards, but neither did she deserve the reputation for having—as black performers liked to put it—"the ugliest face in show business." However, with her thick, straightened hair going in every direction, large gold-capped teeth, a fan of ostrich plumes in her hand, and a long triple necklace of shiny twenty-dollar gold coins hugging her neck, Madame Rainey was a sight to behold. "Ma, there are two things I've never seen," vaudeville performer Billy Gunn once told her. "That's an ugly woman and a pretty monkey." "Bless you, darling," she replied, obviously comforted.

If she thought the audience had been rude to her, she didn't show it. Ruby marveled at how cleverly Ma seemed to turn insults to her own advantage, and she soon realized that even Bessie could not find a more enthusiastic audience. "These people down there loved her," she said, "and she loved them. Ma Rainey was a real entertainer, but she was also very real—like Bessie." Ma rarely appeared in the North, where she was considered too "country," but many Southerners preferred her less polished, earthier delivery and rustic accompaniment to Bessie's.

> . . . . Now all the people wonder why I'm all alone;
> A sissy shook that thing, and took my man from home.

Her fans screamed. "Amens!" pierced the air. Three songs left them whistling for more, but it was time for Danny Rainey, "The World's Greatest Juvenile Stepper," to go into his act. Danny was the Raineys' adopted son. Those who knew the Raineys said that was the only way they could possibly have had a child; the mere idea of Ma in a mother's role made them laugh.

During Danny's performance, Bessie emerged from the wings and signaled Ruby to come backstage. "There's a phantom . . . ," Ruby began, but Bessie hushed her up. "Don't say that in front of Ma," she said. "She's a sweet lady, and I want you to meet her." When Ma joined them, she embraced Bessie warmly and seemed genuinely delighted to see her. As Ruby sat quietly and took it all in, the two women who would become the personification of a Blues Queen reminisced and gossiped. "They were laughing and carrying on like a couple of schoolgirls," Ruby recalled. "People used to talk about them being jealous or angry at each other, but you can forget that—they were friends, very good friends."

One of the things they laughed about was an incident that had taken place earlier that year when Ma found herself in an embarrassing tangle with the Chicago police. She and a group of young women had been drinking, and they made so much noise that a neighbor summoned the police. The impromptu party was getting intimate, and as bad luck would have it, the law showed up just as everyone began to let their hair down. Pandemonium broke loose as girls madly scrambled for their clothes and ran out the back door, leaving Ma, clutching someone else's dress, to exit last. Ma did not get away, however, for she had a nasty fall down a staircase and practically into the arms of the law. Accused of running an indecent party, she was thrown in jail, where she stayed until Bessie bailed her out the following morning.

Bessie ended her brief TOBA tour with an early October engagement at Sam Reevin's Liberty Theater in Chattanooga. Three thousand two-color posters were distributed to advertise the event, and Bessie chalked up another triumphant homecoming. Then it was time to return home to Philadelphia and unwind. Bessie's life was beginning to take on a pattern where hectic touring schedules led to drinking sprees, inevitably followed by a period of sobriety during which she became a homebody, eager to enjoy a period of quietude with Jack. "I never did understand how Bessie changed when she was home with Jack," said Ruby, "but I guess she was trying to make him happy—she'd act like she didn't even like partying, but you know she did. I will never forget it, but one time I came to Philadelphia with my aunt, and there was Bessie, running around in her slippers and acting like she never even seen a stage. I started talking about something funny that had happened on the road when we were all having a good time, and Bessie gave me a look that could kill—oooh, I think she would have beat me up if Jack hadn't been there. That's when I learned never to talk out of turn with Bessie."

During these cooling-off periods, Bessie stayed in, cooked for Jack, jumped over the fence in her housecoat to visit with neighbors, and enjoyed an occasional card game. It was the closest she ever came to leading a normal married life, but it was never long before she was called back to fulfill some career-related commitment such as a recording session or charity appearance. Once the quiet home life was interrupted, it was as if someone had reignited her restless, naughty side.

Bessie's respite from work was over by mid-October, when she began rehearsing in New York for new record dates. Frank Walker had scheduled four sessions between November 17 and December 9, which meant that she would have a fairly long stay in New York. She liked Harlem's bustling nightlife, but complained about having to dress up whenever she went out. As Ruby put it, "Bessie liked Philadelphia, because she could be herself, run around in her slippers and housecoat, and talk to the neighbors over the fence."

During Bessie's stay in New York, Columbia released her new duet with Clara Smith, "My Man Blues." Clara's summer run at the Lafayette Theater had gone well, and Frank Walker may have wished to take advantage of that, but he coupled the release with Bessie's "Nobody's Blues but Mine," which made it look as though Clara was making a guest appearance on a Bessie Smith recording.

Clara and Bessie had never performed together in public, but Columbia's promotion department arranged for them to make a joint appearance on October 21, 1925. The event was a "blues night" held at the New Star Casino, a large dance hall at 107th Street and Third Avenue. Sponsored by a group of black songwriters, the event was supported by various record and piano-roll companies, which bought reserved seats and filled them with staff and friends. It promised to be a memorable social event with an impressive musical program. Two "well-known recording orchestras" were scheduled to accompany such singers as Mamie Smith, Sara Martin, Edna Hicks, Eva Taylor (Mrs. Clarence Williams), and Clara and Bessie.

The affair was set up by Clarence Williams and Perry Bradford, primarily as a profit-making venture, and Bessie—still feeling some animosity toward Williams—at first refused to participate, but the ever-persuasive, promotion-minded Frank Walker changed her mind. Things, however, did not go as anyone had planned.

"I don't know *what* happened," said former chorine Bucher Swan forty-eight years later, "but Bessie never sang that night. The place was full of people—everybody was there—and, all of a sudden, there was this great big commotion near the band, and I saw Bessie throw a chair at somebody who was mashing his way through the crowd, trying to get away from her. Then I saw them drag her out of there, cussing and carrying on. It took three strong men to get her out of there—she was a powerful woman and she could cuss worse than a sailor."

Bessie was also scheduled to perform at the California Rambler's Inn that week, but the incident with Clara may have given her second thoughts, for there is no evidence that she ever showed up for that engagement. Perhaps she felt a need to make up for the New Star Casino incident when she agreed to record with Clarence Williams on her November 17 session. Time had not completely healed their scarred relationship, and it certainly had not improved Williams's performance, but Bessie was giving in to Walker's wishes. Two of the selections scheduled for that day were Clarence Williams tunes: "Florida Bound Blues" and "New Gulf Coast Blues," the latter a remake of Bessie's early hit, with new lyrics.

Around this time, Leigh Whipper, then manager of Newark's Orpheum Theater, offered Bessie a thousand dollars to play there all of Thanksgiving week. A few days after she accepted the deal, Whipper attended a meeting called by Carl Van Vechten to plan what would later become the James Weldon Johnson Memorial Collection of Negro Arts and Letters. Aware of Van Vechten's abiding interest in black culture, and his particular fondness for Bessie, Whipper mentioned that she would be at the Orpheum for the holiday week and extended to Van Vechten an invitation to attend. The forty-five-year-old journalist and former music critic for the *New York Times* was delighted; he had collected Bessie's records for two years but had yet to hear her in person—this would be a good opportunity to arrange a small theater party.

Whipper reserved a box for the ten-o'clock Thanksgiving night show and Van Vechten filled it with nine prominent friends, including humorist Robert Benchley and Arthur Spingarn, an early supporter and later president of the NAACP.

"I must say all of us enjoyed a mood of the highest anticipatory expectation," Van Vechten wrote years later in 1947. "It would be no exaggeration to assert that we felt as we might have felt before going to a Salzburg Festival to hear Lilli Lehmann sing Donna Anna in *Don Giovanni*."[8] By the time Van Vechten wrote his description of the 1925 event, black music had its own critics and had ceased to be regarded as a novelty. The wide-eyed wonderment of the 1920s had changed to a more straightforward appraisal of the music and its performers, so even in the postwar years, Van Vechten's account must have seemed anachronistic, but it does provide a white intellectual's impression of Bessie at a time when few such people recognized her talent:

> As the curtain lifted, a jazz band, against a background of plum-colored hangings, held the full stage . . . The hangings parted and a great brown woman emerged. She was at this time the size of Fay Templeton in her Weber and Fields days, which means very large, and she wore a crimson satin robe, sweeping up from her trim ankles, and embroidered in multicolored sequins in designs. Her face was beautiful with the rich ripe beauty of southern darkness, a deep bronze, matching the bronze of her bare arms. Walking slowly to the footlights, to the accompaniment of the wailing, muted brasses, the monotonous African pounding of the drum, the dromedary glide of the pianist's fingers over the responsive keys, she began her strange, rhythmic rites in a

voice full of shouting and moaning and praying and suffering, a wild, rough, Ethiopian voice, harsh and volcanic, but seductive and sensuous too, released between rouged lips and the whitest of teeth, the singer swaying slightly to the beat, as is the Negro custom:

"Yo' brag to women I was yo' fool, so den I got dose sobbin' hahted Blues." Celebrating her unfortunate love adventures, the Blues are the Negro's prayer to a cruel Cupid.

Now, inspired partly by the expressive words, partly by the stumbling strain of the accompaniment, partly by the powerfully magnetic personality of this elemental conjure woman with her plangent African voice, quivering with passion and pain, sounding as if it had been developed at the sources of the Nile, the black and blue-black crowd, notable for the absence of mulattoes, burst into hysterical, semi-religious shrieks of sorrow and lamentation. Amens rent the air. Little nervous giggles, like the shattering of Venetian glass, shocked our nerves. When Bessie proclaimed, "It's true I loves you, but I won't take mistreatment any mo," a girl sitting beneath our box called "Dat's right! Say it, sister!"

After the curtain had fallen, Leigh Whipper guided us back stage where he introduced us to Bessie Smith and this proved to be exactly the same experience that meeting any great interpreter is likely to be: we paid our homages humbly and she accepted them with just the right amount of deference.

I believe I kissed her hand. I hope I did.

The Orpheum had made a good investment in Bessie. During her seven-day engagement she played to capacity audiences at each performance, despite the fact that ticket prices had been raised for the occasion: matinees were twenty-five cents in the balcony and fifty cents downstairs; evening prices doubled those amounts. The police were called in several times to control the crowd outside the theater. Such overwhelming turnouts and continued high record sales belied contentions that Bessie's type of blues was on the wane. Just two weeks before her Orpheum engagement, the *Chicago Defender*'s William Potter had taken a pessimistic look at the future of the blues ladies:

THE BLUES SINGER

The profession is facing another climax. The day of the straight blues singer is passing. No doubt, there are many who will discount this statement, nevertheless, it is true and, being on the inside looking out, it is an easy matter to see how things are breaking. In the first place, as an attraction theatrically the blues singer has lost a hold. People will not go to the theater just to hear a blues singer. They have their radios and phonographs and they don't have to attend the theater to hear them. Salaries, according to direct reports, are cut. This proves that the straight blues singer generally is not an attraction within herself. They must feature some sort of novelty along with their regular line of

> work in order to even get over. This means necessarily that the styled "blues singer" will either take a company along in revue or eventually slide off the boards. Her records stand in the way of high salaries on the stage.[9]

Potter's prediction was at least three years premature, and when it came to pass, it was for reasons he could not possibly have imagined in 1925.

5

I got a letter from my daddy,
He bought me a sweet piece of land;
I got a letter from my daddy,
He bought me a small piece of ground;
You can't blame me for leavin', Lawd,
I'm Florida bound.
"Florida Bound Blues"

The Florida land boom reached its peak in the mid-1920s. A spectacular real estate venture, it sent thousands of American nouveaux riches to the Sunshine State in search of fun and fortune, rivaled the California gold rush of 1849, and gave birth to that capital of gaucherie, Miami.

It should surprise no one that African Americans were excluded from the Florida frolics, even those who had the means. Bessie's world was as far removed from the Addison Mizner architectural mishmash that characterized the new resort as her "Florida Bound Blues" was from Jan Garber's rendition of "When the Moon Shines on Coral Gables." Thus there was bitter humor in her tale, and the last verse contained parental advice in the form of a warning to any black who might seriously be Florida-bound:

My papa told me, my mama told me, too;
Don't let them bellbottom britches make a fool out of you.

As it turned out, the "bellbottom britches"—the white elite who romped around Palm Beach and Coral Gables in yachting outfits—were making fools of themselves: the release of Bessie's record, in February 1926, coincided with public exposure of giant real estate frauds and so devastating a collapse of the new empire that it has been described as a dress rehearsal for the stock market crash of 1929.

Although African Americans did not profit from the Florida land boom nor enjoy its accompanying decadent lifestyle, many were well aware of it. Some found employment there as servants and—in a tradition that dated back to slavery—gained, by way of personal observation, a window unto the white world. What they witnessed traveled fast by way of Pullman porters, who traversed the country and added their own observations. Black Americans knew more about white Americans than white Americans knew about them, and that often made whites the object of perceptive black humor.

Unlike most white show business stars, whose private lives were carefully shielded and fictionalized for public consumption, top black entertainers lived in glass houses—it was virtually impossible for artists like Bessie to lead a private life in a black neighborhood, nor was that always desired. Many black artists opted not to isolate themselves from their own community, preferring the freedom to let their hair down and enjoy the esprit de corps that exists when one is among one's own people. Bessie did not have to move through life as cautiously as her white counterparts; her private life was more or less an open book, and if it reflected the stories she told in her songs, all the better. Jack was the only person from whom she regularly had to conceal her indiscretions, a practice that escalated as her career progressed and he spent less time with her on the road. Jack never adjusted to the nomadic, uninhibited life of a touring company, but although the novelty of show business quickly wore off, the novelty of making money didn't. "I often wondered if Jack didn't stay away so that Bessie could mess around," said Maud, "because he knew that's what she did, and all he cared about was the money." Ruby disagreed. "Jack was dumb," she insisted. "He didn't know what was going on when he wasn't around. Sure, he caught Bessie a couple of times, but he was too dumb to know that she was always having her fun with this one and that one—and what was *he* doing? Now Bessie used to say that she missed Jack, and I guess she did, sometimes, but what did they have to talk about? And if it was sex, you know Bessie could get better sex than Jack gave her—she told me that herself." It is a wonder that the marriage lasted as long as it did, considering Bessie's thirst for a good time and how little they had in common: Jack rarely if ever drank liquor, he did not share Bessie's sense of humor, and he appeared to be a bit of a prude, although that turned out to be a mere facade. Ruby had a hard time recalling an occasion when Jack seemed to enjoy himself. "Jack was more interested in money than he was in Bessie," she said, "you can be sure of that. But he had his fun, too, I guess—just not around Bessie." Yet although Jack turned out to be less strait-laced than he pretended to be, the Gees' disparate lifestyles were clearly putting a wedge between them. Jack was the occasional anchor Bessie needed, but no legal document was going to change her way of living; she turned back to her old tricks as soon as Jack was out of sight, though it was a nerve-wracking game she played, for he developed a habit of returning when least expected.

She did change her ways, however, whenever Jack turned up on the road, which he often did without warning. "Bessie and I were always on the lookout for Jack," said Ruby. "In fact, the whole show was on its toes, because we knew that when Jack caught Bessie doing something bad, he was ready to beat up everybody—he didn't even like to see her drunk, which she was a lot of the times." Jack's sudden appearances sometimes sparked violent fights, but there always followed a reconciliation and a period of relative tranquility with Bessie on her best behavior.

This cat-and-mouse game became a regular pattern that eventually affected the entire troupe. Bessie's periodic binges alerted a stressful cast to the looming possibility of Jack showing up, poised to fight. "Jack was the fightingest man you've ever seen," recalled Ruby. "He'd walk into a room hittin'. Every time they had their fights he'd hit her so hard I'd think he was going to kill her, and I'd butt in and he'd slap me down like I wasn't even there—and I got *tired* of getting beat up on account of Bessie."

The year 1926 saw Bessie's popularity level off but not decline; she still commanded higher salaries and sold more records than her blues-singing contemporaries,[1] but more sophisticated singers like Ethel Waters and Josephine Baker, who aimed their talent at urban white audiences, attracted wider attention: in Paris, Baker was an international sensation in *La Revue Nègre,* and she would soon open at the Folies-Bergère; in London, Waters prepared to entertain the Prince of Wales. Bessie was never to travel farther east than Long Island.

While the blues divas enjoyed greater visibility, and thus were more marketable, the less polished rural blues of their male counterparts did not escape the attention of record companies. Starting in the mid-1920s, male blues artists, some of whom were obscure itinerant storytellers, were listed in record catalogs, but not given significant live exposure. Even though they now made recordings, their performances continued to be relegated to street corners, back roads, traveling medicine shows, and juke joints. Eventually, the bigger labels, Victor and Columbia, sent crews south to make field recordings of country blues and gospel artists, but these were strictly for local consumption and usually made at the request of record dealers who sensed a vicinal demand. Such local artists remained obscure until the 1950s and 1960s, when record collectors brought attention to them. Their recordings became valuable collector's items, because of the small number of copies pressed.

Such major black publications as the *Chicago Defender* and *Baltimore Afro-American* regularly carried advertising for country blues records, but the genre was otherwise ignored by the press. This neglect probably has more to do with the fact that music was never seriously critiqued in these publications, so write-ups had more to do with backstage gossip, on-stage visuals, and, one supposes, getting a free theater ticket. The writers were often fellow performers, which put them on the inside and certainly reduced their objectivity. Then, too, there was the lack of access to such singers as Blind Lemon Jefferson and Blind Willie Johnson, whose audiences were not found in the urban areas of the North; their recordings were generally sold through mail order or their label's regional dealer. The classic blues women were not competing with the country blues and gospel singers, for there was no real crossover. The guitar-playing rural singer was regarded as a folk artist, with a limited audience; the Toby diva belonged more to the realm of popular music, and—their blues repertoire aside—that categorization was apt for most of them.

As the refined styles of Ethel Waters and Josephine Baker took them to another level, some singers began to focus less on blues and more on Tin Pan Alley fare, but Bessie's recordings were still outselling even the most glamorous of her colleagues and—despite predictions that blues queens faced a gloomy future—Columbia continued to renew Bessie's contract each year.

What *did* affect Bessie financially was her heavy drinking. Liquor could turn the hardworking performer who ran her shows with military discipline into a mean drunk who thought nothing of breaking a contract and leaving a troupe stranded penniless in some godforsaken town. As the novelty of fame wore off and her marriage to Jack became increasingly threatened, this side of Bessie emerged more often. The attentive Jack, who had accompanied her on the first tent tours, discouraged her appetite for alcohol, and taken a positive interest in her work, now spent most of his time pursuing other interests. He no longer sat in the audience, ready to fine those who got out of step. When he did show up, it was usually because he needed money. "Most of us didn't mind Jack not being around so much," said Ruby, "but sometimes I felt sorry for Bessie, 'cause I know she missed him—not always, but sometimes. When he left us on the road, Jack used to say that he was goin' hunting. He would ask Bessie for money and say that he was going to catch up with us later. I thought he really went hunting—at first—and I don't know what Bessie thought, but I'm sure she suspected something."

"Bessie once told me that Jack must not be aiming right, because, with all that hunting, he never seemed to catch anything," said Maud. "I just smiled. I think she knew that he was up to no good, but what could she do? She wasn't being no angel herself."

After two and a half years of marriage, the Gees were still childless, and Bessie may have been attempting to save what plainly was a failing marriage when she decided to add another member to the immediate family: Maggie's niece had long been ready to make good her promise to let Bessie have Snooks, and now Bessie let it be known that she, too, was ready.

A few weeks later, in the spring of 1926, the six-year-old boy was brought aboard the railroad car in Macon, Georgia. "Bessie was very proud of Snooks," recalled Maud, who immediately assumed the unofficial role of governess. "He cried, screamed, and hollered that day when I gave him a needed bath, but Bessie was so thrilled that it sounded like music to her." Snooks was taken along for the rest of the tour, and Bessie named him Jack, Jr. Forty-five years later, Jack Gee, Jr., remained under the impression that he had been legally adopted, but when he sued Columbia Records for back royalties on Bessie's recordings, no official adoption papers could be found, and it was largely for that reason that he lost the case. To Bessie, Snooks was her son, and whether or not the adoption had ever been legal, she treated him as such. Now she had both the means and legitimate motivation to follow through on an old promise: to bring her family up from Chattanooga.

Bessie had often reminded Jack of her intentions, but it was a sore subject that only came up during heated arguments. The idea still did not sit well with Jack, but Snooks mellowed him somewhat. He had to agree that someone was needed to take care of the boy in their frequent absences, and it was Bessie's argument that it would have to be a family member.

To soften the blow, Bessie pulled one of her old tricks and engaged in a bit of bribery by making Jack a gift of the finest car she could find, a custom-built 1926 Cadillac. The two-year-old Nash had been stolen earlier in the year, or so he claimed, but Maud believed that he had gambled it away.

The Cadillac, like the Nash, was an impulse purchase. According to Ruby, Bessie and Jack were waiting at a trolley stop in front of the Scott and Smith Cadillac showroom at Broad and Fairmount when Jack turned around and spotted a strikingly unusual convertible in the dealership's window.

"That's a beautiful car," Bessie commented. "Do you like it?"

Jack nodded.

"Then I'll get it for you tomorrow," said Bessie.

The following day, she went to the showroom, where she immediately caught the salesman's attention. It became one of her favorite stories and the way she told it, the salesman was about to politely ask her to leave when she startled him by pointing to the convertible and declaring, "I'll take that one."

Taken aback, the salesman explained to Bessie that this was a very special and quite expensive automobile, which was intended as a showpiece, and that only two such cars had been made. Then, still not sure that she was a potential customer, he tried to talk her into looking at some of the less expensive models, but Bessie's mind was made up.

"That's the car I came here for," she said, "and I ain't buyin' any of them others."

The salesman made a final attempt to discourage her: "Lady, if you want that car it will cost you five thousand dollars."

"I'll take it," she said, "and I'm going to pay cash for it." One can only imagine the stunned look on the salesman's face as Bessie went beneath her skirt, dipped into her carpenter's apron, and produced a fistful of money. "Bessie said the white man nearly fainted," said Ruby, "she loved to do stuff like that."

The new car performed as intended, that is to say it lessened Jack's pain at the thought of having Viola and the rest of the Smiths move up from Chattanooga. One consolation was they would not be living with the Gees, but Bessie did not want them too far away, so she rented adjoining houses in her neighborhood: 1143 and 1147 Kater Street. One was for the oldest sister, Viola, her daughter Laura, and grandson Buster; the other for her sisters Lulu and Tinnie, and Tinnie's two sons. Clarence Smith was already living in Philadelphia, working as a comedian with her show and handling her business.

Reconciled to the fact that the Smith family was coming to stay, Jack was not prepared for Bessie's next step: he was to transport the family in the new car. Jack grumbled, but with Bessie controlling the purse strings, there was nothing he could do but obey, and to make matters worse, the move required two trips. As Jack reluctantly motored south, Bessie went to New York for a March 5 recording session with Clarence Williams.

Even though Bessie took Frank Walker's advice and patched up her differences with Clarence Williams, Jack could not forgive the fact that Williams had tried to swindle her out of money. Bessie, therefore, went out of her way to hide from him the renewed association, even requesting that Williams's name be left off the label. Williams probably did not readily agree to being anonymous, but he may have rationalized that having Bessie Smith record your songs was money in the bank. His playing is as pedestrian as ever on these sides, but Bessie is unusually exuberant on "What's the Matter Now?" and "I Want Ev'ry Bit of It," and she almost outdoes herself on "Squeeze Me," a tune with a colorful history.

"Squeeze Me" appears to have its origin in an X-rated ditty called "The Boy in the Boat" (the title is a euphemism for clitoris). Fats Waller reworked it and presented it to his music publisher, Clarence Williams, as "Boston Blues." To further complicate matters, the lyrics were a parody of "Kiss Me Again," a song by Victor Herbert, who took a dim view of all the rewrites and threatened court action. Waller reworked the lyrics once again and this time they satisfied everyone. It would have been interesting to hear Waller accompany Bessie, but that was never to be. However, there is a touch of Fats's style in Williams's accompaniment, which—as usual—he played, somewhat cautiously, from the sheet music. The song does not really lend itself to Bessie's style of delivery, which tended to be quite personal even when she had not written the lyrics; surely a line such as "pick me up, on your knee" gave her pause. This was actually her second try at "Squeeze Me," the first one—made three months earlier with a better pianist, Fred Longshaw—failed to produce a satisfactory performance. This time around, she takes full advantage of that innate musicianship that inevitably separated her from the majority of her colleagues: she tailors the song to fit Bessie Smith. Leaning, stretching, and bending her words, she delivers "doggone" and "cry" in at least four distinct notes and—at the midpoint of each chorus—she extends the word "more" to include a heartfelt "Oh, Lawd." The title, too, becomes customized as Bessie lends her own sense of urgency to the request; it was originally meant to be no more than a teasing invitation, but she turns it into a demand. We don't know how Waller felt about Bessie's highly personal approach to his song, but he should have been delighted. It had been a session of Clarence Williams tunes, and though he didn't *write* "Squeeze Me," he collected royalties as its publisher—Williams was back and up to his old tricks.

Bessie returned to the studio twelve days later, this time with Fletcher Henderson at the piano and Buster Bailey on clarinet. The resulting two selections are worth noting. "Jazzbo Brown from Memphis Town" is a gusty novelty, typical of the light musical numbers that Bessie interpolated into each show. The words and music to "Jazzbo Brown," as well as ten other compositions Bessie recorded, are credited to "George Brooks," a pseudonym used by Fletcher Henderson. There may have been a real-life Jazzbo Brown (years later, George Gershwin used the name for a piano player in *Porgy and Bess*), but Henderson relegates the role to Buster Bailey, who, indeed, hailed from Memphis. Bessie dons her lighthearted personality for this song, wringing the comedy potential out of each line with a deliberately rough, yet smiling voice.

Not being into classical music, Bessie may not have understood such lyrics as "He don't play no fancy stuff like them Hoffmann Tales, but what he plays is good enough for the Prince of Wales," but she sings the tale of the "clarinet hound" with great high spirits and characteristic authority. Buster Bailey plays his part with appropriate humor, occasionally teetering at the edge of novelty. A polished musician, he would later tackle the classics with John Kirby's band, and he was probably familiar with Jacques Offenbach's music.

The session's second selection was "The Gin House Blues," a song that critics still like to refer to as autobiographical although it was written by Henderson (this time under his real name), with lyrics by Henry Troy. It should not be confused with Nina Simone's recording of the same title, which is actually "Me and My Gin," another song from Bessie Smith's repertoire. When Bessie sang of gin, her audiences knew that she was close to her subject, but they also knew enough not to take the lyrics literally. Her drink of choice was not gin, for she had no taste for commercial alcoholic beverages, but in the South, "gin" was a generic term for any kind of hard liquor; Bessie's preference was for moonshine or, as Ruby called it, "bad" liquor.

Autobiographical or not, "The Gin House Blues" is one of Bessie's most moving recordings, a stark twelve-bar blues which she delivers eloquently, proving that when it comes to the blues, no man-made instrument can match the power of the human voice. Her reading of Troy's poetic lyrics has all the intimacy and conviction of a personal tale, thoroughly in keeping with that of a woman who, as a last resort, might have taken her trouble to "the conjure man." She sings five choruses, bending some notes, gliding through others, using some that no acoustic keyboard could duplicate. She never sings two choruses in precisely the same way, but the variations are subtle and the apparent repetitiousness gives the music a near-hypnotic quality as it relentlessly builds tension. Henderson and Bailey accompany with great restraint, unobtrusively blending their music into Bessie's story, like a good film score.

At this point in her life, Bessie's happiness easily outweighed her sorrows: her family was with her at last, and she had a son. Those who knew her could hardly imagine her in a mother's role, but she took to it heart and soul. Nothing was too good for little Snooks; Bessie was generous with gifts and affection, and she spoke of the child with tremendous pride. Although he made no attempt to conceal his intense dislike for Viola and resentment over having Bessie's family in Philadelphia, Jack seemed genuinely pleased with Bessie's decision to adopt Snooks, at least in the beginning.

As planned, Viola was given the job of caring for the boy in Bessie's absence. Clarence and Teejay were the only working members of her immediate family, but Bessie saw to it that the others lacked for nothing. Stories of her purchasing a house for total strangers or casual acquaintances, and rumors that she and Jack had squandered some sixteen thousand dollars on an early 1926 spending spree, became a part of the myth that people liked to build up around Bessie. The implication was that Jack had mismanaged his wife's affairs, but the fact is that he never had that much control over Bessie's finances, and—even in the 1920s—a special model Cadillac, the rental and furnishing of two houses, and moving seven people from Chattanooga to Philadelphia could easily consume such a sum.

With the family in Philadelphia, at last, Bessie decided to forgo her usual summer schedule in 1926. She looked forward to spending some time with Snooks and getting her family properly situated. Her sisters and their children had never before lived so well, and they did not seem to have any problem adjusting to their upgraded lifestyle. Maud noted that the family also quickly grew to take Bessie's generosity for granted. If Bessie was aware of that, she didn't seem to care, but Jack knew that neither Viola, Tinnie, nor Lulu had any intention of working, that Viola considered all of this to be payback for time spent raising her siblings in Chattanooga, and that a good portion of their allowance went to support escalating drinking habits. Viola, Tinnie, and Lulu, in turn, were well conscious of Jack's jealous resentments. They knew how opposed he was to their living in Philadelphia, and Maud thought that Viola in particular relished the fact that Bessie repeatedly turned a deaf ear to Jack's complaints.

A competition for Bessie's attention developed between Jack and Viola. She became annoyingly smug around him, so he did his best to avoid her, but Bessie seemed more and more to enjoy pitting one against the other. "Viola had a mean streak in her," said Ruby. "That woman knew that she could get away with just about anything, because Bessie loved her, so she used to always go after poor Jack—well, he wasn't so nice himself." Bessie added fuel to Jack's resentment by giving Viola the upper hand. "She sent all her money home to Viola," Maud remembered. "It was all deposited in the First National Bank, but in Viola's name. When Jack wanted money, he had to wire Bessie, and she would tell him to get it from Viola, so he would have to go to the bank with her and wait while she drew out whatever amount Bessie said Jack could have. As for Bessie herself, when she needed money on the road she always wired Frank Walker or Sam Reevin for an advance." Ruby saw the financial arrangement as part of a divide-and-conquer scheme on Bessie's part: "Bessie opened a bank account," she said, "and it was supposed to be used by the family when she was on the road. Well, she knew that Jack and Viola hated each other, so she had the bank set up the account so that he had to get Viola's signature each time Bessie gave him money. Ooooh, Jack was mad as hell over that, but Bessie didn't give in to him. Now, you know she did that just so she could keep them mad at each other. It was her way of saying 'y'all are gonna do what I say!' "

In mid-1926 Bessie eased up on her professional activities, but she didn't stop working altogether. A May recording date with Fletcher Henderson and Joe Smith catches her in splendid form on each of the session's four selections, "Money Blues," "Baby Doll," "Hard Driving Papa," and "Lost Your Head Blues." Bessie is credited with writing "Baby Doll," but there is a conflicting recollection in Ethel Waters's autobiography. Waters claimed to have sung the song at Atlanta's "91" Theater six or seven years earlier, when sharing a bill with Bessie. Under those circumstances, it is doubtful that Waters would have chosen a Bessie Smith song, so either the composer credit or Ethel Waters's memory is wrong. As we will see, it is probably the former.

Reading like a want ad, the slightly cryptic lyrics of "Baby Doll" express a woman's unfulfilled love requirements, complete with specifications for an ideal lover. Rather than following the traditional twelve-bar blues format, it has the pop song's familiar verse and refrain structure. Joe Smith's cornet is given deserved prominence on Bessie's recording, demonstrating to good effect the influence of Louis Armstrong, whom he replaced in Henderson's big band. He plays a long cornet introduction that beautifully paves the way for Bessie's stentorian, rock-steady voice. She sings the song with immense feeling, incorporating some of her own patented mispronunciations: "I went to see the doctor the *ruther* day," she sings before drawing the conclusion that the cause of her troubles might be "something they call a *Cuban* dart"—which probably should be Cupid's dart. That latter mispronunciation suggests that Bessie at least did not write the lyrics.

Artistically, the four sides rank high in Bessie's discography; commercially, they also did rather well in the stores, selling fifty-three thousand copies within a few months of their release. This figure hardly compared with the sales of Bessie's first recordings, but the initial blues boom had long since peaked and made a dip. Then, too, the race record market had become even more competitive as electric recording techniques brought needed clarity to instrumental jazz. Ironically, there was also competition from two white artists: Charles Correll and Freeman Gosden. This was a comedy team that achieved enormous popularity on the Victor label through a series of racist comedy dialogues. As "Sam 'n' Henry," Correll and Gosden portrayed fumbling, scheming stereotypical blacks in skits that were every bit as racist as the Sambo cartoons of the day, and paradoxically, African-Americans accounted for a high percentage of sales. This team would later gain an even bigger cross-racial following as radio's "Amos 'n' Andy." Considering the strong competition, and measured against other sales figures of the day, Bessie's fifty-three thousand records is arguably an equivalent to today's million sellers. The record business was back on its feet, and Columbia, once teetering on the edge of bankruptcy, was now doing well enough to acquire Okeh, one of its major competitors in the race record field.

As Labor Day 1926 approached, it was time for Bessie to go back to work in earnest. Her summer in Philadelphia had been quiet and unusually sober, but it had also been costly; having the family to support had dramatically raised her expenses, and as Jack was quick to point out, Bessie's income was exceeded by her expenditures. She was probably also being pressured by Frank Walker to resume a normal schedule. This was the time of year when Bessie usually packed up her tent and embarked on a TOBA tour, but the circuit was undergoing a reorganization, so—having skipped the tent tour—she decided to hit that trail while the weather was still warm enough and give her new railroad car another run.

In New York, Bessie assembled and rehearsed a troupe of entertainers that included her brother Clarence and some of her previous performers, such as comedian Dinah Scott, who doubled as stage manager. Among the chorines were Scott's wife, Gertrude, Bessie's sister-in-law Maud, and Boulah Benbow, the wife of Bill Woods, whose six-piece band formed the musical accompaniment. As they boarded the train for Atlanta, Ruby was conspicuously absent. Many years later, she couldn't recall why she stayed behind but remembered (or surmised) that it had not been her choice.

The production was actually a bill of previously featured skits and routines, with minor amendments and a few new musical numbers—the name, too, was familiar: *Harlem Frolics*. The first month of the tour went without incident. Remarkably, Bessie remained sober even after Jack had left the tour, allegedly to go on a hunting trip. Bessie herself took off for New York in mid-October, to make more recordings—she left her brother Clarence in charge. "When Bessie wasn't with the show, we didn't pull in as many people," Maud observed, "but we could still make money—the people down there were starved for entertainment."

Ruby had often asked Bessie if she could tag along for a recording session, but Bessie routinely turned her down. On October 25, she finally acquiesced, but told Ruby that it was against her better judgment and that she had better stay out of the way. The session was barely begun before Ruby made Bessie wish she had followed her original instinct. She and Fletcher Henderson were running through the first number, "Honey Man Blues," when Bessie saw Ruby approach Frank Walker. "I was just telling him that he should record me, too, because I knew Bessie's style and he could probably use another singer," said

Ruby. "I had no idea Bessie would go off like she did—it was embarrassing." Bessie was in the middle of her song when she spotted Ruby talking to Walker, and when she caught the drift of their conversation, she threw her sheet music in the air and screamed: "You ain't gonna take *my* place, you little bitch." Then she vowed never to take Ruby to another recording session—and she kept her word. "I should have known better," said Ruby, as she related this incident, "but I never dreamed Bessie would get that mad. She didn't stay mad, though—that's one thing about Bessie, she could cuss you out one minute and give you a big hug a few minutes later."

Bessie gave Ruby more than a hug—before the day was over, she had agreed to let her come along when she rejoined the tour. At the end of the session, Walker had given Bessie a six-hundred-dollar advance, which she used as an excuse to spend the rest of the afternoon and evening taking Ruby on a round of favorite Harlem haunts. "We'd walk into a joint," Ruby recalled, "and Bessie would say, 'Here's a hundred dollars. Set the house up and don't let nobody out and nobody in.' And she enjoyed getting everybody drunk with her. I would be running behind her saying, 'Give me the change,' because people used to take advantage of her and keep the change."

Bessie tried to keep several aspects of her private life from Jack. When she spent money extravagantly, she told him about it only if it served her purpose. Of course it never served her purpose to let him in on the scope of her sexual activity, and there was little danger of gossip reaching his ears, because he was simply not the sort of person people confided in. She could also take comfort that her troupers—who knew everything—had as little to do with Jack as possible.

Fortunately for Bessie, Jack was virtually illiterate, otherwise he might have seen a short item in the *Interstate Tattler*, a black gossip sheet whose publisher, Floyd Snelson, made other people's business his own. Very little escaped Snelson, for he had a small army of informants, often back-stabbing show people, who tipped him off to the latest dirt from different parts of the country. "Look out for Snelson" was common advice in Harlem, where the enterprising publisher had more than one violent clash with an irate victim. His thinly veiled item on Bessie appeared under the byline "I. Telonyou" in the paper's "Town Tattle" column, February 27, 1925: "Gladys, if you don't keep away from B., G. is going to do a little convincing that he is her husband. Aren't you capable of finding some unexplored land 'all alone.'" Fortunately for Snelson, Bessie, who was rumored to be chummy with male impersonator Gladys Ferguson at that time, neither saw nor heard about the item.

It is not known at which stage of her life Bessie began to embrace her own sex. Some have assumed that it was a similarly inclined Ma Rainey who initiated her, but that conjecture is supported by no more evidence than the improbable story of Bessie's "kidnapping." We do know from eyewitness accounts that Bessie's sexual relationships included women by late 1926, when Lillian Simpson entered her life.

Lillian had been Ruby's schoolmate, and like many young girls of her age, she romanticized about show business life. Her mother had once worked in theater, so she grew up hearing backstage stories, but it was listening to Ruby's tales of life on the road that filled Lillian's head with hazy fantasies and set her heart on becoming, at the very least, a chorine. Knowing how easily she had learned Bessie's routines, Lillian persuaded Ruby to teach her a few dance steps and set up an audition. The last thing the show needed was another chorus girl, but Ruby knew how to soften Bessie's stance, and when it turned out that Lillian's mother had briefly served as Bessie's wardrobe mistress, the deal was all but clinched. Bessie agreed to hold an impromptu audition in the Gee living room on 132d Street. "I knew Bessie would like Lillian," said Ruby, "I just didn't know how much. She even got up and started teaching her more steps, and she got Mrs. Simpson, Lillie's mother to agree that we could take her with us."

And so Bessie headed south with Ruby and Lillian, joining her *Harlem Frolics* company in Ozark, Alabama, on the first of November. When they arrived, Bessie's private railroad car was still parked on a dead track, waiting to be coupled to an outgoing train. Jack had returned to the tour, but he had gone into town to make last-minute arrangements for their departure. Bessie was giving Lillian the grand tour of her railroad car when one of her chorines approached and asked to speak to her privately.

She told Bessie the startling news that Jack had carried on with one of the chorines while she was away. It appeared that Jack—perhaps thinking that turnabout is fair play—had become rather careless around the cast. "He used to love to flirt with all the girls on the show," Ruby recalled. "He would pat them on the ass, pinch them, and go to bed with them if he had a chance, but most of the girls was afraid to go with him because they was afraid that Bessie would get a hold of it." Because Bessie had such a volatile personality, and there was already enough offstage drama to suit everybody, the show's cast and crew had always kept mum about the Gees' individual escapades, and that had made it fairly safe for them to play around in each other's absence. "I don't know what made the girl rat on this other girl, but she blabbed it out. The girl who had been messing around with Jack was in the stateroom, asleep—poor thing. Well, Bessie went in the room and jumped on her and, before she knew what happened, Bessie was beating that poor girl to pieces. Then she got tired of hammering on her and threw her out on the tracks."

In great physical pain and suffering intense embarrassment, the unfortunate chorine screamed at the top of her lungs while Bessie stood on the car's rear platform and cursed back. Then Bessie ran back into the car and reappeared moments later with an armful of the girl's personal effects, which she dumped out on the track. Next she stormed through the railroad car looking for Jack.

"Come out, you motherless bastard," she shouted as the object of her husband's indiscretion continued to scream. The rest of the *Harlem Frolics* troupe huddled in fearful anticipation of the inevitable spousal clash. Though Bessie couldn't find Jack, she found his gun and stormed out to the rear platform wielding it. But Jack had in fact returned and Bessie saw him bent over the sobbing girl, trying to calm her down and find out what had happened.

Bessie fired a shot.

"You no good two-timing bastard," she shouted, waving the gun in the air. "I couldn't even go to New York and record without you fuckin' around with these damn chorus bitches. Well, I'm gonna make you remember me today."

Jack started toward her. "Put that gun down, Bessie," he pleaded, but Bessie answered with another shot. That sent Jack racing down the track. Bessie jumped off the platform and went in pursuit, emptying the gun as she ran. "I've never seen Jack run so fast," said Ruby, "you could play checkers on his coat. Everybody was scared to death that Bessie would kill him this time, but she didn't really want to shoot him." A couple of hours later, the troupe left Ozark without Jack.

Bessie had been on good behavior for several months, but now she was ready for some fun. Jack's hasty departure following the alleged indiscretion provided both the opportunity and the excuse. A month after the incident, having played the smaller communities—Eufaula, Alabama, and the little Georgia towns of Dawson, Americus, and Albany—it was time to pack up the tent, mothball the railroad car in Atlanta, and continue the tour on the reorganized TOBA theater circuit.

The troupe spent Christmas of 1926 on the road somewhere in Tennessee, where Bessie threw a small party for her gang. She bought eggs, milk, and liquor for eggnog, but after the girls had beaten the eggs and added sugar and liquor, Bessie had second thoughts about the milk—it seemed a shame to dilute that good corn liquor with milk, so she reversed the ratio. The resulting concoction left no one sober.

As the party showed signs of ending, Bessie approached Ruby, cocked her head in Lillian's direction, and whispered, "I *like* that gal." Ruby assumed that she was referring to Lillian's dance routine, which had improved in the past month but still could use some work. "I'm glad you like her—she's doing good, ain't she?"

"No, I don't mean that," Bessie replied. "I'll tell her myself, 'cause you don't know *nothin'* child, and when you don't know nothin', you can't tell nothin'." Whereupon she walked over to Lillian, whispered something to her, and led her out of the room.

Ruby shared a room with Lillian, and it became clear to her the following morning that she had spent the night alone. She had to get used to it, for Lillian and Bessie now began sleeping together regularly. That surprised no one in the *Harlem Frolics* troupe, but it heightened the fear of all hell breaking loose upon Jack's inevitable return.

Lillian had adapted remarkably fast to life on the road and all its unorthodox aspects, and now she surprised Ruby by adjusted with equal ease to a lesbian relationship with Bessie. It was a development that she shared with Ruby from the start, revealing her intimate secret the day after her initiation. Ruby had already concluded as much, but she was somewhat taken aback when Lillian suggested that she "try it" with another chorine, and specifically named a suitable candidate: Boulah Benbow, the wife of the show's musical director, Bill Woods. "I knew Boulah was liking me, I knew she was like that," said Ruby, "but Bessie didn't want me to mess around anybody on the show. Lillian had gotten into that mess, and now she was trying to get me into it, too, but I wasn't into that, I liked boys."

Several days later, as the chorus stood in the wings of Bessemer's Frolic Theater, poised to kick up their heels and join Bessie on stage, an incident caused Boulah to make an untimely but innocent move. It was one of the show's big production numbers; Bessie was center stage and the chorines formed two lines in the wings, facing each other from opposite sides. Because she was to lead the line at stage left, Ruby stood closest to the stage, in clear view of Bessie. She had developed a nasty boil in her left armpit, and, to ease the pain, she held the arm in the air as she awaited her cue. Everybody in the show had become aware of Ruby's boil, and all were tired of hearing her make such a fuss over it. "They were sick of seeing me petting my boil," Ruby recalled, "and they kept telling me to puncture it, but I was too scared to do it." Seeing her stand there with her arm extended, Dinah Scott decided to take action, so he sneaked up behind Ruby and grabbed the boil under the arm—Ruby let out a scream.

Bessie kept singing, but she jerked her head in Ruby's direction and frowned, because she never tolerated noise from backstage during a performance. Scott's unexpected move had the desired result, and now Helen Hill, another chorine, ran forward with a tissue, put her arms around Ruby, and gently daubed at what was left of the boil.

Standing in line on the opposite side of the stage, Boulah observed the little drama, but she had not seen Scott kick it off, so she completely misread the incident. Amazingly, the number went as choreographed, but as soon as the curtain came down, Boulah stomped over to Ruby and asked her to step outside. Eager to keep all this from Bessie, Ruby complied and followed Boulah into the alley behind the theater. "You ain't gonna mess around with them other bitches," said Boulah, as she lunged forward and scratched Ruby's face. "I didn't know what she was talking about," said Ruby, "but she was jealous, because she thought something was going on with me and Helen. Anyway, I fought back." The two were deeply entangled when Bessie suddenly appeared on the stage door steps.

"I know Jack's gonna blame me for this," she said as she swiftly moved forward to separate the two women. Then she knocked Boulah clear across the small alley. It was important for Bessie to calm things down expeditiously, because Jack was due to rejoin the show that night, and she had stayed sober for that reason. "Poor Lillie," said Ruby as she reflected on Jack's return, "she didn't know how Bessie could just drop her when Jack came around, but Bessie somehow managed to make her understand—at least I thought she did."

Later that night, following the last show of the evening, several members of the troupe were seated in Bessie's hotel room when Jack entered. "What y'all doin' up here," he asked, looking around, "drinkin'?"

"Nobody been drinkin' any liquor, nigger," said Bessie. "You're not in the police force, you're in show business, so don't come in here pushin' on people all the damn time."

To conceal her battle-scarred face, Ruby turned it away from Jack, but she wasn't very subtle about it, so he asked her to turn around and face him. Ruby obeyed, but before Jack could comment on her face, she nervously and unconvincingly blurted out a story that Bessie had concocted for her. Her face was scratched, she explained, because she and some of the girls had fought over costumes.

"You know how these girls are," Bessie injected, "they're always going to be fighting over costumes." That's when Bill Woods, who had stood quietly in a corner, blurted out, "It was one of them bulldykers who's after Ruby!"

"What do you mean *one* of them?" Bessie shouted angrily. "It was *your* wife!"

That's all Jack needed to hear. He grabbed Boulah, dragged her kicking and screaming into the hall, and threw her down the stairs. Then he turned to Woods, who stood transfixed, staring into space. "Send the bitch home." As Woods ran out of the room, Bessie noticing the expression of fear on Lillian's face, turned to Ruby and whispered, "Whatever you do, you better not tell on me and Lillian."

Another incident from this tour involved the "sweet singer." Bessie would not allow another female blues singer on her show, but she often hired a so-called sweet singer to render the Tin Pan Alley fare of the day. Ruby recalled what happened: "There was a woman on our show that sang popular songs. She hated Bessie and every time she had a chance, she would criticize her, saying to the girls, 'Oh, that old black bitch is always drunk.' Of course she never did it when Bessie was around, but one night Bessie walked in on her."

That evening, the theater was packed and it was almost curtain time. Jack, having seated himself in the audience to check out the show, had no inkling of what was taking place backstage. "He would sit where we couldn't see him," said Ruby, "waiting and watching and hoping that we would do something wrong on the stage so that he could fine us. Well, Bessie overheard that woman talking about her like shit, and so she hit her in the mouth. Now Bessie believed in a whole lot of diamonds, in fact, diamonds was her weakness and she sometimes wore as much as ten or fifteen thousand dollars worth on her hands, which she did when she hit the woman."

The impact unseated a sizeable diamond from one of Bessie's rings, which angered her even more. The bleeding chorine had fled the room and the rest of the girls were on the floor looking for Bessie's diamond when Jack came backstage to find out what was holding up the show; behind him were a couple of policemen who had been called by the sweet singer. "The people out front was yelling, stomping their feet and clapping their hands, because they wanted the show to go on. Oh God, more excitement. But the cops were good enough to let us do the show, otherwise, the manager would have to give the people their money back. I guess they was doing the theater owner a favor, because he would have had to give the people back their money. But right after the show, they took us to jail, including my uncle who didn't know what it was all about. It was after eleven and they had to wake up the chewing judge, that's what we called him, because he was always chewing tobacco. He came in grumbling that everyone would pay for this—waking him up. He wasn't kidding."

"He fined all of us—the girls, Bessie, the other singer that she beat up, and even Jack, who wasn't even there when it happened. The judge would say, 'I fine you,' then he would peep over his glasses, chewing all the time, spit and say, 'Five dollars.' Then he would spit again, chew and say, 'Fifty dollars,' spit again, chew again, look over his glasses at that woman all beat up and say, 'Umm,' seventy five dollars.'" The show continued the following day without a sweet singer.

On January 10, 1927, *Harlem Frolics of 1927*, as it was now called, opened for a week's engagement at the Booker Washington Theater in St. Louis. Disgusted with Bessie's backstage fight, Jack had taken off again, leaving her and Lillian free to continue their affair. Lillian was still a bit shy whenever Bessie made overt moves on her in someone else's presence, as she did on the show's first day in St. Louis. Ruby recalled that Bessie entered their room, walked up behind Lillian, leaned forward, and kissed her.

Embarrassed, Lillian threw a glance at Ruby and jerked away. "Don't play around with me like that," she said.

Bessie grabbed her around the waist. "Is that how you feel?"

"Yes!" Lillian said. "That's *exactly* how I feel."

"The hell with you, bitch," Bessie shouted. "I got twelve women on this show and I can have one every night if I want it. Don't you feel so important, and don't you say another word to me while you're on this show, or I'll send you home, bag and baggage."

For three days and nights, Bessie demonstratively ignored Lillian, and on the fourth night, when Lillian failed to show up at the theater, Ruby offered to look for her. Bessie told her not to bother, they would do the show without Lillie, she said, but no sooner had the final curtain dropped, than Bessie began to show concern. "She's just tryin' to pout," she told Ruby, feebly making light of the situation, and before Ruby could answer, the door burst open and Maud handed Bessie a piece of paper. "I went into the hotel and saw an envelope sticking out from under Lillian's door," Maud recalled, "and I pulled it through, opened it up and read it. It said she was going to commit suicide, so I ran back to the theater and got Bessie, and we busted through the door."

Bessie didn't take the time to read the note—Maud's panic had said it all. She rushed out of the room with Ruby and Maud at her heels, and ran to the hotel, next door. As they approached Lillian's door, they smelled gas, and Bessie panicked. They made an unsuccessful attempt to force the door open, then Bessie scurried downstairs to get the proprietor. When he let them in, they saw Lillian lying across the bed, unconscious but breathing. She had nailed the window shut, so the hotel owner broke the panes and instructed a member of his staff to call an ambulance. Lillian was taken to the nearest black hospital where a doctor assured them that she would be alright. "I didn't think we would ever see Lillie again," said Ruby. "I thought she was dead when they took her out. And Bessie, poor Bessie, she kept saying it was her fault—which it was—and she couldn't sleep that night, but it turned out that Lillie was alright, so Bessie went to the hospital in the morning and brought her back to the hotel. I guess everybody learned their lesson, and from that day on, she didn't care where or when Bessie kissed her—she got real bold after that."

Bessie and company played Cincinnati's Roosevelt Theater for the week of January 17, and opened in Chicago, at the Grand, on the following Monday. The *Defender*'s review was shorter than usual, but no less enthusiastic:

> Bessie Smith and her unit fairly took Chicago by storm last Monday night, Jan. 24, when the curtain descended on her fine show. The house was packed and a large crowd waited outside for the second show. You know one show a night will not accommodate the Chicago lovers of the empress of the blues. She is a real blues artist and an actor, too. She works all through the show, well showing her versatility. Bessie Smith is the largest box office draw the T.O.B.A. has today.

After the opening night's final show, Richard Morgan sent a car to bring Bessie and her party to one of his popular after-hours gatherings. As usual, the place was packed, the noise level so high that it threatened to drown out the music. A pianist (Ruby believes it was Cow Cow Davenport) worked the ivories hard, competing with the din of chatter and laughter as he accompanied a weak-voiced young lady who struggled to be heard.

The poor singer got help from an unexpected source when Bessie stood up and commanded in a loud voice: "Hold *every*thing, this young lady is *singin'*, and I say we should listen."

As one might expect, everybody did.

It was during their stay in Chicago that Lillian first tried to leave the show. Although she had lost her inhibitions, her fear of Jack remained. She knew that it was only a matter of time before he discovered her liaison with Bessie, and she was anxious to get out of it before things came to a head. Each time she voiced her apprehension, Bessie persuaded her to stay, but Lillian's fears were well founded and now adversely affected their relationship. Shortly after the show opened at the Detroit's Koppin Theater, in the first week of February 1927, Bessie decided that it would be best for Lillian to go home. She bought her a train ticket for New York and saw her off at the station without making any last minute plea for her to stay. "I think Bessie felt a little guilty," said Maud. "I told her she should let the girl go and that she was being selfish by keeping her on. Bessie pretended that she wasn't listening to me, but I knew she was."

Having maintained a state of relative sobriety since Lillian's suicide attempt, Bessie cut loose on the night after seeing her off for New York. If one wanted to let one's hair down, there was no better place than the Motor City, said Ruby, recalling a particularly dramatic visit which she and Bessie made to a white establishment. "One night in Detroit we went down to a night club, which was all Italians and they didn't like blacks down there," Ruby recalled.

"We didn't know that and we got into an argument with the waiter, who didn't want to wait on us. They didn't know who Bessie was, of course, but they soon found out, because she jumped up and knocked over the table while they were watching her. I got behind the bar, and started to throw some bottles of liquor to Bessie. Between the two of us, we really straightened that place out. We went out of the door backwards and ran until we found a cab. And to our surprise, no one followed us. We finished our week there and no one bothered us, which was another surprise to both of us."

On previous visits to Detroit, Bessie had befriended a woman[2] who operated a buffet flat. Sometimes referred to as goodtime flats, these were small, privately owned clubs whose customers could indulge in all sorts of illegal activities. Besides the usual drinking and gambling, buffet flats offered erotic shows that featured sex acts of every conceivable kind. These establishments were usually owned by women, who ran them with admirable efficiency, catering to the occasional thrill-seeker as well as to regular clients whose personal preferences they knew in detail. Often the hostess also served as a bank, a trusted person into whose hands a customer could safely entrust valuables and sizable amounts of cash. Withdrawals could be made at any time in the course of an evening.

Buffet flats, which were almost always housed in private homes, served as models for outwardly legitimate "high-class" night clubs whose tuxedoed maître d's discreetly set up sexual liaisons for "important" patrons. With the right people on their payroll, flats enjoyed a reputation for being safe; police rarely raided them, and there were remarkably few incidences of violence and theft. Buffet flats became a part of urban nightlife in the 1920s. They were originally set up to cater to Pullman porters,[3] whose extensive travels, contacts with the white upper class, gentlemanly manners, and good income earned them considerable respect in black communities, but as lifestyles loosened up and the Prohibition made drinking tantalizingly naughty, respectability gave way to hedonism. When asked to describe a buffet flat, Ruby replied, "It was nothing but faggots and bulldykers, a real open house. Everything went on in that house—tongue baths, you name it. They called them buffet flats because buffet means *everything*, everything that was in the life."

Linear apartments were called railroad flats, because one walked through them in very much the same manner as one walks through a railroad car, so it is reasonable to believe that buffet flats derived their name from a combination of that and the fact that its original clients, Pullman porters, were associated with buffet cars. But Ruby's description was apt, for buffet flats did indeed offer a cornucopia of pleasures: bootleg liquor flowed freely, though not inexpensively, gambling was a popular feature, and each room had a different "show." The aim was to satisfy every known sexual inclination, and patrons who wished to partake in pleasures of the flesh were welcomed to do so, for an added fee.

Whenever Bessie appeared at the Koppin, her friend, the buffet flat proprietress, sent one or two limousines to the stage door to whisk her and a coterie of "girls who knew how to keep their mouths shut" off to her notorious, well-protected establishment. On the night following Lillian's departure, Bessie visited the buffet flat with Ruby and four other girls, and as they stepped into the limousine, she issued the usual caution: "If any of you tell Jack about this, you'll never work in my shows again."

Ruby remembered that night well: "Bessie took her favorite girls and, of course, me. We was all dressed up, she had five fur coats. Each one of us would wear one of the coats. It made us feel like we were very important and loaded. I would always wear the mink. The coat was so big on me, I could wrap it around me three times. I didn't care, I just liked to wear the mink. Bessie would have me carry the bad liquor and anything else we wanted to sneak around with, under the mink. By being so big, no one noticed. As usual, when we went into a joint with Bessie it would start jumping; she was like a magnet, she attracted everyone. She wore a white ermine coat and looked like a million bucks. One girl wore Bessie's chinchilla coat, one had on her black seal. Her nephew's wife had on her sable. Even the horse had a monkey on her back, what I mean by horse, was a girl named Eva, who reminded you of a horse when she danced — so we nicknamed her horse. We looked very nice."

Drinks in hand, an eclectic crowd of pleasure-seekers packed the house. While some leisurely ascended and descended the linoleum-covered steps, others lined the staircases that connected the three floors. The air was thick with smoke, giggles, and clashing perfumes; two pianists, on separate floors, pounded the ivory competitively, and oooh's and ahh's emanated from activity rooms on each floor. Puffed up by their furs, Bessie and her young ladies negotiated their way down one of the corridors, to a room reserved for coats. It was not a cloakroom in the ordinary sense, but rather a bedroom with fur and wool piled high. "There were so many fur coats that it looked like a zoo," recalled Ruby.

As usual, Bessie more or less restricted her participation to voyeurism. She could ill afford to exhibit her prurient interest in public lest word of it got back to Jack. It was bad enough that she was drinking and patronizing a buffet flat, neither of which activity would have come as a complete surprise to her husband. "Jack knew she wasn't being no angel," observed Ruby, "but Bessie was kinda careful — well, let's say she would only go so far when strangers were around — but not always. Bessie was well known in that place."

Although the flat's most popular attraction that season seemed to be a young man who expertly made love to another man, Bessie was most intrigued by an obese woman who performed an amazing trick with a lighted cigarette, then repeated it in the old-fashioned way with a Coca-Cola bottle. "She was real great," said Ruby, "she could do all them things with her pussy—an educated pussy, you know." Bessie, being a Southerner, was, of course, inordinately fond of Coca-Cola.

Ruby had to admit that she often didn't see everything. "I wasn't as used to drinking as that bunch was," she said, "so I usually passed out. That night, they laid me out on a bed with all the coats and I threw up all over the fine furs. And when I came to, some white woman had messed with me—and it was the prettiest white woman you ever seen. And somebody had messed with Bessie, or Bessie had messed with someone—I don't know which way that mess was put down."

The Koppin engagement ended the following day. It had been a good week: every performance had gone smoothly, the newspapers had raved, and there had been no unpleasant backstage incidents. Bessie was in a splendid mood, and everybody looked forward to unwinding at Kate's boardinghouse after the final show. Kate's place was typical of the small guesthouses that catered to entertainers and could be found adjoining many TOBA theaters. In an era of widespread, legal racial discrimination, these small hotels answered a need,[4] and not just in the South, for African Americans were not always welcomed by Northern hotels and guest houses. Cities like New York and Chicago had well-appointed hotels that catered to blacks, but most didn't. "It was hard to get a room in some of them towns," Ruby recalled, "because sometimes people there were afraid of show people and Gypsies." Though any form of discriminatory practice was unacceptable to Bessie, she actually preferred the informality that a boardinghouse offered: a place where the atmosphere was down-to-earth, people could cook their own meals, and everyone could dress comfortably. Kate's was typical: no lobby, just three floors of long, narrow corridors and rows of sparsely furnished rooms.

It had almost become a theatrical tour tradition to follow up the final show of an extended engagement with a night of relaxation. "We used to put on our nicest pajamas and nightgowns, and go to each other's rooms and show off and drink and have a good time," said Ruby. "You know, a regular show crowd." On this night, most of her gang ended up in Bessie's room on the first floor. Marie, a young woman who did a ballet–tap dance number in the show, wore a pair of bright-red pajamas that had been a gift from Bessie. Eager to show them off, she performed a few comic steps that had everybody in stitches, and nobody laughed harder than Bessie. "C'mon, Marie, show your stuff," she shouted, encouraging the young lady to escalate her twists and turns. Ruby sized up the moment as she perceived the gleam in Bessie's eyes—it was clear that Bessie had found Lillian's replacement.

"We were drinking, clowning, and having ourselves a ball in Bessie's room, and, as usual, I was the first one to pass out—I just couldn't keep up with that crowd," recalled Ruby. When the drinks got the best of her, someone carried Ruby to her room, which adjoined Bessie's, and laid her on top of the bed. A couple of hours later, she was rudely awakened by shouts and the sound of footsteps moving swiftly down the corridor. She jumped out of bed, dashed to the door, and opened it just in time to see a red streak whizz by—Marie in her red pajamas. "She tore down the hall and disappeared around the corner," said Ruby. "The next thing I know, here comes Bessie. She pushed past me into my room and almost knocked me down, then she slammed the door and locked it." Jack had made one of his surprise returns and caught his wife in a compromising situation with Marie—all hell was breaking loose.

Bessie was as terrified as only Jack could make her. "If Jack knocks, you don't know where I'm at," she whispered to Ruby as the sound of his heavy footsteps passed the door. "Come out here, I'm going to kill you tonight, you bitch," he shouted, pacing back and forth. He knew that Bessie was in one of the rooms, but not which one, and when his bellowed threats failed to bring her out, he began pounding on one door after another. For a while, no one responded, then Kate stepped out of her room and pleaded for calm.

"I think I know where she is," they heard Jack say in a softer tone, "but when she comes back, you tell her I'm lookin' for her." His voice trailed off as he descended the wooden stairway that led to the street.

Bessie waited a few seconds, then asked Ruby to open the door and check the lay of the land. Other members of the troupe began to appear in their doorways and at the top of the stairs, waiting for Bessie to make her move. The show's railroad car was parked on a dead track within walking distance, so she told everybody to gather whatever belongings they could carry and quietly head for the train depot. No one took the time to dress; within minutes the Bessie Smith show, carrying armloads of clothes and other personal effects, was stealthily making its exodus through the dark February night. Jack had seemed angrier than ever before and Bessie wasn't taking any chances, so she ordered that the lights be left off as they boarded the car. They were still sitting in darkness an hour later when workers hitched the car to the next outgoing train. Soon thereafter, the Empress and her entourage, still dressed for bed, quietly slipped out of Detroit and no one was more in the dark than Jack.

6

There's two things got me puzzled,
There's two things I don't understand,
There's two things got me puzzled,
There's two things I don't understand;
That's a mannish-acting woman,
And a skipping, twistin' woman-acting man.
"Foolish Man Blues"

Of course Bessie was not as naive as the lyric to her song might indicate, nor were most urban blacks. Whether they indulged or not, they generally accepted homosexuality as a fact of life. Jack probably did, too, but not when it was so close to home. Not that he was totally straitlaced — he obviously had heterosexual escapades, and as Ruby opined, "Jack did a lot of hunting, but I don't think the stuff he was chasing had four feet." If he had an inkling of Bessie's ambisexuality before catching her with Marie, he kept it to himself, but now it was out in the open and he had to confront it. Clearly it was more than he was prepared to accept, but did it warrant his abandonment of the good life Bessie made possible? "He liked money too much," said Ruby, "and I knew he wasn't going to give it up just like that, but I expected him to be mad as a bull that had been stuck — and he was."

Their nocturnal getaway successful, Bessie and her company headed for Columbus, Ohio, for a scheduled February 7, 1927, opening at the Pythian Theater. Fortunately, most of the costumes and all the drops had been put on the train right after the last show in Detroit, but many of the troupe's personal effects remained behind at Kate's. "That's how I lost the only fur coat I ever had," Ruby recalled. "I had to leave it at Kate's — Bessie took us out of Detroit almost naked."

Following the first evening performance at the Pythian, some local admirers joined members of Bessie's troupe in her dressing room for a drink between shows. Bessie knew that she hadn't heard the end of the Detroit incident — Jack had the show's itinerary and was bound to catch up with her before long, but she did not expect him to appear as soon as he did.

Any performer who had spent time with a Bessie Smith show was conditioned to be on the alert for a sudden appearance by Jack, but this time he caught them all off guard — all but Ruby, that is. She spotted him as he headed for Bessie's dressing room, but there wasn't time to issue a warning, so she high-tailed it in the opposite direction.

Ruby had made an educated decision, for Jack charged into the crowded dressing room and knocked Bessie to the floor. "I'm not going to do any more to you now," he said, looking down at her, "but wait until the show is done tonight — you ain't a man, but you better be like one because we're gonna have it out." He would be waiting at the hotel, he said as he walked out.

Bessie wasn't ready to face Jack. "I'm in real trouble now," she told Ruby after clearing her room of performers and guests, "and I ain't about to mess with Jack as mad as he is. Fix my feathers, baby, and let's get this show over with and get out of town."

Bessie rushed everybody through the grand finale, made a quick change into street clothes, and took Ruby with her to the station, where they caught the next train for Cincinnati. Never one to worry about contractual obligations, Bessie was an old hand at walking out on her shows, even if it meant leaving her troupers stranded — somehow things always seemed to work themselves out. As always, someone else had to gather up and assemble the pieces, and Clarence Smith was becoming an expert at consoling stranded performers and calming irate theater owners.

When the two runaways reached Cincinnati, Bessie wired Frank Walker for money, and they spent a few days "relaxing" before traveling on to New York. What did they do in Cincinnati? "You should ask what we *didn't* do," said Ruby, her face lighting up at the memory. "Did we have a ball! We went to every joint, and Bessie knew more joints. I don't know that woman knew so many joints, but she could take you into more beat-up places, honey. And we just did everything we were big enough to do, from one place to the other, and when we walked in, there was no telling when we'd walk out again—Bessie stayed drunk, and me right along with her." They also visited some of Bessie's more versatile, uninhibited friends, people who derived pleasure from activities Ruby couldn't even have imagined—Bessie was on a hedonistic spree and her little niece was loving every minute of it.

The show caught up with them in Cincinnati. "Bessie wanted to go to New York and not hook up with the show, because she thought Jack would be with it, but I found out that he had gone off somewhere—as he usually did—so I talked Bessie into having us rejoin the gang."

When the *Harlem Frolics of 1927* company left Cincinnati, they did not get very far before a flood forced them to abandon the train. Maud recalled the event: "After we left Cincinnati, we came to this little town, which was flooded, so everybody had to step off the train into little rowboats that took us to where we were staying. It was an undertaker parlor next door to the theater, and we were supposed to stay in some rooms they had upstairs there. So after we had put our bags down, Bessie looked around and said, 'No, no, I can't stay *here* tonight.' But there was a lot of other people there, and they were trying to get her to stay, so they started hollerin', 'Miss Bessie, please sing the Back Water Blues, please sing the Back Water Blues.' Well, Bessie didn't know anything about any 'Back Water Blues,' but after we came back home to 1926 Christian Street where we were living, Bessie came in the kitchen one day, and she had a pencil and paper, and she started singing and writing. That's when she wrote the 'Back Water Blues'—she got the title from those people down South."

On February 17, 1927, she recorded it with James P. Johnson:

> When it rains five days, and the sky turns dark as night,
> When it rains five days, and the sky turns dark as night;
> Then trouble's takin'place in the lowlands at night.
> I woke up this mornin', can't even get out of my do',
> I woke up this mornin', can't even get out of my do';
> There's enough trouble to make a poor girl wonder where she wanna go.
> Then they rowed a little boat about five miles 'cross the pond,
> Then they rowed a little boat about five miles 'cross the pond;
> I packed all my clothes, throwed them in,
> And they rowed me along.
>
> Back Water Blues done caused me to pack my things and go,
> Back Water Blues done caused me to pack my things and go;
> 'Cause my house fell down, and I can't live there no mo'.

Mmmmmmmm Mmmmmmmm,
I can't move no more,
Mmmmmmmm Mmmmmmmm,
I can't move no more;
There ain't no place for a poor old girl to go.

The session, which also produced another of Bessie's compositions, "Preachin' the Blues," marked her first collaboration with James P. Johnson. Of eleven pianists who accompanied her on records, Johnson was unquestionably the best. None of the others could begin to approximate his invention and sophisticated musicianship. The acknowledged master (some say, creator) of the complicated, highly rhythmic Harlem "stride" piano style, Johnson was the inspiration for such future stride pianists as Fats Waller and, in turn, Count Basie. His richly embroidered, two-fisted style embellished and complemented Bessie's voice in much the same manner as Louis Armstrong had done two years earlier.

Because she was still not quite ready to face Jack after the incident in Detroit and his outburst in Columbus, Bessie chose not to stay at the Gee home on this New York trip. Instead she used the apartment near the Lafayette Theater that she had rented in Ruby's name, ostensibly to carry on her affair with Fred Longshaw, a couple of years earlier. She felt safe in that apartment because Jack did not know about it, but she knew that hiding was only a temporary solution — sooner or later she would have to face him. That started her thinking about a solution to one of their principal problems: the rather large sums of money that went to support her transplanted relatives. This was a source of ongoing friction between her and Jack, so, to remedy the situation, Bessie decided to make her sister Viola self-supporting.

To realize that plan, she purchased a small restaurant for Viola and her daughter, Laura, at 1244 South Street in Philadelphia. Viola had always been a good cook and Bessie figured that Laura could wait tables, but Maud recalled that Laura ended up doing most of the cooking. "It was a pit barbecue," Ruby recalled. "They built a pit in the ground and Bessie went to the slaughter house and told the man in charge to keep her sister supplied with those little suckling pigs. One time when I was there, I ate some. I never before or since ate such a good barbecue meal. Believe it or not, they went to the lumberyard and got lumber and made tables and long benches and they had the best potato salad and slaw. Bessie ordered 100 pounds of potatoes in a bag, 25 or 30 cabbages at a time. She saw they got everything that they needed and they did good business. Soon they didn't need Bessie's money."

Bessie knew that it would take more than Viola's independence to solve her marital problems. There was also the fact that the restaurant would not be self-sufficient for some time. She was still spending enough money on her family to warrant Jack's continual complaints over "Viola and that bunch," as he called them. His aggravation and, one suspects, Viola's unceasing taunts, culminated in a nervous breakdown, or so he said. He had in the past at least appeared to be on the brink of a nervous collapse, but this had all the makings of "the big one," so Bessie sent him to Hot Springs, Arkansas, where friends of hers operated a small spa for black people.

Rather than view Jack's apparent mental exhaustion as yet another strike against their marriage, Bessie took it as a blessing in disguise, and made the most of it. "I know he went there, because Bessie made a trip to visit him," said Ruby, "but I always thought she just wanted to make sure that he wasn't going to pop up suddenly, like he usually did. She was checking up on him—that's what I think, because a big bully like that don't get no nervous breakdown. He didn't look sick to me—he never did when he had them breakdowns, but Bessie made a big fuss over him each time."

Playing the Samaritan, Bessie did indeed make a trip to visit Jack in Hot Springs. It was a sign of her genuine concern for his health, and it appeared to whisk away his resentments. All was well again, at least for the time being, and Bessie returned to Philadelphia with a sense of accomplishment. "Oh, she was all smiles, like everything was going to be peaches and cream," said Maud. "He said he had a nervous breakdown, but I never believed it—Jack was so devious. He did go to Hot Springs and rest, or whatever they do down there. The truth is, Jack never had no nervous breakdowns. We were the ones who should have had nervous breakdowns. He wasn't sick. Bessie would do anything for him, so she'd give him all the money he wanted, and tell him to go and take a rest."

On March 2, it was back to business for Bessie: an unusual recording session with Fletcher Henderson and five members of his orchestra, including Joe Smith and Coleman Hawkins. What made it unusual was the repertoire of four popular songs: Creamer and Layton's 1918 hit "After You've Gone," Irving Berlin's "Alexander's Ragtime Band," a 1926 Tin Pan Alley favorite called "Muddy Water (a Mississippi Moan)," and a popular rallying song from the Spanish-American War, "There'll Be a Hot Time in the Old Town Tonight."

Blues purists—who, oddly enough, don't complain about Bessie's 1923 recordings of lesser-known pop fare—have bemoaned her "commercial" repertoire for this session, and critics have rationalized it as an attempt to regain lost ground. But Bessie's popularity was not threatened at the time, and her recordings reflected only a part of her actual repertoire. Her treatment of these

Alberta Hunter (left) and Lil Armstrong flank trombonist J. C. Higginbotham in a photograph taken at a New York club during the late 1940s. From the author's collection.

songs offers delightful evidence of her talent for turning banal material into something special.

When writer Studs Terkel asked blues singer Big Bill Broonzy if blues was folk music, Broonzy replied: "It's all folk music—horses don't sing." He was reflecting the feelings of many performers, who dislike being segregated into idiomatic boxes. To them it is all music. Ida Cox recalled starting out with "Put Your Arms Around Me, Honey," and Alberta Hunter's premiere song offering was a straight-from-the-sheet-music rendering of "Where the River Shannon Flows." It was only later in their careers that these women turned to blues; to them a song frequently was nothing more than a loose guideline upon which to build an act. Just as the sudden popularity of theatrical blues (as opposed to the street corner variety) had turned "sweet" singers into blues divas overnight, so it was easy for blues singers to venture beyond their regular domain.

Bessie did this routinely on stage, but even a song like "After You've Gone" almost became a blues when she handled it, for she seemed incapable of treating even the most insignificant tune casually. Following a vaudeville-style introduction, Bessie bellows out the rarely heard verse, her clear voice cutting the air with an ease that belies the power behind it. It is a fitting beginning and Bessie maintains the momentum as she thunders through the song and makes it one of the best recorded examples of her ability to endow rather ordinary material with unexpected profundity. In the process, she mercilessly adapts the melody to her purposes, again twisting single-syllable words until they seem likely to snap apart. For example, Bessie spends five notes in the first chorus to sing the title's last word, "gone," and when she shouts against stop-time chords at the end of the final chorus, she has turned this pop song into a hard-driving spiritual. Except for banjoist Charlie Dixon's brief transitional passage, there are no instrumental solos, but Joe Smith's brassy cornet spearheads the ensemble to an awesome finish — Creamer and Layton's song was rewritten by Bessie.

"Muddy Water," subtitled "A Mississippi Moan," was a fair-sized hit at the time of Bessie's recording. Written by Tin Pan Alley's Peter Dew Rose, Jo Trent, and Harry Richman, it was featured by Richman in his show. He recorded the song a couple of months before Bessie did, and within a few months it was available on recordings by Jack Pettis, Gene Austin, Bing Crosby and the Whiteman band, and Fats Waller's manager, Ed Kirkeby (who made it under the pseudonym Ted Wallace).

Bessie picks her way through this theatrical number with the deliberate pace of a behemoth, one at which most singers would sound languorous. Henderson's star-studded band remains remarkably inconspicuous, and Coleman Hawkins's presence is barely evident. Although the composers probably lacked firsthand knowledge of such a flood as they depict in their song — or, for that matter, the big river — Bessie had experienced such disasters on more than one occasion. There is barely a trace of blues in this "moan," and surprisingly, Bessie avoids injecting any, but if one needed proof that she could sing the most banal lyrics with conviction, this is it. In her skillful approach, even such a trite line as "Dixie moonlight, Swanee shore" becomes acceptable, and when she sings "my heart cries out for muddy water," we have to believe.

On the following day, March 3, 1927, Bessie recorded four more sides, including her own "Hot Springs Blues," which may have been inspired by her visit with Jack, and a lusty bit of musical comedy, "Trombone Cholly," written by Fletcher Henderson under the George Brooks pseudonym. It is a comedic routine à la "Jazzbo Brown from Memphis Town," but this time Bessie's admiration is directed at Charlie Green rather than Buster Bailey. As might be expected, Green responds in a marvelously witty fashion, aided by Joe Smith's cornet — it all inspired Bessie to be as peppy as ever.

At the time of these recordings, Bessie was at the Lincoln Theater on Lenox Avenue, headlining a show that boasted thirty "famous artists" in its advertisements. It was called *Bessie Smith and Her Yellow Girl Revue*, but, since Bessie had always expressed monumental disdain for light-complexioned women, and none were to be found in her own troupe, one suspects that she did not create this production. She was also preparing for another tent tour, but it involved little rehearsal time, for the lineup was almost the same as it had been the previous year, and "new" routines were usually mere variations on old ones. Her brother Clarence and the husband-and-wife team of Gertie and Dinah Scott were the featured co-performers. Musical director Bill Woods was no longer with the show, having been totally humiliated by the incident that involved his wife, Boulah. His replacement was Thomas Hill, an elderly tuba player who, as Ruby put it, was "old enough to have some sense." Bessie's nephew, Teejay, was still the troupe's secretary, and Jack was scheduled to join the company in the South, being "well enough" to resume his "managerial" role, according to the *Chicago Defender*.

On April 1, Bessie made more recordings with James P. Johnson, "Sweet Mistreater" and the high-spirited "Lock and Key," both written by Johnson with lyrics by Harry Creamer. It would appear that Bessie had exclusive rights to the latter song, because no one else recorded it at that time, but perhaps it only seemed proprietary because she renders it so superbly ("A song is only as good as it sounds," cornetist Rex Stewart wryly observed after suffering through a singer's mistreatment of "Body and Soul"). Only Bessie could so splendidly deliver the song's challenge to her two-timing man. With her vocal engine revved up and her wit in high gear, she clearly had this song under her own lock and key, and she must have found it a great audience pleaser, although it is the seamless interplay between her and Johnson that makes this recording so extraordinary. What we hear here is a refined Bessie (the word "subdued" might be appropriate in this context if it were not otherwise such an inappropriate term for the rambunctious diva); it almost sounds as if she is listening in wonderment and delight to the piano. After singing the song straight through, she enlarges on the message with some patter, suggesting that she may have been a source of inspiration for Pearl Bailey.

With two more excellent recordings in the can, Bessie headed for Atlanta to pick up the railroad car. Jack was already there. A cured man, he had spent a few days having the railroad car made tour-ready and painted to his own specifications. Emblazoned on each side were the words: "Jack Gee presents Bessie Smith and Her Harlem Frolics of 1927." Delighted to have her husband back in the fold, Bessie went along with his touch of self-promotion, but his managerial role was more or less pro forma; Clarence Smith and Teejay continued to handle the show's business, with occasional help from Bessie, who—among other non-performing chores—personally dealt with Hatch

Bessie dances the Charleston in a 1925 Columbia publicity photo. From the author's collection.

Show Print, the Nashville company that made her posters and flyers. Bessie often submitted rough sketches of what she wanted, and she was not afraid to ask professional advice, as in this letter from Monroe, North Carolina, dated July 27, 1927:

> Dear Sir—
> I am riting you to ask you would this picture standing make a better three sheet, than the bust picture. Let me hear you tearm at once so I will no what to do ship letter head to Florence N.C. at once
> Bessie Smith
> Tent Show

Before embarking on the first stretch of her tour and heading to the first stop, in North Carolina, Bessie's show spent a week in Atlanta. During that

July 27 — 1927
Monroe N.C.

Dear Sir.—
i am riting you to
ask you would this picture
standing make a better three
sheet, than the buck picture
lets me hear you term at once
so i will no what to do
ship letter head to Florence N.C.
At once

Bessie Smith
Tent Show

Bessie, who handled many business chores herself, was touring with her tent show when she dashed off this note of instructions to Hatch Show Print, a Nashville printing company that is still in business. From the files of Hatch Show Print.

time, a minor incident occurred involving a chorine named Elsie Ferbee. It seems that she got into a skirmish with one of the musicians that ended with his pushing her down a flight of stairs at the hotel. She was not seriously hurt, but her injuries were deemed bad enough to exclude her from the tour. Bessie fired the musician, paid Ferbee's medical bills, and in general, gave her more personal attention than the circumstances warranted.

Two weeks later, as Bessie's show played Asheville, North Carolina, a letter from Elsie Ferbee appeared in her hometown newspaper, the *Pittsburgh Courier*. Annoyed at having been left behind in Atlanta, she accused her former boss of unfair treatment. Bessie's reply was prompt:

Ashville, N.C.
May 14, 1927
Theatrical Department
Pittsburgh Courier
Pittsburgh, Pa.

Gentlemen:

In regards to the letter sent you by Elsie Ferbee, she or no one else can truthfully say that I did not do anything for her when she was ill, because I did. I paid her room rent and board and she was treated by one of the best specialists in Atlanta from Grady Hospital and her doctor bill was paid by me. I had her moved in where I was staying so I could be near her to see that she got the best attention. As for my mistreating anybody who is sick, I have given and helped more people in and out of the profession than I ever hope to be repaid for on earth, but I will get my reward later from the man higher up.

However, I wish Elsie success in what she undertakes to do.

Yours professionally,
BESSIE SMITH
Care the Bessie Smith Show

Bessie probably dictated the content of the letter, if not the wording, to T. J. Hill, who took care of most correspondence, and seized the opportunity to throw in a little plug for the show: a postscript—obviously meant for the *Courier* to publish—described a successful tour and listed the itinerary for the rest of the month.

The letter's reference to a reward from "the man higher up" is a little hard to reconcile with Bessie's worldly lifestyle, but she was actually quite religious. "In every town that we would get in, if we got in on a Sunday morning early enough, we'd all go to church," Maud remembered. "Bessie could sing some of the most beautiful church hymns, and she often did that around the house." Did the mixture of debauchery and divinity cause Bessie any inner conflict? "No," said Maud, suggesting that Bessie might eventually have taken the high road. "I truly believe that Bessie was getting ready to turn." Ruby did not agree, but blues ladies have been known to give religion more than a casual squeeze in their latter years. Ethel Waters became a regular in the Billy Graham camp, Lizzie Miles affirmed her Catholic faith, and Ma Rainey devoted her energies to the Friendship Baptist Church in Columbus, Georgia.

Bessie had, after all, grown up in a religious household, and there was general agreement among those who heard her in person that her vocal delivery and coordinated movements evoked the fervor of a Southern Baptist prayer meeting. "She was real close to God, very religious," recalled drummer Zutty Singleton, who often accompanied her at the Lyric Theater in New Orleans.

"She always mentioned the Lord's name. That's why her blues seemed almost like hymns."

"If you had any church background, like people who came from the South, as I did," said guitarist Danny Barker, "you would recognize a similarity between what she was doing and what those preachers and evangelists from there did, and how they moved people. Bessie did the same thing on stage. She, in a sense, was like people like Billy Graham are today. Bessie was in a class with those people. She could bring about mass hypnotism."

If the winter had left them starved for entertainment, the smaller rural communities of North Carolina had nothing to complain about after the 1927 tent season got under way. Several touring companies had blazed the trail for Bessie's *Harlem Frolics,* including shows headed by Clara Smith and Ma Rainey, with Rainey showing off her new thirteen-thousand-dollar Mack bus and Koehler electric generator.

Ma's show, *Louisiana Blackbirds*, preceded *Harlem Frolics* in Asheville by less than a month, but Bessie and her troupe were able to generate enough interest to justify a week's stay. For some shows, more than a hundred standees lined the walls of Bessie's huge tent, in addition to the fifteen hundred seated ticket holders. The success was repeated as *Harlem Frolics* worked its way eastward across the state, stopping in Hickory, Statesville, Salisbury, High Point, Reidsville, and Greensboro during the month of May. June found the show in Burlington, Chapel Hill, Durham, Raleigh, Louisburg, Oxford, Henderson, and Franklin, Virginia. In July, the show headed south.

So far, it had been a highly successful tour in every respect. Capacity audiences were the norm, there had not been a single major backstage incident, and the Gees were enjoying a period of tranquility following their fight over the Detroit debacle. Keeping her promise to Jack, Bessie stayed off the bottle and concentrated on her work. Perhaps spurred by the fact that its release coincided with the worst flood disaster in the history of the Mississippi River,[1] "Back Water Blues" enjoyed phenomenal sales, which probably also had a positive effect on show attendance.

Although Bessie could count Southern rural whites among her staunchest fans, there was of course still a segment of the population that resented the success of any black artist. Revived and reorganized in 1915, the Ku Klux Klan claimed its largest membership in the mid-1920s, a time when its effort to establish white supremacy took its most virulent form. Trading on the fears and suspicions of rural whites, the Klan became a law unto itself in many communities and included many law-enforcement officers among its membership.

Having grown up and spent much of her life in Klan-infested territory, Bessie was well aware of the threat this hate group posed. The Klan, however pernicious, had become a fact of life in Southern society. But, other than ignore it, what could anyone — especially an African American — do to fight this menace? Bessie undoubtedly knew that many of her Southern followers, the same people who flocked to her tent, laughed at her jokes, and applauded her singing, were Klansmen who had left their sheets at home. Like many Southern blacks, she did her best to ignore the hooded hate mongers, assuming that she would receive no more malice than she gave. Bessie's complacent attitude changed to one of defiance on a July night in 1927 when the show pitched its tent in Concord, North Carolina.

The following is based on the recollections of Ruby and Maud, who, except for insignificant details, told virtually the same story:

It had been a hot and humid day, and the relief that usually accompanied nightfall was nowhere to be felt. Further aggravating the situation, the show's electric generator and lights heightened the temperature inside the packed tent, making it particularly unbearable for the cast, which had to wear costumes and makeup while performing energetic movements. Bessie and the dancers held up remarkably well, but when one of the musicians came close to passing out halfway through the show, he put down his instrument and stepped outside.

There was sufficient moonlight for him to take a little walk around the tent without tripping over the ropes, and he had not gone far when he heard soft voices and grunts nearby. Walking in the direction of the sound, he came upon a frightening sight: a half-dozen hooded figures, their white robes eerily bathed in the moonlight, were busy doing something to the tent. For a few minutes, he stood frozen in his steps, then he noticed that the Klansmen had pulled up some stakes and were obviously getting ready to collapse the canvas. The musician ran back to the performers' area, reaching it just as Bessie walked off stage and her audience loudly clamored for an encore. Before she could raise hell with him for not being inside with the rest of the band, the musician managed to blurt out what he'd seen.

"*Some* shit!" Bessie declared, ordering the prop boys to follow her around the tent. When they reached within a few yards of the Klansmen, the boys — who had no idea what this was about — took one look at the white-robed figures and hastily withdrew to a safe distance. Bessie seemed fearless as she ran toward the intruders, stopping within ten feet of them. "I was told that she confronted the Klan with her hand on her hip, as she always did when something bothered her," said Maud, "and that she shook her fist at them! I'm telling you, it's a wonder they didn't kill Bessie down there, the way she stood up to them crackers." According to Ruby, Bessie shouted: "What the fuck you think *you're* doin'? I'll get the whole damn tent out here if I have to. You just pick up them sheets and run!"

The Klansmen, apparently too stunned to move, just stood there and gawked. Bessie hurled obscenities at them until they finally turned and disappeared quietly into the darkness.

"I ain't never *heard* of such shit," said Bessie, using one of her favorite expressions, and walked back to where her prop boys stood. "And as for you, you ain't nothin' but a bunch of sissies." Then she returned to the tent as if she had just settled a routine matter. "I don't think she told us what really happened until that night," said Maud, "but she had sent those boys out to fix the tent, and I think they said something about Bessie having chased the Klan away." What did Jack do? "I don't think Jack even knew what was happening," said Ruby.

There was trouble of a different kind on the following night, when the show played in nearby Charlotte, North Carolina. The show's orchestra leader, Thomas Hill, went into town after the final performance and got into a fight with two young men who beat him up rather badly. When the band members, a close-knit group, heard what had happened to Hill, several of them set out to look for his assailants. Meanwhile, Bessie's railroad car was ready to be hitched to the next southbound train. There was no set schedule for these tours; the troupe's movement depended entirely on the sometimes erratic timetable of the railroads. This meant that the cast had to board the car as soon as the tent and other equipment was put in place, and wait until it was pulled out.

On this night, Bessie's car was pulled out before Hill's colleagues returned from their mission. Unaware of the incident, Bessie did not notice their absence until the following day, when the train stopped at Sumter, North Carolina. Thinking that this was a case of musicians getting drunk and acting irresponsibly, she flew into a rage and threatened to fire Hill unless his musicians arrived in time for the evening's show. Fortunately for everybody concerned, the avenging musicians, though somewhat disheveled, found their way back to the railroad car in time for that night's performance. They had accomplished their mission—located the two men and given them such a severe beating that there was even talk of them possibly having killed one of them. Bessie was not supposed to hear that part of the story, but someone told her and she issued a threat: "If anybody comes lookin' for y'all, I'm gonna let 'em have you."

Throughout August and most of September, *Harlem Frolics* did one- and two-nighters in Georgia and Alabama. The tent tour had been Bessie's most successful to date, but it had been long and tiring. It was now time for the show to make its traditional homebound theater tour. The first stop was Dallas, Texas. It was Bessie's first appearance in that state, and it did not go well.

"They really hated the blacks there," Ruby said, "so when we came into town, you could feel the tension and those hostile looks, but everything went as smooth as could be expected until Bessie got into an argument with the stage manager, who was white." Bessie's anger was precipitated by what she considered to be unprofessional staging. "She would finish her song and we girls followed her," explained Ruby. "They were supposed to bring the curtain down so we could dance in front of it while they took the piano away. Well, now they had to push the piano while we were dancing. It was a grand shuffle, the stage help was in our way trying to get the piano off stage. We needed all of that room, because we danced in two lines, six girls in front and six girls in back. It really looked bad and the audience started laughing. Bessie always treated the help backstage fine when they did their work on time and right, but this time she really got mad, I never saw her get that mad before. She ran over to the stage manager, who was standing there talking to some white woman—which turned out to be his wife—and said, 'What is the matter? Are you drunk, you was late getting that curtain down, standing here talking to that white bitch.' The man got so mad when Bessie called his wife a bitch that he drawed back to hit Bessie, but Bessie knocked him down. His wife yelled, 'Let my husband alone.' He got up and never said another word, and made his wife shut up. When the show was over, I said to Bessie in her dressing room, 'I don't like it, he took it too quietly.' Bessie said, 'Fuck him, he is getting paid to do his job, black or white he is suppose to do the right thing by every act.' We went through all of our shows and nothing more happened, then. Bessie was calm, but I was uneasy."

After the last show, Ruby waited for Bessie—they had planned to get something to eat at a restaurant that adjoined the theater. "When we came out of the theater, no one was around," she recalled. "There was one car standing in front of the theater, and no other cars anywhere. Somebody in the car said, 'Miss Bessie Smith?' Bessie answered 'Yes.' 'Would you please come here?' Bessie told me to wait and went over to the car and leaned over to see who was calling her. Two men jumped out of a four-door car, grabbed Bessie and held her mouth." Bessie put up a good fight, which brought two more men out of the car. "So all four of the men got her in the car. By that time I had come out of my astonishment and started screaming and running near the car, but they speeded down the street. Luck was with us, because there was two cops near the restaurant where we were going to eat, near the theater. When I screamed, they came running out, I yelled, 'They got Bessie Smith, the singer, in that car.' They put their siren on and followed, but the car had disappeared."

A man who had just pulled up in front of the restaurant signaled Ruby to get in his car, which she did. "Some of the boys on our show jumped in and we followed the police car. We looked everywhere about ten or twenty minutes until we came to an empty lot and saw some men horsewhipping Bessie. When they saw us and the cops coming, they dropped Bessie to the ground and jumped into their car and disappeared again. The cops didn't even try to stop them. We brought Bessie to the hotel, she refused to go to the hospital. She said if they got her there, they would really beat her to death. One man had a whip that had hit Bessie and cut her clothes through to her skin, just the same as a knife. The cops said, 'Don't worry, we will find them,' but they never did. As for the stage manager, he was in the restaurant with his wife through the whole thing. He or his wife must have made a phone call after Bessie knocked him down. We only had one more day in Texas and we was glad to get out. After that, when we start our tour for the summer and Bessie go to the TOBA office to sign her contract, they always give her a list of the towns that we were going to play for the summer, and the dates. Whenever they would have Texas on the list, Bessie would cross it off—they could never get her to play there again."

Bessie was not easily shaken by adversity, but this incident so affected her that she canceled the rest of the tour, disbanded her troupe, and headed back to Philadelphia. The bad news that awaited her there did not improve her spirits. She had suspected that things were not going well with her sisters' restaurant, but no one had informed her of its closing. "Laura said it was too much work for her," said Maud when asked why the business had failed, "and Viola was up in age." Ruby offered a different explanation, attributing the restaurant's short life to inexperience, excessive drinking, and a general lack of interest. Bessie took care of the outstanding bills and promised to continue her support, but Jack was less forgiving: the gesture that was designed to ease the tension between Jack and Viola had instead escalated it. Against all predictions, this did not send Bessie on a major spree, but it broke her four-month dry spell.

In late September Bessie made four recordings with Porter Grainger, her new accompanist. They worked well together on their initial collaboration, "A Good Man Is Hard to Find" and "Mean Old Bedbug Blues." Both songs had the makings of hit material, and Frank Walker decided to market the coupling as a "special release." "Good Man" was written by Eddie Green and popularized by Alberta Hunter, who introduced it in Chicago around the end of World War I. "I used to sing it at the Dreamland," Miss Hunter recalled, "and, if I remember correctly, the song wasn't even copyrighted when I introduced it, but it went over very big, and all the white entertainers wanted it for their own acts." The song was recorded as early as 1918, but it didn't really take off until ten years later. It went on to become a staple in both pop and jazz repertoires, and remains a favorite among traditional bands. On Bessie's recording, Grainger and guitarist Lincoln Conaway kick off with a typical vamp-until-ready vaudeville introduction, but while Bessie forges ahead with characteristic force, Conaway's guitar lends a an unusually soft texture to the accompaniment, quite different from anything previously heard on a Bessie Smith recording. Imagine a raging bull stomping through a field of delicate flowers, yet leaving no smashed blossoms in its wake. Bessie pressed hard on the tempo, repeatedly jumping in ahead of the beat, as if impatient with its deliberate time. Refusing to be stampeded, Grainger and Conaway placidly proceed to the end in perfect unison. "Mean Old Bedbug Blues" is a Kafkaesque song that gives Bessie full opportunity to demonstrate her sense of humor and ability to build a perfectly structured story within a song.

Billed as "the snappiest revue on the road," Bessie's *Harlem Follies* opened at the Lafayette on October 17, 1927, for a week's run. On the big screen was *What Price Glory,* advertised as "the world's greatest motion picture," and, substituting for the Duke Ellington Orchestra was the Royal Balalaika Orchestra, which may or may not have driven Bessie to the bottle. She was, in fact, drinking heavily again, and her trips to the nearby speakeasy were so frequent that it was said she often had to be propped up on stage. This may well be an exaggeration; Frank Schiffman, then the owner of the Lafayette, did not recall anything of the kind, but he does remember that Bessie never missed a show. "She had love problems all the time, and they might have impaired some of her performances, but we could always count on Bessie to be there, and to put on a show—a good one."

It was impossible to keep Jack from finding out about Bessie's drinking. He also knew where her hangouts were, and that her favorite place whenever she was at the Lafayette was a bar whose side entrance faced the alley next to the theater. Knowing that Jack might be looking to catch her in the act, Bessie had a special arrangement with the bartender—she and her friends would take their drinks in the one place Jack couldn't surprise her: the ladies' room. It worked until the day he caught her coming out of there, glass in hand, and knocked her down in front of everybody. "He almost knocked me down getting to her," Ruby recalled. While some of the patrons restrained Jack, Bessie picked herself up and took off down Seventh Avenue, with Ruby following close behind.

It wasn't long before Jack was chasing them down the street. They were almost a block ahead of him when Bessie stopped a cab and jumped in with Ruby. "I don't know what that poor taxi driver thought," said Ruby, "but Bessie told him, 'Hurry up. That man back there just held up somebody and he's after us because he knows we seen him—hurry up, he's gonna kill us!' "

It was back to the old cat-and-mouse game for Bessie and Jack. As usually happened following these explosive encounters, Bessie entered a period of sobriety and bought back Jack's affection with material offerings. But this routine had happened too many times, and Bessie found it increasingly difficult to summon control for a dry spell and good behavior. And Jack was beginning to fall apart again.

On October 27, four days before leaving New York, Bessie recorded two of her finest sides, "Dyin' by the Hour" and "Foolish Man Blues," with a trio assembled by Fletcher Henderson. By this time, Columbia no longer credited Bessie on its labels as "comedienne," but the original label on "Foolish Man Blues" was almost as fatuous. It read: "Vocal, Novelty accomp." Someone at Columbia was not keeping up with the times, for while jazz indeed was a novelty after World War I, it had since become the beat to which America danced. Still, most Americans were listening to jazz cloaked in Tin Pan Alley garb.

Bessie's accompaniments on this date were not novel, but the instrumentation was a bit unusual. Besides Henderson's piano, it featured a young Louisiana-born cornetist who was new to Bessie but was actually one of the most widely traveled musicians in jazz. Tommy Ladnier appeared on Ma Rainey's earliest recordings and was her favorite trumpeter. He had also worked with Ollie Powers and King Oliver in Chicago, performed with Sam Wooding's extraordinary big band in Berlin and Leningrad, and with the Louis Douglas Revue in Poland. At the time of Bessie's session, Ladnier had spent a year with Henderson's orchestra in New York. A fine musician, his style was blues-drenched and prepossessing in its simplicity. He never dazzled with displays of brilliant technique, but he was capable of generating enormous heat when that was called for, and he made moving statements with a compelling raw tone.

Bessie must have been pleased with the opening he gave her on "Foolish Man Blues," a cascade of plaintive blue notes that seem to plunge to the low levels of June Cole's tuba. Just as the notes hit bottom, Bessie's resonant voice rises and cuts through to the very heart of the blues. She delivers her message firmly and with a great deal of her sardonic humor, her words and Ladnier's appropriate asides floating superbly over a bed of deep tuba and subtle

Hendersonian piano. She is out for blood. "Men sure are deceitful," she sings, her notes ringing out loud and clear as she uses the full power of her magnificent voice to deliver the mock-serious statement.

When Bessie returned home to Philadelphia that weekend, bad news again greeted her. Jack, having run up a considerable gambling debt, was having another "nervous breakdown." As she had done for Viola and Laura, Bessie dutifully paid off Jack's debt, then she sent him off to Arkansas for another stay at the Hot Springs spa. "I really felt sorry for her," said Maud. "Clarence was still upset over what Viola had done to Bessie, but he kinda laid off her because she was his sister, too, and she had worked so hard for all them kids when they were down home. But Clarence never cared much for Jack, so he just thought that Bessie should have dropped him long before this happened." There were many who believed that Bessie should never gave married Jack Gee, but as Ruby said, "you couldn't tell her what to do, not Bessie—she was going to do anything to hold on to my uncle. I was grateful for him being the reason I met Bessie, but, to tell you the truth, I think she made a mistake marrying him—and he was my blood!"

Between Jack and her sisters, Bessie's money was now going faster than she could make it, so—depressed though she was—she had no alternative but to work. On Monday, October 31, she fulfilled her obligation to Gibson's Standard Theater, which was within walking distance of her house. She stayed in Philadelphia all of November, then embarked on a brief theater tour with a slightly updated production of *Harlem Frolics*.

The show opened on December 3 at the Grand Theater in Chicago. Business was good but, by Bessie's standards, disappointing. A "Free Marcus Garvey" movement had just culminated in President Calvin Coolidge's commutation of a prison sentence that the self-appointed "Provisional President of Africa" had been serving in Atlanta Penitentiary since 1925. To some, he was a con man, to others a hero, but regardless of how people viewed his controversial "Back to Africa" movement, Garvey sparked a growing political awareness among urban blacks. Some saw this as the reason why attendance was down, and most black theaters registered 1927 as the most disastrous box office year to date. It was an urban black phenomenon, they rationalized, pointing out that business along the tent trail was at its peak and that the white legitimate theater—with a record 268 Broadway openings—had never had a better year.

The simple truth was that urban black audiences had become more demanding—what knocked them for a loop in Concord, North Carolina, could fall flat in Chicago—and black vaudeville, a throwback to minstrel days, was becoming as outdated as the parlor piano and ankle-length skirts. Bessie herself had not lost her drawing power; as a singer she was certainly in a class by herself, but her talent was not limited to that. We think of her as a singer because recordings reveal only her extraordinary voice; those who experienced her on the stage also saw her as an actress, comedienne, dancer, and mime. And in all these guises she had no equal when it came to communicating with her followers; she had a remarkable ability to command an audience's involvement in whatever she was doing and to control and even shape its responses.

For the week of December 12, Bessie's *Harlem Frolics* commanded packed houses in Indianapolis, proving that she could still attract urban audiences, and a thousand people were turned away during a subsequent run at the Lincoln in Kansas City. Jack, having again recuperated, rejoined her on the road in time for Christmas, and things were swell again as they journeyed home to Philadelphia and New York.

Five years had passed since Bessie first faced Columbia's recording cone and turned it into a horn of plenty. If somebody hadn't told her that 1927 had been a very bad year for her profession, she would never have known it, but a real threat did loom on the horizon, for only three months earlier, New York's Warners' Theater had premiered *The Jazz Singer,* a film that talked and sang.

7

There ain't nothin' I can do, or nothin'
I can say, that folks don't criticize me.
But I'm goin' to do just as I want to anyway,
And don't care if they all despise me.
" 'Tain't Nobody's Bizness If I Do"

In the early months of 1928, Harlem still mourned the recent death of Florence Mills,[1] a popular star who gained international fame when producer Lew Leslie brought her to Europe. Leslie's latest revue, *Blackbirds of 1928*, was about to make stars of Adelaide Hall and Bill "Bojangles" Robinson. At the Cotton Club, Duke Ellington was packing in the white elite, and in midtown, Helen Morgan introduced the "torch" song with a heart-wrenching rendition of "Bill," a P. G. Wodehouse–Jerome Kern collaboration that had come to the Broadway musical *Showboat* as an afterthought. Bessie was on the road for most of January but staying close to New York because Frank Walker had scheduled several sessions for February.

The first of these took place February 9, with trombonist Charlie Green, Fred Longshaw, and Demus Dean. Joe Smith was originally booked for the date, and when he canceled, Dean, a young cornetist from the *Blackbirds of 1928* pit band, became his last-minute replacement. "I was very, very nervous," Dean recalled in a 1971 interview, "because Charlie Green, who was a friend of mine, had told me that Joe was Bessie's favorite trumpeter. Well, here I was, somebody she never heard of, replacing her favorite. I played in Lucille Hegamin's band for a while, so I was used to accompanying a singer, but Bessie was . . . well, I'll just say I don't think there was anyone could touch her when it came to the blues. Now, I hadn't heard her sing before we made those records, but I knew she was good, and I had also heard she'd fly off the handle if something didn't sit right with her, but she turned out to be very sweet—an attractive big brown-skin woman with a nice smile and great legs! We ended up doing more sessions a few days later, so I guess Bessie didn't think I was too bad."

Dean recalled that the only written music was a lead sheet on Longshaw's piano. "After meeting Bessie, we went right to work," he told writer Bill Reed.[2] "She turned us over to her pianist, Fred Longshaw. The only thing that was interesting to him, as far as any rehearsal we might have done, was the introduction. We played an eight-bar introduction, then Bessie sang. We'd never heard those numbers before, no music, but you're supposed to know the blues. If you didn't know the blues, you were like a lost ball in the tall grass.

"Every number she sang told a story. One was 'Pickpocket Blues.' When she sang it you knew right away what she was talking about—she was a pick-pocket, her friends were trying to tell her to stop it, but she ended up in jail anyhow . . . 'I'm in the jailhouse now.' It was a short story. You just couldn't stop listening to Bessie and looking at her too when she sang."

To millions of people, Bessie was now a superstar, and on rare occasions she even looked like one. But wearing an ermine coat and conspicuous diamond rings was only something she did when a situation called for dressing up. She still preferred eating pigs' feet and drinking bad liquor in a ghetto alley to sampling canapes and cocktails at the gatherings of a white society that now sought to embrace her.

It was a good hour's walk from the center of black Harlem to midtown Manhattan, but to most blacks who lived around 132d Street in the late 1920s, the midtown area might as well have been the Côte d'Azur. There was, however, an extraordinary flow of traffic in the opposite direction. Whites whose modern counterparts feel ill at ease above Ninety-sixth Street swarmed uptown to the "colorful" ghetto and became tourists in their own city.

Harlem's celebrated nightlife experienced a slump following World War I, but Prohibition gave it new scope and an enticing, frenetic energy. Outwardly, Harlemites appeared to ignore conditions that had them treated as second-class citizens, even in their own community, but the inequities were clear to all who lived there, and to whites who removed their blinders. Night after night, white socialites and celebrities slummed in Harlem, turning this "foreign," fascinating community into a playground for the privileged. Bejeweled and befurred, they came from their homes on Park and Fifth Avenue or Riverside Drive to hear the great black entertainers at Smalls' Paradise, Connie's Inn, and the Cotton Club. There, in what seemed like a congenial atmosphere, the downtown pleasure-seekers were treated to elaborate shows and smiling faces. Some of the smiles were undoubtedly genuine, but many were simply masks in a game of survival. If the racism escaped the notice of most white visitors, it was abundantly clear to Harlem's inhabitants. It is common belief that some of the major establishments, including the Cotton Club, operated on a whites-only policy, looking the other way only if celebrated blacks of the stature of Bert Williams or Madame C. J. Walker strode in. There was no such policy, but few African Americans could afford the high prices, and those who could often did not wish to subject themselves to the curious stares of pale well-to-dos.

Some Harlem cabarets, like Leroy's at 135th Street and Fifth Avenue, maintained a no-whites policy that may or may not have been official, and certainly was broken on occasion.[3] Other clubs, like the Ubangi, discouraged white patronage, but there were no racial barriers in the community's many after-hours spots—at least not official ones. Feeling adventurous among the friendly natives, many whites shed their inhibitions and rounded off an evening in Harlem by slumming it in a variety of speakeasies. The truly uninhibited frequented buffet flats that bore the names of their proprietors: Eunice's, Minnie's, Mabel's—local Perle Mestas who offered delights that no downtown establishment could match, and assured their patrons anonymity and protection against the law. Even the most perceptive white visitors often failed to sense the resentment behind the smiles that greeted them. They saw blacks as a happy-go-lucky people who laughed infectiously, showed an enviable lack of restraint, and really understood how to have a good time. So they came, laughed, sinned, and slipped back into their Tiffany world before the first rays of dawn struck the ghetto.

Bessie understood how important white tourism was to Harlem, and she was surely also aware of the need for black people to play the game, but she was one native the visitors rarely caught a glimpse of. She loved Harlem but shied away from the tourist spots—that aspect of the black community, the glittery facades, feigned smiles, and demeaning shuffles, went against her grain. She was discomforted by the sight of "them" pulling up in their fancy limousines, cruising the teeming streets for a peek at "the other side," and strutting into clubs flaunting their tuxedos and richly scented Bergdorf Goodman wraps. Bessie didn't envy the women—many of whom she could match, diamond for diamond, fur for fur—but she was bothered by their obvious air of superiority; fame and money had not diminished Bessie's empathy with the less fortunate. "There was never anything hoity-toity about Bessie," said Ruby. "She never forgot where she came from, and she hated to see black people get all fancy and try to act white—she had no use for that."

Neither did class-conscious black social leaders who lived on Striver's Row or Sugar Hill, where Harlem's bourgeoisie could approximate the lifestyle of middle- and upper-middle-class whites. But these well-to-do blacks voiced their strong opposition to the influx for all the wrong reasons. Distancing themselves from the black masses, they were inclined to identify themselves with the visiting whites.

In an article for the black *New York Age,* Archie Seale wrote:

> Our reactions toward these white people are not what the whites would expect them to be, because we find that the white people visiting Harlem are very courteous and very considerate, and all around democratic . . .
>
> There are many of our social leaders who resent it from the standpoint that there isn't anything to be credited to the community through these visits because, as one of the leaders pointed out, when the whites visit Harlem for entertainment they do not come in contact with the better class of Negro residing in Harlem. They are seated by and with many undesirables of the community and these same undesirables leave the impression with the visitors that the type of people residing in the community of Harlem are really those whom they meet in these various places.

Carl Van Vechten—or "Carlo," as friends called him—was one white man who shared the rather twisted concern of Harlem's social leaders. Since hearing and meeting Bessie at the Orpheum Theater on Thanksgiving night in 1925, he had become assistant music editor for the *New York Times* and more deeply involved in what was already a strong emotional and intellectual tie to some of the era's aspiring black poets and writers. Van Vechten gained national prominence as a writer in 1926 when his controversial but well-meaning book *Nigger Heaven* sparked the anger of blacks and whites alike. The first novel ever written about middle-class blacks in Harlem, it seemed to say that there were "good niggers," too.

Van Vechten typified the upper-class white liberal of his day. His snobbism and condescending attitude toward blacks is painfully evident in an embarrassing paragraph from the author's notes, written for a 1950 paperback edition of *Nigger Heaven:* "When I am asked how I happen to know so much about Negro character and Negro customs, I can answer proudly that many Negroes are my intimate friends. The Negro magazine *Ebony* once alluded to me as the white man who had more friends among colored people of distinction than any

Carl and Fania Van Vechten at the 1955 wedding of Geoffrey Holder and Carmen Delavallade. Photo by Sol Mauribu, courtesy of Mr. and Mrs. Holder.

other white person in America. With a high degree of accuracy, I can still boast that many Negroes are still my friends."

Certainly Van Vechten's writing, even in the 1950s, was characterized by a Great White Father tone that patronized as it commended, but this "innocent" racism should not obscure his positive contributions. Regardless of what motivated it, Van Vechten's attitude represented a new liberating voice for his time, and his support of black artists like Bessie must be seen within that context. At first, his efforts benefited only a select few, but he had sown the seeds for the Harlem Renaissance of the 1920s, a cultural movement that brought attention to the works of Langston Hughes, Claude McKay, and others. Thus he was an important force in what came to be a landmark in the history of African-American culture.

In their spacious, lavishly decorated apartment on Manhattan's West Fifty-fifth Street, Van Vechten and his wife, the former Russian ballerina Fania Marinoff, presided over a remarkable salon whose guest list traditionally comprised some of the New York cultural community's foremost figures, inevitably including a sprinkling of uptown notables. Having black people on one's guest list was a novelty in white upper circles, so Van Vechten's parties might be regarded as precursors to Leonard Bernstein's radical chic gatherings of the 1960s.

But Van Vechten's interest in African Americans was not limited to their artistic offerings. Along with his deep fascination for the ghetto's pulsating music, Carlo had a weakness for its strapping young men. To accommodate that interest, he maintained a small Harlem apartment whose decor sharply contrasted that of his midtown residence: painted entirely black, its ceilings were decorated with silver stars that glowed pink from strategically located red lights. This place was used solely for Van Vechten's intimate nocturnal gatherings—asides that only a small inner circle of his downtown friends knew about. "It was a seductive place," recalled entertainer Jimmy Daniels, who only once visited Van Vechten's uptown pad but was a frequent midtown guest. "There were no chairs or tables, just red velvet cushions, and some of them were more like beds—well, I guess they were beds. It was a decorator's nightmare, and Carlo acted quite differently when he was there. I don't think Fania even knew about the place."

To feed his public uptown fascination, Van Vechten collected records by black artists, particularly the female singers of whom his favorites were Ethel Waters, Clara Smith, and Bessie. Because 78-rpm discs were easily broken or worn out, he purchased two or more copies of each, always making sure that one was preserved in pristine condition. He eventually donated these records to the James Weldon Johnson Memorial Collection of Negro Arts and Letters, which he founded in the Yale University Library.[4]

Since first experiencing Bessie in person at the Orpheum, Van Vechten had seen her perform on several occasions, and his enthusiasm never diminished. But memorable as she was on stage, Bessie made a more lasting impression when she played jester to Van Vechten's court of celebrities on an April evening in 1928. That week, Bessie was at the Lafayette Theater with her latest production, *Mississippi Days*, an extravaganza that boasted a cast of forty-five "noted" performers and was billed as a "Musical Comedy Triumph." Much of the show's success was owing to Bessie's new musical director, a shy young man named Porter Grainger, who composed and arranged all the music. Bessie was as impressed by Porter's work as she was by his handsome looks, but she did think him a bit pretentious at times. Ruby recalled that Bessie's reaction to Porter's refined mannerisms and sartorial elegance was often a request that he snap out of it. "C'mon down front, now you're with *me,*" she would order.

Although he had a decided predilection for other men, Porter so respected and feared Bessie that he had on a couple of occasions submitted to her desires and bedded her. Of course Bessie had been around the block a few times, so she knew of Porter's preferences, but he had been a good sport and now there was an opportunity for her to return the favor.

Porter harbored a burning desire to be accepted into Van Vechten's social inner circle. It was a privilege the writer bestowed on few African Americans, but Porter met all the qualifications and so it was no surprise that Van Vechten extended him an invitation to one of his elegant gatherings. There was, however, a stipulation: Van Vechten wanted Porter to bring Bessie. "Of course Porter would have done anything to be invited, so he kept after Bessie to go," said Ruby. "Bessie wasn't interested, she had no use for being around a bunch of rich white people, but she finally gave in—because Porter kept asking her, and I guess she got tired of listening to him." Since the Lafayette ran a film[5] before each stage show, there would be time for Bessie to spend a good hour at the party. Van Vechten made it as convenient as possible by arranging for a limousine to pick them up right after one show and bring them back in time for the next.

There were those who felt that Porter Grainger's neatly pressed suits, spats, and walking stick were his way of commanding attention in the prestigious world of the white man. To gain entry into that world, a black person either had to imitate white standards with some degree of success or, like Bessie, be gifted with an extraordinary talent. In neither case would a black person be accepted as an equal. "Carlo pampered people like Leontyne Price," said the late Fannie Hurst, "but he would never think of inviting a Negro elevator operator to his home." That Bessie and Porter were expected to entertain Van Vechten's guests was a given—African Americans, even the famous, were rarely invited to homes of the white upper class for mere conversation. Grainger, of course, could offer Van Vechten more than his musical talent, but there was considerable competition in that arena—Bessie would smooth the way.

Like most black people, Bessie instinctively sensed class-conscious attitudes and their racial overtones, which may be why she rarely made an effort to befriend white people, and when "dicty"[6] black people rejected her for being too much the image from which they had escaped, she pretended not to care. "Bessie would pay these uppity Negroes no mind," said Ruby, "but I could tell that she was hurt inside when they didn't want nothing to do with her — her own people, you know." Bessie could have played the game, for it was well within her means to take up residence in Merrick Park, Long Island, where successful black entertainers and other well-to-do African Americans had established a colony, but she had no such inclination. "She would have been very unhappy with those people and their fancy homes," Ruby suggested, "because that wasn't Bessie."

It was equally difficult for the Merrick Park crowd to relate to Bessie; her prominence as an artist precluded their total rejection of her, but to them she was unforgivably crude; they were made uneasy by her lack of tact and the fact that she could see right through them. "Sometimes Bessie liked to dress up in expensive fur coats that really looked like money," recalled Ruby, "but she never put on airs, not Bessie. She wasn't going to change for anyone, she just wanted people to like her for what she was — a real person. She pretended she didn't care how people felt about her, but she really felt left out sometimes — not by white people; she *really* didn't care how they felt — she just loved her own people, and she hated to see them trying to act so dicty and white."

Considering her attitude, it is surprising that Bessie agreed to appear at the Van Vechten party. One could speculate that it was a paid engagement, but Ruby thought that to be unlikely; she probably did it strictly as a favor to Porter Grainger, knowing how important such social contacts were to him. Whatever the reason, she did go, and she went in style. Bessie also insisted that Ruby come along, which she gladly did. "We still had one more show to do, so there wasn't a lot of time," Ruby recalled, "but Bessie wanted to show these people some style. She really didn't want to go, but she was doing it for Porter, because she was kind of sweet on him. They had a little affair going, but he wasn't too interested in her — not that way, because women wasn't what he really wanted, if you know what I mean. Anyway, Bessie had on her ermine coat, and she had me dressed up in her mink."

As her thoughts went back to that evening, Ruby remembered thinking that this was about the grandest place she had seen. "It looked like the Waldorf or the Astor," she said.

After an elevator ride and a short walk down a carpeted hallway, they were met by a maid at the apartment door. "She was white," said Ruby. "I never saw a white maid before." Beyond the small foyer a sea of faces turned toward the new arrivals; curious guests piercing the smoky perfumed air with stares that blended outer warmth with cautious curiosity. Some of the guests undoubtedly shared their host's genuine admiration for Bessie's artistry, but she could hardly have failed to realize that in this environment she was looked upon more as a novelty than an extraordinary artist and peer.

Van Vechten's own recollection appeared in a 1947 issue of *Jazz Record* magazine. It is at slight variance with those of Ruby and some of his guests:

> George Gershwin was there and Marguerite d'Alvarez and Constance Collier, possibly Adele Astaire. The drawing room was well filled with sophisticated listeners. Before she could sing, Bessie wanted a drink. She asked for a glass of straight gin, and with one gulp she downed a glass holding nearly a pint. Then, with a burning cigarette depending from one corner of her mouth, she got down to the blues, really down to 'em, with Porter at the piano. I am quite certain that anybody who was present that night will never forget it. This was no actress, no imitator of a woman's woes; there was no pretense. It was the real thing—a woman cutting her heart open with a knife until it was exposed for us all to see, so that we suffered as she suffered, exposed with a rhythmic ferocity, indeed, which could hardly be borne. In my own experience, this was Bessie Smith's greatest performance.[7]

It would appear that Van Vechten's memory failed him on one count, for Bessie's singing style and stage demeanor was hardly of the dangling cigarette variety—she didn't even smoke, at least not tobacco. While he was overly dramatic in his description of Bessie's performance, he prudently left out of his story the real drama of the evening. Van Vechten's assertion that "anybody who was present that night will never forget it" was undoubtedly correct, but it was not Bessie's singing that made this party so memorable. The following account is a composite based on the published recollections of Van Vechten and Langston Hughes, and interviews with veteran character actor Leigh Whipper and Ruby.

The maid offered to take her coat, but Bessie's brushed her aside and breezed past the welcoming party into the next room. Barely visible in the oversized mink, Ruby trailed behind her—"It was so big, you couldn't even see me! I could wrap it around me several times," she recalled. Bringing up the rear was Porter Grainger, elegantly dressed and somewhat nervous. As he moved slowly behind Ruby, she remembers looking back and seeing him graciously return smiles, almost apologetically—the smiles Bessie had ignored.

Taking no notice of a chorus of salutatory "Oh, Miss Smiths," Bessie, cold sober at this point, did not come to a halt until someone mentioned a drink. It was her host, Van Vechten, radiating the sort of glee a celebrity hunter might exhibit upon having at last captured his prey. "How about a lovely, lovely dry martini?" he suggested, clasping his hands together.

"Whaaat—a *dry martini?*" bellowed Bessie. "Ain't you got some whiskey, man? That'll be the only way I'll touch it. I don't know about no dry martinis, nor wet ones either."

"Of course," Van Vechten replied. "I think we can conjure up something you like," he purred, and disappeared to fulfill Bessie's request.

Turning to Ruby, Bessie noticed her tripping over the enormous mink. "Take that *damn* thing off," she ordered, handing her the ermine to hold. Thoroughly embarrassed by Bessie's brazenness, Porter pretended to be oblivious to her little scene and began to distance himself from Bessie and Ruby. He sought to blend, as best he could, into the genteel atmosphere of the drawing room as Ruby, hidden behind the huge fur coats she carried, stumbled to the side of the foyer. Because they were only to stay there a short time, no one bothered to relieve Ruby of the coats. "I didn't even get a drink," she complained, "but I had a ringside seat."

Contralto Marguerite d'Alvarez now stood by the piano, talking to her accompanist as guests began to gather around. Returning with Bessie's drink, Van Vechten paused at the opera singer's side long enough to make a brief announcement: Madame d'Alvarez would sing an aria. Then he moved on, graciously making his way over to Bessie. He handed her the drink and she promptly downed it, handed the empty glass back to her host, and said, "I think I'll have another one of those."

D'Alvarez began singing her aria and Ruby remembered hearing it, but she could not see very far into the living room from where she sat. She thus did not notice, as Langston Hughes did, that Bessie was riveted by the operatic performance and that she walked over to d'Alvarez when it was over, slapped her on the back, and advised, "Honey, don't let *nobody* tell you you can't sing." Then she turned and walked back to Van Vechten, mumbling something about her throat being dry.

Porter had been standing off to the side, horrified and embarrassed, but Van Vechten motioned for him to come over—it was time for Bessie's performance. He walked them over to the piano and disappeared briefly to return with another drink for Bessie. She gulped it down and handed her empty glass to Van Vechten for another refill. Someone asked her what she was going to sing. "Don't you worry about it," she said. "My piano player knows."

Porter Grainger smiled shyly and went into the opening bars of "Work House Blues."[8] With her subtle, sensual movements and heaving bosom, Bessie mesmerized her audience. The guests listened attentively as she delivered her tale of hard times. Perhaps not everyone understood Bessie's words, but as they cut through the scented air and novelty became art, they surely understood why Carlo had offered this treat.

Ruby recalled that Bessie sang six or seven numbers, but that is probably an exaggeration. Leigh Whipper recalled hearing only two or three and that each one was followed by enthusiastic applause. There were apparently also further requests for refills, which made Porter increasingly uneasy. Only he and Ruby knew what effect the refills were having on Bessie. It was therefore a relief when she finished a number and announced, "This is it!"

"Bessie was good and drunk when she finished her last song," said Ruby. "So Porter came over to me and said 'Let's get her out of here quick, before she shows her ass.' We got her coat on her and got her to the front door when all of a sudden this woman comes out of nowhere. 'Miss Smith, you're *not* leaving without kissing me goodbye,' she said." As she stood facing her, the diminutive lady raised herself up on her toes and threw her arms around Bessie's neck. Porter's fears were coming true—Bessie was about to fly off the handle.

Almost hanging on her neck, the lady started to pull Bessie down to her level, but she did not get far. Suddenly, she went off. "It was a mess," said Ruby. "Bessie screamed, 'Get the fuck away from me!' and she pushed her arms out, throwing the poor woman to the floor. Then she said, 'I ain't never *heard* of such shit!'—and poor Porter, he would have done anything to be with that crowd, but now Bessie had done shown her ass to all them people. I felt so sorry for him."

Even forty-three years later, Ruby had no idea who the effusive woman was, but Leigh Whipper, whose account of the incident was practically identical to Ruby's, identified the lady on the floor as the evening's hostess: Fania Marinoff Van Vechten.

Following a painful silence, Van Vechten and one of his guests helped his wife to her feet. Surrounded by stunned celebrities, Bessie stood in the middle of the foyer, ready to take on the whole crowd. Porter knew that she had only begun—it was time to get her out of there. Grabbing Bessie gently by one arm, he told Ruby to take the other; as guests—some horrified, others bemused—followed them with their stares, Ruby and Porter escorted the Empress out of the apartment and proceeded slowly down the hall toward the elevator. Van Vechten trailed closely behind, seemingly giving his review of the night's performance.

"It's all right, Miss Smith," he said softly, "you were magnificent tonight."

They had reached the elevator before it dawned on Bessie that she was actually being led away. Shouting "What the fuck are y'all pullin' me all over the damn place for?" she threw her arms in the air and this time almost knocked Ruby and Porter to the floor.

When the elevator door opened, she quieted down, raised her head high, marched in past the startled operator, and sank to the floor in the corner of the car.

"I don't care if she dies," sighed Porter, straightening the tam on his head.

They barely made it back to the Lafayette in time for the final show. Splashing cold water on her face, Ruby and Porter managed to get Bessie sufficiently sober to make it through the show, but barely. "She could work when she was drunk," said Ruby, "as long as she didn't get fall down drunk, but she wasn't singing too well — she'd remember her lines, though."

She muddled through the show and slept it off, but Bessie was now primed for one of her drinking sprees. When she was in New York, she could often be found at Percy Brown's, a speakeasy on 134th Street near the Lafayette. It was a popular meeting place for performers and the kinds of hangers-on show business attracted — people who didn't themselves perform but who seemed to know just about anyone who did.

Bessie took Ruby to Brown's a couple of days after the Van Vechten affair. They had just finished a matinee, and there was time to kill before the first evening show. Again, Bessie wore her ermine — sprinkled liberally with her favorite perfume, a Woolworth's special, Evening in Paris — and Ruby wore the mink. "She loved that perfume and always carried the little blue bottle with her and poured it on her coat," said Ruby. "I don't know why she had us wearing those furs, but they were still in her dressing room, so I guess she figured we might as well look like something." But this time, although Bessie was very much in a drinking mood, the more compatible atmosphere at Brown's inspired an incident of quite a different nature.

Bessie hadn't had a drink all day, but she was in the mood for it, and it didn't take many glasses of bad liquor to get her going again. Most entertainers knew who Carl Van Vechten was, and the story of how Bessie turned his party upside down was already making the rounds of the Harlem gossip mills. Details of the incident varied according to who related them, but the punch line was always the same: Bessie's words to Fania Van Vechten as she threw her to the floor. The story became so famous that Bessie's name soon found its way into the Harlem vocabulary as a code word for "shit." Musicians and entertainers, in the presence of white people, understood such new expressions as "*some* Bessie Smith" and "I never *heard* of such Bessie Smith."

Bessie herself had a hand in spreading the story. She loved to get a good laugh, and that afternoon at Brown's she broke up the crowd with her version, emphasizing how she had sent Porter Grainger into acute, embarrassed shock. Bessie was a good storyteller and an even better mimic. "How about a lovely, lovely dry martini?" she would say, opening her eyes wide and rubbing the palms of her hands together. The crowd roared as she went from emulating the elegant tones of Van Vechten to being the Bessie they knew: "Sheeeiiiit, you should have seen them ofays lookin' at me like I was some kind of singin' monkey!"

She was, as Ruby would say, good and high and in a devilish mood when—having milked that story dry—she stood up and said, "C'mon, Ruby, let's go have us some fun." Knowing that they still had a couple of shows to do, Ruby was beginning to worry about Bessie, but she knew that she had better keep her mouth shut and tag along.

They stepped out into the bright, cool Harlem day and turned right on Seventh Avenue, heading back toward the Lafayette. That was a good sign to Ruby, who couldn't wait to rid herself of the big mink coat. She was struggling in it just a few feet behind Bessie when they reached the small alley that adjoined the Lafayette Theater. Suddenly, Bessie ducked into the alley, seated herself on a garbage can, ermine and all, and let out a laugh so hearty that passersby turned their heads to see what was going on.

Then, with her legs dangling over the side of the garbage can, she swayed back and forth, snapping her fingers and undulating her arms, shoulders, and neck. She was establishing a tempo, and when it seemed right, she turned to Ruby and said, "C'mon, Ruby, let's show 'em!" Then she filled up the alley with her big voice:

> Show 'em how they do it in Virginia,
> Hey, hey; Virginia, do it for me . . . .

It was one of Porter's songs, from the finale of her show, and Bessie delivered it a cappella, letting her powerful voice rise above the garbage and out into the street. Catching the mood, Ruby—her movements largely concealed inside the mink—performed the steps from the "Virginia" dance routine. The crowd grew bigger and some people were moved to join in the song—Bessie had turned the alley into a very special stage, and everybody was loving it. "They came from everywhere, clapping their hands, dancing, and carrying on," said Ruby. "The more people came, the louder Bessie sang. These were her people, and she was giving them something they weren't gonna forget in a hurry. And me, I was so busy doing my dance that I didn't see Jack until it was too late." Totally involved in her song, Bessie hadn't spotted him either.

> If music was action, and action so grand;
> You'd be the leader of a whole . . .

Without warning, Jack jumped out of the crowd and knocked Bessie off her garbage can. There was a loud crash as the metal can toppled and rolled a few feet. Jack stood there, defiantly looking down at his wife, whom he had just reduced to a heap of ermine amid the trash.

"You ain't nothin' but tramps, both of you," he shouted as the crowd withdrew to a safe distance and began to disperse. "People don't have to buy no theater ticket to hear you, all they got to do is come in the alley . . ." Ruby didn't wait to hear the rest of Jack's sermon: "When I saw Jack, Bessie was already in the trash, so I just wrapped that mink around me, ran down Seventh Avenue, and grabbed the first cab I could find — we were used to grabbin' cabs runnin' from Jack."

Nobody seems to know what Jack did or said after that, but it was weeks before Bessie touched another drink.

In May 1928, Bessie skipped her traditional tent tour and took her *Mississippi Days* company on the road for the TOBA. The popularity of classic blues had long since peaked, but Bessie's following remained steadfast. During her spring tour, Columbia released her classic "Empty Bed Blues," in a truncated version that still took up both sides of the record. Even so, part two is forced to a conclusion by skipping four bars in the final chorus. Ruby and Maud recalled that this was a very long narrative when Bessie performed it on stage. A tour de force of blatant double-entendres, the record was allegedly banned in Boston, but that was probably just a promotional ploy. Some works were indeed banned in Boston, but the tag was more often applied to artistic expression, perhaps in order to heighten curiosity and, thus, sales. Here, Porter plays it straight, as it were, but Charlie Green has a field day, especially on the first side, where he plays an open horn and is given greater presence by the audio engineer. Green's wildly humorous trombone comments complement Bessie's tongue-in-cheek delivery, sounding as suggestive as her lyrics. Bessie herself is in top form as she compliments her "coffee grinder" and "deep sea diver" for his expert performances.

At the same session, Bessie continued the mood with "Put It Right Here (Or Keep It Out There)," a song that serves as an excellent example of her timing and comedic talent. "Porter wrote that for Bessie's show at the Lafayette," Ruby recalled, "and it used to get a big laugh when she sang it, because she had one of the comedians onstage with her, and she bossed him around while she sang." Porter incorporated a few bars of stop-time into the song, but the highlight of Bessie's performance is the extended middle section where she departs from the song and addresses the "no good men" in her audience directly. The three-minute limit allowed for only sixteen bars of patter on the recording, but in live performance Bessie stretched it into a lengthy comedy routine.

"Empty Bed Blues" was one of Bessie's biggest on-stage hits and a major factor in the success of the early 1928 theater tour. "You could hear that record all over the South Side," recalled pianist Lovie Austin, then musical director of Chicago's Monogram Theater. "We couldn't book her for the Monogram because she wanted too much money, and the theater wasn't big enough to hold half the people who wanted to hear her. I don't think Bessie had seen such crowds since she first started out making records."

As their fifth wedding anniversary passed, the most one could say for Mr. and Mrs. Jack Gee was that they were still married. Strong-willed and set in their ways, each seemed unable or unwilling to adjust to the other. They fought incessantly and now seemed more tolerant of each other's promiscuities, but Maud suggested that this was only because they needed an excuse for their own behavior. Although they had spent most of their married life playing cat-and-mouse games, Bessie still felt a need for the relative calm that Jack's presence generated: remarkably, she was still trying to save the marriage. In the past, she had often calmed Jack down and restored peace in the household by lavishing on him something of value, like the Cadillac, but such bribery was not as effective as it once had been. Just as the relationship seemed unsalvageable, a telegram turned it around.

The success of the *Mississippi Days* tour had given renewed hope to officers of the ailing TOBA circuit, prompting Sam Reevin to telegraph Jack a request that he put together two shows for the coming season. Reevin, possibly misled by the "Jack Gee presents" prefix on virtually all of Bessie's road shows, obviously did not know that Jack's involvement in his Bessie's business was largely pro forma. Nevertheless, Jack saw an opportunity and seized it. He told Bessie that Reevin wanted him to produce her next show, apparently deliberately failing to mention that the actual request had been for two shows.

Bessie was delighted. She had seen less and less of Jack in recent times; he now rarely traveled with the show, and when he did, a major fight inevitably sent him scurrying off and her reaching for a jug of moonshine. She had on several occasions announced their official separation, but since reconciliation invariably followed, such announcements were taken lightly. Now there was an enticement Jack could not resist; he had always exaggerated his involvement in her business, and this was her opportunity to realize his fantasy and regain his attention. She gave him a budget of three thousand dollars and told him to get started.

For a while, the arrangement worked as Bessie had hoped—*Steamboat Days* went into rehearsal with a cast of twenty-five performers and musicians, and tranquillity, however fleeting, returned to the Gee home. In later years, Jack would claim that Bessie knew all along of Reevin's request for two shows, but subsequent events suggest that he had indeed told her a half-truth and that it was for devious reasons. Three thousand dollars would be regarded as a laughable sum in terms of today's production costs, but it was a small fortune by 1928 black vaudeville standards.

When he heard about the deal, Bessie's brother, Clarence, warned her that she was ill-advised to entrust Jack with the show, pointing out that he had neither the experience nor the imagination required for the task. "There was not a creative bone in his body," said Maud, "so we were *all* shocked when we heard that he was going to produce a show for Bessie—Lord, if you knew Jack, it was just a joke." Ruby attributed Bessie's foolhardy decision to the aftermath of their impromptu alley performance: "Jack was good for getting things out of Bessie. He knew when she was weak, and because of that thing in the alley at the Lafayette, he knew she would have done anything to make him forget that."

In July, Bessie returned to New York where she planned to spend the remainder of the summer recordings and rehearsing for the new show; it was a fairly light schedule that would give her time to also play mother to little Jack, Jr. He had grown into a handsome boy of eight, with light complexion and long, curly hair, but Bessie's usual prejudices against such features seemed to have vanished.

On August 24, 1928, Bessie had one of her most productive sessions at Columbia: three selections before lunch and five more after before calling it a day. Rarely has Bessie given a better demonstration of her ability to rise above mediocre accompaniments; but while one wonders why Grainger picked Bob Fuller and Ernest Elliot—two unspeakably bad dance-hall musicians—for this date, one must also marvel at how well Bessie survived their sobbing clarinets and saxophones. Trombonist Joe Williams was added for the afternoon session, which featured more interesting material, including two selections that became classic Bessie Smith fare. One of these, Bessie's own composition, "Poor Man's Blues," may have been inspired by her memorable visit to Van Vechten's salon four months earlier, but that is pure conjecture. A weave of social commentary, it is the most poignant of all her compositions, and although it is a plea for the "rich man" to open his heart to the "poor man," the song could well have been intended to convey a different meaning. The war had been over for ten years, but Woodrow Wilson's promise of democracy—if it ever included blacks—remained unfulfilled, and neither the Harding nor the Coolidge administration had made any progress in bringing racial equality to "the land of the free." Bessie had no interest in politics, per se, but that did not place blinders on her; it was plain that the postwar boom favored the white man, and Bessie's audiences knew that this song of social protest was as much about racial inequity as it was about economic disparity. Thus "Poor Man's Blues" was, in fact, "Black Man's Blues," the words "white" and "black" being interchangeable with "rich" and "poor." It was a fact that Bessie's audiences understood. Ruby and others recalled that Bessie frequently made racial references, but she probably gauged her audience carefully before doing so, and she never approached the subject directly on her recordings. Her delivery straightforward and purposeful, she sings "Poor Man's Blues" with a minimum of vocal effects. Clearly feeling deeply the song's message, she transmits it with a profoundly moving intensity:

> Mister rich man, rich man, open up your heart and mind,
> Mister rich man, rich man, open up your heart and mind;
> Give the poor man a chance, help stop these hard, hard times.
> While you're living in your mansion,
> You don't know what hard times mean,
> While you're living in your mansion,
> You don't know what hard times mean;
> Poor working man's wife is starving;
> Your wife is living like a queen.
>
> Please listen to my pleadin'
> 'Cause I can't stand these hard times long,
> Aw, listen to my pleadin', can't stand these hard times long;
> They'll make an honest man do things that you know is wrong.
>
> Now the war is over; poor man must live the same as you,
> Now the war is over; poor man must live the same as you;
> If it wasn't for the poor man, mister rich man, what would you do?

Bessie ended the afternoon session with two outstanding sides for which Porter Grainger and Joe Williams provided the only accompaniment: "Me and My Gin," and her own "Please Help Me Get Him Off My Mind." The latter is perhaps Bessie's most autobiographical song; its words became increasingly relevant in the months that followed:

> I cried and worried, all night I laid and groaned,
> I cried and worried, all night I laid and groaned;
> I used to weigh two hundred, now I'm down to skin and bone.
>
> It's all about a man, who always kicks and dogs me aroun',
> It's all about a man, who always kicks and dogs me aroun',
> And when I try to kill him, that's when my love for him come down.
>
> I've come to see you, gypsy, beggin' on my bended knee,
> I've come to see you, gypsy, beggin' on my bended knee;
> That man put somethin' on me;
> Oh, take it off of me please.

The song suggests Bessie's inner conflict: her instinct to hold on to Jack despite all odds against their happiness. "I think she wanted to break away from him," said former Smith chorine Bucher "Bootsy" Swan in a 1971 inter-

The eyes that lured Jack out of Bessie's life: a 1922 publicity shot of Gertrude Saunders with her "good" hair covered. Courtesy of Frank Driggs.

view, "but it seemed like every time they had a fight he'd find some way to sweet her up again. He knew she couldn't leave him — Bessie always wound up feeling kinda sorry for him — but Gertie changed that." Gertie was Gertrude Saunders, Irvin C. Miller's most glorious "brownskin beauty," and she was about to solve Bessie's inner conflict in a most upsetting way.

Although she hadn't written it,[9] "Me and My Gin," the date's other song, could also be taken as autobiographical — Bessie could certainly identify with its lyrics and it was sadly apropos at the time of her recording. Bessie renders the song in full voice and with characteristic majesty, belying reports that heavy drinking was adversely affecting her singing. She delivers the lyrics lustily, with remarkable control and the indomitability that characterized her to the end of her days. Without the pitiful reeds of Fuller and Elliot, Joe Williams's trombone sounds liberated; his attack and tone seems tailor-made for Bessie's robust delivery, and so natural that one might think singer and accompanist were communicating by telepathy.

Bessie's *Steamboat Days* opened at Detroit's Koppin Theater on October 22, 1928. The huge crowds that nightly had clogged up Gratiot Avenue during her first appearances there were now down to a manageable size, and the reviews were still, in the main, favorable. Jack's first stab at production was not the disaster some had predicted, but rehearsals had not always gone smoothly and he had received considerable input from Bessie and some of the more experienced cast members, including comedian Sam Davis (father of Sammy Davis, Jr.). However, commented Ruby, the props and costumes

KOPPIN THEATRE
520 Gratiot Avenue
WEEK OF OCTOBER 22
"Steamboat Days"
WITH
"Bessie Smith"
25 -- PEOPLE 25 -- PEOPLE
MIDNIGHT SHOW SATURDAY

The Koppin, in Detroit, was one of Bessie's favorite stops. From the October 20, 1928, issue of the *Owl.*

looked "cheap." In the October 27, 1928, issue of the *Owl,* Russell J. Cowans had a tip for the chorines:

> "STEAMBOAT DAYS" AT KOPPIN
>
> Bessie Smith's new vehicle, "Steamboat Days," began a week's engagement at the Koppin Monday afternoon with a large audience in attendance.
>
> Assisted by Beulah [sic] Benbow, Sam Davis, Bucher Swan, Lloyd Hollins, Kid Collins, Hack Back and a chorus of eight dancing girls, Miss Smith provides her audience with two hours of entertainment that is embellished with several numbers of her famous "Blues."
>
> Miss Smith demonstrates the fact that she knows how to captivate her audience by scoring several encores with "Some of These Days, Sweetheart," and "Fetch It When You Come." The numbers were vociferously received.
>
> Sam Davis and Bucher Swan carry the comedy roles. This pair put over their jokes with the aid of Lloyd Hollins as the ever-present policeman.
>
> Hack Back is very clever with the ukelele and receives ample applause with his songs and dances. This boy knows what a "uke" is made for.
>
> Beulah Benbow sings "Daddy" in a very pleasing manner.
>
> Kid Collins has some unique steps. His dancing is refreshing after looking at so many tap dancers.
>
> The chorus is smartly attired and go about their work with exuberance spread over their comely brows. The drill is especially good. Just don't wobble so much, girls.

Following successful bookings in Washington, D.C., and Pittsburgh, *Steamboat Days* gave 1929 a lively welcome at the Standard Theater in Philadelphia, then—on January 14—it was on to the Lincoln Theater in Harlem. "While we were at the Lincoln," recalled chorine Louise Alexander, "something happened to make Bessie mad. She showed her anger by marching up and down in front of the theater, dragging her mink coat on the sidewalk. I guess she was demonstrating her independence." Ruby recalled that this incident was indeed a demonstration, "the man didn't pay Bessie when he was supposed to, or he didn't pay her enough — I don't remember which — but Bessie was telling him to kiss her ass, because she didn't need his money."

In the meantime, Jack was busy fulfilling Sam Reevin's request for a second show, which Bessie — for good reason — still did not know about. Rehearsals had already begun at the Knights of Pythias hall, and Jack had picked Gertrude Saunders as his headliner. Saunders had starred successfully as Liza in the title role of Irvin C. Miller's *Red Hot Mama* show during the 1926 season, and she had headed the cast of various subsequent editions, but her most successful shows had been Liza and the 1921 Sissle and Blake hit *Shuffle Along* (which included Josephine Baker in the chorus line). The latter production would probably have secured Saunders's stage future, but she made a fateful decision and allowed herself to be lured from the original cast by an offer that never materialized. Gertrude Saunders's bad move opened the door for the ultimate black beauty of the day, Florence Mills, who took over the role and was such a hit that she became the toast of Broadway. Mills's career was cut short in November 1927, when she died at age thirty-five. The bright spotlight relinquished by Gertrude Saunders was never restored to her.

It is not known when Jack's relationship with Saunders began, but Ruby thought it had gone on for some time before Jack produced her show and that it accounted for some of his "hunting" trips. Gertrude Saunders was the antithesis of Bessie Smith; their personalities and looks contrasted sharply: Gertrude's complexion was light, her hair long and soft, her disposition gentle. She was also slim and quite a bit younger than Bessie — a typical "Miller beauty." The artistic gap that separated the two was equally wide: Gertrude Saunders relied more on her looks than on her voice, which had about it an unfortunate Florence Foster Jenkins[10] quality and a range that could have made her the Yma Sumac[11] of her day.

"She was the opposite of Bessie," said Ruby, making no secret of her disdain for Saunders. "She had light skin and long curly hair and a gorgeous figure, and she knew it. In fact, she thought her shit didn't stink. All she was capable of doing was looking cute and turning up her hairy ass. There was a chick that had hairs on her chest. What Jack should have named the show, was not *Hot* Mama, but *Hairy* Mama."

Jack Gee had financed Gertrude Saunders's show with what was left of Bessie's three thousand dollars. In a 1971 interview for this book, Saunders was asked if she had known that Bessie's money went to back her show. "No," she replied, emphatically, "but Jack could very well have put the money in my show without telling Bessie. Naturally he wouldn't tell me if it was her money, he'd want to act like a big shot." Which, of course, was exactly what he was doing.

"I don't know how he thought he could get away with it," said Ruby, "but he wasn't never too bright and he didn't know anything about show business. He should have known that you can't keep something like that a secret, not with all them blabbermouths around. His show only lasted about five or six months, then it folded up. He couldn't get enough bookings. And," she added acerbically, "his star wasn't strong enough to hold it up."

After a short run in New York, Bessie's own show, *Steamboat Days,* hit the road again—back to Detroit's Koppin Theater, then on to the Globe in Cleveland, and, on March 11, a week at the Roosevelt in Cincinnati. One night, while at the Roosevelt, Bessie and some of her crowd crossed the Kentucky border to visit a speakeasy for a few drinks before the final show. Everything was going well and Bessie was in a splendid mood when she walked over to greet some friends at another table. "This cute young cat who wasn't with our show started giving me the eye, and we started talking. When he saw that I was with Bessie, he pulled out a copy of the *Amsterdam News* and showed me a story about Jack doing well with Gertie's show. I begged him not to let Bessie see it, but he didn't listen to me."

When the man handed her the paper, Bessie looked at the item long enough to read it several times, her facial expression one of utter disbelief. Her friends at the table had been laughing it up, but now they looked at her in silence. Ruby was expecting a major eruption, but none came. Rising slowly to her feet, Bessie calmly handed the paper back to the man, turned to her show crowd, and said in a remarkably controlled voice, "Let's go, it's time to get ready for the show."

She remained silent as they made their way back to the theater. "Bessie cried when we got back to the dressing room," said Ruby, who had never before seen Bessie cry, "because she was hurt. 'Ruby, I'm *hurtin'*,' she said, 'I'm hurtin' and I'm not ashamed to show it. To think that Jack would feature another woman with *my* money!' Well, she didn't know the whole story—not then."

Bessie regained her composure, dried her eyes, and got into her opening costume. "She said, 'Ruby, fix my feathers,' and then she went on stage as if nothing had happened, but she hardly did the show that night, she was so upset. Poor Bessie, I thought she was going to kill herself, but she was a very strong woman and she lived it down like she did with most of her problems. She was *some* kind of a woman."

When the final curtain came down, Bessie ignored the calls for encores, grabbed Ruby by the arm, and went out into the street—feathers and all—to look for a cab.

A cab from Cincinnati to Columbus? Not unusual, said Ruby. "She would do that any time she felt like it, and she could do it because she always kept a pile of cash in an apron under her skirt. We got to Columbus at two o'clock in the morning and spent another half hour running around looking for the hotel where Jack and Gertie stayed. Lucky for her, she wasn't in, but Jack was there and he and Bessie had it out. She was still wearing her costume so there were feathers all over the place. It must have been comical, but I stayed down the hall—I wasn't going to get into the middle of that mess! When I looked, there were pieces of furniture and feathers everywhere."

The noise attracted the night clerk and some of the guests, but they wisely kept a good distance. When the noise abated, there was a deafening silence, then Bessie finally emerged from the room, disheveled and bleeding. The game was over, but neither Bessie nor Jack were prepared to admit that.

Bessie, still unaware of his affair with Gertrude Saunders, decided to give Jack another chance. "She wouldn't have taken him back if she knew he was sleeping around with Gertie," said Maud. "That marriage would have ended there and then, you can be sure of that." Jack decided to abandon Gertrude and go with Bessie back to the Wallace Theater in Indianapolis.

"Jack was looking pitiful after they fought like two bull dogs, but he won, as usual," said Ruby. "He lied so well and Bessie acted like she believed him, but her trouble was, she loved him so much."

But this time the game was really over—their relationship was beyond salvation. Bessie could not even follow her usual pattern of post-battle abstinence; from the moment they got to Indianapolis, she stayed drunk, and they fought incessantly. Before *Steamboat Days* finished its run at the Wallace, Bessie had packed her things and walked out on the show. Jack tried to save the engagement by going against his own best judgment and putting Ruby in Bessie's place: "They padded me up and put me on stage. I went along with it only because Bessie wasn't there, she was very jealous at the time, and she didn't want anybody to sing that was halfway good."

Perhaps Bessie learned the truth about Jack and Gertie's relationship, perhaps she heard that Ruby was stepping in her shoes—whatever the reason was, she suddenly backtracked and made an unexpected reappearance at the Wallace. "Someone must have told her about me singing in Indianapolis," said Ruby, "because she came back, and ran me off the stage." Bessie also ran Jack off for the last time—he returned to Gertrude Saunders's show and stepped out of Bessie's life for good. It would appear that the finality of Jack's departure gave Bessie renewed energy. She finished her engagement in Indianapolis and took the show to St. Louis and Chicago. There she disbanded it and finished her tour playing Pittsburgh, Philadelphia, and New York with a smaller group of Chicago entertainers.

Not everybody was surprised to hear of Jack's affair with Gertrude Saunders. "A lot of nights when we'd be on the train," recalled Maud, "I'd get off to go in the station and get sandwiches, or something like that, and I'd catch Jack and that woman in there, but I never told Bessie, because then we'd never have reached our destination — Bessie would have killed both of them, so I just kept my mouth shut."

Until his dying day, Jack maintained that he and Bessie eventually made up, but others who were around Bessie insist that she never forgave him nor expressed a desire for reconciliation. One thing is certain: their married life ended in that Columbus hotel room.

On April 22, 1929, Bessie took her new, hastily assembled *Harlem Frolics* to the Lincoln Theater on West 135th Street. The *Amsterdam News* hailed it as her best show to date, and packed houses roared approval all week long. By all accounts, Bessie took the breakup of her marriage very hard. She now knew the true nature of Jack's relationship with Gertrude Saunders, and it made her all the more determined to show him that he was, in fact, dispensable.

So far, no voice had posed a threat to the Empress of the Blues, but now talkies were catching on and during her run at the Lincoln, Bessie found herself sharing an audience with Alice White, whose talking picture *Show Girl* was the theater's photoplay feature.

8

It's raining and it's storming on the sea,
It's raining, it's storming on the sea;
I feel like somebody has shipwrecked poor me.
"Shipwreck Blues"

May Day had particular pertinence for Bessie in 1929: although the handwriting had been on the wall for a long time and Bessie at first seemed relieved, Maud sensed that time was not healing the wound. The longer Jack stayed away, the more depressed Bessie seemed to get. "I'd find her in the stateroom, crying. She would sit up in bed, unable to sleep, and she said she was lonesome," said Maud. Bessie might also have missed Ruby, whom she had not seen since she chased her away at the Wallace theater. In a sense, Bessie might well have felt shipwrecked.

Although her *Harlem Frolics* was doing good business at the Lincoln, songwriter Maceo Pinkard[1] proposed a new venue for Bessie. He told her that he was producing a Broadway show with an all-black cast, and he offered her a starring role. To most stage performers, being cast in a Broadway show was the ultimate engagement, and a lead role was the top of the ladder. Such an offer held an even deeper meaning for African-American performers, for it represented a potential gateway to the prestigious, lucrative white entertainment world, and it was sometimes a first step toward Hollywood and Europe.

It was clear that Bessie's brand of blues had lost its broad appeal, although she continued to do well with it, but the talking picture was a reality and it was already beginning to threaten vaudeville. Considering the turmoil of her private life, shifting public taste, and the bleak outlook for show business as Bessie had known it, Pinkard's timing was perfect. His production of *Pansy,* a musical story of college shenanigans, was slated to open at the Belmont Theater on May 14, which left her only two weeks for rehearsal, but there were no lines to learn, just songs. Pinkard had enjoyed success as a songwriter, yet he was totally inexperienced as a producer, and things had not been going well at rehearsals. Although Bessie didn't know it, she was being brought onboard as a last-minute fix, a desperate attempt to salvage what Pinkard had been told was a hopeless situation.

The short rehearsal time was not a problem, because Bessie's role was limited to singing a couple of songs in the final act. She was the star only because she was the only "name" on the bill, and she was on the bill only because Pinkard had come to the uncomfortable realization that he had little else to offer a Broadway audience.

Irvin C. Miller, who was still one of the most successful black producers of the day, attended one of the rehearsals and noted that nothing seemed to be working out. When Pinkard noticed Miller standing in the wings, he approached him and asked for his professional advice. "The only way I can help you," said Miller, "is to knock you unconscious and drag you back to Harlem."[2] If she did not see it with her own eyes, Bessie probably soon discovered that she had signed up for a catastrophic production, but, veteran trouper that she was, she stuck it out.

As she prepared for *Pansy,* Bessie found time for another recording session. More than three years had passed since she last worked with Clarence Williams in a reunion that she kept from Jack, and now there was no longer a need for secrecy. Joining Williams on this date was Eddie Lang, the twenty-six-year-old son of an Italian mandolin-maker who played guitar in the Paul Whiteman orchestra and eventually became Bing Crosby's accompanist. They recorded three of Bessie's most blatantly pornographic songs: "I'm Wild About That Thing," "You've Got to Give Me Some," and "Kitchen Man."

The unrestrained bawdy nature of these songs has been interpreted as an attempt by Bessie to bolster a fading popularity, but her recording repertoire was strictly in the hands of Frank Walker, whose position in the recording field gave him an overview of changing musical tastes, including the diminishing appeal of blues records. It is not unreasonable to assume that Walker, wishing to test the market, suggested the use of ultra-blue material.

"I'm Wild About That Thing" and "You've Got to Give Me Some" were written by Spencer Williams, a prolific composer with many hits to his credit[3] —

which makes it even harder to understand why both songs share the same simple, repetitive melody and neither have lyrics that are up to his standards. Not surprisingly, Bessie seems to rattle them off without inspiration, but even against such artistic odds, her performance is worthy of one's ears. The session's third and last number, "Kitchen Man," is a much better song, a whimsical hymn in praise of a man with special gifts. Filled with memorable double-entendres, it was written by royalty: Andreamenentania Paul Razafinkeriefo, the nephew of Queen Ranavalona III of Madagascar. Tin Pan Alley knew him as Andy Razaf.[4]

A week later, Bessie was accompanied by an excellent five-piece band for an altogether different and—from a musical standpoint—far more rewarding session that yielded two of her finest performances: the commanding, assertive "I Got What It Takes (But It Breaks My Heart to Give It Away)" and a stirring song that would be forever associated with her: "Nobody Knows You When You're Down and Out."

> Once I lived the life of a millionaire,
> Spending all my money, I didn't care;
> I carried my friends out for a good time,
> Buyin' bootleg liquor, champagne and wine.
>
> When I began to fall so low,
> I didn't have a friend, and no place to go;
> So, if I ever get my hands on a dollar again,
> I'm goin' to hold on to it 'til them eagles grin.
>
> Nobody knows you when you're down and out,
> In my pocket, not one penny,
> And my friends, I haven't got any;
>
> But if I ever get on my feet again,
> Then I'll meet my long lost friends;
> It's mighty strange, without a doubt,
> Nobody knows you when you're down and out.

Bessie's interpretation was both cynical and poignant. Following a moving solo by trumpeter Ed Allen, she returns and lends a brilliant touch to this all-too-timely tale by humming the first half of her lines. They didn't talk about "hooks"[5] in 1929, but had the record business used such a term, Bessie's humming would surely have qualified—it is what the listener remembers most vividly and it expresses the song's mood more effectively than any words could do. Had she hummed the entire chorus, the effect would have been powerful enough, but Bessie's combination is inspired. Relating directly to instrumental blues and jazz expression, it exemplifies the innate aesthetic sense and artistic judgment that gave her so much more than a magnificent voice with which to make her indelible mark:

Mmmmmmmmmmm when you're down and out,
Mmmmmmmmmmm not one penny,
And my friends, I haven't any.
Mmmmmmmmmmm never felt so low,
Nobody wants me aroun' their door,
Mmmmmmmmmmm without a doubt,
No man can use you when you're down and out,
I mean when you're down and out.

"I don't think anybody in the world will ever be able to get as much hurt into one song," said Alberta Hunter, "and I dare anyone to say they aren't thinking of Bessie when they sing 'Nobody Knows You.'" The song was written by vaudeville singer Jimmy Cox, whose daughter, Gertrude, as "Baby Cox," growled extraordinary vocals with the 1928 Duke Ellington orchestra.

It is impossible to say to what degree, if any, Bessie's circumstances contributed to her powerful reading of "Nobody Knows You When You're Down and Out," but she had every reason to feel depressed on the day of that recording; *Pansy* had premiered at the Belmont on the previous night, and the morning's papers carried devastating reviews, which the evening's papers echoed. It came as no surprise to anyone in the cast, because the opening night had seen more drama unfold backstage than onstage.

Disheartening as the rehearsals and three preview performances at the Lafayette Theater had been, the opening night gave new meaning to the term *jitters*. As Pinkard had hoped, the first-night audience comprised a relatively well-balanced racial mix, but, unfortunately, it also included the cream of New York's theatrical press. As they slowly filed into the theater from West Forty-eighth Street, these first-nighters were blissfully unaware that six principal players had just walked out, declaring the show to be an inevitable disaster. What remained of the cast, Bessie included, paced nervously backstage, awaiting delivery of costumes for which some had not even been fitted. A series of frantic telephone calls produced six substitute performers, none of whom had much of an idea what *Pansy* was about. They were handed scripts to read and, as it turned out, given a little more time than anyone had expected, because it was an hour past curtain time before the costumes arrived. Given all that, it is a wonder that the show went on at all, and even more astonishing that there were still people in the audience when the curtain finally rose.

The reviews speak for themselves, one writer noting that it was "as if the dancers were meeting each other for the first time on stage." Some of them were. Under the innocuous heading "To Be Read into the Records," the venerated Brooks Atkinson wore at least one kid glove when he reported the following to his *New York Times* readers:

> Purely for purposes of historical record let this bema quietly announce that the worst show of all time was good-naturedly produced at the Belmont last evening by a handful of colored entertainers . . . Until the audience had succumbed to the fatal fascination that always surrounds the successive "new lows" of the theatre, hisses and boos came out of the darkness with a vehemence that optimistic newspaper men expected to see transformed into a Big Demonstration.
>
> By the time the second act staggered behind the footlights, however, those who still remained in the audience had decided to entertain themselves, and succeeded after a fashion. Presently the obese and wicked orbed Bessie Smith was shouting in splitcord tones, that "If the blues don't get you" neither she nor the devil would know what to do. Since she was the only practiced performer in the company, and a good one, too, the audience thereupon howled "Bessie Smith" until the poor woman, with a moon-shaped face, was completely exhausted. Three times she came from behind the scenes to break the shock of complete defeat . . . By this time "Pansy" is well on the way to forgiveness and limbo.

Under the heading "A 'Musical Novelty,' Bad Beyond Belief," Richard Lockridge of the *Sun* took aim:

> "Pansy" is not a show in any possible construction of that loosely applied word . . . It is, with one momentary interlude of professionalism, the sort of thing that children of five might put on in somebody's barn with costumes borrowed from their elders . . . Bessie Smith furnished the contrast by which the least initiated could perceive how far even from amateur standing were the others. She sang and danced with gusto. She did more—she performed. And those of the audience who had waited for her shook the little theatre with cheers. Those cheers kept her out until she was weary and laughingly protesting. But they could not, finally, stave off the rest.

Wilella Waldorf of the *Evening Post* insisted that the audience had come to hear Bessie and that their staying through the first act, in which she did not appear, was "a remarkable testimonial to her powers as an entertainer." Her description of Bessie's appearance adds a detail or two not found in the other reviews:

> Miss Smith, a rather weighty personage of great good humor, sang a song called "If the Blues Don't Get You" over and over and over to wild applause, likewise executing sundry dance steps at intervals by way of variety. Just as it looked as though she might be kept there all night, Miss Smith announced breathlessly that she was tired and that she was too fat for that sort of thing, anyhow, whereupon she was allowed to retire.

A poster for the 1929 short film *St. Louis Blues* bears a poor likeness of Bessie. From the author's collection.

Only Arthur Pollock of the *Brooklyn Eagle* seemed unfamiliar with Bessie. "A stout colored lady named Bessie Smith," he wrote, "sang as if perhaps she had sung somewhere before."

It is a wonder that Pinkard's bomb did not fold on opening night, but on May 16, after three unremarkable performances, *Pansy* finally met the fate Brooks Atkinson had predicted. Even the closing, however, was a minor disaster.

Still owing many cast members money for the Lafayette tryouts, Pinkard had promised to pay them following the May 16 performance at the Belmont, so when he failed to show up, the cast nearly rioted. Regarding this as the last straw, the apprehensive theater management, to whom money was also owed, ordered the immediate removal of the show's effects. Not one to give up so easily, Maceo Pinkard announced five days later that a "considerably revised" version of *Pansy* would soon open. It did, somewhere in the Bronx, where it quickly gasped its final breath.

As far as Bessie was concerned, it was just more water under the bridge. Her Broadway debut had come and gone, and she was none the worse for it—she had been good, the show hadn't, and now it was time to move on. She wisely did not get involved in *Pansy*'s ill-fated Bronx revival, for something more

This full-page ad from the September 4, 1929, issue of *Variety* shows that Bessie's film had a downtown run on Broadway.

interesting loomed on the horizon. While the rest of Pinkard's cast faded into obscurity, Bessie embarked on a totally new venture.

She had long been fascinated by movies, having over the years seen a good number of them from backstage, viewing the reversed screen image in a hand-held mirror. So far, the film industry had not shown interest in her services, but now that pictures featured sound, she was a natural. The advent of talking pictures was revolutionizing not only the film industry but entertainment in general. New film companies were springing up overnight, and all were searching for suitable material. White filmmakers did not have a large demand for black performers, yet African-American entertainers were hard to dismiss if one was going to make a music film that reflected the times.

When Kenneth W. Adams and W. C. Handy collaborated on a short scenario based on Handy's "St. Louis Blues" and submitted it to RCA Phototone, the company accepted the proposal and commissioned Dudley Murphy to direct a two-reel short. At Handy's suggestion, Murphy cast Bessie in the lead. She had, after all, made the definitive recording of the title tune, and she would have no trouble raising her powerful voice above the projected accompaniment of a forty-two-voice mixed choir, jazz band, and strings.[6]

Filmed in Astoria, Long Island, in late June 1929, the seventeen-minute

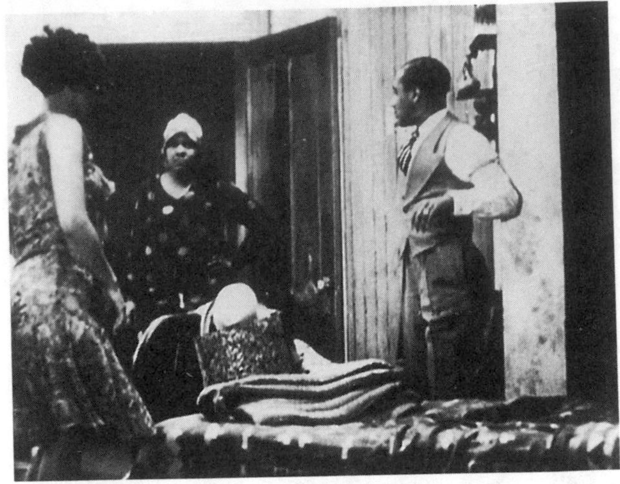

Bessie catches her boyfriend (Jimmy Mordecai) with a new girlfriend (Isabel Washington Powell) in a scene from *St. Louis Blues*. From the author's collection.

short's thin plot centers around Bessie's delivery of the title song. She portrays a woman named Bessie who is driven to drink by her boyfriend, Jimmy, a handsome, opportunistic philanderer portrayed by Jimmy Mordecai. The opening scene has her stepping over a crap game on the ground floor of a Memphis rooming house, climbing the stairs to her room, and catching Jimmy in a compromising situation with a young lady, played by Isabel Washington.[7] A shouting match turns physical, and Bessie, clearly stricken by a severe case of the blues, is thrown to the floor. As luck would have it, she has landed within arm's length of a bottle of liquor, which she grabs and slurps from before launching into a slow a cappella introduction to "St. Louis Blues."

James P. Johnson's piano joins in, and the scene shifts to Bessie leaning against the bar in a crowded, smoke-filled dive. Looking ever so depressed, she continues her song, targeting a stein of beer with her powerful voice. Portraying patrons, the Hall Johnson singers (including Handy's daughter, Catherine) are seated at tables from which they provide an impressive choral accompaniment. Their well-orchestrated voices and an off-camera string section give this Bessie Smith performance an opulent sound that is unlike any found on her records. There is a glimpse of the band as it picks up the tempo for a lively instrumental passage that has patrons dancing and waiters performing gravity-defying twirls with their trays. In contrast to all this, Bessie remains gloomy as she stares into her beer. The place is really jumping—except for Bessie—when the door bursts open and Jimmy enters. Everybody seems to be happy to see

Bessie beams a smile as she dances with her boyfriend (Jimmy Mordecai) in a scene from *St. Louis Blues*. From the author's collection.

him, including Bessie. As the music modulates to a slow grind, they fall into each other's arms and start percolating on the dance floor. But this is not the happy ending it appears to be, for Jimmy, taking advantage of Bessie's blissful state, deftly reaches into her rolled up stocking and extracts a wad of money. With cash in hand and a gleam in his eye, he pushes his victim back to the bar and struts out of the joint. She stares into her drink, continues her song, and the film fades to a sad finish.

For decades, stories were circulated that *St. Louis Blues* had been banned because it was deemed too demeaning and that all prints had been "lost." When one turned up in Mexico, in the mid-1940s, it was regarded as a major discovery, but the film had actually been available all along, it's just that nobody bothered to look for it.[8] Theater advertisements and reviews attest that the film was shown fairly often between 1929 and 1932, and there is no basis for believing that *St. Louis Blues* was ever considered too racy to be released. It may have been forgotten for fifteen years or so, but it was never lost.

In 1950, a group of white liberals petitioned the NAACP to buy and destroy the print found in Mexico, which they believed to be the only copy extant. Taking understandable offense to the film's stereotypical portrayal of dice-shooting, eye-popping blacks, they lost sight of the fact that the film industry had a long history of stereotyping virtually every ethnic group—*St. Louis Blues* was but a drop in a celluloid ocean of prejudice. More astonishing is that the protesters failed to consider the historical value of this seventeen-minute

Saddened by her boyfriend's philandering, Bessie hugs the bar in a scene from *St. Louis Blues*. From the author's collection.

film, which represents the only footage of one of the greatest performers America has produced. Without *St. Louis Blues*, Bessie Smith's body movements and animated facial expressions would have died with the memories of people who saw her in live performance, and we would all have been the poorer.

As the talkies put show business through major changes, Bessie underwent a few changes of her own. When Ruby called to tell her that she missed the fun they used to have, Bessie, eager to let bygones be bygones, told her to come back and work with her. She was still earning a good living, despite the uncertain state of the entertainment industry, but she confessed to Maud that she had not overcome her jealousy. It apparently surfaced whenever she thought of Jack, who was still working with and, as far as she knew, romancing Gertrude Saunders. Resolution was out of the question, for whatever love she once had for Jack dissipated in Columbus—it was now a matter of bruised pride: that light-skinned woman with her "good" hair had triumphed, and it did not sit well with Bessie Smith.

"People would see Gertrude and Jack together and they wouldn't tell Bessie because there was no way in the world that Gertrude could ever beat Bessie," Maud remarked. "But Gertrude did know how to handle Bessie—she stayed out of her way." Saunders denied any romantic attachment: "It was strictly a business relationship," she said in a 1971 interview for this book. "Jack managed my shows, but I never loved him—how could I? He was just an ignorant darkie, but he had a good business head on him, and he was perfect for Bessie; those two belonged together."

The evidence belies Gertrude Saunders's assertion, suggesting that her relationship with Jack Gee was neither brief nor platonic. Jack, Jr., recalled that the affair started long before Bessie found out about it: "I've seen times when Mama was on the road and he'd bring Gertrude right to our house." Maud, who was present when Jack, Jr., contradicted Saunders's denial, nodded in agreement. The hatred between the two women was so intense, especially on Bessie's part, that some people were convinced that one would sooner or later kill the other. "Bessie told all of us, including Jack, that if she ever saw that bitch, that he was running around with, she would get back every cent that Jack ever spent on her by whipping her ass," said Ruby. The predicted fatal confrontation never came to pass, but the rivals did have at least two stormy meetings, both of which were said to have been near-fatal to Gertrude Saunders.

Gertrude Saunders confirmed Bessie's jealousy and certain details of the incidents, but denied that they ever came to blows. Her claim that Bessie could be dealt with verbally did not ring true, yet while she was quick to berate Jack Gee, Saunders spoke of Bessie in surprisingly sympathetic, though patronizing, terms: "I really think she loved Jack, but he didn't treat her right, and she would get violent because that's all she understood—neither one of them had any education, and they just didn't fit in with the crowd."[9]

Their first encounter took place on the road, not long after Jack and Bessie had fought it out in the Columbus hotel room. Because of a flood, Bessie and her troupe were forced to spend a night in a small midwestern town. A barge transported them to higher ground across a particularly deep stretch, bringing them close to the town's only black boarding room. Leaving the barge, they had to walk for about a block through a muddy, slushy street. The barge was moored to a pole where they had left it, ready to take people back to the other side. As Bessie and her company trudged toward the boardinghouse, another group of people left it and came in their direction, headed for the barge. Suddenly, Bessie stopped, put her suitcase down in the mud, and muttered, "You motherless bitch!" She had spotted Jack and Gertrude in that other group. Before anyone could stop her, Bessie started running toward Gertrude, splattering mud and water in every direction. It was as if someone had fired a starter gun, and the race was on, Maud recalled.

Gertrude stood frozen in her tracks as Bessie splashed toward her, and before Jack knew what had happened, Bessie had grabbed Gertrude by her long hair, dragged her through the mud, and begun beating her in the face. Jack struggled to separate the two women as they rolled around in the slush, but they were too active and slippery for him to get a grip on either one. "They looked like two mud pies, you could hardly tell one from the other," said Maud.

Ruby recalled seeing Bessie beat Gertrude unmercifully. "I'm go-ing to make you beau-ti-*ful* for the show. I am go-*ing* to make you beau-ti-*ful* for the show to-night," she remembered Bessie grunt as she emphasized each syllable with a blow to her rival's bleeding face. When Jack finally managed to pry Bessie loose and push her back into the mud, she was clutching a fistful of Gertrude's long "good" hair, and ready for another round. Before she could get up, Gertrude and Jack had made it to the barge and pushed themselves out over the deep water, to a safe distance.

"I'm gonna get a gun and kill you," screamed Gertrude, hysterically.

"I'll make you eat it, bitch," Bessie roared back, "and every time I see you, you yellow bitch, I'm gonna beat you. One of these days, when you're up on stage, I'm gonna be in the audience and I'm comin' up and grabbin' you off."

It was rumored that Gertrude applied for a gun permit, purchased a weapon, and carried it with her for protection against Bessie. Others said that Jack gave her his gun, but Saunders denied ever having owned a weapon.

The second incident happened much later, in the early 1930s, when Bessie was living in an apartment on Harlem's West 133d Street. With equipment supposedly purchased for him by Bessie before their final breakup, Jack had opened a barbershop on Seventh Avenue, near the Lafayette Theater and almost directly across the street from Bessie's apartment. Saunders owned an adjoining candy and tobacco store, and the two establishments were separated only by a rest room, which was accessible from either side.

One evening around closing time, Saunders was counting up the day's receipts when she saw Bessie approach the store. The story goes that Bessie, missing some valuable jewelry, had just learned that Jack had given it to Gertrude. Storming into the store, Bessie came ready for a fight, but Saunders claimed to have calmed her down by simply maintaining her own composure. Yes, she told Bessie, Jack had indeed made her a gift of some jewelry, but she had "given it to uncle," and Bessie was welcome to the pawn tickets. Bessie grabbed the tickets, and left the store.

It had been a remarkably civil encounter for which Saunders complimented herself, but she had been too hasty. Within half an hour, an explosive, fiery Bessie Smith stomped back into the store and, with great drama, threw the pawn tickets into the air. They had yielded some cheap costume jewelry, not the expensive items she was missing. This time there was no calming her down.

When she saw what was coming, Saunders reached for the gun in her purse, but Bessie was too quick. She jumped over the counter, knocking change in every direction, grabbed Gertrude by the hair, and, in an encore performance, dragged her screaming and fighting out into the street.

"I'm goin' to get you this time, bitch," Bessie said, beating the poor woman until she dropped unconscious to the sidewalk.

Hearing the commotion, Jack came running out of his barbershop and tried to intervene, but Bessie was in such a rage that it took more than one man to hold her down. The police were quick to arrive on the scene, and Bessie was given a summons. For Gertrude Saunders, this was the final straw; she vowed never to have anything to do with Jack again. Although she denied it, word was that she did not keep her vow.

It is hard to ascertain how much of this story is true. Bessie's police record, and it surely exists, is harder to obtain than her rarest phonograph record. The above account is the story as Ruby and Maud heard it, secondhand—presumably from Bessie. Saunders's own recollection of the incident, as retold for this book, is far less dramatic:

"Jack had bought this barbershop from someone in the South, at a time when he had money, and put it in storage in New York so that he could open it when the show business went bad. He got it all fixed up beautiful on Seventh Avenue, and I took the next-door store myself, because my mother was having heart trouble and I had to stay in town and look after her.

"I don't know what Jack had told Bessie, but she just came into my store and started to cuss and raise hell. She was so vicious, but I was always calm, and you know if you stay calm and cool you can handle these people, but if you're going to rant like they do, somebody's going to get hurt. I think she had a reason to do the things she did, I guess, because I think she loved Jack, but she had this other man and it was all a big confusion.

"When she came into my store I told her, 'Bessie, go sit down now and calm yourself, this is my store and I'm busy, so you just sit down.' She cussed me out, but I just went on talking calmly. 'We're not going to fuss, I've got to count my change here—these pennies. Want to help me count these pennies?' So she just raised Cain, and when she found out she wasn't getting no fight out of me, she walked out. But I was always ready for her because she was drunk, you know, and she was bigger and stronger than me. I figured I was smarter than she was, I could help her and myself by not fighting with her. I had a reputation of being kind of fiery, too, but I wouldn't shoot no woman over no man, unless somebody was going to kill me and I could get to a gun, but I never carried one."

Considering Bessie's attitude toward Gertrude Saunders and the fact that she was drunk, it is not very likely that she would have passed up an opportunity to duke it out.

By the summer of 1929, talkies were firmly established and the demise of vaudeville was becoming more than a prediction. It was clear that the great days of the TOBA were numbered. Although it had provided employment for many black artists, the organization itself had always been considered second-rate. Most of its theaters had been in shameful condition during vaudeville's heyday, and now they were even worse.

Working conditions, too, had become far less tolerable. Because the TOBA was the only game in town, performers traveling the circuit had for years put up with inhumane schedules, bad lighting, and inadequate or even nonexistent dressing-room facilities. Now the quality of the shows themselves had begun to deteriorate, the public was beginning to complain, and attendance was down. The *Chicago Defender* noted all of this in an article called "The Death Trail of the T.O.B.A."

The Empress of the Blues could still pack them in—even in New York, which had long since ceased to be considered blues territory—but her record sales were falling off, and the talk she heard around town was not encouraging. Still, Columbia exercised its option for twelve additional sides, and on July 25 she recorded the first two with Clarence Williams, "Take It Right Back ('Cause I Don't Want It Here)" and "What Makes Me Love You So?" The latter remains unreleased and is presumed lost. Shifting their focus, record companies were now recording more male country blues singers (for less money) and promoting them almost as heavily as they once had Bessie and her female rivals. This trend, and the fact that most theaters were installing sound projectors, indicated to Bessie that her branch of show business was taking a major step in a new direction, one that was likely to profoundly affect her career.

In August 1929, she opened as a single at the Standard Theater in Philadelphia, but modest as that was, the days of Bessie Smith extravaganzas were not over; she soon returned to New York to begin rehearsals for *Late Hour Dancers,* which featured a cast of forty and was billed as a "rollicking musical comedy." *Late Hour Dancers* began a week's engagement at the Lafayette Theater on August 19. It was such a success that it reopened the following week a few blocks away, at the Lincoln. The Lafayette's new attraction was King Vidor's *Hallelujah*[10]—an all-talking, all-singing, full-length black movie.

It was during that same week of September 2—in a world as far removed from Bessie's as any could be—that the Big Bull Market reached its peak. Before long, the Empress—who rarely read a newspaper and had not the slightest interest in anything that went on below 132d Street—would feel the sting of Wall Street's misfortunes.

Columbia picked Friday, the thirteenth of September, to release Bessie's "Nobody Knows You When You're Down and Out." Certainly it was prophetic of her future, and the way the country was heading, it could have served as the national anthem.

9

I'm gonna straighten up,
Straighter than Andy Gump;
Ain't no use of me tellin' that lie,
'Cause I'm down in the dumps.
"Down in the Dumps"

When panic swept through the corridors of America's financial houses in October 1929, the impact on the average American was not immediate; only a relative few foresaw the long-range effect of Wall Street's tumble. Fortunes were lost overnight, but only by those who possessed them to begin with. In the early months of the Depression, not everybody found reason to jump out the window, apples were still something one purchased from a fruit dealer, and naive optimism delayed the broader effects to come.

The October 30 issue of *Variety* bore one of the paper's most famous headlines, "WALL STREET LAYS AN EGG," but the show went on, and it would be some time before the impact of that egg hit the entertainment industry at Bessie's level. Vaudeville—black and white—was still suffering its severest setbacks at the hands of the talkies, and the clearest victims were blacks, whose only alternatives were to stick it out as long as they could, seek another profession, or retire.

White vaudevillians found new doors opening to them: they could turn to Hollywood and join the competition—often portraying black people—or become household words via the three-year-old medium of network radio. Blacks appeared in films, too, but they were mostly low-budget shorts with limited distribution to black theaters. Network radio wasn't ready for blacks, but the old white team of Freeman Gosden and Charles Correll converted their racist Sam 'n' Henry dialogues into a situation comedy, and had millions of white Americans from coast to coast laughing at them in their new stereotyped roles as *Amos 'n' Andy*. It became the country's most popular home entertainment, and even black people were known to chuckle.

For Bessie, business continued as usual, at least for a while. Between October 1 and October 11, she recorded several sides with James P. Johnson, including "Dirty No-Gooder's Blues," which she may have written with Jack in mind. The lyrics appear to be autobiographical, at least in part, and her delivery has the ring of sincerity—but that was true of almost everything she sang. What is particularly interesting about this lyric is Bessie's poetic imagery: "He treat you nice and kind till he win your heart and hand." That may not be original, but it is pretty fancy for Bessie, and she includes at least one example of her wry humor: "There's nineteen men living in my neighborhood; eighteen of them are fools, and the one ain't no doggone good." When she devotes the greater part of the final chorus to growling "Lawd, lawd," her voice becomes a brass instrument. Johnson is full of high spirit on these sides. Like Bessie, he understood how flexible the blues idiom is, and that it need not always be mournful.

Another side from these sessions is "You Don't Understand," a pop song that in Bessie's reading brims with delicate nuances. It is eminently suited for a study of her style and the artful subtleties she employed to make every song her own. This one was not her own—the composer credit is split among Johnson, Spencer Williams, and Clarence Williams. They obviously pushed the song heavily, for it was recorded five times during a ten-week period,[1] but it remains fairly obscure, and when it occasionally creeps into a traditional band's repertoire it is probably because someone has remembered Bessie's authoritative reading to Johnson's clipped, rhythmic accompaniment. Bessie could give a song twists and turns without sounding contrived.[2]

Even during her marriage to Jack, Bessie had never denied herself a little amorous side trip. Ruby observed that Bessie continued to act as if Jack might show up at any time. While touring with her *Midnight Steppers* show, she carried on an affair with one of her performers, blues singer and guitarist Lonnie Johnson. "It was a constant thing to see Lonnie coming in and out of Bessie's stateroom, and he kept her company on the whole tour," Ruby recalled. "I thought it was strange seeing her messin' around with someone her own age, but they really carried on together." That Lonnie Johnson was a blues singer makes his intimate association with Bessie all the more unusual, but she may not have regarded a male singer as competition. "She was sweet on me," said Johnson in a 1959 interview, "but we never got real serious—Bessie had too many things going for her."

About the only thing Bessie had going for her in the last weeks of 1929 was that she was still in business. The country was experiencing the Big Depression, but Bessie seemed impervious to it—she had her own slump to worry about, sad turns in her personal life. Still, to think of Bessie as a dejected and bitter anachronism during that period is to do her indomitable spirit an injustice. When the downhill ride of Bessie's career is discussed, drinking and waning public interest in the blues are the most common reasons given for the decline, but it is an explanation not borne out by facts. It is true that, by 1930, the blues idiom had lost whatever popularity it once enjoyed in New York, but the South continued to embrace it and Bessie's own popularity continued to exceed that of anything she did on stage. Hers was still the strongest voice in the business, and her style and repertoire had never been limited to blues.

The periodic drinking had indeed been excessive, but never to the point where it threatened to end her career; suggestions that she drank herself out of business are largely based on misinformation from John Hammond, the producer of her last record session—the truth is that Bessie drank less as her career lost its momentum.

While Bessie's shows continued to play in one-horse towns where she cooked her greens in scrubby theatrical boardinghouses and put up with woefully inadequate performance facilities, many of her colleagues moved on to worldwide fame. Alberta Hunter was a big hit starring opposite Paul Robeson in the long-running London production of *Show Boat;* Sam Wooding and his orchestra—who had accompanied Bessie at Smalls' Paradise—made records in Barcelona, and toured the Continent with great success; Josephine Baker, winding up a two-year world tour, could boast over two thousand marriage proposals, at last count; Ethel Waters headlined at the London Palladium and hobnobbed with such notables as Tallulah Bankhead and the Prince of Wales while considered tempting offers from Paris.

Bessie kept up with such news from abroad through the black press and grapevine, but she showed no signs of envy—the world of European high society was one about which she knew nothing and cared even less. People close to her during this period recalled that she did not feel left behind, nor regarded her professional future with anything but optimism.

Her private life was something else again. Bessie made no further attempts at a reconciliation with Jack. When interviewed in 1970, surviving members of the family maintained that the Gees had obtained a divorce and that Bessie lived to see Jack remarry, but there is no proof of that. "Jack was not the type to stay single," said Ruby, weighing the possibility of his having remarried. "He loved yellow women with pretty hair. That's why every time Bessie saw Gertie, she beat up on her. She said she was going to get her money's worth—and she did, almost."

During the first two years of the Depression, Bessie managed to maintain a comfortable apartment in New York, and a housekeeper who looked after Jack, Jr. She started off the new decade with what was to be her last TOBA tour, but it was not at all like the old days: the railroad car had been sold and her salary had dwindled from a peak of two thousand dollars a week to half that amount, which, by 1930 standards, was still considered substantial.

It has been said that the TOBA dropped Bessie, but the truth is that theater audiences dropped the TOBA. By 1930, the rapidly declining quality of the circuit had led to a virtual boycott of its shows. White producers—widely and justifiably criticized for underestimating the ability of the TOBA's black audiences to distinguish between artists and amateurs—hastily assembled third-rate touring companies that regularly had to face humiliating boos, hisses, and walkouts; only the talkies—which now preceded the live shows—continued to lure audiences to TOBA theaters. Another reorganization of the circuit took place in mid-February; new officers were elected, policies changed, and improvements planned. But it was too late—the TOBA was on its last leg.

Against all odds, Bessie's TOBA show, *Moanin' Low,* with a cast of twenty, was well received—patrons remained in their seats after the movie, and reviewers praised the show for its "ginger and pep." But beneath Bessie's energy there lingered a certain sadness: everything she loved seemed to be slipping away from her. Viola, Tinnie, and Lulu, still drinking up a storm, had not taken well to the necessary cut in their allowance and occasionally even showed open hostility toward their generous sister. Bessie lost Ruby again, this time pressured by Jack, who made arrangements for her to join Gertrude Saunders's show. "Jack made me leave Bessie and threatened me by saying he'd better not catch me with Bessie's show any more," said Ruby. "So I had to go with Gertie Saunders, but she couldn't stand me because she knew how close I was to Bessie."

Most heartbreaking, however, was the loss of Jack, Jr. Jack Gee had lost interest in his adopted son, but he found him useful as a pawn in a game of vengeance against Bessie. Though he was only ten at the time, forty years later, Jack, Jr., remembered vividly how it happened:

"One day, when Mama wasn't home and he was living with Gertrude at her house, he came and got me. He told me to get in the car and said that he wanted to take me somewhere. So I got in the car and wound up at the SPCC [Society for the Prevention of Cruelty to Children]. They kept me down there for about two weeks — he told the people that Mama let me stay out all night, which was a lie, and that I wouldn't go to school, which was true. She heard about it, of course, so she came down to the court, and they asked her if she ever let me stay out all night. Well, she raised no uncertain hell in that particular court, she said it was a lie. So they eventually let me go on the condition that she would take me and send me to Viola in Philadelphia. Well, she sent me to Aunt Vi in Philadelphia that Monday, but I was very restless, and about two weeks later I was making my way back to New York. I was caught in Newark, New Jersey, and taken to this home. They notified Pop and he and Gertrude came over and got me at about four o'clock that morning, and took me back to New York. Gertrude hated me, and she wouldn't let me stay in the house, so they let me sleep down in the basement with her brother. So the brother got me up the next morning, made me clean all the halls, and so on, then gave me a quarter to go get something to eat. I seized the opportunity and ran away from there. As my luck would have it, I wound up at the SPCC again the next day, and this time they sent me away for good."[3]

The SPCC sent Jack, Jr., to a home in Valhalla, New York, and for several anxious days Bessie didn't know his whereabouts. Of course, Jack Gee — having achieved what he set out to do — offered no help, so Bessie's anguish continued. Unhappy with his situation Jack, Jr., wrote letters to Bessie, Teejay, Maud, and Maud's brother, Johnny Nabors, whom he liked and who was now Bessie's drummer. He never received any letters back, because, before anyone could respond, he had been transferred to yet another home, a farm in Delaware.

If Bessie made any attempt to get Jack, Jr., back, no one was aware of it; if she wrote him letters, he never received them. At least she knew that someone was taking care of the boy, and she probably also knew that her sometimes nomadic show-business life greatly reduced any chance of her regaining custody of him. Dispirited and lonely, Bessie's tears of grief seemed to have dried up, and all that was left in her was a heightened hatred for Jack. "She wouldn't cry, she'd just sit there, staring," recalled Eufalia Williams, a dancer with the *Moanin' Low* company. "It was strange, Bessie used to carry on so when her and Jack were together, but — I don't know — sometimes I just couldn't believe this was the same woman. That man really broke her down, strong as she was."[4]

During the ensuing months of loneliness, Bessie drowned her personal problems in hard work. When the *Moanin' Low* company played Pittsburgh, Wheeling, and Cleveland, she proved that she was still able to fill theaters with enthusiastic audiences, but there was now a void in her life, and Jack, Jr., was but a part of it. When she returned to New York toward the end of March, she told Maud and Clarence that, although her tour had been a success, there was too much "worry" out there and she didn't believe things would ever be the same again.

Bessie's observation was not unfounded. Tin Pan Alley's latest hit was "Happy Days Are Here Again," but the song's sentiment was wishful thinking. The shadow of hard times loomed over the country: large corporations took drastic economy measures; small businesses went bankrupt; servants were either dismissed or "allowed" to work for room and board instead of salary. With thousands of workers joining the ranks of the unemployed each day, and with those who had jobs saving their money, performers' salaries and ticket prices had to be reduced. The Depression was becoming a way of life.

On March 27, 1930, Bessie and Clarence Williams were reunited in the recording studio after five years. His playing had not improved, but Bessie's delivery was as strong as ever, and remarkably high-spirited. They recorded "Keep It to Yourself" and "New Orleans Hop Scop Blues," a coupling that in better times would have done well, but the Depression was also having a devastating effect on record sales. Bessie's 1929 recordings had been pressed in quantities averaging eight thousand each, a small figure compared to her earlier efforts, but now even that was cut in half. Frank Walker later admitted that in 1930 he saw little hope for the future of the recording industry, explaining that whether to release a record had become a major decision, because the cost of manufacture could easily exceed the profits. Such considerations might have been what prevented the release of "See If I'll Care" and "Baby, Have Pity on Me," two doleful sides Bessie recorded with Clarence Williams and Charlie Green on April 12[5]—the Empress, too, was slowly becoming a victim of the Depression. But Walker may have had another reason for shelving these sides, especially the latter one: Bessie was changing her tune to keep up with the times. She had already begun to consider including pop ballads of the day in her stage program, and "Baby, Have Pity on Me" fell somewhere between such ballads and the blues. Walker may have felt that the new era's hit songs would not be marketable when rendered by a blues queen of a previous era, and the economy was such that he was less inclined to experiment than he had been in better times. According to Maud, Walker definitely did not endorse Bessie's desire to streamline her act. It is unfortunate that he didn't see fit to record Bessie doing such songs as "Smoke Gets in Your Eyes" or "Stardust," which had become a part of her updated repertoire. "Baby, Have Pity on Me" gives only an inkling of Bessie's new approach, but its uninspired melody and lyrics make it a weak substitute.

On May 5, Bessie began a week's engagement in Philadelphia, at the Pearl

Theater on Twenty-first Street and Ridge Avenue. Billed as a "Record Recording Star" and "Originator of the Blues" — an immodesty she herself would not have been guilty of — she headed a large "get-together show" assembled locally by Quintard Miller. Actually she was appearing as a single; her regular song-and-dance routines were simply woven into an existing, flexibly staged show.

Five years of improved recording techniques had inspired changes in Bessie's accompaniments, and Frank Walker had experimented somewhat with her repertoire, but her stage presentations remained basically the same, at least in terms of her style and the type of songs she sang. As the new decade began, Bessie realized that it was time to shed the look that had so successfully carried her through the old one. In what amounted to a complete makeover, she trashed the fancy headgear and elaborate costumes. She and her audiences had loved them, but they were cumbersome, costly, and now quite outdated. The new Bessie wore simple but elegant evening gowns, trimmed, perhaps, with a modest sprinkling of sequins, to give her a sleek look, which she accented with an updated coiffure. Gone were the wigs she had loved to wear. Now she dyed her graying hair, straightened it, and swept it back for an elegant look.

As Bessie opened in Philadelphia, her film, *St. Louis Blues,* began a short run at the Alhambra Theater, on Harlem's 126th Street, "in answer to public demand." Now she could actually appear in more than one theater at a time, but there was noting like the real thing, so, twelve days later, she graced the Alhambra stage in person, headlining a small revue. The ad read "BESSIE SMITH — Herself — In Person." Admission was relatively high for those times, twenty-five to fifty cents, but that did not seem to discourage her devoted followers.

During the second week of June 1930, Bessie recorded two sides that again represented a departure from her previous repertoire. Frank Walker's earlier attempt to boost the sales of her records with lewd material had not worked, so this time he took Bessie in the opposite direction and had her do a couple of pseudo-gospel sides, accompanied by James P. Johnson and a smoothly harmonizing male vocal group, the Bessemer Singers. It was a blatantly commercial foray into the spiritual realm, and clearly a part of Walker's ongoing attempt to find a new audience for Bessie's recordings. The resulting sides, "On Revival Day" and "Moan, You Mourners," have been berated by collectors and scholars who feel that Columbia took its experiments with Bessie's repertoire too far. Certainly, in terms of lyrical content, these sides starkly contrast her naughtiest double-entendre sessions, but it is interesting to hear the Empress taken out of her usual context to deliver mock sermons against a sanctified Tin Pan Alley tapestry. Uncomfortably commercial though these sides may be, they have an engaging quality.

With that session Bessie completed her contractual obligation to make a minimum of twelve selections, and for the first time since signing up with Columbia, she was not asked to exceed that number. The handwriting was on the wall, and Bessie read it loud and clear.

The Depression had not yet taken the sparkle out of Harlem's nightlife. White socialites, movie stars, and foreign visitors still flocked uptown for a good time. One 1930 visitor was the English musical comedy star Gracie Fields, whose report—published in the *London Sunday Dispatch*—received deserved criticism in the *Chicago Defender.* American racism, said the *Defender,* was spreading to Europe: "One evening we went to the famous Cotton Club in Harlem, the colored quarter. They give a marvelous show of dancing and there is a grand orchestra, a real nigger band. It was a place of rather low order and I went there especially for that reason. I wanted to see Harlem in its natural state. There were white women and black men dancing, and black women and white men dancing. If you wanted to dance with a black man you could do so. There were gigolos just waiting to be asked." In a footnote supplied by singer Ivan H. Browning, its London correspondent, the *Defender* excused Fields, but failed to point out that she seemed to have confused the Cotton Club with the Savoy Ballroom. Fields "actually holds no racial animosity," reported Browning, "but picked up her idea of Harlem from white Americans."

In one respect, Harlem *was* changing—block by block, its black population was spreading south, toward Central Park. Since Bessie's arrival there in the early 1920s, it had expanded beyond 125th Street, which was becoming the hub of activity—main street. There, between Seventh and Eighth Avenues, sat Hurtig and Seamon's Burlesque, which at the outbreak of World War I had been a music hall offering beer and wine with its light entertainment. It eventually became a home for Yiddish burlesque shows featuring such performers as Fannie Brice, George Jessel, and Sophie Tucker, and not until 1934 was the name changed to the 125th Street Apollo.[14] That is when it officially became a black vaudeville house. However, black acts were included on the bill as early as 1930, when the Fourth of July weekend attraction was *The Jail Birds,* featuring the team of Drake and Walker with a cast of sixty. Bessie's name appeared at the bottom of a bill. One might wonder how she so quickly slipped down from being the headliner, but the explanation may well be that this was essentially still a white theater and that she saw in the engagement an opportunity to reach a new audience.

A week later, she was back in Philadelphia, headlining her own revue at the Standard with a cast of forty-five, including some well-known names. The Standard's management, fearing that the term *blues* might scare off a

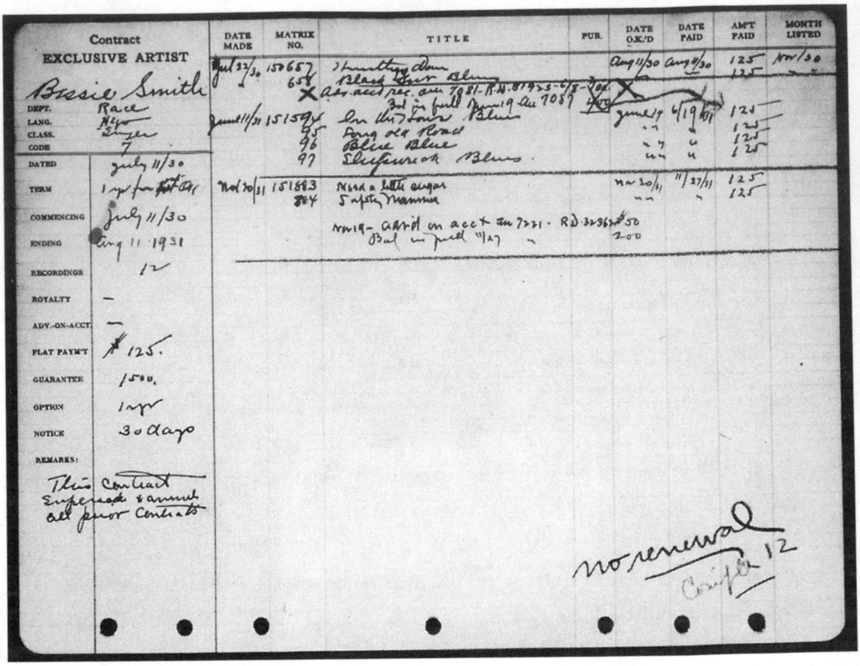

Contract
EXCLUSIVE ARTIST
Bessie Smith
DEPT. Race
LANG. Negro
CLASS. Singer
CODE 7
DATED July 11/30
TERM 1 yr from
COMMENCING July 11/30
ENDING Aug 11 1931
RECORDINGS 12
ROYALTY —
ADV.-ON-ACCT. —
FLAT PAYM'T $125.
GUARANTEE 1500.
OPTION 1 yr
NOTICE 30 days
REMARKS:
This contract supersedes & annuls all prior contracts

DATE MADE	MATRIX NO.	TITLE	PUB.	DATE O.K.'D	DATE PAID	AMT PAID	MONTH LISTED
Jul 22/30	150657	Hustlin' Dan		Aug 11/30	Aug 11/30	125	Nov/30
	658	Black Mountain Blues				125	
June 11/31	151594	In the House Blues		June 17	6/19/31	125	
	95	Long Old Road				125	
	96	Blue Blue				125	
	97	Shipwreck Blues				125	
Nov 20/31	151883	Need a little sugar		Nov 20/31	11/27/31	125	
	884	Safety Mama				125	

no renewal
Comple 12

There is a note of finality to the last page for Bessie in Columbia Records' ledger. Her fee was reduced to the original $125 per usable selection and the twelve-side contractual obligation was waived. Notice the descriptions in the upper left-hand corner; it would appear that Columbia regarded "Negro" as a language. From the author's collection.

Depression audience, billed Bessie as "The Queen of Recording Artists." The engagement was so successful that Bessie was rebooked for August 11. In the meantime, she returned to New York to rehearse a new production for that engagement. It was an elaborate show with the wishful title *Happy Times,* and it would be the last big production she starred in.

These were far from happy times at Columbia Records; the company continued to record its established artists but hesitated to sign new contracts or pick up options. Frank Walker had obviously not given up on Bessie; she was offered a new contract on the same terms as her previous agreements, but the fee was reduced from $200 to $125 per selection. Bessie was back to square one at Columbia, and she had no choice but to accept the cut.

On July 22, 1930, Bessie began recording under her new economy contract. With an obscure pianist, Steve Stevens, and cornetist Ed Allen, who had played so superbly for her on "Nobody Knows You When You're Down and Out," she cut "Hustlin' Dan," a tune structured after the widely performed pseudo-folksong "Stackolee," and a memorable J. C. Johnson tune, "Black

Mountain Blues." The clever lyrics and Bessie's superb delivery has made the latter a favorite among Bessie Smith fans. How can one not be intrigued by a place where the inhabitants are so bad that "a chile will smack your face," babies cry for liquor, people sweeten their tea with gunpowder, and "all the birds sing bass"? This is Bessie the comedienne at her best, telling her tale with an engaging lilt and a fuzzy burr:

> Back in Black Mountain, a child will smack your face,
> Back in Black Mountain, a child will smack your face;
> Babies cryin' for liquor, and all the birds sing bass.
>
> Black Mountain people are bad as they can be,
> Black Mountain people are bad as they can be;
> They uses gun powder just to sweeten their tea.
>
> On this Black Mountain, can't keep a man in jail,
> On this Black Mountain, can't keep a man in jail;
> If the jury finds him guilty, the judge will go the bail.
>
> Had a man in Black Mountain, sweetest man in town,
> Had a man in Black Mountain, sweetest man in town;
> He met a city gal, and he throw'd me down.

When she sings about returning to Black Mountain to seek violent revenge on her unfaithful man, Bessie clearly means business.

> I'm bound for Black Mountain, me and my razor and my gun,
> Lawd, I'm bound for Black Mountain, me and my razor and gun;
> I'm gonna shoot him if he stands still, and cut him if he run.
>
> Down in Black Mountain, they all shoot quick and straight,
> Down in Black Mountain, they all shoot quick and straight;
> The bullet'll git you if you start dodging too late.

The final verse is delivered with a dramatic flair that few singers could equal. As she leaps up to the high notes on "devil," Bessie sounds unusually carefree, almost girlish. She was clearly feeling playful when she recorded this song, and it is very effective.

> There's a devil in my soul, and I'm full of bad booze,
> There's a devil in my soul, and I'm full of bad booze;
> I'm out here for trouble. I've got the Black Mountain Blues.

The record was released in October 1930, with the number of pressings again cut in half: 2,095. Not many years before, Bessie's records had often sold more copies than that in a single day. Her performance on these sides is magnificent, but phonograph records were becoming a luxury that the average

American could ill afford. The handwriting on the wall now seemed etched in stone and Frank Walker gave Bessie the bad news: Columbia had come full circle since she signed on, and now it was once again on the verge of bankruptcy.

New York had become the hub of black as well as white show business, the home of the big record companies, the great theaters, the big-time black producers, songwriters, and talent. Some of the biggest African-American stars lived in New York, because that's where the action was—there had been good reason for naming the city "The Big Apple," but the opportunities that inspired that sobriquet were less apparent by the summer of 1930. Many black stars were not working, because the high salaries they once commanded could no longer be met. Taking advantage of the situation, Sam Reevin, now manager of the entire TOBA circuit, visited New York in hopes of signing up major talent at bargain fees for a last-ditch effort to save his dying organization. "This will either make us or break us," he told a reporter with a modicum of optimism, but his efforts failed: the TOBA did not survive the summer.[6]

With the TOBA dead, Bessie had to make other arrangements for her fall theater tour. Working together, Frank Walker and her brother, Clarence, charted and booked a tour through the Deep South and into Texas. Considering the state of the economy, this was a brave venture. Even in the best of times, touring companies sometimes found themselves stranded in far-off places, but the Depression had made such occurrences more commonplace, and Texas was known to be a particularly hard state to get stuck in. Bessie had sworn never to play Texas again, but these were abnormal circumstances and one took what one could get.

As "Black Mountain Blues" shipped to a reduced number of dealers, those who somehow had managed to stay in business, Bessie and her small troupe of entertainers embarked on their long tour. Their first stop was Chicago, where Bessie routinely looked up Richard Morgan on her first day, but this time there was nothing routine about the reception Richard gave her. "She came back to the hotel with this big grin on her face," Maud recalled. "I don't think I had ever seen her in a happier mood—she was ecstatic and all she wanted to talk about was Richard. Richard said this, did that, you know what I mean. You'd think she had fallen in love—well, actually, she had. Her and Richard were sweet on each other—after all those years." They found each other on the rebound—Richard had left his common-law wife, Lucy, and he knew of Bessie's separation from Jack, so they were in the same boat, and a long-standing friendship quickly developed into an intimate relationship. "He was good company for her," said Maud. "After Richard joined the show, she became another person. Before that, she's stay up and say she had a lot of things on her mind, and I know it wasn't the business, because Clarence was taking care of that, and we were making money."

As Bessie's troupe continued its southern journey, Richard became its new manager. "He was good for her because I think he really cared for her," said Maud, "and he was a smart business man who knew the show life. Clarence thought it was a terrific idea for them two to hook up like that, and so did I."

Bessie had paid little attention to the Depression, though she was keenly aware of the adverse affect it was having on show business. Still, she had felt its sting only slightly, but that was about to change. The entertainment sections of such major black papers as the *Chicago Defender* and *Baltimore Afro-American* were downright gloomy at times; many theaters had replaced their stage shows with talking pictures, others had closed altogether. Unable to sustain her latest show, *The Arkansas Swift Foot,* Ma Rainey found herself touring with Boise De Legge's *Bandanna Babies,* and not doing too well at that. After five disastrous weeks on Broadway, the traditionally successful producer Lew Leslie had to close his *Blackbirds of 1930,* even Ethel Waters had failed to attract the audience needed to keep it going.

Amid all this bad news, Bessie could take some comfort in knowing that she hadn't lost her grip on Southern audiences. From Mobile, Alabama, to the Lincoln Theater in New Orleans and the Central in Dallas, they came to hear the Empress with as much ardor as ever. Still, the big-money days were over. Bessie commanded only five hundred to seven hundred dollars a week for most engagements, and her twenty-five troupers had to be paid out of that.

Even when her success was at its highest, Bessie never really pampered herself, so her reduced income made little difference to her lifestyle. The concealed apron was undoubtedly lighter, and outlandish impulse-buying had to be shelved, but Richard was no Jack Gee in need of appeasement through material offerings. His bootlegging business had not suffered nearly as much as Bessie's profession, and when funds were low on the road, he frequently made up for the losses from his own pocket. Maud recalled that Bessie and Richard had their differences, but—at least in the early part of the relationship—they never amounted to more than a brief argument.

In Houston, Bessie and Richard held Christmas dinner for the troupe. The holiday spirit was somewhat dampened by the absence of Jack, Jr.—who, unknown to Bessie, had now been moved to a home in Easton, Maryland—but Richard's presence seemed to fill the void. Bessie bought presents for all. "She didn't have a whole lot of money, like in the old days," Maud recalled, "but it wasn't cheap stuff. She gave me a very expensive chiffon scarf and a nice bracelet that matched it, and I think Clarence got a coat with a fur collar.

"She was like a new person. Richard was everything that Jack should have been. They got along very well, they both loved a good time, and they respected each other. Richard was very jovial when he'd had a few drinks, but he never got nasty, and when he was sober you had a hard time getting a word out of him. He was a good businessman, he didn't throw money around, but he wasn't tight either. Also, he was tall and handsome, a real sharp dresser. He was perfect for Bessie, he understood her."

Bessie's *Broadway Revue,* as her show was now called, toured Texas in January, appearing in Beaumont, Austin, and San Antonio, and stopping over in Monroe, Louisiana, before heading north. She had not followed Jack's activities since their final separation, but an item in the January 3, 1931, *Defender* indicated that he hadn't exactly become the new Flo Ziegfeld. According to the paper, Jack had left a company stranded in Detroit and taken off with the receipts. With the help of the Koppin Theater's booking agent, the enraged crew had sworn out a warrant for his arrest. Bessie must have smiled.

On May 13, 1930, *Broadway Revue* opened at the Pythian Theater in Wheeling, West Virginia. Booked for three days, the show was so successful that the management asked Bessie and company to stay a week. On Saturday night Bessie, having just been paid for the first three days, started drinking. An hour before the last show of the evening, she armed herself with a gallon of corn liquor and slipped away from the theater. She was not trying to hide anything from Richard Morgan who, unlike Jack, did not get upset by her drinking, nor demanded that she account for her time. It was all perfectly innocent—Bessie wanted to look up some old friends and bring along refreshments—but one jug led to another, and when it was time for her to return to the theater, she was thoroughly drunk. Unable to get a cab, she roamed the streets in a stupor, occasionally breaking into songs or curses that disturbed more than the quiet night air, and when someone called the police, Bessie was arrested and jailed for violation of the Volstead Act.

Meanwhile, the last performance had gone on without her. Angered by the star's absence, the theater manager informed Richard that the show would forfeit a whole day's fee as a consequence. When word of this reached members of the cast it quickly spread from room to room at the Panhandle Hotel, where the troupe stayed. Richard did not learn of Bessie's arrest until two o'clock that morning, by which time the cast was on the brink of mutiny. Richard went straight to the jail and bailed Bessie out. He explained the situation to her, told her to expect trouble from show's cast, and sneaked her into the hotel to avoid a confrontation. Bessie decided that it was time to pull an old trick and abandon ship. "She had Richard wake me and Clarence up, and we all tried to talk her out of stranding the show, but she would hear none of it," Maud remembered. "When Bessie made up her mind about something, it wasn't easy to make her change it. I felt sorry for Richard, because he really wanted to keep the show going. Anyway, we finally gave in and Bessie had me and Clarence go to the theater and pack up all the costumes and props. Then they rented a truck and, at that time, we was traveling in cars. Bessie closed the show and she asked if anybody would come with us, so I went to the hotel and called all of them downstairs, my nephew [Buster Smith] and his girl, my brother [Johnny Nabors] and his girl, Annie Mae, and Jewell Cox. Jewell had been with the Silas Green show and we picked her up in Dallas. I asked them if the wanted to come to Philadelphia, but they wanted to stay there, they didn't want to come with us, so we got in the car, which the trombone player, a little thin fellow, drove for us.

"When we got to Philadelphia, Gibson wanted us to come to the Standard Theater, so Bessie said, 'I don't have my show together, most of my girls left me in Wheeling.' So Laura, Bessie's niece, who was Buster's mother, said 'I'll go and get Buster.' Anyway, Laura and myself went back to Wheeling and we brought them back here [to Philadelphia], Jewell Cox and the whole show, and we opened at the Standard Theater. I don't know where the story came from, because there was nobody else, left except them, that didn't want to leave. It was unfair to Bessie, because we sometimes picked up people that other shows had left, like one time we picked up one of Ida Cox's girls in Dallas."

The "story" Maud referred to is the one that appeared in the black press. It contradicts her own recollections and cites Bessie's own advance man, Billy Tucker, as the source. According to Maud, the advance man was a "Mr. Healey," not Billy Tucker. The *Pittsburgh Courier*'s May 23, 1931, edition reported:

> BESSIE SMITH ACCUSED OF DESERTING COMPANY DOWN IN WHEELING, W. VA.
>
> WHEELING, W. VA.—May 21—Bessie Smith, well-known Columbia Recording Artist of "Broadway Revue" left her company at the point of starvation in Wheeling Sunday morning after having been jailed for violating the Prohibition act Saturday night. Bessie, her husband and brother packed their trunks while the rest of the company slept, and left for Philadelphia. She left without paying anyone of the company their well-earned salaries.
>
> Miss Smith was jailed when found on the street intoxicated, according to the story as told by Billy Tucker. Tucker, advance man for Bessie Smith, billed the show like a circus for at least 75 miles around Wheeling. The first three days were very good and the show decided to stay over the balance of the week.

> Had Bessie paid off her co-workers, allowance might have been made for her disappearing on the strength of embarrassment for being put in jail, but leaving the company stranded puts her in a bad light.
>
> Mail will reach the entire company at the Pan Handle Hotel at 1043 Market Street, Wheeling, W. Va.

The happy ending described in the following week's *Chicago Defender* also did not help Bessie's image:

> ALBERTON PAYS STRANDED ACTORS' FARE BACK HOME
>
> WHEELING W. VA.—May 29—Brother Alberton, a true trouper, came to Wheeling last week with his *Mose from Birmingham* company and found 25 performers, formerly with Bessie Smith, stranded at the Panhandle Hotel.
>
> Alberton gave them all a week's work at the Pythian temple here and gave them transportation to their respective homes. Now in the *Mose from Birmingham* company, which travels in its own bus, are listed thirty people in the show with a ten-piece band.

Bessie may not have succeeded in gathering up a cast in time, for she appeared at the Standard Theater as a single in a show headlined by dancer Peg Leg Bates. The Wheeling incident became popular grist for the gossip mills, but it does not appear to have hurt Bessie's popularity. On the contrary, it may have stimulated business, for the Standard held Bessie over for another week. During her second week Bessie shared bottom, but prominent, billing with Viola McCoy, a blues singer who had launched her recording career on Columbia a month after Bessie made "Down Hearted Blues." Since Bessie had always insisted on being the only blues singer on a bill, McCoy's presence could be taken as a sign of either diminished authority or increased tolerance, but it is also possible that Viola McCoy was the program's only blues singer—Bessie was beginning to distance herself from her repertoire of the previous decade.

On June 11, 1931, Bessie broke another long-standing rule of her own by recording with a drummer. It was a quartet date with cornetist Louis Bacon, trombonist Charlie Green, Clarence Williams, and Floyd Casey, a drummer with a fondness for cymbals, wood blocks, and rim shots. Since the introduction of electric recording, six years earlier, the technology had seen further development and reached a stage where Bessie's earlier apprehensions were no longer justified. Bessie was still wary of recording with drums, but Frank Walker assured her that it would be okay. As it turned out, Walker was wrong, but only because this session was uncharacteristically sloppy from a technical standpoint. The drums do indeed, as Bessie feared, seem dangerously close to drowning out her vocals, and the balance is in every respect poor. Bacon's cornet sounds as if it came from another room, Green's trombone appears to be swallowing the microphone, and Bessie's voice has a shrill sound. Musically, the session fared better. The ensemble playing is occasionally a bit rough, but Bessie delivers four solid performances of superb tunes that she composed for the occasion: "In the House Blues," "Long Old Road," "Blue Blues," and "Shipwreck Blues." This is not the spirited, witty material Bessie so often performed, but these were also different times; Bessie had good reason to sing tales of despair, for the country itself was depressed and she was seeing the music business deteriorate around her.

"Long Old Road" is a bitter song of unrewarded determination. "You can't trust *nobody*, you might as well be alone," sings Bessie, with fervor, but we are not allowed to wallow in her misery, for the singer's sadness is offset by a barrel-house atmosphere. It is an intriguing contrast that has the musicians clearly enjoying themselves and Bessie pushing a gloomy forecast aside to wade with great enthusiasm into the number. In the process, she generates an awesome presence that in the end triumphs over Columbia's uncharacteristic technical flaws. Perhaps no one cared any more. Only four hundred copies of "Long Old Road" (paired with "Shipwreck Blues") were pressed, and seven hundred of the other coupling. With figures like that the label could not expect to break even.

Bessie returned to the Standard for a two-week engagement on July 6, following on the heels of *Trouble on the Ranch*, an all-black musical Western starring Clara Smith and a relative newcomer named Jackie Mabley.[7] Although *Gossiping Liza* was advertised as a Bessie Smith extravaganza with a cast of forty, it was not a cohesive production but rather a variety show held together by a thin plot line. Her booking extended, Bessie was actually in the show for three weeks, but the acts around her kept changing, as did her accompaniment. For several performances it was Hack Back, "The Ukelele Wonder," a far cry from Louis Armstrong, James P. Johnson, and Joe Smith—times had indeed changed.

While Bessie was at the Standard, an enigmatic notice found its way into a *Chicago Defender* gossip column: "William W. Christian, trombonist, has just finished recording with Bessie Smith. He grabs his mail at 800 1/2 W. Moore St., Richmond, Va." Columbia's files show no evidence of Bessie having recorded with Christian, but, her days at the label being clearly numbered, there is the unlikely possibility that she might have made recordings for another company. If so, they were never released.

As the stock market crash passed its second anniversary, even the most optimistic observers had to concede that the Depression was not going to be over soon. Bread lines became longer and box office lines dwindled. Theater business had never seen such a slump; even New York City, the country's entertainment center, seemed to have lost much of its glitter and flash. Harlem's Lincoln Theater, whose mighty organ Fats Waller once had commanded, now reverberated to a different tune as the Mount Moriah Baptist Church; a few blocks away, the Alhambra Theater, which had dropped live vaudeville shows at the beginning of the Depression, announced its closing as of December 1931.

Rumors abounded and some had very long legs. In his 1959 biography of Bessie Smith,[8] English blues historian Paul Oliver states that Bessie's financial situation at one time was so dire that she "came to selling chewing gum and candy in theater aisles." Another story in Oliver's book is equally fanciful: "Now Bessie was obliged to accept parts in seedy night-club cabarets where, dressed in a long gingham dress, an apron and a kerchief tied about her head to represent that evergreen of American sentiment, the lovable Negro 'mammy,' she sang 'coon songs.' At other times she was submerged in the obscurity of cellar clubs to sing pornographic numbers to the habitués of 'drag parties,' her blues forgotten." John Hammond may well have been Oliver's source,[9] for he gave an almost identical description in an interview for this book. "That's not Bessie," said Ruby after hearing the tape. "The only night clubs she sang in were in Philly and here in New York, and she would never, *never* wear her mammy costume when she was doing that—you can be sure of that. And what are those songs, coon songs? Oh, my God! Bessie never sang those type of songs in her life." Did she sell candy in theater aisles? "Are you kidding?" Ruby exclaimed. "Bessie never had to do anything but sing, baby. Nobody but God could have stopped Bessie from singing, you can believe that, because that was all she knew how to do, and she always did it so much better than anybody else." Indeed, Bessie wore her mammy outfit only in earlier years, when she was doing skits in the South; she had long since abandoned them when Hammond heard her in person. In the early 1930s, Bessie was even trying to get away from blues and build up a more modern repertoire. As for her financial situation, she had lowered her fees considerably, and her voice was affected at times by her hard living, but Richard Morgan's business continued to thrive. Even at its worst, Bessie's voice remained commanding and her legions of fans remained loyal—there was always some place for her to display her talent.

As the Depression entered its third and most devastating year, Bessie's most lucrative offers came from Philadelphia, which meant that she could spend more time at home and less money on travel expenses. She became a regular at the Standard, Pearl, and Forrest theaters, often accompanied by a band led by Maud Smith's brother, Johnny Nabors. The Depression had slowed Bessie down and given her career a bit of a U-turn, but she still fared better than many of her colleagues. Although her direct income from Columbia Records had always been paltry, Bessie owed much of her success to the fact that she was heard on a major, widely distributed label, but that, too, was about to change. On November 20, 1931, when she went to New York to record two sides, Frank Walker confirmed what she had foreseen: these would be her last for Columbia, the label was dropping her.

Almost nine years had passed since Bessie signed her first recording contract. It had been a mutually beneficial relationship: the label thrust Bessie to stardom, and her recordings established Columbia's successful "race" division. One can imagine what the mood must have been as Bessie and Frank Walker now ended their long business relationship. There was also a sense of déjà vu, for as it had been in the beginning, so it was now: Clarence Williams at the piano.

If the technical deficiency of Bessie's previous session had bothered the people at Columbia, they more than made up for it now, for, of all her Columbia recordings, none reproduced her voice with as much clarity and presence as "Safety Mama" and "Need a Little Sugar in My Bowl." There is a trace of wear in Bessie's voice, but her phrasing and timing remain stunningly intact on "Need a Little Sugar in My Bowl," a song featuring the kind of sly double entendres her theater audiences loved. Nina Simone included the song in her act forty years later, changing the title to "Want a Little Sugar in My Bowl" and listing herself as the composer. Actually, the song was originally credited to three writers, including Clarence Williams. "Safety Mama" is one of Bessie's own tunes, a well-structured song that offers advice on how to handle a man. As things stood, Bessie probably did not expect these sides to be released, but some pressings were shipped to dealers just ten days later. Columbia seemed to have instituted a supply-on-demand policy, for an unusual order accompanied the masters to Columbia's pressing plant: "Ship parcel post only. Manufacture against shipping orders only." Times had indeed changed.

With these two selections, Bessie had completed only eight of the twelve sides needed to meet her contractual obligation, but there would be no further recording—Columbia found it prudent to pay her five hundred dollars and cancel the agreement. In all her years with Columbia, Bessie never had a royalty arrangement, thus her total recording fee income amounted to a mere $28,575[10]—a fraction of what many young performers of lesser talent today receive on signing a contract.

Although there was widespread belief that the recording industry had seen its last days, Bessie found that the Depression had not killed the demand for her brand of entertainment. She spent the last three weeks of December on the road, arriving back home in time for New Year's Eve, which she and Richard celebrated with Clarence and Maud. "She was beginning to look a little tired," Maud recalled. "I don't think it was from working too hard, I just think she felt depressed because things happened so fast — it wasn't like the old days. We all suffered. Clarence understood it better, I mean what was happening, so he wasn't going to let it get to him. Bessie . . . well, she had those sisters to take care of, and they didn't understand anything, it was just gimme, gimme, gimme — you know what I mean?"

On February 1, 1932, Bessie opened as a single at the Grand in Chicago, the scene of many past triumphs. A reviewer from the *Pittsburgh Courier* was there:

> BESSIE SMITH AND "GANG" CLICK AT GRAND THEATRE
>
> Bessie Smith, herself, is back in town at the Grand theatre. And we don't mean maybe. She's singing "Please Don't Talk About Me When I'm Gone" and "Safety Woman Looking for a Safety Man" ["Safety Mama"]. Bessie has a real humane personality, and when she "puts it her way" it's really put over. She's a scream when she takes full possession of her 200 pounds averdupois [sic] and steps around like a finale-hopper on a ballroom floor.

The review did not mention that Bessie's week at the Grand netted her only two hundred dollars, or that a local critic — a professed fan of Bessie's — attributed the packed theater to the screen offering *Possessed,* starring Joan Crawford and Clark Gable.

Pianist Art Hodes, a devoted fan, described one of Bessie's Chicago appearances in the September 1947 issue of *Jazz Record:*

> Now comes the big hush. Just the piano goin'. It's the blues. Somethin' tightens up in me. Man, what will she look like? I ain't ever seen her before. Then I hear her voice and, gosh, I know this is it . . . my lucky day. I'm hearing the best and I'm seeing her, too. There she is. Resplendent is the word, the only one that can describe her. Of course, she ain't beautiful, although she is to me. A white shimmering evening gown, a great big woman and she completely dominates the stage and the whole house when she sings the "Yellow Dog Blues."
>
> There's no explainin' her singing, her voice. She don't need a mike; she don't use one. I ain't sure if them damn nuisances had put in their appearance that year. Everybody can hear her. This gal sings from the heart. She never let me get away from her once. As she sings she walks slowly around the stage. Her head, sort of bowed. From where I'm sittin' I'm not sure whether she even has eyes open. On and on, number after number, the same hush, the great performance, the deafening applause. We won't let her stop.

Following a spring tour through Alabama and Louisiana, Bessie and Richard went to New York, where they stayed at the house of Jack's mother, who obviously was an open-minded woman. "My grandmother liked Bessie," said Ruby, "and she never blamed her for her and Jack breaking up. I don't know if she liked Richard much, but she put up with him because of Bessie." The Depression had put a damper on Harlem's nightlife, but people still partied, only now the fun and frolic was more likely to be a rent party at somebody's apartment. Many landmark commercial establishments were feeling the squeeze: several Harlem clubs had already folded; rumor had it that the Lafayette Theater, Connie's Inn, and the Cotton Club were about to close, and even the Palace Theater, in the heart of Times Square, had seen it necessary to reduce ticket prices.

Bessie may have worried over such things as club and theater closings, but she had more personal concerns, a major one being that she had lost track of Snooks. He was still at the home in Easton, Maryland, and he had tried the best he could to locate Bessie, but letters went unanswered and Jack Gee claimed not to know her whereabouts. Snooks felt a glimmer of hope when he dashed off a note to Frank Walker. "They sent a letter back saying that she wasn't with Columbia Records anymore," he recalled, "and told me her address was 1139 Kater Street, but she wasn't even living in Philly then—I think her and Richard had moved to New York. I don't know if Mr. Walker told her how to find me, but they moved me, about a month later, to another home in Maryland, in St. Martin, so she couldn't find me either, I guess."

There was another problem Bessie had to face. Lucy, Richard's former common-law wife, wanted him back. Ruby had never been fond of her Uncle Jack, but neither did she care much for Richard, whom she viewed as an adversary, someone who had come between her and Bessie. "I know he didn't break them up," she said, "but she might have gone back with Jack if Richard wasn't always there."

Ruby had not worked with Bessie since Jack put her with the Gertie Saunders show, and Bessie was still treating her somewhat frostily whenever they saw each other at her former mother-in-law's house. Ruby blamed Richard for that and all the recent changes in her life—he was the reason she could no longer get into mischief with Bessie, and he had reduced the happiest days she had ever known to mere memories. It may well have been Ruby's jealousy at play, but she insisted that Richard never really let go of Lucy. "When Bessie used to come to New York to record," she said, "half of the time Bessie would not see him. He would go off somewhere, which we later found out was to his wife. He was a married man with three children, the youngest was five months old. He was running from Bessie to his wife and begging Bessie to hurry back to Philadelphia. We would not have been any the wiser if it had not been for his wife. She had heard about Bessie and her husband and found out Bessie was staying with my grandmother. One night, after we had finished supper, the doorbell rang. I answered and here stood a young woman. She once had been an attractive woman, but she had that tired, worried look that every woman gets when she has a man that is too much for her. She said to me, 'Are you Miss Bessie Smith?' I said, 'No, but I will call her,' which I did, and invited the woman in. I gave her a chair and called Bessie. She looked at Bessie a long time and said, 'I am surprised that you are the one, I thought this young lady,' she meant me, 'was the one. Why, you are older than I am.' That did it. Bessie got mad and said to the woman, 'Who are *you,* sad-looking bitch? The census taker? Outside of my age, do you want to know if my mother was there when it happened? Enough? or do you want more?' Bessie scared the poor woman to death. But I guess she had made up her mind, come high water or low, she was going to have her say, so she said, 'I'm Richard's wife,' and she stopped and looked at Bessie pitifully to see what impression it would have on her. After seeing none, she went on and said, 'I have three children, the youngest is only a five-months'-old baby, and they need their daddy, Miss Smith. You don't love my husband and you are in a position to have any man you want. So please, for God's sake, give me back my husband, we need him.'

"I thought that would move Bessie, but hell no, not in the least. Bessie said, 'So what?' took the trembling woman by the arm, led her to the door, and said, after she opened the door, 'Take the bullshit out of here and find your husband and bend his ear, 'cause I don't want to hear it.' I watched the woman going up the street until she got out of sight. She looked as if she did not care what happened to her, and I asked Bessie, 'How would you feel if you heard later that that woman committed suicide, wouldn't your conscience bother you? Would you be able to sleep again?' Bessie said, of course I would sleep like a baby. If it hadn't been me it would have been some other woman.' "

Maud recalled that Lucy did, indeed, pay a visit to Bessie, who made it clear that no one was forcing him to stay with her, but she did not believe that Richard ever returned to his common-law wife, even briefly. "I think Ruby made that up, because she would have done anything to get Bessie back into her own family," said Maud. Lucy died not long after that. "I think she grieved herself to death, just as my uncle Richard grieved himself over Bessie," Lionel Hampton observed.

Bessie and Richard had long since returned to Philadelphia in November 1932, when Snooks finally succeeded in getting a letter to her. He wrote that he was back in New York with Jack and that he wanted to be with her in

Philadelphia. Bessie immediately mobilized a delegation that included Richard, Maud, Teejay, and Maud's brother, Johnny Nabors. They paid Jack a surprise visit in New York and returned to Philadelphia with the boy. Now Bessie was truly happy. "You could see it in her face, hear it in her voice," said Maud. She closed out the year at Philadelphia's Lincoln Theater, sharing top billing in *Hot Stuff of 1933* with the popular vaudeville team of Butterbeans and Susie.

Nineteen thirty-two had been Bessie's leanest year since achieving stardom, and the outlook for 1933 was worse. In March she took second billing at Harlem's Lafayette Theater, which had stayed in business despite gloomy predictions. It was her first New York appearance in two years, and she was almost guaranteed an audience because the headliner was Jules Bledsoe, a popular baritone who five years earlier had originated the role of Joe in the Broadway musical *Show Boat* at the Ziegfeld Theater. "That didn't hurt Bessie none," said Ruby, "because Bledsoe was very popular—a fine-looking man with a beautiful deep voice. Bessie wasn't trying to do blues, like she used to do, because she knew that's not what most people wanted anymore. Jules Bledsoe drew a different kind of crowd than Bessie, more sophisticated, so it was actually good for her to get a new audience. She probably would have worked with anybody at that time, because times were bad, and you took what you could get."

Although she was now making far less money and her career was floundering somewhat, Bessie continued to lead a fairly active professional life through 1932, touring and make local theater appearances. However, by the spring of 1933 the nation's inclement economic situation had worsened, and Bessie began to feel its effects in earnest; she received fewer bookings, and her fees were almost back to where they had been before she signed with Columbia. Consequently, she found herself spending more time at home in Philadelphia, which is where John Hammond, a wealthy, well connected twenty-three-year-old jazz enthusiast, looked her up and offered to record her.[11]

In the decades that followed, Hammond would become a powerful mover in the jazz business, a man credited with more talent "discoveries" than the facts bear out. But when he claimed to have had a special affinity for Bessie, he was probably speaking the truth. "I heard Bessie for the first time in 1927, at the Alhambra Theater," he said, "and that's when I realized that there was more to jazz than instrumental improvisation." Bessie actually did not appear at the Alhambra until 1931, but he might have heard her at the Lafayette in 1927. There were so many made-up stories about John Hammond over the years that it sometimes seemed difficult even for him to distinguish between fact and fiction. It is a fact that he contributed significantly to jazz for about three decades and that his actual accomplishments alone would have secured for him a prominent place in the history of jazz, but he was prone to embellish his input.

Somewhere along the line, all those stories of discoveries and charitable acts gave Hammond a "Great White Father" image, which he seemed to enjoy. Many believed that he had done more for African Americans than any other white individual in the jazz community; that was not true, but Hammond never discouraged such stories. Indeed, he often contributed to the myth, either by allowing stories of his alleged deeds to remain in circulation or by adding slight coloration, such as when he described his 1933 meeting with Bessie in Philadelphia.

She was, he claimed, working as a singing hostess of a speakeasy on Philadelphia's Ridge Avenue, the implication being that he more or less rescued her from a demeaning job. The truth is that Bessie actually did work in a Ridge Avenue club, Art's Café, but not as a hostess, and not until the summer of 1936. Art's was not a speakeasy, Maud recalled, "just a nice little club that nobody had be ashamed to work in."

"She had given up all hope for a comeback, and was drinking more than ever," Hammond wrote in a 1951 article for *Down Beat* magazine. "I was able to persuade the timid officials of the bankrupt American Columbia company to arrange a session with Bessie for their Okeh 'race' label. She agreed to come to New York to do the record date, but refused point blank to record the type of blues that had made her famous. Her argument was that people didn't want to be depressed by blues, that they wanted something in a jazz vein." In his 1977 autobiography, he quotes Bessie as saying: "Nobody wants to hear blues no more. Times is hard. They want to hear novelty songs." Though she probably did not suggest novelty songs, Bessie was clearly trying to move with the times.

In a 1971 interview for this book, Hammond said that he had persuaded Bob Miller, Okeh's recording director, to give him free use of the studio and engineers if he agreed to pay the artists out of his own pocket. Okeh had been purchased by Columbia to serve as its lower-priced label, and he was given the go-ahead to cut four sides for which Bessie agreed to accept a flat fee of $37.50 each, with no royalties. That is plausible, for she was probably eager to record again and she had always regarded recordings as promotional tools rather than a source of direct income; from that perspective, a low fee was inconsequential. A slightly different account appears in Hammond's autobiography, where he states that Bessie "was not wanted abroad," and therefore could not be recorded under a contract he had with an English company. "Still," he adds, enigmatically, "Bessie Smith was a star. She had to be paid even though she had made no records since 1931 . . . I offered to pay her way to New York, I could offer no more." Bessie was drunk, broke, and "amazed to find that someone actually wanted to record her again," he wrote. "She didn't think anyone loved her any more, and I don't think she really believed me." Ruby and Maud reacted to Hammond's statements with disbelief and amusement. Bessie, they insisted, was never so broke that she couldn't afford a train fare to New York. "She probably told him she didn't have any money," Ruby suggested, "but that was just to get him to cough it up—we all can play that little number."

Neither the declining popularity of the blues, the shift from live to mechanical entertainment, nor prevailing national economic conditions ever left Bessie without money; she still commanded a decent, if not extravagant, fee for her work, and Richard Morgan kept his under-the-table liquor business going. Bessie may well have viewed Hammond's offer as an empty promise, for she knew that record sales were abysmal and that the depressed state of the record industry had not improved in the year and a half since she left Columbia. She probably did not know that the record companies were devouring each other through corporate consolidation: Victor had been absorbed by the Radio Corporation of America; Brunswick was acquired by Warner Brothers; and the Majestic Radio Corporation, seeking an established worldwide distributorship, bought the bankrupt Columbia company, which earlier had acquired the Okeh label.

Bessie's Okeh session was scheduled for the end of November 1933. In the meantime, Hammond made a trans-Atlantic trip to finalize plans for bringing an all-black satirical revue to London, with music by Duke Ellington. Bessie spent the summer at home, making only a couple of local appearances. In September, she played Pittsburgh's Roosevelt Theater as a single and did so well that management extended her one-day engagement to three weeks—she could still pack them in. On September 22, while at the Roosevelt, Bessie made a Friday evening guest appearance at an Emancipation Day celebration in Mapleview Park, near Little Washington. She was no longer with Columbia, nor had she signed with another label, but her billing read: "Bessie Smith and her Victor Recording Orchestra." It had a nice ring to it.

Performing from an improvised canvas-enclosed stage, Bessie sang several songs to which the sizeable outdoor audience was highly receptive, but the event turned out to be more memorable than anyone had intended. After delivering her concluding number and taking her bows, Bessie started to walk off stage. To the approving roar of the crowd, she sashayed to the side of the small makeshift stage and began to descend a rickety set of steps. Turning to acknowledge the applause, she lost her footing and grabbed a pole that just happened to support the canvas roof. This brought the entire stage covering down on her and the orchestra, creating a scene reminiscent of that which eight years earlier had ended the tent experiment at Columbia's studio. This time, calamity turned to comedy as Bessie—seasoned trouper that she was—emerged from beneath the canvas and went to work uncovering the band. That done, she faced her audience once more and announced that things had gone better at rehearsal.

Bessie spent October at home in Philadelphia, where Richard's bootleg liquor business still brought in money. That compensated for her increasingly sporadic work schedule, but the extra income was now threatened by the long-awaited repeal of Prohibition, which was only a month away. The election victory of Franklin D. Roosevelt was already changing America's drinking habits; even members of the Women's Christian Temperance Union could—were they so inclined—drown their tears in a hearty legal brew or glass of wine at a local "beer garden."[12] The noble experiment had backfired, boosted alcohol consumption, and laid the foundation for gangster empires that would plague law enforcement for decades to come.

The happy tune of the day was "We're in the Money," but prosperity was as yet only on a dim hope on the horizon. Still, things were already looking up for black entertainers: radio network executives were beginning to eye black talent, and Hollywood was learning that black films need not be for African Americans only; Ethel Waters, having scored a tremendous hit in Irving Berlin's *As Thousands Cheer,* signed a radio contract for a reputed $1,250 per broadcast, and Dudley Murphy—the man who in 1929 directed Bessie in *St. Louis Blues*—was enjoying a successful first run of his latest film, *Emperor Jones,* starring Paul Robeson.

Bessie, too, had reason for optimism. She opened at Harlem's Lafayette Theater on November 18, sharing feature billing with comedian Dusty Fletcher and Mandy Lou, a Fred Waring singer who billed herself as "The Greatest Colored Radio Star." It wasn't top billing for Bessie, but it was more than she had been getting in the Big Apple for quite a while.

Then, on November 24, 1933, John Hammond's promised recording session took place. After an absence of two years and four days, Bessie returned to the studio with an all-star interracial band, a voice that had lost nothing in the intervening years, and the outlook for a reasonably bright future.

10

Picked up my bags, baby, and I tried it again,
Picked up my bags, baby, and I tried it again;
I got to make it, I've got to find the end.
"Long Old Road"

When Bessie headed downtown on the subway that Friday morning in November 1933, she could hardly have expected that the records she was about to make for Okeh would do much for her career. But the mere fact that she had been asked to make them was a sign that times were improving. People had, after all, been saying that, with Roosevelt in the White House, things would soon get better, and the anticipation continued to have a good effect on the nation's morale. For the first time in a long while, people were optimistic, and so were some businesses; Radio City Music Hall showed its confidence by accepting checks dated three months in advance.

Things seemed to be looking up for Bessie. Her engagement at the Lafayette had been encouraging, and she was scheduled to open at the Lincoln in Philadelphia on her return from New York the following day. Richard was also negotiating for her to headline a special Christmas show at the Harlem Opera House.[1] The downward momentum of Bessie's career had clearly gone into reverse gear.

Columbia and Okeh, under new ownership, now had studios downtown at 55 Fifth Avenue, where the entire company was housed on two floors. This being his first vocal date, John Hammond was nervous, especially since the artist was someone whom he considered to be without peer. It had been his intention to use drummer Big Sid Catlett on the session, but Bessie's previous experience of recording with drums had only strengthened her original resolve never to include them in her studio accompaniments. She argued over it with Hammond during the week and got her way; who was Hammond to argue with the Empress? At her suggestion, Coot Grant and "Socks" Wilson (Leola B. and Wesley Wilson), a husband-and-wife vaudeville team with a long list of Paramount, Okeh, and Columbia records to their credit, were commissioned to write four tunes, none of which would qualify as a novelty song, but neither were they blues. In later years, Hammond said that the songs in his opinion "do not compare with Bessie's own material of the 1920s" and that the band "lacked the special qualities essential to good accompanists," but many critics and collectors disagree, declaring this session to have been one of her finest. It also had a sound quite different from any heard on Bessie's previous recordings, one that moved her up from the languid blues of the past decade and into the brisk urban style that was beginning to shape the swing era. Helping her get there was a formidable band led by pianist Buck Washington: trumpeter Frankie Newton, trombonist Jack Teagarden, tenor saxophonist Leon "Chu" Berry, guitarist Bobby Johnson, and bassist Billy Taylor.

In his autobiography, Hammond admits that he had a different kind of session in mind. Clearly bothered by Bessie's desire to make this date more modern than her previous ones, it seems that he was determined to give it a rough edge. "I purposely went out of jazz when I hired Buck, who also couldn't read a note," he wrote, "hoping the fact that none of the other musicians had played with him might be an asset." Washington and Bessie were a good combination, he thought, because both were basically vaudeville performers.

Kicking off the session with "Do Your Duty," a spirited admonition, Bessie's stentorian voice is in glorious form, her mood clearly uplifted by the high caliber of this group and undoubtedly also by the fact that she is back in the studio after a two-year absence. Solos by Newton, Washington, the twenty-three-year-old Berry, and Teagarden lead into a marvelous stop-time chorus; except for a slight, compelling husky quality, Bessie's singing contains all the familiar attributes, the bent notes, superb timing, clear, trumpetlike tone, and masterful control.

The next number, "Gimme a Pigfoot and a Bottle of Beer," would become one of the most widely performed songs from Bessie Smith's repertoire. It is a rollicking tale of a Harlem rent party, the kind that flourished during the

Depression and never disappeared entirely. Frankie Newton contributes another spirited solo, but it is Bessie, in her role as Hannah Brown (from 'cross town), who ignites the band as she imbues the song with appropriate rowdiness and makes her lusty call for a pig's foot and a bottle of beer. In the final verse, she modifies her demand and asks for "a reefer and a gang of gin." The reference to marijuana was common in lyrics and titles of the period. Tunes like "Reefer Man," "You'se a Viper," "Kicking the Gong Around," and "Viper's Dream" carried messages about drugs that few whites understood, but "Gimme a Pigfoot" contains the only such reference by Bessie on records. (It is omitted from subsequent versions of the song, made by Billie Holiday in the late 1940s and Nina Simone in the early 1960s, when the use of marijuana was illegal and of widespread concern.)

In the 1930s, marijuana smoking was as common in Harlem, on Chicago's South Side, and in other black ghettos as it became at love-ins in the 1960s.[2] White society cared very little about what blacks did, as long as it didn't affect whites, but some African Americans saw the widespread smoking of "tea" as a threat to the future of their people. The September 9, 1933, issue of the *Defender* carried on its entertainment page an article referring to it as "this deadly puff," and warned that marijuana left young blacks "weak-minded and without will."

Smoking "reefers" was so common in Harlem during the 1930s that many older blacks find it hard to believe that today's highly controversial "pot" is the same thing. "No, no," said Ruby, "Bessie didn't smoke pot, not Bessie, nothing like that—just regular reefers."

It is perhaps appropriate that on this session, which marked her move into the modern age of swing, Bessie was joined by the man who would eventually be hailed by the media as the "King of Swing." His clarinet is barely audible, but Benny Goodman (who later became John Hammond's brother-in-law) happened to be recording with Adrian Rollini's orchestra[2] in one of two adjoining studios, so he dropped by Studio A long enough to make his presence known, if not felt, on "Gimme a Pigfoot."

"Take Me for a Buggy Ride" is another lusty double-entendre song. With characteristic gusto, Bessie gives her partner an endorsement for consistent good performance. There are no instrumental solos, but Frankie Newton's trumpet livens up the busy ensemble background. The session's final number, "Down in the Dumps," is about a young lady who wakes up after a nightmare and finds an empty pillow. It is the date's only sad song, but at the end of her tale of love lost and suicide contemplated, Bessie comes out growling with optimism. Again, there are no solos, but Teagarden, Berry, Washington, and Newton take turns playing marvelous things in the background. Bessie seems to have enjoyed this session, and it is almost as if she refused to end it on a dim note. Of course no one could have suspected it, but this was to be Bessie's swan-song recording; the session affords us the only opportunity to hear Bessie with swing accompaniment, the flexible rhythm of a string bass, and a saxophonist who doesn't sound like a refugee from a dance hall—a tantalizing hint of what might have come.

There is an interesting footnote: following Bessie's session, the studio closed for the weekend. But when it opened again, Monday morning, a nervous eighteen-year-old Bessie Smith–inspired singer named Billie Holiday made her recording debut. Fate had neatly arranged a changing of the guard.

Back in Philadelphia, Bessie had good reason to feel optimistic as audiences flocked to hear her at the Lincoln Theater during Thanksgiving week. The bill was a "Triple Attraction" featuring Mandy Lou, Bessie, and Jackie Mabley. Completely ignoring Mabley, one critic wrote something that must have pleased Bessie: "Mandy Lou has made a name for herself with Fred Waring's Pennsylvanians, but Bessie Smith, 'Philadelphia's favorite daughter,' will always be the main attraction wherever she appears." Such praise only faintly echoed past accolades, but things seemed to be looking up. Pleased with the way her recording session had gone, Bessie was now gradually modernizing her stage act by including such popular tunes as "Smoke Gets in Your Eyes" and "Tea for Two." Many of her fans still demanded to hear blues, so she did not abandon them altogether, but she was now presenting even her old songs with a slight 1930s polish. Knowing that Bessie's biggest following was still in the South, Richard urged her not to give up blues altogether and began to make plans for another tour.

Bessie's family was still in Philadelphia, depending on her for support. "Viola was drinking more and more," Maud recalled. "She used to come around and ask Clarence for money and she'd say that Bessie let her down, but Clarence knew the truth. He knew that Bessie gave them sisters of theirs as much as she could afford, and they just stayed drunk—that's why he never gave them much. Maybe a couple of dollars here and there, but that was all. Bessie paid their rent and bought them food, and the only reason she could do that was because Richard helped out—he was still selling liquor."

Ruby was no longer around, but Bessie had less need for her company, because she and Richard did not go through the ups and downs that had characterized her life with Jack Gee. Bessie had always had a warm spot for children, possibly because her own childhood had been so hard, and now that she had more free time, she turned her attention to local kids. The Lincoln featured a weekly talent show for youngsters, and Bessie always took time to talk to them and give them advice. Juanita Green recalled vividly her first meeting with Bessie: "I was just a little girl singing in this talent contest at the Standard Theater," she said. "My mom called me 'Baby Allen,' and the whole family was hoping that I'd grow up to become a famous singer, like Bessie. Well, that one afternoon I sang my little number and walked off stage. Bessie happened to be standing in the wings and she said 'Come here little girl,' so I walked over to her. She bent down and asked me, 'Is you in school?' I said, 'Yes ma'am,' and she said to me, 'Well, you better stay there, 'cause you can't carry a note.' I was crushed, but it turned out to be the best advice I ever got. You understand, she wasn't being mean or anything. Bessie loved kids and she always had some of them escorting her to and from the theater — we called her 'Miss Bessie' and she treated us so nice." Later, when she was about fourteen, Juanita went to Bessie's house every Saturday and scrubbed her kitchen floor. "Bessie paid me for it," she recalled, "and many a day she'd greet me at the top of the stairs, singing. Sometimes she cooked chitterlings, boiled with scallions, dipped in flour, and fried. For being so famous, she was very down to earth."

The Volstead Act was officially repealed within the next two weeks, but bars did not open overnight, nor did bootleggers go out of business. Heavy taxes on alcohol actually prolonged the economic rewards of bootlegging by several years and encouraged the smuggling of liquor from abroad. Repeal had little effect on Bessie's drinking habits: "She was liking the bad stuff even when the good stuff was in," Ruby recalled. But Bessie did take advantage of the beer gardens, which were the first establishments to open after Repeal.

While preparing for her four-day 1933 Christmas show at New York's Harlem Opera House, Bessie treated some fifty Harlem beer-garden patrons to an impromptu performance. Maud was not present, but she heard the story many times, as did Ruby. Apparently, Bessie was seated at a table with Richard Morgan and two friends when she overheard a young, light-complexioned chorine brag that she would be appearing in the Lafayette's *Yuletide Vanities* show. Obviously vying for attention, the girl — who was seated with her back to Bessie — raised her voice in order that people at nearby tables might also hear what she had to say. Thus having secured attention to herself, she was ready to bask in it for a while, and proceeded — in an equally loud tone of voice — to make catty remarks about other performers. When she mentioned a couple of singers, someone — perhaps aware of Bessie's presence — mentioned that Bessie would be appearing at the Harlem Opera House.

"Bessie Smith!" exclaimed the chorine disdainfully. "Who cares about *that* old bag, and all them ugly Ma Raineys liftin' their legs."

Her friends were still laughing when Bessie slowly rose from her seat, ignored Richard's advice to stay put, and tapped the chorine on the back. As the young lady turned and looked up at her, Bessie said: "You little yellow bitch.

Billed as "Queen of All Torch Singers," Bessie headed a cast that included Jackie (later, "Moms") Mabley and a dozen dancing mermaids who "worked like bitches." Swing was on the horizon, Benny Carter led the band—Bessie was beginning to shake the blues. From the December 23, 1933, issue of the *Amsterdam News*.

Them Ma Raineys got more high-class movements in their toes than you'll ever have in your whole body, and don't you talk about my girls like that, 'cause you ain't gonna be in *no* show when I'm through with you!" Then she jumped the startled girl and within minutes the beer garden was a free-for-all. Some patrons fled to the street; others remained and took sides. The police were summoned, but Richard Morgan managed to hustle Bessie out of there before they arrived.

Whether the indiscreet chorine appeared in the Lafayette's holiday production the following week is not known, but Bessie, now advertised as "Queen of All Torch Singers," launched her *Christmas Revels* at the Harlem Opera House with "twelve dancing mermaids" whose looks sent no one scurrying for the exit.

In early 1934, when it became apparent that Roosevelt's New Deal wasn't turning things around after all, the 1933 euphoria that had swept Bessie and others into a flurry of promising activity subsided. The New Deal would eventually have a more obvious positive effect on the economy, and the 1933 election of Mayor Fiorello La Guardia was already being felt in New York and beginning to directly alter Harlem's nightlife. La Guardia campaigned vigorously against burlesque, which had become increasingly risqué and light on the wardrobe side. The result was that several bump-and-grind establishments, including Hurtig and Seamon's Burlesque, were forced to close. In the January 19, 1934, issue of the *New York Age* an advertisement heralded the Hurtig and Seamon's Burlesque's historic transformation:

> MESSAGE TO HARLEM THEATRE-GOERS
> Dear Friends and Patrons,
>
> The opening of the 125th Street Apollo Theatre[3] next Friday night will mark a revolutionary step in the presentations of stage shows. The most lavish and colorful extravaganzas produced under the expert direction of Clarence Robinson, internationally known creator of original revues, will be a weekly feature.
>
> The phrase "the finest theatre in Harlem" can be aptly applied to this redecorated and refurnished temple of amusement.
>
> Courtesy and consideration will be the watchword of the management, truly a resort for the better people.
>
> High-Fidelity RCA sound equipment, the same as used by Radio City Music Hall, and an innovation in public address systems, has been installed, and we feel certain that the 125th Street Apollo Theatre will be an entertainment edifice that Harlem will take pride in showing off to neighborhood communities.

Having spent the first two weeks of January at home, Bessie traveled to New York to rehearse for her first appearance at the new 125th Street Apollo on February 3, 1934. The show was *Fan Waves*, and as the announcement promised, it was no skimpy offering. A benefit for the Harlem Children's Fresh Air Fund, it was a musical extravaganza that seemed designed to defy the prevailing economic slump. Besides Bessie, the cast included the dancing team of Meers and Meers, comedians Dusty Fletcher and Gallie De Gaston, "Noma," a fan dancer, and "the Sepia Mae West," a mystery star who was featured with sixteen chorus girls in a special production and said to be "the sensation of Chicago." It was not uncommon for black performers to be billed a dusky version of some white star; the irony was, of course, that the white stars often were but pale versions of black performers—Harlem had its own Mae Wests and Sophie Tuckers long before those two ladies made the scene.

One can easily imagine Bessie's surprise at discovering the identity of the Sepia Mae West, for it was none other than blues singer Ida Cox, and the whole show was built around her act. A few years earlier, Bessie would not have shared the stage with another blues singer, not even for a charity performance. Back then, when days were better and she commanded the field, she

Blues diva Ida Cox, "the Sepia Mae West," in a 1939 photograph. She began her recording career on the Paramount label in the 1920s and ended it in 1961. From the author's collection.

might have torn down half the theater, or—at the very least—staged a quick exit at the mere idea. But Bessie was more tolerant now that she no longer had the world in a jug and the stopper in her hand. Times were changing and so was she, at least as far as her career was concerned; she knew that her attitude had to be more flexible than before, and since she was now updating her own act, she might have seen Ida Cox's old blues as a welcome contrast. Bessie was gearing up to move with the times.

"When Bessie saw me at rehearsal, all dressed up like Mae West, she just laughed her head off," said Ida Cox years later. "I thought for sure she would be mad." Bessie was, of course, in no position to be. During the run of *Fan Waves*, the two singers became as friendly as Bessie would allow. Ida had recently toured the South with some success, and it is possible that she provided the encouragement Bessie and Richard Morgan needed to implement their touring plans. In any event, it wasn't long before they got some money together, assembled a small group of entertainers, and took to the road with a show called *Hot from Harlem*. Unfortunately, Southern audiences found it only lukewarm, so Bessie and Richard returned to Philadelphia without hav ing made any money on the tour. For the first time she seemed depressed by the way her career was going. Until now she had been able to blame the Depression for everything; the tour convinced her that even Southern audiences were ready for a change and that there was a very good reason why Mamie Smith, having abandoned the blues that had made her famous in 1920, now enjoyed tremendous success even among the South's rural audiences. Bessie didn't need further proof, but she got it during the last week of October when she appeared at the Harlem Opera House, headlining with a supporting cast of fifty and a band led by Don Redman. A saxophone player who had accompanied her at the peak of her recording career, Redman was now himself climbing to the top as the leader of a trendy, swinging big band. The *New York Age* rated the show one and a half daggers out of a possible five and proved to Bessie, once and for all, that it was time for a change:

> If it were not for the rather clever and different arrangements played by Don Redmond [sic] and his band, the show at the Harlem Opera House this week would hardly rate one dagger . . . the rest of the show is very little out of the ordinary. The chorus rates mention for their performance, especially in what might be called the "production number," in which they put across a nice routine and tableau to the tune of "Out in the Cold Again." . . . Bessie Smith is undoubtedly a good blues singer—but blues singers don't seem to rate as highly as they used to. Her reception by the audience, although warm enough, seemed to be actuated by appreciation of her personality rather than her act. Of course the usual risque lines evoked the usual obscene howls of laughter, but—she wasn't called back at all.

Most singers who shifted from pop to blues during the blues craze had long since switched back. Bessie had been a blues singer from the start, but she had always included non-blues songs in her repertoire, giving them blues characteristics by her interpretation. Out of her blues and that of her contemporaries had evolved the jazz singing of Louis Armstrong, such women as Ivie Anderson—a former dancer with Mamie Smith who became a celebrated vocalist with the Ellington orchestra—and newcomer Billie Holiday, who cited Bessie and Armstrong as her major influences. Ivie Anderson's 1931 rendition of Ellington's "It Don't Mean a Thing, If It Ain't Got That Swing" was almost a manifesto and certainly an accurate prediction of things to come. Benny Goodman's swift rise to the swing throne was only a few months away, and Bessie already found that many regarded her as a living relic.

During the week at the Harlem Opera House, Bessie did receive some encouragement from Will Marion Cook, a distinguished black composer who had studied classical music in Europe and been a pupil of Czech composer Antonin Dvořák in New York. With Dvořák's encouragement, Cook turned to the music of his own ancestors for inspiration and became a successful writer of musicals, including several for the popular team of Bert Williams and George Walker. Cook telephoned Bessie to offer her a featured part in *Dusk and Dawn*, an ambitious musical production that was in its planning stages. Destined for Broadway, it had a projected cast of two hundred and an intriguing storyline that shifted from the shores of Africa to the slave ships and the cotton fields.

Bessie accepted the offer, the press made the announcement, and that was the end of that — like so many adventurous theatrical dreams, *Dusk and Dawn* never materialized. Stories of Cook's inability to get the show off the ground began to appear before the end of the year, closing 1934 with another disappointment for Bessie. It had been her worst year, but friends recalled that, although she was now more depressed than they had ever seen her, she remained extraordinarily optimistic and more determined than ever to get in step with the times.

Bessie's personal life became relatively uneventful as the pace of her professional life slowed down. Barely able to support herself, she became increasingly reliant on Richard, who still did rather well with his liquor operation. It was around this time that Viola's daughter, Laura, suddenly passed away. To economize, Bessie moved Tinnie and Lulu into the top floor of Viola's house, spending a great deal of money on special plumbing installations and the interior work that was needed to convert the floor into a self-contained apartment.

The arrangement was short-lived. The three sisters fought incessantly, each feeling entitled to the larger share of Bessie's favors. The situation became so unworkable that Viola soon had the house to herself again. "They were mean bitches, those sisters," said Ruby, perhaps not without bias. "All they ever did was to try to get as much out of poor old Bessie as they could. They drank up her money and then they had the nerve to call her names behind her back. I can see why Jack didn't like them, there was all this jealousy. But poor Bessie, she didn't know half of what they was doing to her — she was blind to the facts, because she just loved her family." Clarence, who had quit show business and opened a beauty parlor, was less forgiving; he told Bessie that she was wasting time and money because their sisters had no sense of responsibility and the more they got the more they wanted. "Times were hard," said Maud, "and Clarence thought Bessie was foolish to keep Viola and the rest of them in Philly — it would have been a lot cheaper to send them back to Chattanooga. I think Andrew was still there, and he had a job, so why couldn't he help look after them? But you couldn't tell Bessie nothing when it came to her family."

The entertainment pages of the black press carried mixed news during the early months of 1935. The *Defender,* taking a slap at Mae West, proclaimed Ada Overton-Walker, wife of comedian George Walker, the original "Queen of the Curves"; Ma Rainey retired in Columbus, Georgia, on the death of her sister Malissa; Clara Smith died of a heart attack at the age of forty; the swing era was heating up as big bands led by the likes of Chick Webb and Willie Bryant met in "savage battles" at the Savoy Ballroom; the Lafayette Theater, having done away with stage shows a few weeks earlier, closed down;[4] the 125th Street Apollo Theater was taken over by Leo Brecher and Frank Schiffman, who vowed to pick up where the Lafayette had left off, and continue a tradition of black vaudeville.

Jazz was now making great inroads on the other side of the Atlantic, and there was no American musician who was more familiar to Europeans than Louis Armstrong. In 1935, following a stormy dispute with his European manager, N. J. Canetti, Armstrong cut short his triumphant Continental tour[5] and returned to New York, where he would celebrate his homecoming at the Apollo during the week of February 15. He was to be featured as soloist with Al Jenkins and his Fifteen Rhythm Makers, but he failed to show up. Rumors spread quickly, suggesting that Armstrong was ill, or even dead, but the truth was that he simply needed a rest. When Bessie was called in as a last-minute, unadvertised replacement, the disappointed *Amsterdam News* reviewer gave her a mere one-line mention. Three months later, in the first week of May, she was again booked at the Apollo, this time receiving third billing in a revue featuring Lil Hardin's band, which was billed as "Mrs. Louis Armstrong and Her Orchestra."

Bessie was to appear with a group of her own chorines as a separate act, and she was making calls to assemble her chorus line when a telegram came from Ruby.

"I had just finished a show with Gertie Saunders and we were going off. Just as the final curtain came down, Gertie said, 'Everybody stay on stage.' She told us to go through a rehearsal, and said, 'Especially you, Ruby. You didn't keep your lines straight. If you were on Bessie's show you wouldn't do that.' She was just trying to embarrass me in front of everybody—that woman really hated me. That night I didn't care if Jack killed me, I sent a telegram to Bessie saying, 'I can't stay on here, Gertie keeps picking on me.' Bessie wired me back, 'Come back with me and let Jack try to stop it.' That's how I went back on Bessie's show, and it was very different, because Bessie wasn't doing those old blues we used to feature on the road. Well, she'd throw in a couple of them, but she wanted to do up-to-date stuff—and so did I."

Lil Armstrong recalled a problem in connection with that engagement: "Bessie Smith was furious because Mr. Schiffman was going to change her show. I had heard so much about her mean temper that I figured I'd better get on the right side of her, so I went out and bought her a chicken sandwich. She didn't say much to me, but she ate the sandwich and I never had any problems with her—she was real mad at Schiffman, though."

Lil did not know the details of Bessie's rift with Schiffman, but Ruby remembered. Bessie and her new group of chorines, including Ruby, were rehearsing for the Apollo appearance. When they took a break, Frank Schiffman, who had been a silent observer, told the young ladies to get some fresh air while he spoke to Bessie. He knew who Ruby was, so he did not ask her to leave—besides, she was already at work rubbing Bessie's back, as she so often had done in earlier days. What follows is the conversation as Ruby remembered it:

"Bessie," said Schiffman, standing in front of her, "you got a dancing bunch of girls with you this time, but they are *so* black that with the makeup on they'll look gray—especially that little one at the end of the front line, she's *exceptionally* dark, and I wouldn't want to bring this bunch into the Apollo."

"A little harder on the left side, baby," Bessie instructed Ruby, without looking up.

"I have a bunch of girls that we can put in the line," Schiffman continued. "It shouldn't take them long to rehearse up the routine."

Ruby could feel Bessie tensing up. She rose to her feet, placed a hand on her hip, and looked Schiffman straight in the eye.

"If you don't want my girls, you don't want me."

"Bessie, I . . ."

"No Bessie nothin'. The only reason those girls look gray out there is because I don't get the proper lighting. We're coming in there, and you get me some amber lights to put on those girls—that is, if you want the show, and if you don't, I don't give a damn, because I'm tired of wearin' myself out. I can go home, get drunk, and be a lady—it's up to you."

Schiffman gave in.

The story spread quickly, with help from Bessie. "Mr. Schiffman had to take all those gals," Ruby remembered. "He didn't mind me, because I was the lightest in the bunch, but all the street cats had heard the story, and they were standing out there on the corners saying, 'I ain't gonna miss the show *this* week, all those Ma Raineys are gonna be there.' So, honey, when we fell in there we stopped the show. You never saw people give applause like they did for us girls—we broke it up! And Bessie told them girls, 'Now the man don't even *want* y'all in here, so don't let me down.' You should have seen us go, we worked like bitches, and each time we went out there, they would applaud for us to come back. We really let them know that we was stewin'—every leg came up together, every smile was turned on just right. All those half-white

Having shed her horsehair wigs and feathers, Bessie combed her hair back, donned evening gowns, modernized her repertoire, and reinvented herself in the mid-1930s. From the author's collection.

gals who'd come in there just couldn't work like Bessie's crowd. 'You can say what you want about them Ma Raineys,' Bessie said, 'but they know what they're doin' when they're out there working.' And you can believe that—we worked our asses off."

Frank Schiffman did not recall this particular incident, "But," he pointed out, "that is not to say that it didn't happen."

Bessie, who had worked for Schiffman at the Lafayette Theater, was eager to show him that she was quite capable of performing in step with the times. Many new singers were emerging: Billie Holiday had made her Apollo debut two weeks earlier, and word was getting around about Ella Fitzgerald, Chick Webb's new vocal discovery, who would make her professional debut at the

Apollo a few weeks later. Determined not to let the new trend toward swing music leave her behind, Bessie was updating her material, and *New York Age,* having all but labeled her act passé the year before, now took note of her updated material and gave her a three-dagger rating: "Bessie Smith of the old blues singing school is probably the first of her clan to modernize her type of singing. She does one number in particular which boasts of 1920 rhythm and 1935 lyrics, employing such phrases as 'trucking,' 'tea,' and similar expressions."

Though New York reviewers were somewhat subdued in their praise of Bessie, Frank Schiffman—who had been one of her most frequent employers, going back to the Lafayette days of the mid-1920s—recalled no corresponding waning of enthusiasm on the part of her audience. "Bessie was sometimes a little shaky, but she never ceased to be a drawing card for us," he said. "She was a difficult and temperamental person, she had her love affairs, which frequently interfered with her work, but she never was a real problem. Bessie was a person for whose artistry, at least, I had the profoundest respect. I don't ever remember any artist in all my long, long years—and this goes back to some of the famous singers, including Billie Holiday—who could evoke the response from her listeners that Bessie did. Whatever pathos there is in the world, whatever sadness she had, was brought out in her singing—and the audience knew it and responded to it."

Although some reviewers noted the change in Bessie's presentations, most still regarded her as a leftover from the 1920s. On July 26, when she appeared at the Apollo after a three-month absence, the *New York Age* again acknowledged her "modernization," but noted that the context within which she appeared placed her historically as far back as 1918:

> Roland Holder, plenty good with the taps, makes his appearance, following which Shelton Brooks turns—musically speaking, of course—the pages of Life back to the days of the Armistice to present a fitting introduction to Bessie Smith, hailed as the Queen of the Blues. Bessie, incidentally, is one blues singer who has ever been a pleasure to hear, and the fact that she has kept step with the times has been all to her credit.

During Christmas week, 1935 when Bessie made her last appearance of the year at the Apollo, Jane Withers[6] was on the big silver screen in *This Is the Life,* but 1935 hadn't exactly reflected the kind of life Bessie sought. The recordings she made for John Hammond remained unreleased, and her performance credits for the whole year added up to a mere four weeks at the Apollo. Richard Morgan's ongoing bootlegging business became increasingly important as a source of income, but that was all about to change as a twist of fate sent Bessie's career in a new direction: downtown.

In February 1936, Billie Holiday's future looked as bright as Bessie's looked bleak, but the young singer was about to give her idol's career the boost it needed, and she inadvertently accomplished that by eating the wrong thing. While appearing in *Stars over Broadway* at Connie's Inn—a one-time Harlem nightspot that had moved downtown to Forty-eighth Street between Broadway and Seventh Avenue[7]—Billie came down with a case of ptomaine poisoning and was forced to take a leave. When the show's producer, Nat Nazarro, was asked to come up with a replacement, he recalled hearing Bessie sing some of her current material, and recommended her. Bessie's gradual streamlining was paying off—this was her most prestigious engagement in several years, a venue unlike any she had tried before, and she made the most of it.

Connie's Inn brought Bessie a whole new audience, the chic crowd that used to find its way to Harlem's Cotton Club and breathe in its Ellingtonian elegance. If any of them had heard Bessie belt out the blues through her feather boa and shift her beaded derriere suggestively, they were in for a surprise, because this was the opportunity Bessie had waited for, and she was quick to seize it. Bathed in Connie's spotlights was a new Bessie Smith; gone were the blues—except for an occasional request—and gone, too, was the earthy raw sensuality. The gaudy headdresses and horsehair wigs had given way to a simpler, more elegant look, and Bessie's hair was now swept back and her full figure smartly poured into a silk or satin evening gown. All that remained of the old Bessie was that glorious voice, perfect timing, and innate ability to mesmerize her audience. She had always been adaptable when it came to choosing songs, and if she sounded dated, the blame lay with the accompaniment rather than her delivery. At Connie's, she sang current Tin Pan Alley material to a "modern" swing beat, and her new audiences loved it. Bessie had been unsuccessful when she tried to do the same thing at the Apollo, for there she carried the "stigma" of an old-time blues singer. Her uptown audience was generally most receptive when she reverted to a familiar, old-styled blues song, and much as she had tried, she never seemed able to convince them that her talent stretched beyond that. There was no such problem at Connie's Inn and word of the reborn Bessie Smith spread quickly.

Now that she was getting back on her feet again, the "long lost friends" Bessie sang about on her 1929 recording of "Nobody Knows You When You're Down and Out" came out of the woodwork. During the first week of February, Carl Van Vechten invited her to his studio for a photo session. She arrived between shows "cold sober and in a quiet reflective mood," Van

Bessie in performance, possibly during her successful 1936 midtown Manhattan engagement at Connie's Inn. From the author's collection.

Vechten later recalled. "She could scarcely have been more amiable or cooperative. She was agreeable to all my suggestions and even made changes of dress. Of course, on this occasion she did not sing, but I got nearer to her real personality than I ever had before and the photographs, perhaps, are the only adequate record of her true appearance and manner that exist."[8]

Van Vechten was justly proud of the thirty-six photographs he took that day. They show Bessie in a variety of moods, wearing two outfits and captured—in typical Van Vechten fashion—against backgrounds of busy wallpaper and curtain. Though posed, they are remarkable studies—the most intimate portraits of Bessie available, and probably the only ones taken in the years of her decline. She smiles and throws back her head to look at the white plaster face of a Greek god; looks askance and with a hint of apprehension at a bizarre, racist, stereotyped Sambo face that seems to rest on her shoulder; dances the "truck," beaming a broad, mischievous smile. There are poses with a feather fan and funereal shots with an armful of flowers, but perhaps the most honest picture of all is one in which she stands behind a dining room chair, clutches its back, and lets us look behind the mask.

While February 1935 seemed to take Bessie into the new era musically, her success at Connie's Inn also gave her social life a boost. One might have thought she had been in Siberia instead of Harlem, the way people now fussed over her, and as she strove to move her career off its beaten track, time was making its own transitions: the Lafayette Theater was scheduled to reopen, but not for vaudeville—it would now become a part of the Works Progress Administration theater project. Bessie also heard sad news about two of her favorite accompanists: trombonist Charlie Green was found frozen to death on the steps of a Harlem tenement, and trumpeter Joe Smith was slowly fading away in a Long Island sanatorium.

Shortly after the Van Vechten photo session, Bessie made her only appearance on "The Street," a block of Fifty-second Street in midtown Manhattan, between Fifth and Sixth Avenues. Jazz first came to the block in the late 1920s, when a bootlegger named Joe Helbock opened a speakeasy called the Onyx, but Repeal made the Onyx legit, and soon other jazz clubs began popping up there, prompting promoters to call it "Swing Street." By the late 1930s, this block of brownstones was virtually lined with intimate jazz spots on both sides. Here the most celebrated performers of the day jammed and paid each other bandstand visits. Remarkably, it was not until the mid-1940s that Fifty-second Street audiences became totally integrated, but black and white performers jammed together at such Street landmarks as the Onyx, the Three Deuces, the Spotlite, the Yacht Club, and the Famous Door.[9] Located at number 35, just off Fifth Avenue, the Famous Door was one of the first jazz spots to open on the block; like the Onyx and other clubs on the Street, it was a converted speakeasy. Bessie made her only known Fifty-second Street appearance there on a cold February day in 1936, appearing in an upstairs room where the club's regular Sunday afternoon jam sessions were held.

"She came in," reminisced Robert Paul Smith in the *Record Changer*, "she planted those two flat feet firmly on the floor, she did not shake her shoulders or snap her fingers. She just opened that great kisser and let the music come out." Others recall that she wore a fur wrap and kept it on during her

Carl Van Vechten found Bessie to be gracious and cooperative in 1936, when he asked her to his apartment studio for a photo session. She obviously was a good sport, agreeing to some of his bizarre poses. Photos by Carl Van Vechten.

performance. Guitarist Eddie Condon remembered Bunny Berigan's muted trumpet backing her up on half a dozen numbers from her old repertoire and singer Mildred Bailey refusing to follow her on the bandstand for fear of breaking the spell. "That's true," said guitarist Brick Fleagle in an interview for this book, "and I think Mildred was wise not to sing. Bessie left as soon as she was through—no liquor was served at these upstairs sessions—so she just came, sang, and left us all in a daze."

Mildred Bailey and her musician husband, Red Norvo, were among the people who had recently befriended Bessie and Richard Morgan. "Bessie was crazy about Mildred," Norvo recalled in a 1968 interview with Whitney Balliett for the *New Yorker.* "She and Mildred used to laugh at each other and do this routine. They were both big women, and when they saw each other, one of them would say, 'Look, I've got this brand-new dress, but it's too big for me, so why don't *you* take it?' "

Harlem's latest dance craze was "the truck," and trucking contests were all the rage with the ballroom set. During the first week of March, Mildred encouraged Bessie to attend a contest at the Savoy Ballroom, popularly called "The Home of Happy Feet." The judges were English musical comedy star Beatrice Lillie and Bessie's old rival, Ethel Waters, and the music was furnished by the big bands of Chick Webb and Fess Williams. The featured singers were Mildred and seventeen-year-old Webb protégé Ella Fitzgerald, but newspapers reported that Bessie also did a few numbers, accompanied by her old friend James P. Johnson, and that she demonstrated her versatility by executing a few dance steps in the latest style. Was Bessie trucking? Of course she was, just as she had done before Carl Van Vechten's camera a month earlier. She was certainly no longer going to be treated as a museum piece.

As Bessie's professional activities increased, so did attention from the press. Allan McMillan had erroneously reported in his syndicated column "Theater Chat" that Bessie's Connie's Inn appearance registered a "no click" with Broadway audiences and that another singer was replacing her. Two weeks later, his column contained an apology:

> Well, I thought I was right in my report and it didn't exactly mean that La Smith was slipping. Nevertheless, Impresario Nazarro had me know that I must make another visit to Connie's Inn for the express purpose of hearing one of our foremost exponents of blue notes in a cycle of new songs.
>
> So, Sunday night I went to Connie Immerman's hot spot on the Gay White Way and waited for Miss Smith to do her turn. To say the least, I was amply repaid for having waited, because I had an opportunity to see one of the most enthusiastic demonstrations of approval ever recorded in a night club.
>
> The portly blues singer came out and knocked them dizzy and then came

> back to do W. C. Handy's "St. Louis Blues" for an encore. To Miss Smith I apologize because when any performer is received by a Broadway audience as you were on Sunday night, he's absolutely the tops.

A week after his apology, McMillan reported that Bessie, now in her sixth week, had been held over at Connie's. He also wrote a lengthy piece for the *Chicago Defender*'s March 28, 1936, issue. Considering that Bessie in the preceding two years had performed almost exclusively, though sporadically, in New York, the heading was misleading. It should also be noted that Allan McMillan was a press agent, which explains why the article reads like a publicity release, full of misinformation. Some of the twisted facts came from Bessie herself—she had been in the business long enough to know how to feed the right line of jive; the important thing was that she was getting attention again:

> NEW YORK SEES BESSIE SMITH; WONDERS WHERE SHE'S BEEN
>
> It's a long way from Tennessee to Broadway, but Bessie Smith made it even though it did take an extra year or so. The highway leading to the glamorous white lights of the gay white way is filled with many disappointments, but the portly delineator of blue notes never allowed such trivials as hard knocks and disillusions to thwart an innerborn desire to reach the top.
>
> Miss Smith is right now in her seventh week of an extended engagement at Connie's Inn and backed by Broadway approval she has taken on new life. "I'm feeling better now than ever in my life," Miss Smith confided in an interview with this writer last week, "and I feel as though I am on the brink of new successes. I am most certainly optimistic concerning the upward trend of the theatre."
>
> *Began Career at Nine*
>
> "Things have changed quite a bit," reminisced the jubilant chantress, "and I realize that we are living in an entirely new era of entertainment—far different from the one in which I began many years ago."
>
> It was here that the stylist of blues songs blushed (actresses never like to appear old), but that was because she started her career as a child and has been active in the theater for 27 years.
>
> She was born in Chattanooga, Tenn., April 15, 1898, appeared in school plays, was the champion roller skater of the state, made her first professional appearance at the age of nine at the old Ivory Theatre in her home town . . . used her first weekly salary of $8 to purchase a new pair of ball-bearing roller skates. Got a severe tanning for it from her mother, but it didn't dull that childish enthusiasm. Has since appeared in theatres all over the United States. Also had shows of her own in the old T.O.B.A. days. Her Columbia phonograph records of famous "blues" are played the world over. Very fond of sports but is much fonder of diamonds and fur coats. Once had a box full of

> genuine sparklers. Plays guitar and piano. Initial inspiration came from Cora Fisher and W. C. Handy. Made the "St. Louis Blues" in a motion picture short for Handy a few years ago. Favorite stage star is Ethel Waters. A lover of pets . . . says she will retire in 1960, maybe (accent on the maybe) and settle down in the country. She's got rhythm in her soul.

With Billie Holiday set to return to Connie's Inn the following night, Bessie closed on April 17, but Nazarro didn't keep her idle for long. A week later she opened at the Apollo as part of a Nazarro package, which also included W. C. Handy's fifteen-piece orchestra, the popular team of Buck and Bubbles — one half of which was Buck Washington, the leader of Bessie's last recording orchestra — and three additional acts. One gets a good idea of Depression fees from the cost of this package: $2,434.40 for the entire week.

Although she was no longer recording, Bessie continued to write songs. Pianist-composer Eubie Blake remembered being called to W. C. Handy's office on Broadway during her Apollo engagement. Bessie was there with an idea for a blues, and Handy suggested that Blake set it to music. "They weren't prepared to pay me anything for it, so I said I couldn't do it," Blake said, "but I remember that it was a very good idea — I wish I could remember it — I had never met Bessie before, and I never saw her again."

In the middle of May, Richard took Bessie to the Earle Theater in Philadelphia, where his nephew, Lionel Hampton, was appearing with Benny Goodman's band. "It was obvious that Bessie and my uncle were very devoted to each other," Hampton recalled, "and I don't believe there was anything he wouldn't do for her. I introduced her to the members of the band, but she really didn't need an introduction — she was the star. I'm convinced that if she had lived, she would have been right up there with the rest of us in the swing music, she would have been a national figure."

"STILL TOPS" read the heading over Bessie's photo in the May 30, 1936, issue of the *Defender.* "One need never worry about Bessie Smith holding her own as a blues singer. Although the type of songs she featured have gone out of style, Miss Smith is singing torrid songs which will keep her in the limelight." What a shame it is that Bessie was not recorded singing the "torrid" song of her "modern" period. The 1933 Okeh recordings give us but a small hint of the emerging, updated Bessie.

The next engagement Nazarro lined up for Bessie proved to be the longest of her career: she would head up her own show at Art's Café, a night club at Twenty-second Street and Ridge Avenue in Philadelphia. She was booked from June 18 through September 3, 1936.

The engagement at Art's was an unqualified success; the comfortable blend of the old and the new worked well. There were three shows nightly with a rotating program that included such new tunes as "It's a Sin to Tell a Lie" and "Pennies from Heaven," a blues, and a risqué song from the old repertoire. The last was presented as a duet and comedy skit with Billy McLaurin. "Philadelphia's night life has been enriched," reported the *Tribune* after Bessie's closing on September 3.

Although her act had changed, Bessie, by all accounts, was more like her old self at Art's—perhaps too much so. She rode around in her own car, an old Packard that Richard kept in pristine condition, played nightly to a packed audience, performed material that did not make her come across as a flapper-era leftover, and saw a new generation of fans come to see "that famous radio star," as advertisements billed her. Further contributing to Bessie's euphoria was the fact that Snooks—now a somewhat restless teenager—was back with her.

With her career on the upswing, Bessie began once again to meet life and its pleasures with characteristic excesses, including a bit of philandering. "I'm not sure if Richard knew that Bessie had eyes for other men, but he kept it quiet if he did," said Maud. "As a matter of fact, I can't tell you for a fact that she did anything more than flirt with a couple of guys." According to Ruby, Bessie was back in full swing, at least for a while. She had her eyes on Eddie Mitchell, a young, handsome dancer in the show who dressed sharply and was "just Bessie's type." It so happened that he was also Ruby's type, and Ruby was having an affair with him.

One night, toward the end of Bessie's engagement at Art's, a barmaid called Ruby aside, pointed out one of the girls in the show, and said that she was syphilitic. She knew of Ruby's involvement with Eddie and advised her to keep him away from this chorine. Not long after that, Ruby caught Eddie and the girl locked in a passionate kiss and abruptly ended the romance. Thinking it wise to warn Bessie, she cornered her downstairs in the bar and relayed what she had been told about the girl and what she herself had observed. "I was doing her a favor by telling her," said Ruby, "and when I suggested that she drop Eddie, too, she just got an attitude and said, 'If he's that common, what do *you* want with him?' You see, she didn't believe me. Bessie thought I was jealous of her and that I just made up this story so I could have Eddie for myself."

Unable to convince Bessie that she was expressing concern rather than jealousy, Ruby decided that she might as well quit the show and return to New York. The engagement at Art's was about to end anyway, and Ruby did not wish to be present when Bessie discovered the truth. She later learned that

Bessie did have an affair with the young dancer and that he had indeed caught "something" from the girl, but she never found out if it had been passed on to Bessie.

One advantage of working an extended engagement in Philadelphia was that Bessie got to spend her days at home, but at times that could be painful. Still drinking heavily, Viola played on Bessie's conscience by constantly reminding her of the years when she kept the family together. "Bessie sometimes got all teary-eyed when Viola reminded her of how hard she had worked to support the brothers and sisters down south," said Maud. "Clarence didn't think it was right for Bessie to keep giving their sisters money, and when he saw that Bessie was about to do something foolish—well, he thought it was foolish—he'd say to her, 'Remember how Vi used to lock you up in the toilet?' he didn't say toilet, but you get the idea. Bessie didn't pay him no mind—she was very much into blood sticking together."

A similar situation faced Bessie in Snook's case. He was now close to seventeen and seemed to be suffering from the effects of his nomadic childhood. "We couldn't keep up with him," said Maud. "He would come home and Bessie would give him any amount of money that he would ask for, she'd dress him up, and the next thing you know he'd be gone. He had a lovely home and everything, but he just wouldn't stay in one place. I think the longest he stayed home was about two months. He'd be all dressed up, Bessie would give him a hundred dollars, and good-bye, he was off again."

Confirming his aunt's recollections, Jack, Jr., admitted that he never got along in school, and told how Bessie constantly tried to impress upon him the value of a formal education: "I'll never forget the only time Mama put a hand on me. The truant officer had told her that I wasn't going to school, and she asked me about it. 'You don't want to go to school,' she asked, 'tell me, and I'll take you out of school if you don't want to go.' She was just trying to trick me into telling her the truth, so, like a fool, I said, 'No, I don't want to go.' Well, she beat me up all over the room."

Bessie never gave up trying to get Snooks interested in school. "Mama was a real bug on education, and I remember when I was about seventeen or eighteen she wanted me to become a lawyer. 'Baby,' she said one day, 'if you go back to school, I'll buy you anything you want. I'll buy you all the clothes you want, pay your tuition, and I'll even buy you a car.' I should have listened to her."

Bessie ended 1936 as she had 1935, with a week at the Apollo. Jane Withers was on the screen again, this time in *Can This Be Dixie?* a film that also featured Hattie McDaniel (who three years later would become the first African-

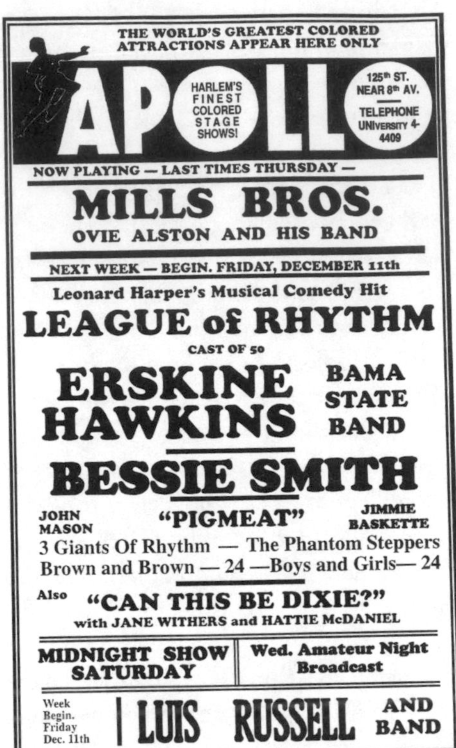

As this 1936 Apollo Theater advertisement in the *Amsterdam News* shows, Bessie was keeping up with the times. From the author's collection.

American Oscar winner for her performance in *Gone with the Wind*). Still steering her act into the modern age, Bessie was backed in the latest style by the pulsating big band of trumpeter Erskine Hawkins.

During her Apollo engagement, owner Frank Schiffman refused Bessie a request for an advance, but it was a decision he would soon regret. Bessie stormed out of his office, headed straight down to the crowded lobby, threw her two hundred pounds to the floor, and gave the theater's startled patrons a dramatic, impromptu performance. Lying on her back, she kicked up her feet, furiously pounded the floor with her fists and hollered, in a voice that could be heard clear across 125th Street: "I'm the *star* of the show, I'm Bessie Smith, and these fuckin' bastards won't let me have my money." It wasn't long before she got what she wanted. When this incident was brought up in an interview, Schiffman again conceded that it might well have taken place, although he did not recall it.

In the course of the week, Bessie met with Ruby at the Braddock Bar.[10] A favorite entertainers' hangout, it was located on the corner of 126th Street and Eighth Avenue, and shared a back alley with the Apollo. The rivalry over

Eddie Mitchell was behind them, and it was time to mend fences again. It was early afternoon and the place was practically empty. Bessie and Ruby seated themselves at the far end of the long bar and were enjoying what Ruby called a "catch-up chit chat" when a man entered, ordered a drink, and engaged the bartender in conversation.

"You see Bessie Smith at the Apollo this week?"

"No," replied the bartender, knowing that Bessie was within earshot at the other end of the room. "How is she?"

"Oh, that bitch, she thinks she's some big shit. I knew that bitch when she was right down in Atlanta, and don't you know she passed right on by me and didn't even speak?"

"That ain't like Bessie," said the bartender, nervously.

"Well, you don't know her like I do."

At this point Bessie got off her barstool. Wearing her dark glasses and a turban, she was not immediately recognizable. Approaching the man, she walked into the daylight that distinguished the front of the bar from the rear.

"Hey," she said.

Ruby braced herself.

"Hey, lady," the man retorted.

"Have a drink on me—bartender, give this gentleman a drink." She leaned on the bar and smiled. "So tell me more about Bessie."

"That black bitch, I know her well."

"You really know her, huh?"

"You're damn right I know her—from way back in Atlanta, when she wasn't nothin'."

"And she passed right by you and wouldn't speak—ain't that some shit?" Bessie was obviously enjoying her little game.

"Yeah, that bitch wouldn't even open her mouth."

With that, Bessie kicked the man in his most vulnerable spot. "That bitch opened her mouth *this* time," she said, "and the next time I see you, you black bastard, I'll do the same damn thing. C'mon, Ruby."

Just like the old days, Ruby thought, as they walked out of the bar. But it was the last time she ever saw her aunt and friend.

On February 4, 1937, Bessie began another nightclub engagement in Philadelphia. She was booked for only three weeks at the Wander Inn Café on Eighteenth and Federal Streets, but her stay stretched into the summer.

In his autobiography Sidney Bechet recalled dropping into the Wander Inn around that time. He had married since he last saw Bessie, and his wife was with him: "Bessie just showed up and came over to our table and sat down. She'd been drinking and she wasn't too careful about how she'd do things. She just came over and sat down and started fooling around with me, talking in a way that could lead on to things.

"My wife was one of those real pretty girls and she wasn't having any of this. The way it was, Bessie must have known how much my wife had been hearing about me and Bessie, all what people had been telling her about our going together; 'Bessie this and Bessie that' whenever old friends meet. Bessie must have known that pretty well; it was the kind of woman-knowing she'd been born with. And she started in deliberate-like, needling my wife. Only my wife got to needling right back and it seemed like she was a little better at it because before long I could see that Bessie was ready to haul off and pull hair. She wasn't one to stand for anything, Bessie. She was really a hell of a woman.

"Lucky though, before anything really happened, the woman who owned the place, who liked my wife, came over and got Bessie to go with her. She brought her into the back of the club and got her calmed down . . . That night at the club, it was the last time. That woman led Bessie away to the back of the club and I never saw her again."

As the summer of 1937 drew to a close, Bessie faced a busy schedule. The record industry had recovered from the near-fatal wounds of the early Depression years; "race records" were still labeled as such but since the mid-1930s had concentrated mostly on big bands, small swing groups, and such blues singers as Leadbelly, Leroy Carr, Big Bill Broonzy, and Charley Patton. The first jazz record collectors were emerging, and the concept of reissuing old material was around the corner as renewed interest in older jazz forms, including the classic blues, heightened. This also had a new generation of blues women lining up, but Bessie was not interested in re-creating her past. She had transcended the idiom and slipped gracefully into the swing era.

"I had planned to record her for Columbia's Brunswick series, the lower-priced pop label," John Hammond recalled. "I was going to use Jo Jones, Walter Page, Buck Clayton, Jack Teagarden, and Hershal Evans or Chu Berry—I was even going to sneak Basie in on piano."

If that is true, Hammond was not the only one who had plans for Bessie: "We were going to make records," Lionel Hampton recalled. "I told everybody in the Goodman band about Bessie being tight with my uncle, and Benny said, 'Oh, man, we *gotta* make some records with her.' And I had just signed a contract with Victor Records to do a lot of small-band dates with people like Johnny Hodges, Nat King Cole, and all those guys, so Eli Oberstein of Victor told me, 'Be sure to get Bessie,' because she was just coming back into prominence then. You know, what she sang was so relaxed, the stories she sang became so true—this was reality. She always adapted the 'now' sound, whatever that became, but we never got around to recording it."

Bessie was also scheduled to make another film, this time in Hollywood. Her career seemed to be undergoing a complete makeover—it was 1923 all over again. Into her forties, her huge frame scarred by two decades of reckless living, Bessie still radiated vitality. She had weathered the storms of her personal and professional life, and now she defied those who would relegate her to the past. Maud and Ruby agreed that Bessie felt life had been good to her, and she had remarkably few regrets.

Although she had felt the love of millions whom her artistry profoundly affected, she had not always found love at home, where she sought it most. Performers to whom she had been an inspiration now stood where she had been fourteen years earlier, but rather than sit back and observe, Bessie was moving on, prepared to break new ground. "I never saw so much life left in someone who had lived so much," said Bernice Latelle, a gospel singer who lived in Bessie's neighborhood and heard her at the Wander Inn. "I don't think anybody or anything could break that woman's spirit."

In September, Bessie accepted a feature spot touring the South with Winsted's *Broadway Rastus* show. Jack Gee claimed that she paid him a surprise visit in New York to ask his advice on accepting the *Broadway Rastus* engagement. He recalled the alleged meeting in the 1965 *Down Beat* yearbook:

"The last time I saw my wife living, she was at 48 West 127th Street in New York. I was out late that night, when I came home I stumbled over some bags in the hall. I asked my mother what it was all about, and she told me my wife was in my room. I went in and Bessie was in bed. She said she come to talk to me about doing a carnival show. I went out and bought a half dozen Cokes, which Bessie was a lover of a long time before then.

"We decided that night to let bygones be bygones and get back together as before, and I agreed with her to accept the carnival show at $250 a week. We figured after the season we'd reinstate ourselves back to normal. This never happened, I'm sorry to say."

Not surprisingly, those who knew Bessie well during this period say that this "last visit" with Jack never happened. Jack, they contended, invented such clandestine meetings with Bessie in order to justify his rights to her estate. "Yes, she loved Coca-Cola, but that's the only truth in that statement," observed Maud, adding that Southerners of Bessie's generation were practically weaned on that drink.

Bessie did go on the tour, and she took Richard Morgan with her—a fact that hardly supports Jack Gee's story. Morgan had remained remarkably faithful during the years when Bessie faced hard times with hard liquor and hope. Rather than take the train, she decided to travel in her old Packard, with Richard at the wheel—Bessie never learned to drive a car.

The show did good business in the Memphis area and was scheduled to open in Darling, Mississippi, on Sunday afternoon, September 26. Early that morning, having just finished the last Saturday night performance, Bessie seemed to be in a restless mood. She suggested to Richard that they get a head start on the troupe, drive down to Clarksdale, and spend the night there. As he would later tell Bessie's family, the idea of driving through the night did not sit well with him. He later admitted that his real reason for not wanting to go was his desire to "get into a card game with some of the boys." A heated argument ensued, and when Bessie threatened to get another driver, Richard gave in.

They left Memphis at about one in the morning and headed south on a straight stretch of Route 61. The heat of the argument had produced an aftermath of painful silence, which they maintained as they drove seventy-five miles toward Clarksdale. Richard was tired. The road was dark and seemingly endless. Suddenly, there loomed before them the rear end of a huge truck—Richard tried to avert a collision, but it was too late.

11

"BLUES SINGERS' QUEEN" DEAD
MEMPHIS, Sept. 26 (AP).—Show folk on Beale Street mourned today the death of Bessie Smith, 50, "queen" of blues singers, who was killed in an automobile accident. In 1917 Bessie sang the blues in a Beale Street show house, attracted attention of Eastern theatrical agents and was soon famous. Broadway welcomed her. She made many phonograph recordings. Two weeks ago she returned to Memphis to join the "Broadway Rastus" show on Beale Street. Early today an automobile in which she was riding overturned.
New York Times, September 27, 1937

The brief Associated Press report of Bessie's death appeared in white-readership newspapers across the country; it was inaccurate, but it was more press than most of these publications had given Bessie in her lifetime. The black press covered the story in greater detail, and gave it more prominence, but here, too, the facts were wrong. The *Chicago Defender*'s banner headline, "BESSIE SMITH, BLUES SINGER, KILLED," ran across the front page, followed by wildly contradictory capsule biographies and accounts of Bessie's final hours. It was clear that black reporters also knew little about Bessie's life, and even less about how it had ended.

Her funeral, a week and a half later, inspired more write-ups and photos in newspapers that for six years had all but forgotten her existence. Some made fragmentary, inaccurate references to the accident, but most merely pointed out that it had occurred. Other papers printed lengthy real and imagined descriptions of Bessie's accomplishments, often in terms more fanciful than any press release. The *Afro-American* told its readers that she had made 1,023 records for Columbia, "including many with accompaniments by white orchestras," and that she had in the course of a few weeks spent seventy-five thousand dollars in cash; according to the *Philadelphia Tribune,* she "pulled the Columbia Recording Company back to its feet after it had collapsed on the verge of bankruptcy," and George Gershwin "refused to write the final score of *Porgy and Bess* until he had sought her opinion."

Rumors of Bessie having been the victim of a Southern hospital's racist policy soon began to circulate, but no such circumstance was implied by the press until an article appeared in the November 1937 issue of *Down Beat,* a reckless piece of journalism that opened the floodgates to a stream of misinformation that would run for more than thirty years. It bore John Hammond's byline:

> DID BESSIE SMITH BLEED TO DEATH WHILE WAITING FOR MEDICAL AID?
>
> A particularly disagreeable story as to the details of her death has just been received from members of Chick Webb's orchestra, who were in Memphis soon after the disaster. It seems that Bessie was riding in a car which crashed into a truck parked along the side of the road. One of her arms was nearly severed, but aside from that there was no other serious injury, according to these informants. Some time elapsed before a doctor was summoned to the scene, but finally she was picked up by a medico and driven to the leading Memphis hospital. On the way this car was involved in some minor mishap, which further delayed medical attention. When finally she did arrive at the hospital she was refused treatment because of her color and bled to death while waiting for attention.
>
> Realizing that such tales can be magnified greatly in the telling, I would like to get confirmation from some Memphis citizens who were on the spot at the time. If the story is true it is but another example of disgraceful conditions in a certain section of our country already responsible for the killing and maiming of legitimate union organizers. Of the particular city of Memphis I am prepared to believe almost anything, since its mayor and chief of police publicly urged the use of violence against organizers of the CIO a few weeks ago.

Hammond ended his extraordinary piece with an ill-timed, shameless pitch; the first harvest of Bessie Smith's death was about to be reaped: "Be that as it may, the UHCA [United Hot Clubs of America] is busy sponsoring a special Bessie Smith memorial album[1] . . . the album will be released by Brunswick-

Columbia around the middle of November with pictures of the performers and details about each of the discs. Take it from one who cherished all the records that this will be the best buy of the year in music."

Although totally unsubstantiated, Hammond's report was quickly picked up and perpetuated by the black press, which made no attempt to determine its veracity.[2] It was only when Hammond's negative comments regarding Memphis drew angry protests from the city's mayor and hospital authorities that *Down Beat* did its homework. In a second article, the magazine reported that Bessie was taken directly to the Afro-American Hospital in Clarksdale, Mississippi, where she died due to loss of blood. It correctly refuted all stories of her having been refused admittance to a white hospital, but the truth lacked the intrigue of the original rumors, so no one seems to have paid attention.

Considering the temper of the times and Hammond's involvement in what was then a disorganized and far from popular fight for racial equality, the image of Bessie dying at the hands of Southern bigotry provided the perfect cause célèbre. From a writer's point of view it represented a fascinating bit of irony: Bessie Smith, the greatest of all blues singers, a powerful symbol of African-American success who had moved millions of Southerners to tears with her songs of misery, killed by Southern prejudice.

In an interview for this biography, thirty-four years later, John Hammond admitted—with some embarrassment—that his article had been based entirely on hearsay and that a few phone calls, made at the time, might have curbed the circulating rumors. He listened with great interest to a tape on which Dr. Hugh Smith gave his eyewitness account, and never challenged any of Smith's statements, but five years later, when his autobiography, *John Hammond on Record,* was published, it contained a convenient, contrived amalgam of his original fable and Dr. Hugh Smith's account:

"There are various theories about how she died. In 1937, during one of my trips to Huntsville, I heard what I thought was the true story. This was about five weeks after Bessie's death. I talked to the owner of the Green show, who told me how the old Packard in which Bessie was riding had been forced off the road and her arm nearly severed. He said that two ambulances had passed her by because she was black. It was a long and convincing story from a man who was in a position to know the truth, and there were two other people there nodding agreement as he told it to me.

When I told him that I wrote for several magazines and was interested, as my readers would be, in what had really happened, he said, 'Don't quote me.' "

If Hammond's final sentence was meant to explain why he waited forty years before telling this version, it stretches credulity. His stubborn perpetuation of the myth is all the more puzzling in view of an article that appeared in the October 17, 1957, issue of *Down Beat.* In it, George Hoefer noted that writers were still ignoring the truth surrounding the accident and its aftermath. He quoted the Hammond article and set the record straight; once again, it made little difference. In 1960 Edward Albee's play *The Death of Bessie Smith* opened in West Berlin; based on the same rumors that had inspired the Hammond article—and perhaps on the article itself—it prolonged the myth. Bessie Smith became better known for the way in which she had allegedly died than for what she had done in life.

Although Richard Morgan was physically unscathed by the accident, it is said to have left him a psychologically scarred, broken man. "He never got over it," said Maud, making an observation shared by Ruby, who remembered meeting Richard in the street a couple of years after the accident. "He didn't even recognize me, I don't think," she said, "and I almost didn't recognize him—he was so thin and sad looking." Lionel Hampton was convinced that Richard blamed himself for Bessie's death: "He kept saying he should have avoided that truck," he wrote in his 1989 autobiography. "He couldn't even say Bessie's name without crying. He was never the same after that. He got real old real fast, and he died just a few years later. I believe that he grieved himself to death over Bessie." Morgan died around 1943 without any reporter having asked him what actually happened on the morning of September 26, 1937. Only he could have described the circumstances that led to the accident.[3] The highway patrolmen who handled the case were reported dead by the mid-1950s, and if there are any records of the accident in the files of the Clarksdale Police Department, the officers there seem unwilling to make them public—letters of inquiry remain unanswered.

Virtually nothing would be known of the accident or the circumstances surrounding Bessie Smith's death were it not for the arrival on the scene, moments after the impact, of Dr. Hugh Smith[4] and Henry Broughton, his fishing partner. Broughton has long since died, taking to his grave any light that he might have shed on the event, but Dr. Smith—referred to in the second *Down Beat* article only as "a Memphis surgeon who came upon the scene of the accident and attended Bessie Smith"—was contacted by that magazine in the early 1940s for a published interview. Further details of his recollections appeared in a 1969 *Esquire* article entitled "The True Death of Bessie Smith," but that piece revealed little more than the fact that Dr. Smith was still alive and contained inexcusable misinformation, such as the detail that Bessie's car was traveling north instead of south.

We will never know the whole story, but the truth probably lies somewhere between the two following accounts based on Dr. Smith's detailed

In September 1937, Dr. Hugh Smith was an intern at the Campbell Clinic in Memphis. A fishing trip brought him to the scene of Bessie's fatal accident and forever linked him to her story.

recollections for this book and a 1938 newspaper interview with Jack Gee, Jr. (Snooks).

Smith and Broughton routinely left Memphis around one o'clock every other Sunday morning to drive south along Route 61 for two or three hours of pre-dawn fishing in a Mississippi lake. Recently married, Dr. Smith had just completed his training at the Campbell Clinic and—in celebration of these two milestones—traded in his Model A Ford for a small 1937 Chevrolet. At one-thirty on the morning of Sunday, September 26, 1937, the two men placed their fishing tackle in the back seat of the new car and headed south. The weather conditions were perfect: a warm, humid night, no moon, no wind stirring.

They were about seventy miles south of Memphis, driving at fifty to fifty-five miles per hour, when the figure of Richard Morgan stepped out of the dark and waved them down with frantic motions. Dr. Smith immediately slowed down, bringing his car to a halt fifty feet from the wreck of a large Packard sedan, which lay on its left side, diagonally across the narrow highway. Also bathed in Dr. Smith's bright headlights was the large, lifeless figure of Bessie Smith—cast from the wreck, she lay in the middle of the road. As Morgan—unhurt, but somewhat hysterical—approached the Chevrolet, Dr. Smith noticed two red tail lights disappearing into the dark night, heading toward Clarksdale. They belonged to the truck Bessie's car had struck, a truck that Dr. Smith believed to have been leased to the U.S. Post Office during the week and used to deliver the *Memphis Commercial Appeal* on Sundays. The truck has also been described as belonging to the U-Need-a-Biscuit Company, but a subsequent lawsuit establishes it as a National Biscuit Company vehicle.

According to information learned by Dr. Smith a few days later, the driver, fearing that his tires were overheated, had pulled up and parked on the side of the road. Dr. Smith pointed out that the shoulders were only two feet wide on this particular stretch, so it would have been impossible for the driver to pull off the road completely. Consequently, most of the truck had to protrude onto the road, resting in the right lane and requiring passing cars to pull into the northbound lane. The truck driver checked his tires, found them to be all right, and climbed back into the cab of his vehicle. His vehicle had just started moving at the time of the impact.

Dr. Smith's theory of how the accident happened is certainly plausible:

> If you've ever driven down a two-lane highway in the middle of the night, you know that it's almost impossible to estimate the distance of a pair of tail lights—they can be a mile, four miles, or four hundred and forty yards away. I would assume Richard Morgan realized there was a truck up there, but didn't realize that his depth perception extended only to his headlights . . . It would be natural to assume he expected those tail lights to be moving at about forty-five to sixty miles per hour down the highway when, in fact, the truck had just pulled back on the highway and hadn't gone two hundred and twenty yards at the time of the accident. So the tail lights and the depth perception all came together just at the instant that Richard Morgan realized he was about to plow into the back of a slowly moving truck on the east side of the highway.
>
> From the skid marks, I don't think there is any question but that he tried to go to the left side of the truck and miss it, but at the same time he applied his brakes, which made it go into a skid and probably almost a 90° angle at the time of impact. It ricocheted backwards and then flopped on its left side. The impact of Morgan's car was on Bessie Smith's side and she had "side swipe" injuries.[5]
>
> So one of two things happened. Either she was asleep with her entire arm out of the car, or else just the point of her elbow was out of the car—I suspect that was true—and it hit the tail gate of the truck as the top of Bessie's old Packard was sheared off. It was a real old car, for instead of a metal roof or metal struts supporting the roof, it was all wood—it was literally splintered like an old piece of dead kindling wood.

Dr. Smith jumped out of his car, rushed toward Bessie, and began a preliminary examination:

> All the bones around the elbow were completely shattered; there was a complete circumferential interruption of soft tissues about the elbow, except miraculously—despite the fact that she had almost had her forearm torn

> loose from her upper arm at the elbow—the three nerves were intact, lying there like telephone wires. The two major vessels, the artery and the nerve were intact. What that boils down to is that hemorrhage from the arm did not cause Bessie Smith's death.
>
> It was a horrible mess, lying out there in the open with maybe a half a pint of blood on the highway. But if that had been her only injury, she would have survived—there's no question in my mind about this at all. In this day and time we might even have saved her arm, but in that day and time there wouldn't have been any question; you'd just amputate, she'd have a seven-inch stump below the shoulder and probably be out of the hospital in twelve or fourteen days. However, that was not the case—she had sustained severe crushing injuries to her entire right side.
>
> I don't recall if Bessie Smith ever uttered a word, I don't think she answered any questions. She was moaning and groaning from excruciating pain and she was having a lot of trouble getting her breath. She was just breathing on the left side of her chest, all the ribs on her right side had been crushed pretty bad, and she probably had some inter-abdominal injuries. She was probably bleeding in her abdomen, because it was very stiff and rigid.
>
> Whether or not she had a head injury is a moot question, she wasn't conscious enough to talk. In the available light and without tools, I could not examine her pupils—at this stage it would have been too early to know if she had an inter-cranial hemorrhage, but she did have only minor head lacerations. Suffice it to say that Bessie Smith was in very critical condition.

As Richard Morgan looked on in silence, Mr. Broughton and Dr. Smith moved Bessie onto the road's grassy shoulder. They covered the major wound with a clean handkerchief, and Dr. Smith asked his friend to go to a house, some five hundred feet off the road, and call an ambulance. About ten minutes had lapsed since the accident, and another fifteen passed before Mr. Broughton returned. By this time Bessie was in shock.

The scene of the accident was still quiet; a few crickets and the voices of the two men seemed loud in the humid night. Having calmed down, Richard Morgan remained the silent observer—there was nothing he could do to help Bessie at this point. It has been suggested that he was intoxicated at the time of the accident, but Dr. Smith refuted that.

As time passed without any sign of an ambulance, Dr. Smith suggested to Broughton that they move the fishing tackle from the back seat of his car to the trunk, and take Bessie into Clarksdale. They had almost cleared the back seat when they heard the distant sound of a car approaching from the north, at high speed. Dr. Smith's Chevrolet was in the middle of the road, making it impossible for the approaching car to pass on either side, and since there was no indication of it slowing down, Broughton, standing on the right running board, suggested that they give some kind of signal. Dr. Smith immediately mounted the running board on the driver's side and, reaching for the dashboard switch, began blinking his lights as a warning to the approaching driver:

> I'll never forget this as long as I live. Mr. Broughton was on the right side hollering "Smith, you'd better jump—he ain't checkin'." Well, I jumped and Broughton jumped just as this car barreled into the back of my car at about fifty miles per hour. It drove my car straight into the wrecked Bessie Smith car and made a real pretzel out of it—it was a total loss. He ricocheted off the rear of my car and went into the ditch to the right. He barely missed Mr. Broughton and Bessie Smith.

The car's occupants were a young white couple who were obviously returning from a party. Dr. Smith now had his hands full:

> Now, my God, we had three patients on our hands. A young lady, curled up under the instrument panel on the right, screamed at the top of her voice, hysterical, scared to death. There was a man draped over the steering wheel, which had broken off completely. Well, we got them out in the grass and started to check them. As far as I could tell, the young lady didn't have any major injuries, but the man had a chest injury and that was about all. It turned out later that he had multiple fractures of his ribs, but fortunately he didn't have any lung injury, he wasn't in shock and he wasn't critical.

Dr. Smith was examining the young couple when an ambulance, a deputy sheriff, and several law officers appeared on the scene. The ambulance, answering Broughton's call, came from the G. T. Thomas Hospital, which served Clarksdale's black community, but as attendants and police placed Bessie on a stretcher, a second ambulance appeared on the scene. This one came from Clarksdale's white hospital, summoned by the truck driver, who had reported the accident without knowing the racial identity of the victims. Considering the course that the accident had taken, and the area's prevailing racist policies, the mix-up was fortuitous: Richard Morgan accompanied Bessie in one ambulance while the white couple was whisked off to the white hospital in the other.

Had these details been reported to the press in 1937—and there is no reason why they shouldn't have been—the controversy would not have arisen. Nor would there have been grounds for speculation if clear heads had prevailed and logic applied. Dr. Smith explained:

> The Bessie Smith ambulance would *not* have gone to a white hospital, you can forget that. Down in the Deep South cotton country, no colored ambulance driver, or white driver, would even have thought of putting a colored person off in a hospital for white folks. In Clarksdale, in 1937, a town of twelve to fifteen thousand people, there were two hospitals—one white and

> one colored—and they weren't half a mile apart. I suspect the driver drove just as straight as he could to the colored hospital.

The driver of the ambulance, Willie George Miller—a black man—confirmed this twenty years later. He remembered taking Bessie straight to the G. T. Thomas Hospital. He also recalled, albeit incorrectly, that she was dead on arrival. "I can't remember for certain," he told a reporter, "but I don't think she died instantly. But she did die within a few minutes after putting her in the ambulance, before we could get her to the hospital." As we will see, that part of Miller's statement is apocryphal.

Dr. Smith pointed out that it took an hour to draw a pint of blood from a donor in 1937. Then, too, both Clarksdale hospitals were country facilities, neither of which was as well equipped as their counterparts in larger cities, like Memphis. Given the same situation today, Smith pointed out in 1971, Bessie would have stood only a fifty-fifty chance of surviving the accident—she certainly would never have been able to sing again.

Of course, none of this can excuse the neglect on the part of the truck driver, who should have stopped, examined the accident scene, and taken Bessie to a hospital, nor Dr. Smith's failure to transport Bessie immediately in his own car rather than waste time summoning an ambulance.

It was only much later that Dr. Smith found out who the woman in the road was. The name Bessie Smith meant nothing to him in 1937,[6] nor did he see Hammond's article when it first appeared, but shortly after learning who Bessie was and how the circumstances of her death were being misreported, he found himself in New York on a business trip and decided to look up Frank Walker. "I wanted to give him the full details as to what actually happened down there in Mississippi," Dr. Smith recalled. "Well, he wasn't very interested and I could tell that he couldn't care less about Bessie—and that was the end of that."

Richard Morgan may well have contributed to the confusion by coloring his account of the accident and its aftermath. Some members of the family felt he was holding something back. "Richard sent for me before he passed," Maud Smith recalled, "but I wasn't able to come to him in time—he said he had something to tell me, but I have no idea what that could have been. He used to talk about Bessie, and he'd start crying. I never would ask him exactly what happened, but there were times when he was in my company that he would start crying and say he was sorry that he asked Bessie to leave that night. Richard and Bessie were *very* close, he was good for her, and he was never the same after Bessie died. He was always quiet when he wasn't drinking, you couldn't get a word out of him."

Rather than rely on his memory, Jack Gee, Jr., produced a newspaper clipping of an interview he gave the Baltimore *Afro-American* in early 1938. It was, he said, based in part on Richard Morgan's account to the family.

> "My mother and her chauffeur were on their way to Clarksdale, Mississippi, where she was to fill a singing engagement. It was on Saturday night, September 25. About 3 A.M., Sunday, just ten miles out of Clarksdale, her car ran into a parked truck belonging to the National Biscuit Company, which was standing on the side of the narrow highway without any lights.
>
> "Before the chauffeur, Richard Morgan, had a chance to stop, or turn out, he ran into the left corner of the truck, wedging my mother between the truck and the car.
>
> "Her left arm was cut almost off, and was hanging just by the skin. She was knocked unconscious. Moore [sic] jumped out of the car and went up to the driver of the truck, a white man, and said: 'What have you done? Pull up your truck.' The truck driver pulled up, but pulled away and had to be run down by State troopers and arrested. He was released on bail and still free.
>
> "A white physician, a Dr. Smith, came along about this time. He stopped to administer first aid, while Moore [sic] hiked to town to get an ambulance. My mother was still unconscious.
>
> "While the doctor was administering first-aid to my mother, another motorist came along and hit his car. A white woman passenger in the car was hurt in this second accident. One of the spectators asked the doctor why he didn't take my mother to town in his car, but he replied that his car would get too bloody.
>
> "About this time Morgan came back with the ambulance. As the men were about to take the stretcher out to take my mother, somebody in the crowd said: 'Wait, let's see what's the matter with this white woman first.' The doctor then administered first-aid to the white woman, and then put her in the ambulance, and sent her back to town. Morgan protested but could do nothing.
>
> "We have never found out accurately yet how my mother was taken back to town, but we do know that she was first taken to a white hospital, which refused to administer first-aid or take her in. She was then taken to the Afro-American Hospital, a colored institution. This hospital didn't have the proper equipment with which to operate. Physicians had to run all over town to get the proper equipment.
>
> "It was about 11:30 A.M. before they administered ether to her. She died at 11:45 A.M. No reason was given as to why she died, but we know clearly that she died from loss of blood and neglect. I believe that if the ambulance had taken my mother back to town, as it was proper for the doctor to have instructed the driver, since the ambulance was sent for her case, she might be alive today."

While it behooved Jack Gee, Jr., and the day's liberal press to keep alive the story sparked by John Hammond's article, it contained too many inconsisten-

A "Black Sheep" Makes Good

JACK GEE, JR., who told the AFRO last week that he, an only child of the late Bessie Smith, blues singer, was considered the black sheep of the family, and that now he is leading the fight to collect $250,-000 from the National Biscuit Company, as an aftermath of her death near Clarksdale, Miss., last September.—Photo by Woodard.

Jack Gee, Jr. ("Snooks"), made news shortly after Bessie's death, when he joined Jack Gee, Sr., in a lawsuit against the National Biscuit Company. "There was a settlement," he said, "but I never saw any of it." From the Baltimore *Afro-American*, early 1938.

cies not to also raise serious skepticism. Among the early disbelievers was folklorist John Lomax, who in 1941 wrote several letters of inquiry and received some interesting and significant responses.

"Sadly, the Country is infested with Negro communists who seek to poison their own people against their best friends," wrote the mayor of Memphis, Walter Chandler, "and I am glad to have the opportunity to join in establishing the facts, which I am sure will disprove the story." In a subsequent letter, dated September 8, 1941, the mayor referred to Hammond's *Down Beat* article, saying that the writer "either lied maliciously, or is an irresponsible writer desiring to foment trouble between white and colored people." If racial incident had played a role in the death of Bessie Smith, the setting was not Memphis, he concluded. Indeed it wasn't.

The most significant letter came a month later, from Dr. W. H. Brandon, the man who had treated Bessie at the G. T. Thomas Hospital and signed her death certificate:

15284

BUREAU OF VITAL STATISTICS **STANDARD CERTIFICATE OF DEATH** State File No.

MISSISSIPPI STATE BOARD OF HEALTH

1. PLACE OF DEATH
County Coahoma — Registered No. 171
Voting Precinct ... or Village ...
or City Clarksdale, Miss. No. 116 4th St. ... St., ... Ward
(If death occurred in a hospital or institution, give its NAME instead of street and number) Afro-American Hospital 615 Sunflower Ave. Clarksdale
Length of residence in city or town where death occurred

2. FULL NAME Bessie Smith 530 (Write or Print Name Plainly)
(a) Residence: No. 7003. 12th St., Philadelphia, Pa. Ward. (Usual place of abode) (If nonresident give city or town and State)

PERSONAL AND STATISTICAL PARTICULARS	
3. SEX	Female
4. COLOR OR RACE	Negro
5. Single, Married, Widowed, or Divorced (write the word)	Married
5a. If married, widowed, or divorced HUSBAND of (or) WIFE of	Jack Gee
6. DATE OF BIRTH (month, day, and year)	
7. AGE Years / Months / Days / If LESS than 1 day, hrs. or min.	42
8. Trade, profession, or particular kind of work done, as spinner, sawyer, bookkeeper, etc.	Artist
9. Industry or business in which work was done, as silk mill, saw mill, bank, etc.	
10. Date deceased last worked at this occupation (month and year)	9/26/37
11. Total time (years) spent in this occupation	25
12. BIRTHPLACE (city or town) (State or country)	Chattanooga, Tenn
13. NAME (Father)	Unknown
14. BIRTHPLACE (city or town) (State or country)	"
15. MAIDEN NAME (Mother)	Unknown
16. BIRTHPLACE (city or town) (State or country)	"
17. INFORMANT (and Address)	Richard Morgan, Philadelphia, Pa
18. BURIAL, CREMATION, OR REMOVAL Place / Date	Philadelphia, Pa. Oct. 3, 1937
19. UNDERTAKER (and Address)	Afro-American Burial Ass'n, Clarksdale, Miss.

MEDICAL CERTIFICATE OF DEATH

21. DATE OF DEATH (month, day and year) Sept. 26, 1937
22. I HEREBY CERTIFY, That I attended deceased from Sept. 26 1937 to Sept 26 1937
I last saw h... alive on Sept. 26 1937. Death is said to have occurred on the date stated above, at 11:30 A.m.
The principal cause of death and related causes of importance in order of onset were as follows: ... Date of onset
Contributory causes of importance not related to principal cause: ... 1-210
Name of operation (if any was done) ... Date of Sept 26, 1937
What test confirmed diagnosis? ... Was there an autopsy? No
23. If death was due to external causes (violence) fill in also the following: Accident, suicide, or homicide? Auto accident
Date of injury Sept 26, 1937
Where did injury occur? (Specify city or town, county, and State)
Specify whether injury occurred in industry, in home, or in public place Public road
Manner of injury
Nature of injury
24. Was disease or injury in any way related to occupation of deceased? No If so, specify
(Signed) W. H. Brandon M.D.
(Address) Clarksdale, Miss.

Filed Sept. 28 1937

CERTIFIED COPY OF RECORD OF DEATH

I, Hugh B. Cottrell, M. D., State Registrar of Vital Statistics, hereby certify this to be a true and correct copy of the death record of the person named therein, the original being on file in this office.

Given at Jackson, Mississippi, over my signature and under the official seal of my office, this the 13th Day April, 1971

Hugh B. Cottrell, M. D. State Registrar

Paul Burnell Hawkins

Paul Burnell Hawkins, Deputy State Registrar

Mississippi State Standard Certificate of Death No. 15284 belies much of the myth surrounding Bessie's final day. From the author's collection.

October 7, 1941
Dear Mr. Lomax:

I am very glad to have your letter with reference to Bessie Smith.

Bessie Smith was injured in an automobile accident several miles out from Clarksdale and was brought to Clarksdale in a colored ambulance. The car in which she was riding was smashed and she was in shock when brought to the hospital.

She died some eight or ten hours after admission to the hospital. We gave her every medical attention, but we were never able to rally her back from the shock.

She was badly broken up, having many fractures of her limbs and internal injuries.

The man who was driving the car was apparently very drunk. As I remember it, he received very few injuries, as is often the case.

You may brand the statement that she was refused treatment as an absolute untruth.

If there is any further information that I can give you on this subject, I will be glad to do so.

Very truly yours,
(signed) W. H. Brandon, M.D.

According to the official death certificate issued by the Mississippi State Board of Health, Bessie Smith died in Ward 1 of the Afro-American Hospital, 615 Sunflower Avenue, Clarksdale, September 26, 1937, at 11:30 A.M. "The principal cause of death and related causes of importance in order of onset were as follows: *Shock. Possibly internal injuries. Compound, comminuted fractures of rt. humerus, radius and ulna.* Contributory causes of importance not related to principal cause: *Rt. humerus, radius and ulna.* Name of operation: *Amputation rt. arm.*"

12

"That woman must be weeping in her grave—poor Bessie, even after she died, people wouldn't let her be."
Ruby Walker

Bessie Smith's stature as an artist is too great for her story to end on that dark Mississippi road in 1937. She left a rich legacy, her musical influence, both direct and indirect, is ongoing, and even as we move into a new millennium, the magic of her name continues to inspire—and ring cash registers.

The entertainment industry inherently thrives on publicity. Vast amounts of money are spent creating stars and keeping them in the spotlight. To this end, promotion people have been dreaming up ingenious devices and gimmicks for more than a century. Today, the Internet allows these hucksters to reach millions of people around the globe in an instant, but although the methodology changes with each technical innovation, some marketing ploys remain the same, and in the record business nothing is as surefire as the premature death of a major star.[1]

As we have seen, the temptation to reap a consumer harvest existed even in Bessie Smith's day; although the posthumous album was already planned at the time of her death, it was quickly dubbed a "memorial album" and John

Hammond shamelessly seized the opportunity to plug it as the year's "best buy." Bessie's recording debut and her immediate success in 1923 had been a lifesaver for the near-bankrupt Columbia company, and now, ironically, her death proved to be just as timely, for it virtually coincided with a renaissance of traditional jazz, which also sparked renewed interest in the classic blues singers. Now Bessie's entire recorded output would forever be the exclusive property of Columbia.

The 1938 Bessie Smith reissues sold reasonably well largely owing to her death, but also because of the enormous popularity of swing music, which had invaded Carnegie Hall via Benny Goodman that January and given the previous decade's jazz a trendy veneer. Jazz had always enjoyed a youthful following, but there was something different about the new jazz fan of the late 1930s. Not content to merely hang out in smoke-filled joints or perform athletic dance steps in ballrooms, this generation of fans searched musty attics and junk shops for original issues of recordings that had come to be regarded as "classic," collected them zealously, and romanticized the past. With the typical collector's mentality, they sometimes seemed to care more for rare matrix numbers than for the performances they identified, but a debt is owed them for preserving valuable information and music. In an era when swing's big band leaders and soloists were glamorized and received with as much adoration as Hollywood stars, the new jazz collector explored the roots of swing, tracing current sounds back to such "colorful" figures as Ma Rainey, King Oliver, Jelly Roll Morton, and Bessie Smith—performers whose exploits, real and imagined, made good subjects for after-dinner conversation. They found a history riddled with ongoing social inequities and racial injustices, which they deplored and romanticized but did little or nothing to correct.

The average white jazz followers readily embraced a black performer's output as art but rarely accepted him or her as a person. "Oh, they loved you when you was up there on that stage, with all those lights and costumes," said Ruby, speaking of white audiences, "but most of them wouldn't give you a second look on the street. And invite you to their home? Ha! Not unless you could perform for their white guests." A few early collectors founded small record companies and devoted them to the music they loved, and as the music changed, several of these independent labels got a jumpstart on the majors and began recording the new sound of bebop.

The swing era brought jazz to the forefront of America's popular music, giving it the greatest prominence it would ever enjoy. The renewed interest brought work and a measure of recognition to many artists—black and white—whose careers had been on the wane, but the material rewards were generally greater for the promoters, impresarios, club owners, and record companies. Exploitation was rampant, but garbed in a cloak of artistic recognition and cultural acceptance.

Like any movement, this one needed its myths and martyrs. It found the latter in people like Joseph "King" Oliver, Louis Armstrong's early boss and lifetime idol, who spent his last days in a janitorial job and chronicled the pain in a series of moving letters to his sister; in Bix Beiderbecke, a white cornet player who died at twenty-eight in 1931, the victim of artistic frustration and alcoholism; and now, too, in Bessie, whose premature death—allegedly at the hands of racism—eminently qualified her. Oliver, Bix, Bessie, and a handful of other jazz performers became legends, and the myths surrounding them so ingrained—because they were tailor-made—that the truth continued to be ignored. But as jazz history began to be scrutinized, there were also some reality checks: Paul Whiteman was not really the "King of Jazz,"[2] nor was it appropriate to regard Benny Goodman as the "King of Swing."

The largely unrecognized black musician of the 1920s became the darling of the late 1930s' and early 1940s' left-wing liberal. Socialists and Communists found in America's black population the proletariat to suit their cause—what better way to show social concern than to have a "colored" man play for your gathering of friends! Carl Van Vechten was way ahead of the game. It was in this milieu that many of the postwar period's established, old-ward jazz writers, record collectors, promoters, and recording executives laid the groundwork for their fortunes. Behind their benign smiles and embrace of black creativity lurked a patronizing attitude that most performers easily detected but—for political expediency—chose to ignore. This is not to say that all people on the business end of jazz were mercenary; many genuinely loved the music and respected the artists, and we would be less enlightened today were it not for their enthusiasm.

Today, we still see interaction between people of different complexions end with the five-o'clock whistle, so it should not surprise us to learn that the cultural gap was even wider sixty and seventy years ago. The early jazz writers (who were white) certainly did not consider themselves to be racist, quite the opposite, but their relationships with black performers rarely extended beyond the jazz scene, which meant that there existed an invisible wall between writer and subject. That accounts to a great extent for the lack of accurate reporting that until very recently marred most books on the subject of black music and its creators. The writers believed only what they wanted to believe, and their sources told them only what they wanted them to hear. The lack of openness resulted in what often amounted to a revisionist history of African-American music, such as the overly simplified and not entirely true Africa-

Wearing an Afro wig and a stylish robe, Ruby Walker Smith has a youthful look in this 1972 photo. Photo by Don Lynn, from the author's collection.

to-New-Orleans-and-up-the-river story, which—as *Jazz,* Ken Burns's sadly flawed monumental TV documentary series demonstrated—refuses to die. The up-the-river approach also formed the basis for John Hammond's successful *From Spirituals to Swing* concert at Carnegie Hall in December 1938, an event that was to have included Bessie among its many stars but was instead dedicated to her memory.

Ruby Walker—who after Bessie's death changed her surname to Smith—represented Bessie at Hammond's concert. Four months later, Ruby made her recording debut for the Blue Bird label, and continued over the next few years to record for Vocalion, Decca, Harmonia, and Victor. She made frequent club and theater appearances into the 1960s, gradually abandoning the imitation of Bessie's dress and mannerisms that Hammond had forced upon her. "He wanted me to *be* Bessie Smith," she recalled, "to walk like her, do her little steps, and sing like her. I went along with it, but I didn't like it, because Bessie herself had gotten away from that old stuff—I wanted to do swing songs, that's all people was listening to back then."

In the early 1970s—with that long-promised "big break" yet to materialize—Ruby continued to sing in public whenever the opportunity presented itself, often dipping back into her aunt's repertoire, which by then somehow seemed less dated than her swing songs. Except for the few times when she gave largely unsanctioned performances in Bessie's place, Ruby had not sung publicly while Bessie was alive, but their long and close association prepared her well for the task. "I could do Bessie well," she said, "every little move—and you know she had a lot of little moves; Bessie didn't do a lot of shaking, she just raised an eyebrow or kicked her hip out, quiet-like. Naturally, I knew all her songs backwards and forwards, even some of the ones she started singing after she changed."

Bessie's influence on Ruby transcended music to include a spirit and a sense of humor that the years had not diminished. Ruby Walker matured from girlhood to womanhood in the shadow of her aunt's triumphs and tribulations, but Bessie's fierce independence had not rubbed off on her. On her own, she lacked Bessie's ability to stand up to those who would exploit her.

Aside from Snooks, Richard Morgan may well have been Bessie's one true love. Wild as she often was, he remained loyal, if not faithful, to the end. From all accounts, he never quite recovered from her death, but began to age prematurely. Ruby had not recognized him when they chanced to meet, and Lionel Hampton thought Richard had "grieved himself to death," yet Maud saw another reason for the rapid deterioration of Richard's health and spirit: "I do think he truly loved her, but I also think he blamed himself for the accident—that's what Clary always said. You know, when you're in an accident and somebody gets killed, but you don't have a scratch on you, you either think God spared you or that you should have died, too. I think Richard felt guilty and it drove that poor man to his death."

Gertrude Saunders survived her eventful relationship with Jack Gee. "She was always a smart woman," recalled Alberta Hunter. "She was investing in real estate long before the rest of us thought of investing in anything." In the 1930s Gertrude continued her career successfully in Hollywood, lending her voice to animated cartoons. When she retired from show business, she settled down as the landlady of a Bronx apartment house, spending "all my time," as she put it, "fighting my tenants in court."

By the end of the 1940s, Clarence and virtually all of Bessie's closest kin

A 1971 snapshot of Jack Gee, Jr. ("Snooks"). Thirty-four years after Bessie's death, he still had lawsuits on his mind. Photo by Maud Smith Faggins.

were dead. The remaining nieces and nephews also died prematurely, before the end of the 1960s; in 1972, when the original edition of this book was published, only Jack Gee, Jack Gee, Jr. (Snooks), and Clarence's widow, Maud, were still living. Maud remarried a man named James Faggins, took a job with the U.S. Marine Corps, and became an active member of the Republican Party; Jack Gee owned a Laundromat in Philadelphia and dabbled in various enterprises, including artist management, but none of his various protégés succeeded. He died at the age of eighty-four on June 6, 1973; Jack, Jr., worked as a bartender in Philadelphia, where he died in the 1990s.

During Bessie's final years, there was no love lost between Jack Gee, Jr. and Sr., nor did her death change that, but money has a way of breaking down barriers, even if only momentarily, so they combined forces to file a $250,000 lawsuit against the National Biscuit Company.[3] It was an attempt to cash in on Bessie's death, and it severed once and for all any semblance of kinship that had existed between Snooks and the rest of the family. Jack, Sr., had always been persona non grata, but he had maintained a tenuous relationship with Jack, Jr.—the lawsuit would eventually also increase the distance between them.

The lawsuit was filed in Clarksdale shortly after Bessie's death. "I've always been looked upon as a sort of black sheep by my family," Jack, Jr., told a reporter at the time, "and that's why I want to fight this thing through. I believe it will in a way help to make up to my mother for some of the trouble I caused her while she was alive. I intend to fight this case all the way. I don't know what luck I'll have, because I know, that despite the fact that we have a good case against the company and the doctor too, the case will come up in Clarksdale, Miss., sometime this month [January 1938], and I feel that it will be hard to get justice down there."

According to the *Afro-American,* the National Biscuit Company offered to settle out of court for $80,000, but "the family is holding out for $250,000, and the establishment of justice in this case."

"As far as I know," recalled Jack Gee, Jr., thirty years later, "my father collected the money—some $58,000, I believe, but we were on the outs then, and in fact, the whole family had a falling out about this."

"After Bessie died," said Maud in 1972, adding to the confusion, "Jack came and everything was signed over to Viola, nobody but she could touch anything until she herself died. I can't understand how Jack can go and make such a big splash now, because he and Bessie was divorced when he died. In fact, Jack was married when Bessie died." Searches have failed to produce documentary evidence of Jack having divorced Bessie and remarried.

Following the lawsuit, Jack, Sr., sought to maintain some form of relationship with Snooks. Waving before him a carrot of financial rewards, all he actually did was to lead Jack, Jr., into a life of petty illegal activities that often resulted in jail sentences and eventually soured their relationship. While Jack, Sr., continued to fabricate the myth of a close bond between himself and Bessie, and to collect whatever monies the estate produced, Jack, Jr., entered middle age without receiving as much as a penny from Bessie's legacy. In fact, his existence was a well-kept secret until Ruby casually dropped his name in one of the interviews for this book. More about the Gees later.

In the 1940s, Columbia Records (which had been acquired by the Columbia Broadcasting System in 1938) continued to reissue Bessie's records or authorize their reissue by such private labels as the United Hot Clubs of America. These releases also included selections that were originally rejected[4] and for which neither Bessie nor her accompanists were paid. Through these recordings, Bessie continued to influence young singers whose followers, ironically, often regarded Bessie's own records as ancient history.

For many years the stigma of Uncle Tomism was attached to the music of Bessie and her contemporaries, scaring off young black would-be followers, but that changed in the wake of the Civil Rights movement of the 1960s, a time that coincided with and boosted a renewed interest in blues and other folk music. In 1951, George Avakian produced for Columbia a reissue of forty-eight of Bessie's recordings on four long-playing albums; it was a fine series that proved to be a slow but steady seller, and Columbia kept the four releases in its catalogue for nineteen years. In 1970, Bessie Smith became the subject of a reissue project more ambitious than any in the label's history: five double albums containing her entire available recorded output. By the summer of 1972, the first four albums of the new series had sold a total of two hundred thousand copies, or four hundred thousand records, exceeding by about 90 percent the combined sales of the four 1951 albums over the nineteen-year period.

In all fairness it should be pointed out that the 1951 reissues were given limited press, whereas Columbia's publicity department began promoting the 1970 series six months before the release of the first album. Press releases and telephone calls resulted in unprecedented advance publicity for a reissue program, and the secret to Columbia's success was that it aimed its publicity at the young, placing advertisements in the so-called underground press—the rock publications—and skillfully couching the advertising copy in terms that are usually reserved for contemporary albums. Such tactics would have been of little use had not the timing been right, which it was: spurred by the folk revival, a new interest in old blues was stimulated by such popular groups as the Rolling Stones, who openly admitted their debt to Robert Johnson, and such resurrected blues pioneers as Skip James, Furry Lewis, Memphis Slim, and Lonnie Johnson.

Within weeks of the release of the first album in the new Bessie Smith series, her name was being bandied about on inane daytime TV quiz shows; a Philadelphia organization voted to strike a silver coin in her honor; contemporary performers were recording tributes; Edward Albee's *Death of Bessie Smith* enjoyed some revivals; her film, *St. Louis Blues*, was shown on TV for the first time; and she became the subject of innumerable term papers. The Bessie Smith albums were awarded four Grammys; critics honored the first album with a Grand Prix du Disque at the 1971 Montreaux Jazz Festival; and the producer was the recipient of *Billboard* magazine's 1971 "Trendsetter of the Year" award. Suddenly, Bessie Smith climbed to the top in jazz critics' polls.

With all this publicity, it was inevitable that someone would discover a rather startling fact: Bessie Smith's grave was still unmarked. This was not the first time the matter had been brought up: newspapers and the music press of the day described successful benefits held during the 1940s and 1950s to raise funds for Bessie's gravestone, but none explained why the grave remained unmarked.

"I never saw three cents of all that money," Jack Gee replied when he was asked why *he* had not purchase a stone, but other surviving relatives contradicted his assertion. According to them, proceeds from such benefits were turned over to Jack Gee on at least two occasions. Ruby recalled performing at such an event in New York's Town Hall during the 1940s: "Jack showed up and demanded the money. He said he'd have his lawyers stop the concert if he didn't get it. He got it, but knowing Jack he spent it on something for himself."

Maud Smith may have been referring to the same event: "When Jack went to New York, he made enough money to buy two stones, but he used the money for something else." She also pointed out that Bessie's funeral did not absorb all the insurance money, and told of a benefit that took place at Philadelphia's Blue Note Club in the early 1950s: "Jack Fields gave the benefit, and the place was packed full of stars and people from Philadelphia and New York, including Juanita Hall. I remember it was a Saturday morning when William Upshur came to the house and gave me a check from the benefit at the Blue Note. I got into Mr. Upshur's car and we went to Jack on South Street. I gave the check to him and we were supposed to go and pick out a stone for Bessie, and that's the last time I saw the check, and every time I would ask him about the stone he said he was busy, that he was waiting on his lawyers, or waiting on somebody. I don't remember the amount on the check, but it was more than enough to buy a stone — and that's what the money was for."

All this time, Jack Gee could well have afforded to purchase a stone on his own, even if the story of his settlement with the National Biscuit Company wasn't true. He received with regularity composer's royalties for Bessie's tunes — many of which were recorded by top artists through the years — and he put that money to work by investing in real estate and several small businesses. Perhaps they simply did not know about Bessie's unmarked grave, but, if they did, affluent "close friends" and admirers of Bessie remained unperturbed by her anonymity at Mount Lawn Cemetery. It would take someone who had never known Bessie to point out the discrepancy more than forty years after Bessie's death.

Epilogue

"My dream is to go to California before my face drops."
Ruby Smith, 1970

In July 1970, inspired by the rash of publicity given the album releases, Barbara Muldow, a black Philadelphia housewife, wrote a letter to the *Philadelphia Inquirer*'s Action Line. She had read some publicity regarding the reissues of Bessie's recordings, and she wondered why there was no marker on her grave. The *Inquirer*'s Action Line reporter, Frank Coffey, saw a human-interest story and decided to follow it up. He called Columbia Records and was switched to the office of Robert Altshuler, the label's vice president of promotion, who also happened to be a collector of traditional jazz recordings. Altshuler immediately recognized this as a PR opportunity and promised to get back to Coffey within a day. It just so happened that one of Columbia's hottest artists at that time, singer Janis Joplin, was an avowed Bessie Smith fan. When Altshuler suggested that she get involved in purchasing the gravestone, Joplin said, "You make the arrangements, I'll pay for it," but when Altshuler got back to the *Inquirer*, Coffey had meanwhile received a call from Juanita Green, a Philadelphia area business woman, who made the same offer. Eager to get Columbia involved in this PR opportunity, Altshuler suggested a compromise: the two women would share the expense. That turned out to be a relatively small amount of money, for a monument firm contacted by Coffey offered to sell the stone at cost: five hundred dollars.

Both women were paying a debt to Bessie. Janis Joplin, a rock superstar, felt she owed her style and urgency to Bessie. "No one ever hit me so hard," she told me one night as we listened to a Bessie Smith recording in one of Columbia's editing rooms. "Bessie made me want to sing." Juanita Green also attributed her success to Bessie, for it had been on her good advice that she shelved her stage aspirations and stayed in school. Little Juanita, who subsequently scrubbed Bessie's kitchen floor on Saturdays and continued to have the importance of education instilled in her, became a registered nurse before acquiring two Philadelphia nursing homes. In 1970, when she made her call to the *Inquirer*, she was also the president of the North Philadelphia chapter of the NAACP.

The unveiling of Bessie's gravestone was set for Friday, August 7, 1970. No invitations were sent out, but a notice in the *Philadelphia Inquirer* attracted a few people, and Altshuler had of course summoned the local media. Juanita Green contacted Jack Gee, offering to send a car to pick him up, but her invitation was greeted with verbal abuse and a threat of legal action against all involved. Jack was being true to form. Later, claiming to have misunderstood Green's intentions, he sent her a letter of apology.

Neither Bessie's sister-in-law, Maud, nor Snooks attended the ceremony, although both had known it was taking place. Janis Joplin's absence was more conspicuous; the official explanation was that she had prior commitments, but the truth was that she did not wish to become the center of attention at this event. "I know the Columbia guys would want me there," she said, "but it wouldn't be cool, because people are just going to say that I wanted publicity, or some shit like that."[1] In a phone conversation that week, Joplin and Green discussed the possibility of establishing a scholarship fund in Bessie's name, and agreed to meet in the near future. The meeting never took place, for, two months later, Columbia had cause to prepare a Janis Joplin memorial album.

John Hammond showed up and made a point of mentioning that he was there in an unofficial capacity, but it later turned out that Altshuler had urged him to go as part of a Columbia contingent that also included a professional photographer and the label's Philadelphia distributor. More than three decades after Bessie's death, Columbia Records continued to cash in the chips.

Also among the thirty or so people who milled around Bessie's grave, including myself, were two local ministers, one representing the company that supplied the gravestone, the other a candidate for office who seemed to be there for no reason other than to pose for the media and hand out his election flyers. Dressed in black and sporting dark shades, the two men looked slightly sinister as they huddled to devise a simple ceremony. Then, as one minister posed for the cameras and handed out campaign leaflets, the other announced

John Hammond's raincoat covers Bessie's new gravestone at the August 1970 "unveiling." In the foreground are the Reverend Wycliffe Jangdharrie (wearing black suit and sunglasses) and the Reverend W. E. Cook. In the center, Juanita Green (black dress and hat) is flanked by John Hammond and pianist John Brown; the woman holding flowers is Barbara Muldow, whose letter to the *Philadelphia Inquirer* sparked the event. Photo courtesy of Columbia Records.

that the ceremony would begin with his dedicatory message, which would be followed by Barbara Muldow's placing on Bessie's grave the rather large bouquet of assorted flowers she held. While that was carried out, the other minister would say a prayer, and we would all step forward to drop a flower upon the grave. As he laid out this scenario, a lady walked among us, handing each a long-stemmed yellow flower. Finally, we were all told to form a semicircle in front of the modest gravestone. It was a simple-enough ritual, but it soon became farcical.

As the minister began to speak and the small group stood poised for the flower drop, it occurred to someone that a covering would be needed if an unveiling was to take place. There followed a moment of confusion and the two ministers once again huddled. "I have something in the trunk of my car," said Hammond as he headed toward the parked vehicle. We all watched as he pulled a wrinkled old blue raincoat out of the trunk and handed it to one of the

John Hammond, Juanita Green, and pianist John Brown, who once accompanied Bessie, accommodate Columbia Records' photographer by reenacting the flower ritual. The author, flowers in hand, awaits his turn. Columbia Records publicity photo.

men in black. It was promptly draped over the stone, and one could just imagine what Bessie might have said about that. The minister finished his dedication, struggling somewhat to lend solemnity to what had developed into a comical scene. Right on cue, the coat was ceremoniously lifted to complete the "unveiling." The political candidate delivered his prayer as scheduled, and everybody filed past the grave, dropping their flower while the cameras clicked. No sooner was the ceremony declared over than the campaigner produced a stack of his leaflets and distributed them with a pearly smile and handshakes. People slowly headed back to their cars, but they had not gone far when Altshuler asked everybody to return. It seemed that the flower drop had taken place too fast, robbing some photographers of the shots they wanted; the charade's principal characters were asked to retrieve a flower from the grave and stand by for a reenactment. This time, the press was satisfied, the photo-op was over, and everyone but Bessie was free to leave.

Following this ceremony, an informal gathering was held in the home of Juanita Green, who announced the foundation of a Bessie Smith scholarship fund for the purpose of "helping a student in a career of music and science." A plate was passed around for donations that added up to three hundred dollars. That figure did not change until a year later, when Columbia Records contributed one thousand dollars and John Hammond added fifty from his own pocket.

That evening and the following day, the quiet event received widespread publicity in newspapers across the country and on the television networks. Most media emphasized Bessie's alleged death at the hands of Southern racism and the involvement of Janis Joplin in the purchase of the stone. Altshuler waited for the flurry of interest to fade, then perked it up with a self-serving promotional announcement dated August 17, 1970. Falsely stating that the label's own John Hammond had contributed to the purchase of the stone and crediting Altshuler himself with authorship of its inscription, the press release deceptively gave the impression that Columbia Records had reached out to Bessie Smith.

> COLUMBIA PARTICIPATES IN TRIBUTE TO BESSIE SMITH
> After Thirty Years, a Marker Is Put on Empress's Grave
>
> Janis Joplin, Columbia Recording Artist, Juanita Green, a registered nurse from Philadelphia, and John Hammond, Director of Talent Acquisition, Columbia Records, among others, shared the cost of a gravestone for legendary blues singer, Bessie Smith, whose grave had lain unmarked since her death in an auto accident in 1937. About fifty fans of the late Miss Smith were present at the unveiling of the stone last week at her grave-site in Sharon Hill, Pennsylvania, near Philadelphia.
>
> Robert Altshuler, Columbia executive and long-time admirer of her recordings, was responsible for the inscription on the stone, which reads, "The Greatest Blues Singer in the World Will Never Stop Singing—Bessie Smith—1895–1937."

The epitaph, at least, was true, but Altshuler soon found himself having to answer embarrassing questions from journalists who wondered if Columbia had short-changed Bessie.

Not long after the gravestone ceremony, as I continued work on the Bessie Smith reissue project, I found myself in John Hammond's office, and it proved to be a most opportune moment. We were a group of two or three gathered on the visitor's side of John's desk when his secretary announced that a Miss Ruby Walker was there to see him. "Oh, send her in," said John, appearing quite surprised by this unscheduled visit. "She's a marvelous singer," he told us, just as Ruby stepped in. We were all introduced and there was some small talk about the old days, but conversation soon gave way to awkward silence. John stood up from his desk, reached into his trouser pocket and handed Ruby what I believe was either a ten- or a twenty-dollar bill. "I know I'll never see this again, but here," he said. It was a remarkably awkward display of tactlessness and, I thought, disrespect, but Ruby took the money. "Why?" I later asked her. "A bird in hand," she replied with a smile. "That man owes me a lot more."

Stunned by John's insensitive, insulting gesture, I broke the silence and asked Ruby if she had eaten. She hadn't, but seemed delighted when I offered to take her to lunch. During the next couple of hours, as we downed a rather ordinary, inexpensive luncheonette offering, Ruby—who had taken to calling herself Smith—gave me some background on her visit.

She had come to John Hammond's office that morning in hopes of cashing in on his thirty-year-old promise to make her "the new Bessie Smith." As proof, she pulled from her purse a time-worn page from the evening's printed program. It stated that Hammond was "grooming Ruby to replace her famous aunt."

It was the old Bessie whom Hammond wanted to re-create, not the smartly coiffed torch singer. That disappointed Ruby, but she bowed to his wishes and became the anachronism Hammond needed her to be, even changing her last name to Smith. If she seemed eager to undergo a retro makeover, it was because Hammond dictated it, and he had the power to make or break careers in the music business.

Unfortunately, as the Carnegie Hall concert slipped into history, Hammond's promise to Ruby slipped from his mind. To appease her, he occasionally booked her to sing at private parties—not the elegant ones thrown on Fifth Avenue by his Vanderbilt-rooted family, but small gatherings of leftist literati and other intellectuals to whom a sprinkling of dark skin lent a visual touch of liberalism. However, fees for such appearances were hardly the stuff of which capitalists are molded, and there was no promotional value in performing at small private parties.

In 1939, Ruby recorded a couple of sides for Vocalion with Bessie's favorite pianist, James P. Johnson. Her own promotional efforts also resulted in a few Harmonia and Victor sides in the mid-1940s, but Hammond had lost interest in her career. In the mid-1950s, Ruby again decided to take matters into her own hands; she noticed that Mercury Records was releasing quite a few albums by singers, so she decided to write the company a letter and offer herself. Hammond, she wrote, had "promised me the moon, but dropped me like a hot potato." Unknown to Ruby, John Hammond was now a vice president at Mercury, so her letter landed on his desk. In typical fashion, he made a blustering phone call, promising Ruby that he would do what he could to ensure that she never recorded again. It was the kind of call Hammond often made when artists displeased him, and this time, he kept his promise to Ruby.

Twenty-five years later, Ruby made her impromptu visit to Hammond's CBS office, fueled by a hope that age had mellowed him. And so it had, to a point.

Ruby and I had developed a close friendship by 1971, when publisher Sol Stein suggested that I write this Bessie Smith biography. "You know how you go to the mirror one day, and your face has dropped?" she once asked me. I told her that I had some idea of that possibility. "Well," she continued, "my dream is to go to California before my face drops." With that in mind, I called Ruby as soon as I got off the phone with Sol. "Has it dropped yet?" I asked. "No," she said. "Good, because here's your chance to get to California."

Accepting the book deal, I offered Ruby a percentage or my entire advance. She opted for the latter, again citing the advantage of a bird in hand. We began recording a series of lengthy interviews, and each time she faced my microphone, Ruby left me numb with her stories. At first, I thought she was exaggerating, but as I researched old newspapers and spoke to other people who were also on the scene, it became clear that this Miss Smith had an extraordinary memory. Even some of the wildest incidents she related were borne out by other witnesses.

With the money I paid her, three thousand dollars (and here I have to say that it was far too meager a sum for what I received in return) Ruby crated up her prized possessions—a huge vintage refrigerator and an oversized early RCA television console—and moved to Placentia, a suburb of Los Angeles where, on a scouting trip, she had found a small, comfortable apartment in a well-kept, quiet neighborhood. When advised that more advanced models of both items could be had for the cost of shipping these hopelessly outdated appliances, she stubbornly refused to listen to reason; it had taken too much hard work and financial sacrifice to acquire them, and there was nostalgia involved, for they had made livable her ramshackle residence, a small, damp, barely converted garage in Jersey City, New Jersey.

It did not take her long to make friends in Placentia; soon she was sending me newspaper clippings with her smiling face: Ruby had become a local celebrity, and she loved it. She never gave up her ambition to sing, and to that end, she had for several years carried a 45 in her purse—not a handgun, a 45-rpm instrumental recording by the Nat King Cole Trio. It was a blues to which she could apply any number of lyrics from her repertoire. Give Ruby a turntable and she'd give you an audition. She also took advantage of any opportunity to give a public performance, as on the night when some new gay friends took her to Dude City, a gay club in Los Angeles. There was no need for the Cole recording, for Dude City boasted a pianist and regularly featured singers. The club's reigning queen and mistress of ceremonies was a drag—literally—who seemed resentful when told that Bessie Smith's niece was in the house and that she wanted to sing a number. Sensing that she might be upstaged, the cross-dressing diva introduced Ruby with unconcealed disdain: "The lady *says* she is Bessie Smith's niece, and she's going to *try* to do some old number," she announced. Telling the pianist to play a blues, Ruby, then in her mid-seventies, delivered—with all the gusto and sensuality Bessie had taught her—a song called "I've Got Ten Tons of Pussy." The crowd went wild. "Them gay guys loved me," she said as she reported the incident to me in one of her wee-hour phone calls. "They had themselves some fag hags, honey, but they had never come across anything like me. I turned out the place, and that tacky drag queen took off!"

In 1972, with African-Americans experiencing a heightened awareness of their heritage and young blacks looking back at the roots of contemporary music, the publication of *Bessie* contributed to a growing interest in past exploitation of African-American artists and songwriters. Partly inspired by the book, New York's public television station, WNET-TV, devoted a prime-time program to an examination into the record industry's treatment of artists. To set the scene, the producers opened with a filmed, documentary-styled segment in which artists and producers discussed the problems facing jazz artists in an industry dominated by big corporations. Since I was among the film's talking heads, the subject of Bessie Smith came up. I noted that she had never been paid artist royalties by Columbia and that the label had posthumously issued recordings for which she had not even received the basic fee.

When the film ended, the station switched to a live studio discussion, which soon focused on Bessie Smith. Seated at a small table, flanked by the program's host and producer, Bruce Lundvall, then Columbia's vice president of marketing, looked very uncomfortable. I was later told that Altshuler also was present in the studio, nervously pacing the floor off camera and seemingly bracing himself for a public relations disaster. The following is a transcript of the live discussion:

> HOST: With me in the studio this evening is an executive of one of the country's largest recording companies, he is Bruce Lundvall, vice president in charge of marketing for Columbia Records. Ray McArthur, the producer of tonight's feature report is also with us. Mr. Lundvall, you're with Columbia Records, this company has produced a lot, a sizeable number of jazz recordings and among them some very good reissues. Is there an attempt to compensate the artists economically, beyond the restrictions of the contractual stipulations?
>
> LUNDVALL: I think so, I think at Columbia and it's really true of other recording companies as well, today, that the kind of compensation that I'm thinking about here is the type of thing where the company will support the artist while on tour, will support an engagement with an advertising cam-

paign surrounding that engagement so that we are also promoting his appearance, trying to get people into the nightclub or into the concert hall to see the artist as well as to sell his album product. I think that in fact the contractual arrangements with all artists today, jazz artists as well as rock artists, gives the artist far more than he would have gotten in a contractual situation 10 years ago or 20 years ago. And furthermore, I rather disagree with much of what I saw in this film although it's certainly to a degree accurate. I think that the outlook for jazz today is indeed very healthy.

MCARTHUR: The economic outlook or the reception by the audience?

LUNDVALL: Well . . .

MCARTHUR: Both?

LUNDVALL: Both certainly go hand in hand.

MCARTHUR: Bessie Smith is once again very much in vogue, I learned that from the film, the book is out by Chris Albertson and her records are again making money. Now in the film we were told that there was no compensation being paid to her estate or so, but what happens in situations like these? Does the money just go back into the company, to be reinvested in company stock or is some support of the art thought about?

Unprepared for that question, Bruce Lundvall improvised an answer. There actually had not been a payment made to the Bessie Smith Foundation, as Lundvall claimed, but he arranged to have a one-thousand-dollar contribution made during the following week. Lundvall was really out of this loop, but Altshuler had put him on the spot. The fifty dollars John Hammond added to the funds collected at Juanita Green's house was declared as a "personal contribution" but he charged it to his CBS expense account.

LUNDVALL: No, absolutely, the latter is the case. There was royalty paid, a payment made to the Bessie Smith Foundation, number one, and secondly John Hammond and Clive Davis, the president of Columbia Records, are attempting to form a scholarship fund in Bessie Smith's name to support needy black students with royalties from the sale of these albums. And indeed they have sold well.

MCARTHUR: In other words, Bruce are you saying then that you are paying royalties on the reissues constantly or did you just make one block?

LUNDVALL: We made one payment initially, but the royalties have accumulated in an account and will be used for a fund for needy black students in the future, and this is being arranged for by the president of the company and John Hammond, who was largely involved with Chris Albertson in putting the repackaging together.

Had Clive Davis and John Hammond really attempted to form a scholarship fund, they would of course have succeeded, but no such attempt was made, and if royalties had indeed "accumulated in an account," they subsequently

Blues singer Pearl Murray looks on as Jack Gee, Jr., addresses a group in Chattanooga during the 1973 Tennessee Arts Festival's tribute to Bessie. Photo by Doug Griffith.

vaporized. When I made an inquiry, no one at Columbia knew of the existence of such an account, nor did anyone seem interested in following this story up. Juanita Green's spur-of-the-moment scholarship fund also seems to have faded into history.

It was around this time that Jack Gee, Jr., joined the Bessie Smith estate to file a multifaceted suit against Columbia Records's parent corporation, CBS. As the court papers noted, the original edition of this biography was the inspiration for Gee's suit:

Albertson has chronicled Smith's life and times in great detail, drawing mainly upon interviews with persons who knew her. His volume sheds helpful background light upon the statute of limitations problem by demonstrating that many, if not most of the people who might have had knowledge of the events of the 1920's surrounding Smith's relationship with Columbia, are now dead. It is worth noting too that the Albertson book (and research) seems veritably to be the wellspring of plaintiff's case. For example, whole paragraphs of the complaint are copied almost verbatim from the volume.

Basically, Columbia was charged with posthumously issuing sides for which Bessie had not been paid and for leaving the royalty clause blank in her contracts, which lawyers for Jack Gee, Jr., regarded as racial discrimination:[2]

> All the recording contracts and copyright agreements entered into by Smith and Columbia between 1924 and 1933 are invalid because of their unconscionability and Columbia's overreaching: Columbia is said to have taken advantage of Smith's illiteracy and lack of sophistication in business affairs. Complementing these allegations are the claims that the invalid contractual dealings were the product of race discrimination. On the average, Smith received a flat fee of $200 per selection recorded for Columbia with no royalties, allegedly in contrast to much larger sums, including royalties, paid to white artists then recording for Columbia such as Eddie Cantor, Ted Lewis, Rudy Vallee, Sophie Tucker and Bing Crosby. The complaint alleges that this corporate racism constituted willful and intentional violation of the civil rights of Smith and of others similarly situated "by failing to afford them the opportunity to make and enforce contracts to the full extent as is enjoyed by white citizens, in violation of 42 U.S.C. § 1981." Plaintiffs have also advanced a novel theory of § 1981 liability by contending that these original contract discriminations are actually direct wrongs to themselves, as Smith's heirs.

The lawsuit brought new information to light regarding Bessie's composer royalties:

> On information and belief, Jack Kapp, a Columbia Records official during the period when Bessie was recording, paid Bessie a few dollars for her tunes during the regular course of business with Columbia. He would then copyright the tunes under a dummy publishing company and collect royalties himself, at the expense of Bessie. On information and belief, these activities were carried on with the actual and constructive knowledge of Columbia and no reasonable payment or accounting to Bessie or her heirs has ever been made as a result of these activities.

There was the anticipated problem of filing a suit after so many years, but the statute of limitations was not Jack Gee, Jr.'s only obstacle. The time problem might have been overcome were it not for the fact that he was unable to document his adoption and, therefore, could not claim ownership of Bessie's intellectual property. The court concluded: "plaintiffs failed to allege fraud facts sufficient to overcome a statute of limitations problem because there was no inherent fraud or fraudulent concealment. The court found plaintiffs' copyright infringement claim insufficient for failure to specify the works, that plaintiffs owned the copyright, that the work was registered, and how defendant infringed . . . Plaintiffs failed to allege required elements of copyright infringement or facts sufficient to constitute fraud."

Snooks later admitted that he had never seen adoption papers but that he had always assumed that they existed.

"I don't think they should have given Snooks anything, anyway," said Ruby, "but Bessie *did* adopt him. Now, maybe there weren't any papers, but that's how it was with black people—nobody gave a damn. How do you think I got married thirteen times? I'd just go to city hall, or wherever, and get a marriage license—didn't nobody ask for divorce papers."

Film studios rely on outside readers for initial evaluations of new books. A 1972 Warner Brothers reader's report on *Bessie* gave a summation of Bessie Smith's life as the book depicted it, but concluded that this was not recommended film material, because "Bessie Smith was not on drugs, and this is not the five-handkerchief stuff that 'Lady Sings the Blues' is made of." Nevertheless, there was no dearth of interest in *Bessie* as film material, and one exploration predated the book's publication. Hollywood producer and erstwhile choreographer Danny Dare called to say that he knew I was working on a biography and that he was going to make a film with or without it, "so you might as well let us option the rights." He went on to inform me that Dionne Warwick was up for the title role—that was all I needed to hear. When I told him Helen Hayes would be as good a choice, he seemed to believe me.

Shortly after the book's publication, another producer called to say that Cicely Tyson and "a very important director" were set to go with a film version. He could not reveal the identity of the director, but the grapevine works in mysterious ways. The following day, Odetta called and asked me why Vincente Minelli was buying so many Bessie Smith albums; a friend in Los Angeles had seen him purchase the complete Columbia set at Tower Records in Hollywood!

Never a Tyson fan, I was not sorry to see that project die, but it was not without considerable effort on the part of Danny Dare. When I proved to be uncooperative, he flew Jack Gee, Sr., to Los Angeles in hopes of striking a deal with him, but Jack's customary million-dollar demand killed that attempt, so Dare turned to Ruby, who was already out there. "They want me to go to Mr. Minelli's house for a meeting," she told me in a phone call, "and I know they just want to pump me for information. I got news for them, *I'll* be the one getting the information, so you stay home tonight, because I'm going to call you as soon as I get back to my place."

Dare made no inroads with Ruby. She took an instant dislike to him and the people he had assembled at Minelli's house. "I didn't tell them nothing," she reported. "They were trying to get all kinds of information out of me, and they even had a black guy there who was supposed to be the writer—guess they thought that would impress me, but he looked like he didn't know what the hell was going on." Dare's next move was to have one of his associates call to offer me a part in their film—it was obviously a desperate measure, and it proved to be a last gasp.

More projects popped up, including an option deal with Columbia Pictures, whose idea of Bessie Smith was Roberta Flack. That production actually went through initial stages of development, with coast-to-coast commutes by Joe Layton, the designated director, and a rough draft script by Melvin Van Peebles, who combined elements from the book with ludicrous fantasies.[3] That approach was promptly rejected and the producers turned to Horton Foote, a wonderful, accomplished playwright who shared my views of how Bessie should be portrayed. Although his screenplay was a bit old-fashioned, Columbia Pictures did not reject it—instead, they dropped the project altogether[4] when an unrelated scandal brought the company to the brink of bankruptcy.

A Broadway play was also optioned, and scripts were written and readings held, but even though people with impressive track records were involved, the curtain never went up on an authorized stage adaptation of this book.[5] The curtain had earlier risen on *Me and Bessie,* a musical in which singer Linda Hopkins vulgarized Bessie's songs in a scenario that bore little or no resemblance to Bessie's own. The idea for this production originated with Geoffrey Holder, who would have given Bessie a proper treatment, but when Holder turned Hopkins down, she stole the idea and ran it into the ground. Originally approached to write Hopkins's show (and knowing full well that it really belonged to Holder), I walked out after a dispute with the producer. I had also concluded that Linda Hopkins, an engaging singer, lacked the intellectual depth to take on this role.

Although she never met Ruby Walker, Hopkins resented her. In a radio interview about her Bessie Smith show, she said, "Chris Albertson got all his information from a drunken old woman who thinks she is Bessie's niece." When she continued her personal attack on Ruby, I had to write Linda a letter suggesting that she put an end to her unwarranted smear campaign. She did.

The author poses with Alberta Hunter in 1971. Photo by Don Lynn.

During the first week of March 1977, I received a call from Ruby, who had earlier in the week been diagnosed with a form of bone cancer. "Get a pen and some paper," she ordered me. Explaining that she did not have long to live, she then proceeded to dictate an impressive list of publications, ranging from the *New York Times* to *Down Beat*. "I've told the doctor to call you as soon as I'm dead," she said. "Now you make sure that all the newspapers know about it." A few days later, the dreaded call came. "What a remarkable woman," said the doctor. "When I asked her why I should notify you, she replied, 'My dear doctor, you seem to forget that I am in show business, and when you're in show business, you don't just die and let nobody know about it.' " Dear Ruby, spirited to the end.

Interest in Bessie Smith has never waned. Sixty-six years after her death, as a world that has become very different from the one she had known transitions into a new century and the next millennium, Bessie Smith continues to be revered and honored around the world. There have been books,[6] major articles, and further reissues of her recordings; small theater groups have staged plays; France Telecom issued a phone card bearing her name and photo; the U.S. Postal Service placed her likeness on a thirty-two-cent stamp; she was inducted into the Rock and Roll Hall of Fame; and her hometown, Chattanooga, introduced an annual event, the Bessie Smith Strut, which has hundreds of people prancing in her memory down a street lined with vendors. Columbia Records, which now belongs to Sony, Inc., issued a five-volume set of her recording, including a compact disc of excerpts from Ruby's interviews for this book, the complete soundtrack from "St. Louis Blues," and five alternate takes.[7] Not to be outdone, Frog Records, a small British label dedicated to vintage jazz, began releasing its own series of Bessie's complete recorded output in 2002, including even more alternate performances.

In Clarksdale, Mississippi, people still come from far and wide to spend a night or two in the room where Bessie Smith took her last breath. They have paid their morbid visits since 1944, when a Mrs. Z. L. Hill took over the small one-story building that in 1937 had been the Afro-American Hospital and turned it into the Riverside Hotel. Clearly, someone knew that Bessie had not died in the nearby white hospital, but the myth was allowed to live on. Over the past fifty years, more people have slept in that small room than ever attended a single Bessie Smith performance.

As the first decade of the new millennium proceeds, there still is not a biographical feature film devoted to the Empress of the Blues—a fact that is to be deplored but perhaps also seen as a blessing, for Hollywood has yet to produce a jazz-related film that does its subject justice. From *The Benny Goodman Story* to *Lady Sings the Blues* and *Leadbelly,* filmmakers have consistently diluted facts to suit what they obviously regard as the simple minds of filmgoers. Even Clint Eastwood's highly acclaimed *Bird* paid disproportionate attention to Charlie Parker's drug addiction, indicating that the values reflected in Warner Brothers' 1972 reader's report on *Bessie* still prevailed in 1988. In 2001, Ken Burns's *Jazz,* a myopic, factually distorted seventeen-and-a-half-hour TV "documentary," proved that jazz remains a victim of tabloid mentality.

Notes

Chapter 1

1. Late, because black newspapers were published weekly.

2. Absent from the family gathering was Ruby and Jack's adopted son, Jack Gee, Jr. Jack, Sr., was driving down from New York and claimed not to have had room for "Snooks" in the car.

3. James Harris, Jack Brady, Cecilus Remson, Louis Siceluff, William Battis, and Herbert Jenkins, who were making a bit of history themselves in that hired pallbearers had not previously been used at a Philadelphia funeral.

4. By extreme contrast, Louis Armstrong's 1971 funeral was a shameless farce staged by his widow, Lucille, for the benefit of TV talk show celebrities. While the likes of Johnny Carson and Merv Griffin were invited, Armstrong's old friends—some of whom had barely managed to make the fare from New Orleans—were turned away for lack of invitational tickets.

5. New York's song-publishing district has been known as Tin Pan Alley since *Hampton's Broadway* magazine introduced the phrase in 1908. The tag was subsequently applied to commercially successful popular songs.

6. Her given name—not Elizabeth, as writer Paul Oliver surmised in his Bessie Smith biography.

7. Who, in fact, were neither classic in any explainable sense nor strictly blues singers.

8. John W. Work, Jr., *American Negro Songs and Spirituals: A Comprehensive Collection of 230 Folk Songs, Religious and Secular* (New York: Bonanza Books, 1940).

9. Sandra Lieb, *Mother of the Blues: A Study of Ma Rainey* (Amherst: University of Massachusetts Press, 1981). This is the definitive biography and treatise on Ma Rainey.

10. "Weary Blues" was published in 1915, suggesting that Leigh Whipper's memory may have been two years off, but it is also possible that Bessie sang a similar tune or that "Weary Blues" was around for two years before its publication.

11. Under the pseudonym "Georgia Tom," Thomas Dorsey wrote and recorded double-entendre songs in the 1920s, but he later turned to gospel music, writing such songs as "Precious Lord" and co-founding the National Gospel Singers Convention. In 1982, he was the subject of an award-winning full-length documentary film, *Say Amen, Somebody.*

12. Thomas A. Dorsey interview with Jim and Amy O'Neal, *Living Blues,* March–April 1975.

13. This is what Jack Gee, Jr., was told by one of Bessie's sisters, who also insisted that Love and Bessie were never legally married.

14. In 1925, Dr. Sabin, a noted medical researcher, became the first woman elected to the National Academy of Science.

15. Nat Shapiro and Nat Hentoff, eds., *Hear Me Talkin' to Ya: The Story of Jazz by the Men Who Made It* (New York: Rinehart, 1955).

16. So called because their unbuckled galoshes made a flapping sound as they walked.

Chapter 2

1. Interview with the author, December 23, 1976.

2. From an unpublished manuscript by Lil Armstrong and the author.

3. On January 10, Victor had gone so far as to record a test with Mamie Smith singing "That Thing Called Love," but it was rejected.

4. Black comedian Bert Williams had previously recorded humorous monologues for Columbia, using a small chorus.

5. The company changed the identification to "race" in the 1930s.

6. Paramount also released a number of hillbilly and foreign-language records.

7. Bechet, then twenty-six, was to become one of black music's leading performers. He pioneered the soprano saxophone as a jazz instrument, leading the way for John Coltrane and other post–World War II players who took up the instrument. Bechet's extraordinary improvisational skills also prompted Ernst Ansermet to write what is generally regarded as the world's first jazz review. He eventually settled in France, where he lived until his death in 1959.

8. Sidney Bechet, *Treat It Gentle* (New York: Hill and Wang, 1960).

9. *How Come?* opened at the Attucks Theatre, Norfolk, Virginia (since renamed the Booker T. Theatre), on January 15, 1923. It played between there, Washington, D.C., and Philadelphia for the next few weeks, but Bessie didn't join the show until its January 29, 1923, opening at the Dunbar.

10. Interview with the author, December 23, 1976.

11. Interview with the author, 1970.

12. Alberta Hunter would later claim sole authorship of "Down Hearted Blues," insisting that she gave Austin half of the tune in gratitude for having shown her the ins and outs of music publishing.

13. No payment was made for rejected recordings. Some of these were subsequently released—in the 1940s and 1950s—without any payment to Bessie's estate.

14. The Reverend Tindley was a prolific composer of gospel songs, his most famous being "I'll Overcome Some Day," which with slightly changed lyrics became the anthem of the civil rights movement "We Shall Overcome."

15. Clarence Williams was originally listed as the song's co-composer, but he probably only published it. ASCAP credits Robert Graham Prince and Porter Grainger; other sources list Grainger and Everett Robbins.

16. In 1923, Bessie recorded two such songs from that period, "Aggravatin' Papa" and "My Sweetie Went Away."

17. The custom of having special performances for whites had originated at the Lyric Theatre in New Orleans, but the practice soon became widespread.

18. The average price of a radio set was $135.

19. Pianist James P. Johnson wrote the music for *Runnin' Wild,* including the famous "Charleston," which was inspired by dances he saw being done by patrons of the Jungle Casino (on West Sixty-fourth Street). The Jungle Casino was frequented by African-Americans from Charleston, South Carolina, whose variations on cotillion steps became the Charleston, a dance rage.

20. Waters won a Best Supporting Actress Oscar nomination for her role in *The Sound and the Fury* (1949) and the New York Drama Critics Award for Best Actress in the stage production of *Member of the Wedding,* a role she repeated in the 1952 film version.

21. Ethel Waters with Charles Samuels, *His Eye Is on the Sparrow* (New York: Doubleday, 1951).

22. At the Bijou Theatre and the Ryman Auditorium.

23. Predecessors of Amos 'n' Andy, the Two Black Crows (Moran and Mack) were actually Irish.

24. Bessie's previous contract had brought her more than double the $1,500 guaranteed her.

Chapter 3

1. Bessie's accompaniment on these two sides was by pianist Jimmy Jones and guitarist Harry Reser. The guitarist gained a measure of notoriety as a member of the famous Cliquoe Club Eskimos and was the first white musician to accompany Bessie.

2. *Billboard,* February 9, 1924.

3. *Memphis Commercial Appeal,* February 2, 1924. This review also appeared in the *Chicago Defender*'s February 23, 1924, issue, under the heading "Bessie Radiates."

4. Ibid.

5. Bessie was accompanied by Irvin Johns and John V. Snow, a violinist who toured with the show.

6. Ma Rainey recorded these songs first in December 1923 and again four years later.

7. Tim Moore later became known nationally as "Kingfish" in the television version of *Amos 'n' Andy.*

8. Joe Glaser, a lower-echelon gangster, graduated from filing serial numbers off stolen vehicles to managing boxers before becoming Louis Armstrong's manager. Armstrong opened the door for his founding of the Associated Booking Corporation, a multimillion-dollar business.

9. Interview with the author, 1971.

Chapter 4

1. A popular stage personality, Jones was also well known as Fae Barnes.

2. Usually a Mr. Emerson.

3. Ma Rainey's label, Paramount, soon began using the imprint "Electrically Recorded" on its labels. Its engineers did employ some form of electrical system, but the quality was so inferior to those of the bigger companies that some said all Paramount did was turn on an electric bulb in the studio.

4. Still under contract to Paramount, Hunter recorded under the pseudonym Josephine Beatty, which was actually her younger sister's name.

5. *Chicago Defender,* April 18, 1925.

6. There is a slight discrepancy in Johnson's story, since *Midnight Steppers,* the show he toured in with Bessie, did not appear in South Carolina, but his report checks out with similar stories told by others who witnessed Bessie's treatment of her prop boys.

7. From an unpublished autobiography, cited in Hans R. Rookmaaker's annotation for the Riverside album *Ma Rainey, Mother of the Blues.*

8. *Chicago Defender,* February 13, 1925.

Chapter 5

1. In January 1926, Columbia pressed 27,675 copies of Bessie's "I've Been Mistreated and I Don't Like It," as opposed to 12,200 of a Clara Smith recording, which was released simultaneously.

2. Immortalized by Bessie in "Soft Pedal Blues."

3. The Pullman Porters Club in St. Louis is said to have started as a buffet flat.

4. In towns where there was no commercial lodging available, entertainers often stayed in private homes or at the local Elks club.

Chapter 6

1. Floods inundated twenty thousand square miles, leaving seven hundred thousand persons homeless.

Chapter 7

1. Mills's premature death inspired Duke Ellington to write a posthumous tribute, "Black Beauty."

2. Bill Reed, *Hot from Harlem* (Los Angeles: Cellar Door Press, 1998).

3. It was said that only one white man, Al Jolson, was ever permitted to visit Leroy's during its thirteen years of operation (circa 1910 to 1923).

4. Van Vechten stipulated that each record could only be played once during any one-year period. His Bessie Smith collection was still in excellent condition in 1970, when the author and engineer Larry Hiller transferred it for Columbia Records's LP reissue project.

5. That week's featured photoplay was Charlie Chaplin's *Circus*.

6. African-American colloquial term meaning "highbrow" (rarely used today).

7. *Jazz Record* magazine, September 1947.

8. Ruby was fairly sure that this was Bessie's opening song; Leigh Whipper recalled only that it was "one of her saddest songs."

9. "Me and My Gin" is credited to H. Burke, a pseudonym for J. C. Johnson, who also wrote "Empty Bed Blues."

10. Florence Foster Jenkins was a Philadelphia socialite who became known for her unintentionally humorous renderings of operatic arias. Before she died, Jenkins is alleged to have told a friend, "Many people said that I could not sing, but nobody can say that I didn't."

11. Sumac's four-octave range made her the object of admiration and ridicule in the 1950s, when Capitol issued several albums that featured her valiantly competing against some of the busiest "jungle" arrangements ever written.

Chapter 8

1. Pinkard's compositions included such standards as "Sweet Georgia Brown," "Sugar," and "Them There Eyes."

2. Phone interview with the author, 1971.

3. Spencer Williams's hits included "Royal Garden Blues," "Basin Street Blues," "I Ain't Got Nobody," "Everybody Loves My Baby," and "I Found a New Baby."

4. Razaf's 1929 output alone included "Black and Blue," "Honeysuckle Rose," and "Ain't Misbehavin'," all written in collaboration with Fats Waller.

5. In the pop music field, a "hook" is a catchy musical or rhythmic line that easily identifies a tune and "hooks" the listener in.

6. The chorus is conducted by J. Rosamund Johnson; the orchestra, comprising mainly members of the Fletcher Henderson band, is under the direction of James P. Johnson.

7. Sister of Fredi Washington, Isabel was the first Mrs. Adam Clayton Powell, Jr. The part was originally supposed to go to Fredi, but she was taken ill. When Isabel was told that her complexion was too light, she asked: "I can be dipped, can't I?" The answer was "yes."

8. Although the print found in Mexico was announced as a "discovery," other prints in superior condition existed all along, and the negative was safely stored in Dudley Murphy's private collection.

9. Interview with the author, 1971.

10. A full-length MGM feature film starring Daniel Haynes and Nina Mae McKinney, with blues singer Victoria Spivey in a supporting role. It perpetuated the Negro stereotype.

Chapter 9

1. Clarence Williams and his wife, Eva Taylor, recorded it for Edison, Johnson recorded it for Victor with Fats Waller and King Oliver, then again the following day with Clarence Williams, for Okeh, and—less than a month later—again for Victor, this time with Eva Taylor.

2. A quality that Sarah Vaughan would consistently demonstrate a couple of decades later.

3. Interview with the author, 1971.

4. Interview with the author, 1974.

5. "See If I'll Care" and "Baby, Have Pity on Me" finally reached the market in 1947.

6. Another unsuccessful attempt was made to revive the TOBA circuit in 1945.

7. Two decades later, she billed herself as Moms Mabley and became a hugely popular standup comic.

8. Paul Oliver, *Bessie Smith* (London: Cassell, 1959).

9. John Hammond had a tendency to exaggerate Bessie's reversal of fortune, possibly to enhance his own role as savior.

10. Plus composer royalties, when applicable.

11. Hammond's entrée to the record industry was its brush with bankruptcy and his inherited wealth. Underwriting the session expenses, he made his debut as a producer with a 1932 solo session featuring pianist Garland Wilson.

12. Legal establishments that heralded repeal, offering light wines and steins of beer for a dime.

Chapter 10

1. So called because it featured grand opera at the close of the nineteenth century, when Oscar Hammerstein built it.

2. Not with Ethel Waters and Ben Selvin, as Hammond wrote in his autobiography.

3. So called to distinguish it from the Apollo Theater on West 42d Street.

4. The Lafayette, as part of the WPA Federal Theater Funds program, soon housed such all-black dramas as *The Swing Mikado* and *Black Macbeth*, produced by John Houseman and Orson Welles.

5. The orchestra continued the tour under the leadership of pianist Herman Chittison.

6. She resurfaced as "Josephine the Plumber" in 1960s TV commercials.

7. It later became the Latin Quarter and, in 1971, was converted into Cine Lido, a movie theater specializing in blue movies.

8. *Jazz Record* magazine, September 1947.

9. So called because many famous jazz musicians had inscribed their names in the small wooden entrance door.

10. It later became the Venus Lounge.

Chapter 11

1. The black press, usually quick to point out incidents of racial injustice, carried no such story in connection with Bessie Smith's death until after the publication of Hammond's *Down Beat* piece.

2. Not long after LPs relegated 78-rpm records to collectors' shelves, record companies established a routine of releasing "memorial" albums to honor their dear departed artists, a practice that escalated with the introduction of CDs to include also previously rejected material, imperfect performances the release of which most living artists would not have condoned.

3. The only other person who might have shed some light on the circumstances, the driver of the truck, was never located or identified. Morgan's account of the accident was given only to the family. It appears on page 264 as recalled by Jack Gee, Jr.

4. A past president of the American Academy of Orthopedic Surgeons, Dr. Smith became a staff orthopedic surgeon at the Campbell Clinic, in Memphis, in 1936.

5. Many Mississippi roads, built during the Depression, were so narrow that two wide trucks could barely pass each other. Because drivers often rode with an elbow protruding from the car's window, it was not unusual for the bed of a passing truck to hit the elbow of a driver going in the opposite direction. These were called "side swipe" injuries—usually a combination of a compound fracture dislocation of the wrist, both bones of the forearm broken, and the elbow itself completely crushed.

6. A strange fact, considering that Dr. Smith even then was a part-time jazz pianist with a Fats Waller–inspired style.

Chapter 12

1. Louis Armstrong's death, in 1971, was anticipated by at least two companies whose "memorial" albums were ready for release at a moment's notice.

2. Actually, Whiteman never claimed to be the "King," and sometimes seemed embarrassed by the label.

3. Documentation of the alleged settlement is not possible because the National Biscuit Company's files from that period have been destroyed.

4. Twenty of Bessie's rejected selections have never surfaced, but Frog Records, a British company, claims to possess previously unissued alternates.

Epilogue

1. Phone conversation with the author, August 1970.

2. The truth is that Columbia also generally struck out the royalty clause in its contracts with white country-music artists and that it retained the clause in contracts with black ministers and gospel performers. The clause was automatically struck out unless the artist demanded a royalty agreement.

3. Van Peebles later turned his script into a play. When threatened with a copyright lawsuit, he claimed that his story was based on rumors that circulated in his neighbor-

hood during his childhood. It was a claim he apparently did not wish to repeat in court—perhaps because he grew up in a white neighborhood.

4. After an expenditure of about two hundred thousand dollars, which was unrelated to the studio's financial woes.

5. A handful of small productions have drawn "inspiration" from this book, but none have succeeded at the box office.

6. Including one by a relatively successful feminist writer, Elaine Feinstein, who so blatantly plagiarized *Bessie* that one reviewer suggested the book should have opened and ended with quotation marks. A lawsuit was contemplated but not carried out because the publication coincided with Stein and Day's declaration of bankruptcy.

7. With extensive annotation by this writer, some of which will look familiar to readers of this edition of *Bessie*.

Suggested Reading

Barker, Danny. *Buddy Bolden and the Last Days of Storyville*. London: Cassell Academic, 1998.

Bechet, Sidney. *Treat It Gentle*. New York: Hill and Wang, 1960.

Dance, Helen Oakley. *Stormy Monday: The T-Bone Walker Story*. With a foreword by B.B. King. Baton Rouge: Louisiana State University Press, 1987.

Fox, Ted. *Showtime at the Apollo*. New York: Holt, Rinehart and Winston, 1983.

Lieb, Sandra R. *Mother of the Blues: A Study of Ma Rainey*. Amherst: University of Massachusetts Press, 1981.

Mezzrow, Mezz, and Bernard Wolfe. *Really the Blues*. New York: Random House, 1946.

Ramsey, Fredric, Jr., and Charles Edward Smith, eds. *Jazzmen*. New York: Harcourt, Brace, 1939.

Schuller, Gunther. *Early Jazz: Its Roots and Musical Development*. New York: Oxford University Press, 1968.

Shapiro, Nat, and Nat Hentoff, eds. *Hear Me Talkin' to Ya: The Story of Jazz as Told by the Men Who Made It*. New York: Rinehart, 1955.

Stearns, Marshall. *The Story of Jazz*. New York: Oxford University Press, 1956.

Taylor, Frank C., with Gerald Cook. *Alberta Hunter: A Celebration in Blues*. New York: McGraw-Hill, 1987.

Welding, Pete, and Toby Byron, eds. *Bluesland: Portraits of Twelve Major American Blues Masters*. New York: Dutton, 1991.

In addition to the books listed above, information pertinent to a study of Bessie Smith and her era can be found in the following news and trade papers (editions published between 1915 and 1937), many of which are available on microfilm at the New York Public Library's Schomburg Collection and in various libraries around the country.

Afro-American (Baltimore)
Amsterdam News (New York)
Chicago Defender
Commercial Appeal (Memphis)
Interstate Tattler (New York)
Journal and Guide (Norfolk, Va.)
New York Age
New York Clipper
Owl (Detroit)
Philadelphia Tribune
Pittsburgh Courier

Discography

The following CD releases relate directly or indirectly to Bessie Smith. All were available at time of publication.

Bessie Smith

Empress of the Blues: The Complete Recordings, vol. 1 (Columbia CK 47091)
Down Hearted Blues; Gulf Cost Blues; Aggravatin' Papa; Beale Street Mama; Baby Won't You Please Come Home; Oh Daddy Blues; 'Tain't Nobody's Bizness If I Do; Keeps on A-Rainin' (Papa, He Can't Make No Time); Mama's Got the Blues; Outside of That; Bleeding Hearted Blues; Lady Luck Blues; Yodling Blues; Midnight Blues; If You Don't, I Know Who Will; Nobody in Town Can Bake a Sweet Jelly Roll Like Mine; Jail-House Blues; St. Louis Gal; Sam Jones Blues; Graveyard Dream Blues; Cemetery Blues; Far Away Blues (with Clara Smith); *I'm Going Back to My Used to Be; Whoa, Tillie, Take Your Time; My Sweetie Went Away; Any Woman's Blues; Chicago Bound Blues; Mistreating Daddy; Frosty Morning Blues; Haunted House Blues; Eavesdropper's Blues; Easy Come, Easy Go Blues; Sorrowful Blues; Pinchbacks—Take 'Em Away; Rocking Chair Blues; Ticket Agent, Ease Your Window Down; Boweavil Blues; Hateful Blues*

Empress of the Blues: The Complete Recordings, vol. 2 (Columbia CK 47471)
Frankie Blues; Moonshine Blues; Lou'isiana Low-Down Blues; Mountain Top Blues; Work House Blues; House Rent Blues; Salt Water Blues; Rainy Weather Blues; Weeping Willow Blues; The Bye Bye Blues; Sing Sing Prison Blues; Follow the Deal on Down;

Sinful Blues; Woman's Trouble Blues; Love Me Daddy Blues; Dying Gambler's Blues; The St. Louis Blues; Reckless Blues; Sobbin' Hearted Blues; Cold in Hand Blues; You've Been a Good Ole Wagon; Cake Walkin' Babies (From Home); The Yellow Dog Blues; Soft Pedal Blues; Dixie Flyer Blues; Nashville Women's Blues; Careless Love Blues; J. C. Holmes Blues; I Ain't Goin' to Play Second Fiddle; He's Gone Blues; Nobody's Blues but Mine; I Ain't Got Nobody; My Man Blues (with Clara Smith); *New Gulf Coast Blues; Florida Bound Blues; At the Christmas Ball; I've Been Mistreated and I Don't Like It*

Empress of the Blues: The Complete Recordings, vol. 3 (Columbia CK 47474)
Red Mountain Blues; Golden Rule Blues; Lonesome Desert Blues; Them "Has Been" Blues; Squeeze Me; What's the Matter Now?; I Want Every Bit of It; Jazzbo Brown from Memphis Town; The Gin House Blues; Money Blues; Baby Doll; Hard Driving Papa; Lost Your Head Blues; Hard Time Blues; Honey Man Blues; One and Two Blues; Young Woman's Blues; Preachin' the Blues; Back Water Blues; After You've Gone; Alexander's Ragtime Band; Muddy Water (A Mississippi Moan); There'll Be a Hot Time in the Old Town Tonight; Trombone Cholly; Send Me to the 'Lectric Chair; Them's Graveyard Words; Hot Spring Blues; Sweet Mistreater; Lock and Key; Mean Old Bedbug Blues; A Good Man Is Hard to Find; Homeless Blues; Looking for My Man Blues; Dyin' by the Hour; Foolish Man Blues; Thinking Blues; Pickpocket Blues; I Used to Be Your Sweet Mama; I'd Rather Be Dead and Buried in My Grave

Empress of the Blues: The Complete Recordings, vol. 4 (Columbia CK 52838)
Standin' in the Rain Blues; It Won't Be You; Spider Man Blues; Empty Bed Blues (Part 1); *Empty Bed Blues* (Part 2); *Put It Right Here (Or Keep It Out There); Yes Indeed He Do!; Devil's Gonna Git You; You Ought to Be Ashamed; Washwoman's Blues; Slow and Easy Man; Poor Man's Blues; Please Help Me Get Him Out of My Mind; Me and My Gin; I'm Wild About That Thing; You've Got to Give Me Some; Kitchen Man; I've Got What It Takes (But It Breaks My Heart to Give It Away); Nobody Knows You When You're Down and Out; Take It Right Back ('Cause I Don't Want It Here); He's Got Me Goin'; It Makes My Love Come Down; Wasted Life Blues; Dirty No-Gooder's Blues; Blue Spirit Blues; Worn Out Papa Blues; You Don't Understand; Don't Cry Baby; Keep It to Yourself; New Orleans Hop Scop Blues; See If I'll Care; Baby Have Pity on Me; On Revival Day (A Rhythmic Spiritual); Moan, You Moaners; Hustlin' Dan; Black Mountain Blues; In the House Blues; Long Old Road; Blue Blues; Shipwreck Blues*

Empress of the Blues: The Complete Recordings, vol. 5 (Columbia CK 57546)
Need a Little Sugar in My Bowl; Safety Mama; Do Your Duty; Gimme a Pigfoot; Take Me for a Buggy Ride; I'm Down in the Dumps; The Yellow Dog Blues (alternate take); *Soft Pedal Blues* (alternate take); *Nashville Women's Blues* (alternate take); *Careless Love Blues* (alternate take); *Muddy Water (A Mississippi Moan)* (alternate take); *St. Louis Blues* (complete soundtrack with dialogue); *Ruby Smith Dialogue / An Interview with Chris Albertson*

The Collection (Columbia CK 44441)
Downhearted Blues; St. Louis Blues; Young Woman's Blues; 'Tain't Nobody's Bizness If I Do; My Sweetie Went Away; Reckless Blues; You've Been a Good Ole Wagon; I Ain't

Gonna Play No Second Fiddle; Weeping Willow Blues; Muddy Water (A Mississippi Moan); Mean Old Bedbug Blues; Empty Bed Blues, Parts 1 and 2; Do Your Duty; Gimme a Pigfoot; Nobody Knows You When You're Down and Out; Black Mountain Blues

Ida Cox

Blues for Rampart Street (Riverside OJCCD 1758)
Death Letter Blues; Hard Times Blues; Fogyism; Wild Women Don't Have the Blues; Fogyism; Mama Goes Where Papa Goes; Cherry Pickin' Blues; Lawdy, Lawdy Blues; Blues for Rampart Street; St. Louis Blues; Hard, Oh Lord

Alberta Hunter

The Legendary Alberta Hunter: '34 London Sessions (DRG 5195)
Two Cigarettes in the Dark; What Shall I Do?; Soon; Where the Mountains Meet the Sea; A Lonely Singing Fool; Long May We Love; Miss Otis Regrets (She's Unable to Lunch Today); Be Still My Heart; Stars Fell on Alabama; Two Little Flies on a Lump of Sugar; I Travel Alone

James P. Johnson

Carolina Shout (Biograph BCD105)
Carolina Shout; Harlem Strut; Charleston; Ole Miss Blues; Muscle Shoals Blues; Ain't Givin' Nothin' Away; Baltimore Buzz; and 7 others (all recorded from piano rolls)

Ma Rainey

Ma Rainey, vol. 1 (Milestone MCD-47021–2)
Jealous Hearted Blues; See See Rider Blues; Hear Me Talking to You; New Boweavil Blues; Prove It on Me Blues; Victim of the Blues; Runaway Blues; Trust No Man; Hoot Owl Blues; Sleep Talking Blues; Sweet Rough Man; Ma Rainey's Black Bottom; and 14 others

Jabbo Smith

Hot Jazz in the Twenties (Biograph BCD151)
Jazz Battle; Croonin' the Blues; St. James Infirmary Blues; Michigander Blues; Ready Hokum; Dyin' with the Blues; That's My Stuff; and 9 others

Various Artists

American Pop: An Audio History; From Minstrel to Mojo: On Record, 1893–1946 (WH-4017[9])
An eclectic 9-CD collection containing 215 selections that form a remarkable cross section of America's popular music. This multifaceted set illustrates the development of the music before, during, and immediately after Bessie Smith's time.

Songs We Taught Your Mother (Prestige Bluesville OBCCD-520–2)

Alberta Hunter: *I Got Myself a Working Man; You Gotta Reap What You Sow; Chirpin' the Blues; I Got a Mind To Ramble.* Lucille Hegamin: *St. Louis Blues; You'll Want My Love; Arkansas Blues; Has Anybody Seen My Corine.* Victoria Spivey: *Black Snake Blues; Got the Blues So Bad; Let Him Beat Me; Going Blues*

Stars of the Apollo (C2K 53407)

A 2-CD compilation of recordings by artists who appeared regularly at Harlem's Apollo Theater. The 28 selections include performances by Bessie Smith, Buck and Bubbles, Bill "Bojangles" Robinson, Ruby Walker Smith, Ida Cox, Butterbeans and Susie, Mamie Smith, Billie Holiday, and Duke Ellington.

Index